JOHN PENTLAND MAHAFFY

THE
EMPIRE OF THE PTOLEMIES

Elibron Classics
www.elibron.com

Elibron Classics series.

© 2005 Adamant Media Corporation.

ISBN 1-4021-7815-8 (paperback)
ISBN 1-4212-8676-9 (hardcover)

This Elibron Classics Replica Edition is an unabridged facsimile
of the edition published in 1895 by Macmillan and Co., London.

THE EMPIRE OF THE PTOLEMIES

AMICO

Giacomo Lumbroso

PROFESSORI ROMANO

DE PTOLEMAEIS ANTE ALIOS OPTIME MERITO

HUNC LIBRUM

D D D

DOCTRINA EIUS SAGACITATE BENEVOLENTIA

CUMULATUS AUCTOR

PREFACE

I HAVE explained at the opening of the following book what need there was for a renewed attempt to write the history of Ptolemaic Egypt. But no intelligent reader will require to be reminded that in a constantly growing subject, where new discoveries are frequent, and are even to be expected in every year of the near future, finality is not to be expected. Though it is, therefore, a humble, it is still an useful task to chronicle what has been discovered for the benefit of those who take interest in this period, even if it be certain that in a few years another book, or a new edition of this, will both amend and enlarge much that is here contained. I have called it the *Empire* of the Ptolemies, to emphasize the fact that this dynasty were not mere kings of Egypt—indeed the very notion of a defined kingdom as the domain of a sovran was a notion foreign to the old world—but that they ruled over a composite Empire, and were suzerain lords over local dynasts and kings.

Instead of stuffing my pages full of isolated references to classical and post-classical authors, of which the best example may be found in Cless's articles on the Ptolemies in Pauly's *Encyclopaedia*, I have rather striven to cite in full such evidence as is not easily accessible; hence the extant Ptolemaic inscriptions, which are important, will be found textually in this volume. The cartouches and coins are added for the convenience of travellers and others who may wish to identify Ptolemaic work in Egypt and else-where. A general inquiry into the sources, primary, secondary and otherwise, of this history is an interesting task, but so full of complications and of controversies, that after considerable labour I have desisted from the hope of giving it in this volume, the size of which it must have unduly increased. Meanwhile I can refer the curious reader to the excellent and learned summary in Prof. C. Wachsmuth's *Einleitung in das Studium des alten Geschichte* (1895) pp. 579 *sq.*, where the literature of the subject up to last year is reviewed.

As regards the chronology, we are confronted at the outset with the difficulty that Olympiad years do not correspond with Julian, and so the accession, say of Philadelphus, seems to be more strictly within 285-4 (November to November) than 285 B.C. This difference in the commencement of the years affects most of the dates. But as the whole scale is only approximate, and as in hardly any cases can we fix the date closer than the year, I regard it sufficient to give the approximate time, simply with a view to the sequence of events. It is for this purpose that there is given a practical chronology, however imperfect, at the end of the Preface. Such col-lateral events as influenced the course of affairs in Egypt, or hindered interference, are given as bearing upon the subject. I have also felt constrained to add, at the end of the book, a few notes containing information either overlooked in the text, or accruing from recent discoveries, while the sheets were going through the press. Even now, since these additional notes were printed, new ideas have occurred to me, and I do not yet know how far my most recent observation—that Egyptian crown-princes did not marry as such, but waited till their accession to do so—may carry us. But when a child has come to the birth, a speedy delivery is the safest and best.

The index has been prepared for me with much care by my friend Mr. J. E. Healy, and will be found a great help through a book full of intricate details, and necessarily containing some repetitions. No teacher of any experience will blame me for these repetitions, seeing that I had no object to gain in changing the original form in which the book was composed. It consists of lectures delivered to my History class in the University of Dublin, without the many digressions suggested by intelligent questions from my hearers, and with the passages given in full (from translations) which the class read in the original texts.

There are many interesting problems for which I have yet found no solution. What was the origin of the pro- verbial 'seven wonders of the world,' which Diodorus knows, but concerning which we have only a late and worthless tract?

What is the real history of the translation known as the LXX and what is its age?

What are we to understand by the joint government of

a king and queen so estranged that each would seek to thwart the other in every detail of the administration?

How far does the observation, that we only know of one crown-prince with a wife (Soter II.) account for the divorce of that wife after his accession, and for other apparent heartlessnesses in Ptolemaic history? Is the hereditary title recognised in the princesses, which no doubt led to their marriages with their reigning brothers, a relic of Pharaonic ideas, or a mere imitation of the successful experiment of Philadelphus? Some day a catalogue of these problems may be set by some Academy for a special essay, and then we may attain to some satisfactory replies regarding most of them. But we may have long to wait before such another prize-essay is published as that of Giacomo Lumbroso, which marks one of the epochs in Ptolemaic studies. Yet even as I write, there are before me the proofs of Mr. Grenfell's Appendix III to our joint edition of the Revenue Papyrus—an appendix which marks another epoch in the explanation of the Ptolemaic coinage.

A few proper names (Polyperchon, Arrabaeus, Trogodyte, etc.) have been altered from their usual form on the ground of better authority for the new form. With regard to the rest, the current forms are not changed where they have become ordinary English words, or where the modern spelling did not affect the pronunciation. In lesser known names I have taken the frequent liberty of preserving the Greek forms; but without any desire to defend this inconsistency, or to impugn any other rule on the subject. Provided the reader is not misled, con-

sistency is not important, and inconsistency quite ex-
cusable. As regards the accentuation of Greek, I have
avoided doing so where our originals (on stone or papyrus)
have no accents ; when I quote from literary texts, handed
down to us accentuated, the accents found in the MSS.
have been retained.

One serious disadvantage under which the historian of
later Hellenism suffers may be noted in conclusion. In
every university the student of classical Greek subjects
finds many highly-trained colleagues to assist and criticise
him. But in the later epochs of Greek life it is not yet
so, and he must work well-nigh alone, were it not for the
broad sympathy of those who come to the subject almost
as a novelty. Hence, though I have received most
valuable aid from several of my younger colleagues, it is
not easy to find, even in so great an array of scholars as
we possess, any specialist to sift and correct the many
statements made, and conjectures hazarded, upon this
wide and intricate field of study.

In a few more years of discovery and criticism we may
expect this epoch to be as carefully surveyed and dissected
as the older epochs of Greek history have been. But as
yet the writer on Ptolemaic history feels himself in some
sort a pioneer, who is liable to be baulked by unexpected obstacles, misled by ardent expectations, diverted
from his path by false informations. Yet are all these
risks and dangers unable to outweigh the intense interest
of penetrating a country either unexplored or imperfectly
described by former travellers.

CONTENTS

CHAPTER VI

CHAPTER VII

CHAPTER VIII

CHAPTER IX

CHAPTER X

CHAPTER XI

CHAPTER XII

CHAPTER XIII

CHRONOLOGY

NOTE.—I regret that after much labour we have not yet been able to fix the closer dates (*i.e.* the months) of the accession of the various kings. Even the year is often uncertain. But I hope ere long to be able to say something more definite on this question.

B.C.

332   Alexander III. of Macedon (the Great) conquers Egypt.

331   Visit to the oasis of Amon. Submission of Cyrene.

331–0 Alexandria founded (winter).

330   Cleomenes practically Satrap of Egypt.
       Ptolemy marries Artakama, daughter of Artabazus.

323   (Summer). Death of Alexander. Philip Arridaeus nominal king.
       Ptolemy Satrap. Intimacy with Lais.

322   Transference of Alexander's body to Egypt.
       Ptolemy's alliance with the kings of Cyprus.

322–1 Subjugation of Cyrene by means of Ophelas.

321   Invasion of Egypt by Perdikkas. His defeat and death.
       The division of Triparadeisus.
       Ptolemy's marriage with Eurydike, daughter of Antipater.

320   Ptolemy occupies Cyprus and Syria.

319   His alliance with Casander. Proclamation of Polyperchon.

317   Alexander IV. (Aegus) nominal king.
       Ptolemy marries Berenike.
       Restoration of the cella at Luxor in Alexander's name.

316   Seleukos flies from Antigonus. Arrives in Egypt.
       (?) Birth of Berenike's daughter Arsinoe.

315   War of Ptolemy (and Seleukos) against Antigonus. Antigonus seizes Cyprus, and the Philistine coast.

314–3 Reconquest of Cyprus by Ptolemy and revolt of Cyrene (?). Meeting at Ekregma.

B.C.

312   Demetrius defeated at Gaza.   Seleukos returns to Babylon. Antigonus recovers Syria and Palestine.

311   Death of Alexander IV. (but his name appears as king till 305).

310   Peace between Antigonus and Ptolemy.

    Death of Roxane (Alexander the Great's widow).

    Grant of land to the temples of Pe and Tep in Alexander Aegus' name, but the titles of the young king are left blank, as he was probably already dead.

    Ptolemy declares the freedom of the Greeks, and so obtains practical possession of the coasts of Cilicia and Lycia.

309   He visits the Cyclades, and puts garrisons into Corinth and Sikyon.

    Death of Alexander the Great's sister Cleopatra, and of his bastard son Herakles.

308   Birth of Berenike's son Ptolemy (afterwards king).

308–7 Demetrius retakes Corinth and Sikyon.

    Ophelas murdered by Agathocles.   Ptolemy recovers Cyrene and sends Magas to govern it.

307   Ptolemy marries his daughter Theoxena to Agathocles.

    He visits Megara.

306   Defeat of Ptolemy at Cyprus by Demetrius, who takes the island.

    Arrival of Demetrius the Phalerean in Egypt.

306–5 Invasion of Egypt by Antigonus.   Its failure.

305   (November).   Ptolemy assumes the title of king.

    Siege of Rhodes by Demetrius.

    (?) Assumption of the title Soter by Ptolemy.

302   New alliance against Antigonus.

    The campaign of Antigonus against Lysimachus in Asia Minor.

    Ptolemy re-occupies Syria and Palestine, but again evacuates them.

301   Battle of Ipsus.

300   Lysimachus marries Arsinoe, daughter of Ptolemy and of Berenike.

    His son Agathocles marries Lysandra, daughter of Ptolemy and of Eurydike.

299   Pyrrhus a hostage in Egypt.

295   (?) Ptolemy recovers Cyprus from Demetrius.   The foundation of the Museum and Library at Alexandria about this time.

B.C.

295 Pyrrhus returns to Epirus as king.

294 Demetrius Poliorketes king of Macedonia.

290 Probable time of Ptolemy's composition of his history of Alexander's campaigns.

289 Begging petition of Demochares (from Athens).

288 Great armaments of Demetrius in Greece.

285–4 Ptolemy practically abdicates by associating his younger son Ptolemy in the royalty.
Eurydike and her children leave Egypt.
She marries her daughter Ptolemais to Demetrius.

283 Death of Demetrius Poliorketes (Droysen).
Death of Ptolemy Soter.

281 Battle of Korupedion. Death of Lysimachus.
Death of Seleukos I. and accession of Antiochus I. (Soter).

280 Pyrrhus lands in Italy. Ptolemy visits Pithom.

278 Antigonus (Gonatas) defeats the Gauls near Lysimacheia, and becomes definitively king of Macedon.

277 Pyrrhus in Sicily. (?) Second marriage of Ptolemy to Arsinoe II.

275 Pyrrhus returns to Italy.

274 Pyrrhus returns to Epirus.

273 Ptolemy sends an embassy to Rome. His second visit to Pithom.
The Romans reply with an embassy to Alexandria.

271 Ptolemy Soter deified.

269 First coinage of silver at Rome.

266 The Canephorus (priestess) of Arsinoe Philadelphus established (?).

265 Beginning of the Chremonidean War (?).

264 The eponymous priests of the *gods Adelphi* first mentioned.
First Punic War. Third visit to Pithom, and religious endowments.

263 Time of Second Syrian War (?). Eumenes succeeds to the throne of Pergamum.

262 The ἀπόμοιρα on wine and fruits settled on the deified Arsinoe.
Death of Antiochus Soter (king of Syria) and accession of his son Antiochus II. (Theos).

260 Progress of the Chremonidean War.

258 Athens subdued by Antigonus. Defeat of Ptolemy's fleet at Kos (?). The Revenue Papyrus.
Death of Magas. Demetrius the Fair at Cyrene. Ptolemy III. (crown prince) declared lord of Cyrene.
Change in the formula of the king's dates.

B.C.

256   Reclaiming of the lake Moeris in progress.

255   Ptolemy II. visits the lake Moeris, and (probably) re-names the
       district as the *Arsinoite nome*.

251   Aratus frees Sikyon.

250   Aratus goes to Egypt.
       Arsaces founds the Parthian monarchy, and revolts from the
       Seleukids.

247   Egyptian victory at Andros.
       Death of Ptolemy Philadelphus, accession and marriage of
       Ptolemy III.

246   Third Syrian War.   Accession of Seleukos II. Kallinikos.
       Ptolemy captures Seleukeia on the Orontes, and Antioch.

245   Ptolemy recalled from the East by domestic troubles.

241   End of the First Punic War.   Accession of Attalus I. at Per-
       gamum.

239   Death of Antigonus Gonatas.

238   Synod of Canopus.   Ptolemy III. and his queen Berenike II.
       deified as *gods Euergetae*.

237   Great temple of Edfu founded.

229   Death of Demetrius the Aetolian (king of Macedon).

228   First Roman embassy to Greece.

226   Accession of Seleukos III. Keraunos.

223   Great earthquake at Rhodes (?).

222–1 Battle of Sellasia.   Cleomenes flies to Egypt.
       Death of Euergetes I. and accession of Ptolemy IV. (Philo-
       pator).
       Death of Antigonus Doson (of Macedon), and accession of
       Philip V.

221–0 Accession of Antiochus III. (the Great, of Syria).   Hannibal
       in Spain.   Fourth Syrian War.

219   Antiochus recovers Palestine from Egypt.

218   Hannibal crosses the Alps.

217   Battle of Raphia and defeat of Antiochus III.
       Peace between Egypt and Syria.

216   Battle of Cannae.
       Decius Magius escapes from the Carthaginians, first to Cyrene
       and then to Egypt.

214   Treaty of Hannibal with Philip V.

213   (?) Insurrection of the natives in Egypt.
       Marriage of Ptolemy IV. to his sister, Arsinoe III.
       They are deified as *gods Philopatores*.

B.C.

211 Scopas praetor of Aetolia.

210 Birth of Ptolemy V.

His mother imprisoned, and after some time murdered by Sosibius and Agathocles.

209 Ptolemy V. associated in the crown.

205 Accession of Ptolemy V. Epiphanes.

202 Battle of Zama.

201 Roman embassy to Egypt.

Battle of Chios between the Rhodians, etc. and Philip.

200 Embassy of Ptolemy to offer assistance to Rome against Philip.

198 Battle of Panion. Scopas defeated by Antiochus III.

Betrothal of Ptolemy V. to Cleopatra I. (of Syria).

197 Battle of Cynoscephalae. Accession of Eumenes II. at Pergamum.

196–5 Anacleteria and divine honours to Ptolemy V. (Rosetta stone and decree of Memphis).

194 Death of Eratosthenes. Apollonius Rhodius chief librarian at Alexandria.

193 Marriage of Ptolemy Epiphanes and Cleopatra I. at Raphia.

192 Antiochus invades Greece.

191 Embassy of Ptolemy with gifts of money to Rome.

190 Battle of Magnesia. Antiochus III. defeated by the Romans.

189 Insurrection in Upper Egypt.

188 Manlius in Asia Minor.

187 Embassy from Egypt to Achaian League (?).

Death of Antiochus III. and accession of Seleukos IV. (Philopator).

186 The concessions of the king's 9th year (Rosetta stone) renewed.

184 The insurrection subdued.

182 Death of Ptolemy and accession of Ptolemy VI. (Eupator).

182–1 Accession of Ptolemy VII. (Philometor).

179 Death of Philip V. and accession of Perseus in Macedonia.

175 Accession of Antiochus IV. (Epiphanes).

174 Death of Cleopatra I.

173 Marriage of Ptolemy VII. to his sister Cleopatra II.

Embassy from Rome to Egypt.

171 Invasion of Antiochus IV. Epiphanes. Ptolemy Philometor defeated near Mount Casius.

Antiochus crowned king of Egypt (?).

170 Ptolemy Euergetes II. made king by the Alexandrians.

B.C.

170   By Cleopatra II.'s mediation, Ptolemy Philometor returns and the two brothers reign conjointly.

170–69 Renewed invasion of Antiochus IV.

168   Battle of Pydna (June). Antiochus checked and sent home by the embassy of Popilius Laenas.

167   Revolt of Dionysius Petosiris.

165   Revolt at Panopolis subdued by Ptolemy Philometor (?).

164   Accession of Antiochus V. (Eupator).

163   Ptolemy Philometor exiled by his brother and flies to Rome. He is restored by the Senate, and Euergetes II. is sent to Cyrene.

162   Accession of Demetrius II. Soter in Syria.

161   Euergetes II. goes to Rome, to obtain new terms (?).

160   Visit of Ptolemy Philometor and his queen to Memphis.

159   Accession of Attalus II. at Pergamum.

155   Embassy of the three philosophers (on the part of Athens) to Rome.

154   Euergetes II. conquered in Cyprus. Settlement of the war between the brothers.

151   Demetrius Soter endeavours to annex Cyprus.

150   Ptolemy Philometor gives his daughter Cleopatra in marriage to Alexander Bala at Ptolemais.

149   Third Punic War.

147   Demetrius Nicator claims the crown. Ptolemy gives him his daughter Cleopatra to wife, and is crowned king at Antioch.

146   Death of Philometor in battle. Accession and death of Ptolemy VIII. (Philopator Neos).
       Fall of Carthage, and of Corinth.
       Renewed accession of Ptolemy IX. (Euergetes II.)
       He marries the queen Cleopatra II.

145   Birth of his son Memphites.
       He issues a decree of Benevolences.

144–3 (?) Euergetes II. marries his niece Cleopatra III. (Euergetis).

143 (?)   Mission of Scipio Aemilianus to Egypt.

138   Death of Attalus II. (Philadelphus) and accession of Attalus III.

137   Antiochus Sidetes king of Syria.

134   Slave war in Sicily.

133   Death of Attalus III.

132   War of the Romans with Aristonicus of Pergamum.

130–29 Ptolemy IX. exiled, and Cleopatra II. reigns. (Nevertheless he appears as king of Egypt in at least two documents of the year 129 B.C.)

B.C.

129   Aristonicus put to death. Death of Scipio Aemilianus.

127   Euergetes II. again recovers Egypt.

123   C. Gracchus tribune.

121   Death of C. Gracchus.

120   Accession of Mithradates VI. (Eupator) in Pontus.

117   Death of Ptolemy IX. His widow Cleopatra rules.

116–5 Association of Ptolemy X. (Lathyrus) with his mother Cleopatra III. in the throne.

       Ptolemy X. marries his sister Selene.

115   Ptolemy X. visits Elephantine (stele of Aswân).

114   Ptolemy Alexander I. appointed king of Cyprus.

114–3 Cleopatra III. and Ptolemy Soter II. assume the title Philometores Soteres.

111   Jugurthine war.

110   Ptolemy Philometor Soter II. (Lathyrus) assumes sole power.

107–6 Ptolemy Lathyrus exiled and Alexander I. recalled to reign with his mother.

105 (?) Ptolemy Lathyrus makes war in Palestine.

       Invasions of the Cimbri into Italy.

104   Triumph of Marius over the Cimbri.

102   Second Servile war in Sicily.

100–99 Berenike III. appears as queen with Alexander I. but also with his mother.

       Saturninus tribune.

99   Lathyrus king of Cyprus.

96   Death of Ptolemy Apion, who bequeaths Cyrene to Rome.

92   First public transaction (by Sylla) between Rome and Parthia.

91 (?) Death of Cleopatra III.

90   Marsian or Social War.

88   Alexander I. is exiled, and slain.

       Soter II. (Lathyrus) returns from exile and again becomes king.

       Mithradates invades Asia Minor and massacres the Italians there. He finds Ptolemy Alexander II. at Kos, but the prince escapes to Rome.

87   Lucullus comes to Egypt to seek aid for Sylla.

86   Athens stormed by Sylla.

84 (?) Destruction of Thebes by Lathyrus.

       Peace between Sylla and Mithradates.

81   Death of Ptolemy X. Philometor Soter II. (Lathyrus).

       Accession of Ptolemy XII. Alexander II., who marries

B.C.

81   Berenike III. Philopator.   Death of both queen and king
         in nineteen days.
         Accession of Ptolemy XIII. Neos Dionysus, Philopator (III.)
         and Philadelphus (II. Auletes).¹

80   Capture of Mitylene by the Romans.   Caesar's first campaign.

79   Auletes marries Cleopatra V. Tryphaena.

78   Death of Sylla.

77 (?) Birth of Berenike IV.   War of Rome against Cilician pirates.

75–4   Bithynia bequeathed to Rome. Cyrene occupied by the Romans.
         Second war with Mithradates.
         Selene and her two sons come from Syria to Rome.

72   The two sons of Selene and Antiochus Grypus leave Rome.
         Wars with Sertorius, Spartacus, and Mithradates in progress.

69–8   Birth of Cleopatra VI.   Selene put to death by Tigranes.

67   Gabinian Law.   Pompey subdues the pirates.

66   Manilian Law.   Pompey against Mithradates.

65   Crassus proposes to reduce Egypt to a Roman province.

64   Betrothal of two infant Ptolemies to two daughters of Mithra-
         dates.
         Pompey in Syria.

63   Death of King Mithradates of Pontus.
         Auletes seeks recognition from Pompey.

60 (?) Diodorus Siculus visits Egypt.

59   Auletes recognised by Julius Caesar as consul.
         The temple of Edfu completed.

58   Auletes is expelled, and flies to Rome.
         Cyprus reduced to a province by Cato.   Death of King
         Ptolemy of Cyprus.

57   Cleopatra V. Tryphaena remains queen at Alexandria.   She
         dies and Berenike IV. her daughter assumes the throne.

56   Berenike marries Seleukos Kybiosaktes, and rejects him.   She
         marries Archelaus of Komana.
         Cicero makes his speech *pro rege Alexandrino.*

55   Restoration of Auletes by Gabinius, with Antony commanding
         his cavalry.   First meeting of Antony and Cleopatra.
         Rabirius over the finances of Egypt.

54   Cicero's speech *pro Rabirio Postumo.*
         Crassus invades Parthia.

51   Death of Ptolemy XIII. Auletes.
         Cleopatra VI. and her brother Ptolemy XIV. appointed to
         the throne by his will.

B.C.

49   Caesar crosses the Rubicon.
      Cnaeus Pompey goes for levies to Egypt.
48   Battle of Pharsalia.
      Cleopatra driven out by her brother.   She returns with an army
         to Pelusium.   Pompey arrives at the camp of Ptolemy XIV.
         and is murdered.
      Arrival of Julius Caesar, who is besieged (with Cleopatra) in
         Alexandria.
47   Alexandrian War.   Ptolemy XIV. drowned.   Cleopatra ap-
         pointed queen with her younger brother Ptolemy XV.
46 (?) Cleopatra goes to Rome.   Reform of the Calendar by Julius
         Caesar.
45   Death of Ptolemy XV.   Cleopatra assumes her son Caesarion
         (Ptolemy XVI.) as co-regent.
44   Caesar assassinated.   Cleopatra returns to Egypt.
43-2 Famine in Egypt.   Triumvirate of Octavian, Antony, and
         Lepidus.¦
42   Battle of Philippi.
41   Antony summons Cleopatra to Cilicia, and returns with her to
         Alexandria.
40   The Parthians invade Syria.   Herod appointed king of Judaea.
38   Ventidius conquers the Parthians.   Capture of Jerusalem by
         Sossius.   Antony returns to Italy.
37-6 Antony returns to the East, and after his Parthian expedition
         rules at Alexandria with Cleopatra.
      War of Octavian and Antony against Sextus Pompey.
      Antony invades Armenia.
34-3 Triumph of Antony at Alexandria.   He distributes Eastern
         provinces to her children.
31   Battle of Actium.
30   Death of Cleopatra VI., Ptolemy XVI. (Caesarion), and of
         Antony and his son Antyllus.
      Settlement of Egypt as an imperial province under Augustus.

CHAPTER I

§ 1. THERE is something unsatisfactory in beginning a history with the mature state of a nation. As in biography so in history, we desire to go back to the cradle, and see the growth of social and of political life from their first rude commencements. There is, moreover, not a little difficulty in finding a later moment which will afford a real starting-point. Each condition of a nation is the result of what went before, and the human mind feels compelled to seek the causes for this, as for every other effect. In undertaking, however, to

ALEXANDER THE GREAT.

begin a special history of Egypt with the accession of the first Ptolemy, these objections lose most of their force. For, in the first place, several competent scholars have written the history of Egypt from its dawn till the conquest of Alexander, so that all the earlier stages can be studied in good books. These eminent men must also have felt some distinct break in the life of the nation, as their work appeared to them concluded when Egypt passed under Macedonian sway. In this impression they have but reproduced the unanimous feeling of Hellenistic writers, who imply or assert that with Alexander a new volume of the world's history had opened, and that the events even of the recent past belonged to a different age, and might be neglected as the decrepitude of a byegone civilisation. Polybius, for example, in his careful and philosophic history of the Greek world of his own century, though he inquires diligently into causes and appreciates traditions, finds no occasion, so far as we know him, to cite Xenophon or Thucydides more than once, Herodotus more than twice. In his mind the break with the past made by Alexander was complete. We are therefore fortified by a general consensus of opinion, when we assume for Egypt what was true of the rest of the nations about the Levant, and treat the Ptolemaic rule as a distinct epoch in the history of the valley of the Nile.

§ 2. That this epoch has hitherto been neglected is not strange. In spite of the great splendour and importance of the Ptolemies in the Hellenistic world, no systematic account of them had survived even in Pausanias' day.[1] We know them through pompous hieroglyphics, which were not intended to instruct us, through panegyrics which were perhaps intended to mislead us, through episodes in the universal histories of Polybius and Diodorus. Recently we have added to these literary authorities a good many stray inscriptions, and a mass of papyrus fragments, which give us multitudinous isolated facts, seldom of public interest,

---

[1] i. 6 ὡς μὴ μένειν ἔτι τὴν φήμην αὐτῶν, καὶ οἱ συγγενόμενοι τοῖς βασιλεῦσιν ἐπὶ συγγραφῇ τῶν ἔργων καὶ πρότερον ἔτι ἠμελήθησαν.

but no connected history. The only writer who has attempted to treat this period in connexion with the preceding and succeeding epochs, was Sharpe,[1] in whose book the Ptolemies have obtained the lion's share. But how antiquated it seems to us now, and how many of his statements are contradicted by recent discoveries! A like fate will inevitably attend his successors. Even now no history of the Ptolemies can claim or desire to be final. Ptolemaic inscriptions, Ptolemaic papyri, are finding their way into our museums every year. Whenever demotic Egyptian comes to be understood, so that its matter becomes accessible to ordinary scholars, a flood of new light may be thrown upon the subject. Yet if the vast body of isolated facts be not gathered periodically, and set in order, it will be impossible to fit further discoveries into their places, and we shall find ourselves in presence of a confused mass of evidence which few will attempt to comprehend. Even now the task of knowing the extant Ptolemaic papyri is arduous enough; were it not for exceptional privileges enjoyed in deciphering and explaining them, the undertaking would have been beyond my ambition. Those who know this vast and partly-explored field best, will be the readiest to make allowance for my shortcomings.

§ 3. None of Alexander's achievements was more facile, and yet none more striking, than his Egyptian campaign.[2]

---

[1] *History of Egypt* by Samuel Sharpe, 5th edition, in 2 vols., 1870. Unfortunately this edition takes no notice of the German translation (2nd ed., Leipzig, 1862), which is corrected and enriched with excellent notes by A. von Gutschmid. These latter I have constantly used.

[2] Arrian ii. 13 *sq.* and Diodorus xvii. 48 are our chief authorities; also Plutarch *Alex.* 26, Justin, and Curtius. It is so easy to find the respective passages in any index to these texts, that I shall often omit the 'chapter and verse.'

His advent must have been awaited with all the agitations
of fear and hope by the natives of all classes, for the
Persian sway had been cruel and bloody, and if it did not
lay extravagant burdens upon the poor, it certainly gave the
higher classes an abundance of sentimental grievances, for it
had violated the national feelings, and especially the national
religion, with wanton brutality.   The treatment of the revolted province by Ochus was not less violent and ruthless
than had been the original conquest by Cambyses, which
Herodotus tells us with graphic simplicity.   No conquerors
seem to have been more uncongenial to the Egyptians than
the Persians.   But all invaders of Egypt, even the Ptolemies,
were confronted by a like hopelessness of gaining the
sympathies of their subjects.   If it was comparatively easy
to make them slaves, they were perpetually revolting slaves.
This was due not to the impatience of the average native,
but rather to the hold which the national religion had
gained upon his life.   This religion was administered by
an ambitious, organised, haughty priesthood, whose records
and traditions told them of the vast wealth and power they
had once possessed—a condition of things long past away,
and never likely to return, even under a native dynasty,
but still filling the imaginations of the priests, and urging
them to set their people against every foreign ruler.   The
only chance of success for an invader lay in conciliating
this vast and stubborn corporation.   Every chief who headed
a revolt against the Persians had made this the centre
of his policy; the support of the priests must be gained
by restoring them to their old supremacy—a supremacy
which they doubtless exaggerated in their uncriticised
records of the past.

§ 4.   There was another class of the population not less
discontented—the military caste, which had long since

been thrust into the background by the employment of foreign, chiefly Greek, mercenaries. Even kings of national proclivities found these Greeks or Carians so much more efficient, that they could not be persuaded to dispense with them and depend upon native troops. The military caste, which denied that these foreigners were necessary,[1] and professed all readiness to fight the king's battles, or mount guard at his palace, was moody and jealous, and the neglect of its grievances must have given great additional force to the rebellions, usually supported by this section of the population. As for the labouring classes, we may assume that then, as now, they desired little more than freedom from forced labour, and security against the exactions of the tax-farmer. There is little mention, in this later Egyptian history, of any nobility territorial or otherwise, such as had flourished under the Middle Empire,[2] though there were still over the administration officials of great importance from their knowledge of the people and their language. But most local magnates or feudal chiefs only asserted themselves during those weaknesses of the central power, which give special opportunities to ambitious and wealthy provincials for making their dignities hereditary. Such a body of nobles does not meet us in any of the records of this period. Yet the insurgent chiefs who rose against the Persians and against the fifth Ptolemy were apparently men of high birth, descended from royal ancestors; no ordinary Fellah would ever think of leading an army.

[1] They could point to the high character of the Egyptian contingents which fought with Croesus against Cyrus (Xenophon *Cyrop.* vii. 1, 45) and with Xerxes against the Greeks (Herod. viii. 17, ix. 32), as historical evidence of their efficiency, when properly fitted out and treated with confidence. In Ptolemaic times they are called οἱ Μάχιμοι.

[2] Cf. Erman's *Aegypten* pp. 135 *sq.*

§ 5. We can only assert these generalities concerning the condition of the oppressed people, who were watching with breathless interest Alexander's attack upon the Persian Empire. All better information is wanting. The satrap of Egypt, Sabakes, had been summoned with most of the garrison to join his master Darius, and had fallen at the battle of Issus.[1] Though his division probably consisted of Greek and Asiatic mercenaries, it is hardly possible that some Egyptians did not accompany them, who must have brought back a startling report of the conqueror and his army. Even if they had not done so, the distinguished people mentioned by Arrian, the deserter Amyntas, Mentor's son Thymondas, and others, who fled straight from Issus to Egypt, as to a land of safety, made matters plain enough.[2] Then came the siege of Tyre, in which Alexander's obstinacy, and his versatility of resource, had overcome apparent impossibilities, and during these many months, so long as the Tyrian fleet was able to keep the sea-way open, traders must have brought news of the gradual change from confidence to alarm, from alarm to despair, in the great naval mistress of the Syrian Levant. And after the fall of Tyre, and the consequent passage of the naval supremacy into Alexander's hands, came in rapid succession the news of his clemency at Jerusalem, his severity at Gaza,[3] and his advent at the Eastern gate of Egypt.

I have elsewhere[4] explained the probable reasons for

[1] Arrian ii. 11, 8.

[2] Amyntas (Diod. xvii. 48, Arrian ii. 13, 2), who had a force of 4000 (Arrian says 8000) men, took possession of Pelusium, and tried honestly to hold the country for Darius, but he and his soldiers were all slain by the natives near Memphis as being lawless marauders.

[3] Arrian ii. 18-26 ; Diod. xvii. 48.

[4] *Greek Life and Thought* etc. p. 470.

his tender treatment of the Jews, whose trading connexions over the world, combined with the regular journeys
of the ' Dispersion ' to Jerusalem, made them invaluable
friends to him, as guides to his intelligence department.
From them too did he learn the passes into Egypt between
marshes and deserts, and they must have announced to
the Egyptians his liberality towards their religion, and his
graciousness towards those who submitted promptly and
unreservedly to his commands.[1] So, when the remaining
Persian garrison and fleet had made hardly a show of
resistance, the Macedonian entered into peaceable possession of the kingdom of the Pharaohs.

§ 6. The various mercenary forces, whether in the pay
of the Persians, or marauding in the country under pretence of defending it for the Great King, had now no
alternative but to submit to Alexander, and swell the
ranks of his army. The priests hailed with satisfaction
the victorious enemy of their recent oppressors. Thus
we may assume that his march along the eastern outlet of
the Nile, from Pelusium to Heliopolis and Memphis, was
a triumphal procession.[2] No sooner had he arrived at
Memphis than he displayed the same conciliatory policy
to the priests which he had adopted at Jerusalem. He

---

[1] Isaiah xix. and Jer. xliv. tell us of settlements of Jews in the
Eastern Delta, and imply frequent intercourse between Egypt and
Judaea ever since Assyria (or Babylon) had been contending with Egypt
for the possession of Syria and Palestine. The narrative of Josephus
(*Antiqq.* xi. 8, 4) is very suspicious, and has been generally rejected. I
have sought to disengage the element of truth concealed in it. Cf.
the citations in Pauly - Wissowa's *Encyclop.* i. pp. 1422 - 23 (art.
ALEXANDROS). Alexander, in reciting his dream to the high-priest says :
διασκεπτομένῳ μοι πῶς ἂν κρατήσαιμι τῆς Ἀσίας αὐτὸς (*sc.* the figure of the
high-priest) ἔφη ἡγήσεσθαί μοι τῆς στρατιᾶς, which means, I think, that
the Jews would show him all the roads, and tell him the distances.

[2] Arrian iii. 1.

sacrificed to Apis and the other gods, and assured the priests of his favour and support.[1]   If the Jewish authorities were to help him in his campaigns through Asia with their knowledge of distances, their correspondents in remote cities, their exceptional geographical knowledge, the Egyptian priests were to serve him in another way; they were to secure to him without disturbance the supplies of provisions and money which in that favoured country seemed unlimited, even in troublous times and under the grossest misgovernment.   Some six millions—the Ptolemies raised the figure to seven and a half—of hard-working fellahs were trained by hereditary oppression to work for their masters, and pay taxes out of all proportion to the size of the country.   This safe and certain source of revenue was at the moment of great importance to the new king, who had not yet seized the great hoards of treasure at Susa and Persepolis.   His own treasury was at the lowest ebb, though his conquests may have already obtained for him considerable pecuniary credit.[2]

§ 7. But we are only concerned with Alexander so far as we can explain through his acts more clearly the policy of his successor in the sovranty of Egypt.   We hear that he appointed two Egyptians, Peteēsis and Doloaspis, *nomarchs* of the provinces, of which he created for this purpose but two, probably Upper and Lower Egypt.   Doloaspis, who presently obtained the whole management, has a name which hardly seems to be Egyptian, Peteēsis, on the other hand, was the name of several native officials of importance in later generations.   There were several

---

[1] With these ceremonies he combined a gymnic and musical contest among artists brought from Greece.   Arrian *loc. cit.*

[2] The Egyptian priests also supplied him with a sentimental dignity which will come before the reader presently.

Greeks and Macedonian grandees also appointed for military purposes, and to look after the treasury.[1] Of these one only, Cleomenes, maintained his importance for some years. He was indeed the chief adviser of the king at the founding of Alexandria, if pseudo-Callisthenes,[2] here apparently well-informed, is to be trusted ; but in the sequel, and when no longer under Alexander's eye, he earned a reputation for dishonesty and injustice. But, of course, all these appointments were merely provisional, pending a reconstruction of the Persian Empire.[3]

§ 8. Two acts only of the king were plainly intended as declarations of a deliberate policy. He had no time to visit Upper Egypt, but took care to send a detachment of troops under Apollonides as far as Elephantine,[4] to exhibit his authority. He himself, having made his peace with

---

[1] B. Niese *Hellenismus* i. p. 87 gives a good summary of the details. I can make nothing of Suidas' note on βασίλειοι παῖδες ἑξακισχίλιοι· οἵτινες κατὰ πρόσταξιν Ἀλεξ. τοῦ Μακ. τὰ πολέμια ἐξήσκουν ἐν Αἰγύπτῳ, and suspect the last word should be Αἰγαῖς (viz. Aegae), the old seat of the Macedonian kings. Diod. (xvii. 48) says that he received reinforcements from Greece before he left Egypt (331 B.C. spring). Possibly this may be the fact concealed in the note.

[2] i. 30. I quote from the βίος Ἀλεξ. edited by C. Müller with Arrian, in the Didot series.

[3] Arrian iii. 5 gives a list of these officers, and notices the subdivision of charges, implying an apprehension on the part of Alexander, lest a single ruler of Egypt might cause him serious difficulties in case of revolt. This fear, he adds, the Romans seem to have learned from Alexander, since they exclude senators from governing it. He also notices that Cleomenes, the general collector of the taxes, was made governor not of Libya, but of Arabia, which lay far away from that person's native town Naukratis.

[4] There is evidence that this was now a penal settlement, probably to utilise the labour of the prisoners in the granite quarries, for Alexander sent there certain Chian political prisoners from Memphis (Arrian iii. 2, 7). I shall produce some evidence in the sequel that it was not yet a town or πόλις, though Arrian calls it so.

the priests of Memphis, and consulted with them—though of course any such consultation was carefully kept a secret —set out by the western branch of the Nile, on his circuitous route to the temple of Jupiter Amon in the oasis now called that of Siwâh. During his circuit the priests were, of course, duly informed of his approach by a detachment sent across the desert from Memphis.[1] They, therefore, were quite prepared for him, and instructed how to receive him.

Meanwhile his sail down the Canopic arm must have led him close by the old Greek city of Naukratis, founded upon a lesser arm, the Herakleotic, more to the west than even the Canopic. And as this Herakleotic arm or canal opened into the Canopic—for we know that the waterway from the sea to Naukratis was to ascend the latter arm —it is most likely that Alexander, who had done everything hitherto to favour the Egyptians, received some petitions or representations from the ancient Greek settlement, and visited it on his way to the sea. Nor is it likely that they should not have claimed wider privileges through the agency of Cleomenes, now a great state-officer, selected from Naukratis, to control the finances of the country; and who is said by Justin (xiii. 4) *to have been one of the architects of Alexandria*, along with Deinocrates: moreover Alexander was bound to show them that he did not mean his new province to be anti-Hellenic.[2] Hitherto the Naukratites had been under all manner of jealous restrictions, which, though relaxed in recent times, might be

---

[1] *Per praemissos subornat antistites quid sibi responderi velit*, Justin xi. 11.

[2] We now know, from the recent discoveries of Mr. Petrie, that the city was allowed to coin, at least copper, during Alexander's reign; this the legends ΝΑΥ and ΑΛΕ render certain. Cf. B. Head in *Numismatic Chronicle* vi. 3rd series, p. 11.

reimposed by nationalist kings or governors. But if
Alexander did visit their city, he found it considerably
decayed, and situated on a water-way quite inadequate
for the increasing trade with the north and west. Therefore I cannot but think that the proximity of Naukratis
had some influence in determining the site of his new
foundation at the western point of Egypt (331-0 B.C.
winter). If the Naukratites asked for privileges, he could
offer them such of tenfold value at the new site he had
chosen, on the sea, and communicating with the old Greek
mart by an easy water-way. It is even likely that a canal
led straight from Naukratis into Lake Mareotis, and so to
the new Alexandria in a few hours.[1]

§ 9. This very obvious reason for Alexander's choice
of the new site is not mentioned by the few ancient
historians who are left to tell us about his famous foundation. They regale us instead with the prodigies which
accompanied it,[2] while their modern successors insist upon
the rare genius which foresaw the suitabilities of the place.
With these latter I am not in harmony. Alexander
possessed undoubted genius, and his city was eminently
successful, but it is almost certain that had he founded it
anywhere else on the coast, say at Canopus or at Aboukir
Bay, it would have made little difference. He plainly
intended it to look to the west for its wealth. The
traders of Naukratis must have always turned in the same

[1] That Naukratis was not absorbed by Alexandria appears from the
buildings there of Ptolemy II., and from the mention of it under
Ptolemies IV., V., and VII., as will appear in the sequel.

[2] Thus Plutarch (*Alexander* 26) says it was a figure (Homer?)
appearing in a dream and reciting a line from the *Odyssey* (iv. 354)
which turned his attention to Pharos. Pseudo-Callisthenes says the
oracle of Amon instructed him, and gives the verses of the alleged
response (i. 30).

direction. The coast has not been sufficiently surveyed
to tell us whether other bays have not equal facilities
for harbouring ships. Aboukir Bay certainly held fleets
in recent days far more difficult to harbour than were the
greatest Alexandrian merchantmen. Nor is either entrance
into the harbours of Alexandria free from great risk. In
fine it appears to me that the moment had come when
any port on the Delta, in communication with an arm of
the Nile, and open to foreign trade, must inevitably have
a great success. It was, I believe, not the eagle eye of
the conqueror, but the proximity of Naukratis, and the
representations of its traders, which led him to choose
the western extreme of the Delta. It replaced at once
the port at the Canopic mouth of the river. It could
not replace Pelusium, which was a great frontier fortress
and which lasted throughout the Ptolemaic epoch, and
probably far later, as the natural harbour for Syrian
traffic.[1]

§ 10. The next point of interest in Alexander's progress is his visit to the remote oasis of Amon,[2] with great
risk and trouble, to accomplish an object which could

[1] Alexander appointed Polemon governor of this fortress, and we
find in the Revenue (or Tax-farming) Papyrus, col. 52 οσοι δε των
εμπορων εκ Πηλουσιου ξενικον ελαιον η Συρον παρακομιζωσιν εις Αλεξαν-
δρειαν ατελεις εστωσαν συμβολον δε κομιζετωσαν παρα του εμ Πηλουσιωι
καθεστηκοτος . . . The title to be given to this important document is
not yet fixed. We hope to publish it in the course of this year (1895).
Its ordinances are dated 262 and 258 B.C.

[2] Some of our authorities, Diodorus xvii. 52, Justin xi. 11, Curtius,
iv. 7, speak as if the city had not been founded till Alexander's return
from the oasis. Arrian and Plutarch are explicit that it was otherwise.
The discrepancy is hardly worth mentioning, for though he may have
planned and given orders about the site before his visit to Amon, he,
of course, resumed the matter and gave more attention to it upon his
return. Justin adds a very significant expression : *Alexandriam
condidit, et coloniam Macedonum caput esse Aegypti jubet.*

apparently have been compassed by consulting the priests of Memphis, or of the accredited oracles in many Hellenic countries. But what was his object? Some modern historians, shocked that so great a person should have coveted the sham prestige of a divine origin, insist that it was only a matter of policy to overawe Orientals, and that on Greeks and Macedonians the conqueror never sought to impose his own divinity. The sceptical spirit of the Greeks, they think, was as ready to scoff at any such assumption as we should be, nor is any really great man likely to promote or trade upon a manifest imposture.

Our ancient evidence on the other hand is consistent that he did advance such claims, and if Arrian only mentions sundry miracles which happened on the journey to the oasis, he in no way contradicts Diodorus and others as to the king's main object, and even assumes that such claims were well known to his soldiers on subsequent occasions. During the mutiny at Babylon they jeer at him by telling him to apply to his father for an army— viz. to Zeus-Amon. When he dies it is decreed that he shall be buried in the temple of the god, not (as Perdikkas ordered, when he saw his mistake) at Aegae among the Macedonian kings. These indirect evidences are quite conclusive. Modern thinkers brought up under the influences of that Semitic spirit which places a single deity at a vast distance above man, are apt to forget that among people such as the Greeks and Egyptians, the divine and the human were not so far apart. Greek legends were full of instances of divine parentage among mortals, and if philosophers scouted such myths as absurd and unworthy of the gods, or as evidences that these gods were unreal, we know that the ordinary public, even long after

Alexander's day, were ready to attribute any extraordinary manifestation of human excellence, or even strange eccentricities in human character, to the fancy of a god for a love adventure with a mortal. There is nothing known to us of Alexander which permits us to picture him as a cool sceptic ridiculing such popular beliefs. On the contrary, the daemonic force, the deep enthusiasm, the absolute confidence in his own primacy among men, which moulded his life and determined his actions, are the very qualities we should expect from a man convinced that his origin was more than human.[1] In Egypt too he learned that the old indigenous kings had all ranked as gods, and had been called the sons of gods quite other than their human fathers, without the smallest disrespect to their mothers, or to the relations between their earthly parents. We may go so far as to say that if Alexander had neglected or refused to accept divine honours in Egypt and the East, it would have been thought strange in those days. That he should accept them in the East, and not require them from his Greek subjects, would imply not only a policy opposed to that of fusing East and West into one common civilisation, but a curious ignorance of the readiness of Greek cities to decree divine honours to any benefactor. The Athens which presently lavished idolatry upon Demetrius the Besieger, was not likely to make difficulties about worshipping Alexander, whenever hope of favour or dread of disfavour might suggest it. Taking it therefore as certain that Alexander as well from exaltation

---

[1] Arrian appreciates this perfectly; cf. iii. 3, 2 Ἀλεξάνδρῳ δὲ φιλοτιμία ἦν πρὸς Περσέα καὶ Ἡρακλέα, ἀπὸ γένους τε ὄντι τοῦ ἀμφοῖν καί τι καὶ αὐτὸς τῆς γενέσεως τῆς ἑαυτοῦ ἐς Ἄμμωνα ἀνέφερε. καὶ οὖν παρ' Ἄμμωνα ταύτῃ τῇ γνώμῃ ἐστέλλετο, ὡς καὶ τὰ αὐτοῦ ἀτρεκέστερον εἰσόμενος ἢ φήσων τε ἐγνωκέναι.

of mind as from policy desired to claim a superhuman origin, it still remains for us to inquire why he chose the difficult and dangerous journey to the far oasis in order to obtain his desire.

§ 11. It is hardly necessary to insist upon the strong attraction which difficulties presented to the royal adventurer. No feature in his character has been more consistently attested by history and by legend.[1] The sober ground of his choice lay in the fact that this oracle of Amon, regarded with awe by the Egyptians as a sanctum of their religion protected by nature from all profane contact, was also the only one in Egypt which the Greeks for centuries back had known and consulted.[2] Possibly the Greeks of Naukratis, and those of Cyrene, had something

---

[1] Cf. Arrian's account of the journey with its marvels, iii. 3.

[2] Pausanias (ix. 16, 1) tells us that Pindar (who alludes to this god : Διὸς ἐν Ἄμμωνος θεμέθλοις, *Pyth.* iv. 28) had written an ode for the Libyan priests of Amon, of which he saw a copy on a triangular stele at the temple of Amon at Boeotian Thebes beside an altar erected in honour of the god by the first Ptolemy. Pindar had also set up a statue of the god there, probably to commemorate his liberal treatment by the Libyans. Lysander was said by Ephorus to have visited this remote oracle (Plut. *Lys.* 25) in connexion with his attempts to bribe other oracles of the Greek world, and Pausanias (iii. 18, 3) says he saw an old temple of Amon at Sparta. He found the same thing at Elis (v. 15, 11). Plutarch tells us (*Kimon* 18) that Kimon sent a secret inquiry to the oasis from Cyprus, and that the god replied to his envoys that Kimon had died during their journey. If these notices are all from late writers, we can show early familiarity with the oracle at Athens from Aristophanes (*Birds* 619, 716), where it is classed with Dodona and Delphi. These references, which are not an exhaustive list, are sufficient to prove the high and general reputation of this temple of Amon in the Greek world. In addition to our ancient authorities for this passage in Alexander's history (Arrian, Plutarch, Diodorus, Curtius, Justin), there are special articles on the oracle by Parthey (Berlin *Abhand.* for 1862) and Blümner (Büdingen *Program*, 1868).

to do with this curious fact. Either of them may have thought it worth while to undertake the journey of 180 miles from Paraetonium, which they could reach by sea, to obtain the trade with the whole series of oases, whose produce comes to that of Siwâh by caravan from the south. At all events, this oracle had a recognised authority throughout the Hellenic world, which none of the shrines of Memphis or of Thebes, however splendid, had attained.

It happened also that on his way westward, Alexander received the voluntary submission of Cyrene,[1] which thus became legitimately a province of Egypt, and gave the Ptolemies that title to its sovranty, which was of great importance in the diplomatic disputes of the Hellenistic world. Upon his return from the oracle Alexander went to Memphis, whether by Alexandria or across the desert directly was a point upon which first-rate authorities, Aristobulus and Ptolemy, differed. From thence, having bridged the Nile and the various arms he required to cross, he brought his army to Phoenicia.

§ 12. We have now reviewed the historical incidents of Alexander's occupation of Egypt, giving stress to those which have been misunderstood, or required explanation, and to those which suggested to the Ptolemies the principles of their administration. Briefly; Alexander had asserted the dignity and credibility of the Egyptian religion, and his determination to support it, and receive support from it. He had refused to alter the local administration, and had even appointed some native officials to superintend it. On the other hand he had placed the control of the garrison and the central authority in the hands of Macedonians and Greeks, and had founded a

---

[1] Diod. xvii. 49 ; Arrian omits this.

new capital, which could not but be a Hellenistic city, and a rallying point for all the Greek traders throughout the country. The port of Canopus was formally closed, and its business transferred to the new city. That of Naukratis found its way there of necessity, though the old site was not abandoned and furnished in after days several distinguished authors to Greek literature.[1]

We hear little hereafter of the other great cities of the Delta—unless it be in the occasional national revolts:—Sais, which had for some time been the Egyptian capital, but which may now have been partly absorbed by Alexandria; farther off, Tanis and Bubastos, the former of which was certainly the scene of a convocation of priests in the third Ptolemy's time. Pelusium, as we now know, remained the port for Syrian merchandise.[2]

During the succeeding decade of Alexander's conquests, we hear of no disturbance in Egypt, beyond stray complaints of the misconduct of Cleomenes, which reached the ears of Alexander.[3] But it is to be noted that on the death of his favourite Hephaestion, Alexander again applied to the oracle of Amon, as to the honours possible for his friend. Even

[1] Philistus, Apollonius, Polycharmus, Charon, Lykeas, Staphylus in the Ptolemaic age; Chaeremon, Athenaeus and Julius Pollux in the late Roman.

[2] It is stated by Josephus (*Antiqq.* xi. 86) that Alexander settled in the Thebaid many Samaritans, whose quarrels with the Jews made them willing emigrants; they had land-lots assigned to them, and the garrisoning of Upper Egypt. I do not believe this statement, though I have found in the Fayyum frequent mention, not only of Jews, but of a village called Samaria, in the middle of the third century B.C. But I do not believe that Samaritans were settled there till the new dynasty was established. This new evidence disposes of the extreme scepticism of Niese (*Gesch. des Hell.* i. 83 note), who thinks this whole Jewish episode in Josephus an invention of the second century B.C.

[3] Arrian vii. 23. Aristotle *Oecon.* ii. p. 1352-3 gives various instances of Cleomenes' dishonesty to merchants and to tax-payers.

in his case, Alexander was ready to admit some admixture of divinity. The account of these things in Arrian's seventh book confirms the view above taken regarding Alexander's deliberate claims.

Such then was the immediate preparation of the country for the rise of a new and glorious dynasty.

COIN OF ALEXANDER (EGYPTIAN).

CHAPTER II

§ 13. AMONG the extant historians none has thought it worth while to tell us whether the future King of Egypt was there attending upon Alexander, and what impressions he derived from his visit. In his own history of Alexander's campaigns, written perhaps forty years after, he seems not to have laid any stress upon this point; and yet it is more than probable that he went to Egypt with Alexander, and was impressed with the richness and the security of this new province. For its fruitfulness was only equalled by its isolation, there being natural frontiers of desert, marsh, and water which bar out all easy access. We are not told that Ptolemy went with the king to the oracle of Amon, and from the discrepancy mentioned by Arrian regarding the miracles on the way and the route of Alexander's return,[1] no safe conclusion can be drawn.

Ptolemy, son of Lagos and Arsinoe,[2] was some years older than the king, probably born in B.C. 367, but still

---

[1] Above § 11.

[2] For the year of his birth we have no better authority than the inference from Lucian *Macrob.* 12. Suidas *sub voc.* Λαγός repeats the fable that when exposed by Lagos, who repudiated the paternity, the child was

young enough to have been one of his companions at
Mieza during his education, and so intimate with him
during the domestic quarrels at the court of Philip that
he was exiled with other friends of the young prince,
and only returned to court on Alexander's accession.[1]
These meagre facts are, however, sufficient to enable us to
contradict the current legend,[2] that Ptolemy was of mean
extraction, a mere soldier of fortune, whose only claim to
blue blood was a possible intimacy of his mother with
King Philip of Macedon.   That some indiscreet flatterer
may in after days have sought to make him a half-brother
of the great king is likely enough, but the fact of his being
the young Alexander's playfellow shows clearly that he
came from one of those high families in Macedon—we
might almost call them feudal nobles—who furnished
the βασιλικοὶ παῖδες or pages for the royal household.
His very exile by Philip shows that his name must have
had some importance at the court.   On the other hand
the historians never cite his noble origin as a cause
of his popularity or position with the Macedonians, as
they do in the case of Krateros, Perdikkas or Leon-
natos.

§ 14. It has been inferred by E. Revillout from Egyptian
inscriptions that he concealed his father's name, and called
himself Ptolemy son of Ptolemy.[3]   We are further told
that the LXX refused to translate the Hebrew word for the
unclean *hare* in Leviticus with λαγώς, as it would be a

taken care of by an eagle.   This fable was probably suggested by the
eagle which figures on the coins of Ptolemy and his successors.   An
anecdote of Plutarch (*de ira cohib.* 9) also implies that Lagos was of
mean birth.   Both Ptolemaios and Arsinoe are very old Greek names,
the former occurring in Homer.

[1] Arrian iii. 6, 5.   [2] Justin xiii. 4.
[3] Revillout *Rev. Egypt.* i. p. 11.

reflection on the royal name.[1] All the evidence to be
had from Greek documents contradicts these inferences.
Pausanias tells us more than once [2] that on votive offerings at Thebes in Boeotia and at Delphi, Ptolemy called
himself merely 'the Macedonian,' though he was king.
This, however, was the correct Greek fashion, and only
shows an absence of needless boasting. We now know [3]
that he dedicated a gold cup at Delos with the
inscription Πτολεμαιος Λαγου Μακεδων. The texts written
in demotic and cited by Revillout, which are dated 'in
the reign of Ptolemy son of Ptolemy,' are therefore not of
the first, but of the second Ptolemy.[4] There is also a
Cyprian inscription (*CIG* 2613) ending—

Πραξαγορας δ ονομ εσχον επικλεες, ον πριν επ ανδρων
θηκατο Λαγειδας κοιρανος ηγεμονα.

But in reply to Revillout's two statements, unproven, and
perhaps even leading to opposite conclusions—for if the
name of Lagos had been indeed suppressed, why avoid an
ordinary Greek word a generation later?—it is enough

[1] The word is δασυπους, used very frequently by Aristotle, and
apparently for the rabbit. The hares of Egypt were noted by him
as a small variety.

[2] vi. 3, 1 ; x. 7, 8.

[3] *Bull. Corresp. Hell.* (*BCH*) vi. 48.

[4] I have published a Greek instance in the *Petrie Papyri* (II. xxiv).
The Revenue Papyrus, col. 24, gives another distinct instance of the year
27 of the second Ptolemy. The theory of Revillout was refuted long
since (*Rh. Mus.* vol. xxxviii. 1883) by Wiedemann, who, however,
infers from the non-occurrence of the formula in demotic papers of
the years 9 and 10 (of Ptolemy II.), before the marriage of Arsinoe II.,
and in the papers of the years 33 and 36 after her death, that it was
first a precaution to secure the succession against any possible children,
afterwards against any schemes, of the second queen. But this conclusion is not confirmed by more recent evidence. For we now put the
marriage of Arsinoe II. earlier, and we have a date of the year 27
attesting the association of the prince. Cf. *Addit. Notes* p. 487.

to state that in the *Encomium* of Theocritus upon the second Ptolemy, his father is formally called Λαγείδας, or son of Lagos.[1] Athenaeus (576 E) mentions a son of the first Ptolemy, called Lagos. I have also found in the papyri of the Fayyum[2] repeated mention of a village *Lagis*, side by side with Berenikis, Philadelphia, and other names in honour of the royal family. Theocritus, moreover, does not think the title Lageidas inconsistent with the assertion that both Alexander and Ptolemy were Herakleids, and became companions of the gods of Olympus on equal terms. Lagos therefore was no obstacle to this glorified genealogy.

§ 15. Secondly, we may infer that Ptolemy's appointment to a place on the new king's staff was secured by the trifling adversity of his early banishment, not apparently by any early display of military genius. He was not among the original A.D.C., if so I may translate σωματοφύλακες, and was only promoted in Areia upon the treason of Demetrius.[3] He was not appointed to any early independent command, such, for example, as Peukestas' command of the Macedonian troops in Egypt. He worked his way upwards by the qualities of diligence, personal bravery and good temper, so as to be one of Alexander's best generals of division. The accounts of his military prowess, notably his part in the attack on Aornos and the capture of Bessus, have not lost in their transmission to us from his own narrative of the great campaigns.[4] He seems to have kept clear of all the jealousies and quarrels among the generals, which even Alexander found it hard to

---

[1] This point from Theocritus (*Idyll.* xvii.) is noticed by Krall *Studien* ii. 23.

[2] Cf. *Petrie Papyri* II. pp. 92, 95, 98.

[3] Arrian iii. 27, 5 in the conspiracy of Philotas.   [4] Ibid. iv. 29.

quell.   These excellent qualities of minding his own business
thoroughly, and meddling with none of his colleagues, may
also explain why we have hardly any personal anecdotes of
him surviving.   There are few eminent men in history who
have left us a clearer general notion, or a fainter individual
image, of their personality.   He was no doubt like many
of his brother-officers a dashing soldier; he was rather a
prudent and safe than a brilliant commander.   We may
say of him that if he had excited no enmity among his
companions, so he had aroused no enthusiasm.   As a
lieutenant acting under Alexander, he was always, if we
believe the histories based upon his memoirs, brilliantly
successful.   When in after days, in the full maturity of
experience, he commanded his own armies, he gained
some signal successes, but also met with some sore defeats.
He was then indeed no longer pitted against Orientals,
but against his own compeers, and this made a considerable difference.   But his readiness to retreat even after a
victorious campaign shows a want of confidence in his own
resources, and we find him throughout his long and
successful life inaugurating that diplomatic habit which
distinguished the court of Egypt in succeeding generations.
Socially he stood in a very leading place.   At the great
' marriage of Europe and Asia,' which Alexander ordered
at Babylon, he was joined to the Princess Artakama,
daughter of Artabazus, of whom we hear nothing subsequently.[1]   The scandal-loving Athenaeus also tells us that
after Alexander's death he formed an intimacy with the
celebrated Greek courtezan Thais, and had by her three
children, Leontiscus, again mentioned as taken prisoner
by Demetrius in Cyprus in 307 B.C., Lagos, and a daughter
Eirene, who married Eunostos, king of Soli in Cyprus.

[1] Arrian vii. 4.

§ 16. In the summer of 323 B.C. the great crisis, which many men must have foreseen as probable, fell suddenly upon the world. Alexander died after a fever of a few days' duration. He was making great preparations, at the moment, for the conquest of Arabia by sea and land, and we may be sure all the information available about the wealth of Yemen, and the sea-way from thence to Egypt by the Red Sea, must have been gathered and brought before the king. Ptolemy, who was then in his intimate counsels, may have seen a new and undeveloped source of wealth likely to accrue to Egypt by this adventurous trade. Moreover, upon the king's death, it is certain that nobody thought of him as the fit man for the regency—there were other Companions of Alexander both senior and more prominent; it is equally certain that he alone among them all had his mind fully made up both as to the province he would choose and as to his future independence of the Royal House. He was the strongest advocate, says Pausanias,[1] that the whole power should not be concentrated on Philip Arridaeus, and that the nations should be distributed into several royalties.[2] He entered upon his province with a full conviction that this quarrel would be fought out in the first instance with Perdikkas, who as guardian and representative of the royal house (Philip Arridaeus and the infant Alexander)

[1] i. 6, 2.

[2] This statement Droysen interprets to mean that Ptolemy persuaded Perdikkas to set separate satraps over the several provinces, thus removing them from the court (which Perdikkas desired), but also giving them an opportunity to fortify themselves in their several countries (which Ptolemy desired). On the events following Alexander's death we have besides Diodorus (xviii.) the good epitome by Photius of Arrian's *Events after Alexander* (in Didot's Arrian, with other historians of Alexander). The compendium of Justin throughout is only of value because we sometimes have no other information.

was determined to maintain his actual authority over
the whole empire.   'Ptolemy,' says Diodorus,[1] 'took
over Egypt without disturbance, and treated the natives
with kindness; received in the country 8000 talents,
collected a mercenary force and organised his power;
moreover, there ran together to him a crowd of his
friends on account of his popularity.   He also sent an
embassy to Antipater to make joint cause with him, seeing
plainly that Perdikkas would attempt to oust him from the
satrapy of Egypt.'   For that purpose Cleomenes, now the
sole manager of Egypt, had not been superseded, but
associated with him.[2]   This policy Ptolemy foiled by
putting Cleomenes to death, an act hardly unjust,
and certainly not unpopular in Egypt, if we accept
the tales of dishonesty and oppression told of that
governor.[3]   Perdikkas, however, turned his attention first
to Ariarathes of Cappadocia, and to the cities of Pisidia
which were disobedient, in both of which cases his cruelty
as a conqueror showed the world plainly what sort of
successor to Alexander's rule they would have in him.
He had thus, before he turned to attack Ptolemy, alienated
the other satraps, and especially Antigonus, who had to
fly for his life.

§ 17.   During the two years that elapsed after the death
of Alexander, Ptolemy had gained several considerable advantages, one sentimental, the others solid.   The council
of generals in Babylon had directed that the body of
Alexander should be set on a magnificent catafalque,
and brought to the oasis of Amon, there to be laid
to rest.   The splendour of the bier, which was drawn
by 64 mules, and its military escort, commanded by Arra-

---

[1] xviii. 14.   [2] Arrian vii. 23.
            [3] Aristotle *Oecon.* ii. p. 1352.

baeus,[1] a distinguished Macedonian noble and staff-officer
of Alexander, excited the deepest interest. All the world
came out to see the splendid procession, which was met
by Ptolemy in Syria with a large force, and, in spite of
Perdikkas having countermanded that the dead king should
go to Egypt, and having ordered him to be brought to
Aegae, the ancient necropolis of the Macedonian kings,
the catafalque was led by Ptolemy to Pelusium, and thence
(probably on a state barge) to Memphis, where the
sarcophagus of gold remained for some time (we know
not how long), nominally on its way to the oasis, really
awaiting its final resting-place at Alexandria. For as
yet the Sema, a special temple for its reception, was not
ready. Moreover, until Ptolemy was assured of his supremacy on the sea, a hostile fleet might carry off the golden
sarcophagus by a sudden raid. To capture it at Memphis
would mean to conquer the whole of Lower Egypt. The
explicit narrative of Diodorus, the recently-recovered fragments of Arrian,[2] and the absence of all contrary statement,
make this episode in our history so certain that we may
well wonder at the boldness of those who assert that
a splendid sarcophagus of some Sidonian king, probably
Hephaestion's nominee,[3] who was buried with members of
his family at Saïda, might be, if not the actual tomb, at
least intended for the shrine of the great king's body.[4]

[1] Diodorus calls him Arridaeus, which Droysen corrects without
venturing to adopt the correction in his text.

[2] These fragments are from a palimpsest in the Vatican found by
Reitzenstein in 1886, containing remains of the seventh book of the
sequel to Alexander's life, written by Arrian. They are published in
the *Breslauer Philolog. Abh.* iii. 3 (Breslau, 1888).

[3] Diod. xvii. 47.

[4] This sarcophagus is now the priceless ornament of the museum at
Constantinople, where it is surrounded by the lesser monuments made
by the same artists for the king's family. The official account of the

This acquisition added more than we can estimate to
the prestige of Ptolemy's satrapy. If the tent of Alexander,
with his imaginary presence, was enough to sway the turbulent Macedonian soldiery,[1] what must the effect have been
of possessing his actual remains?

§ 18.[2] But it brought the satrap of Egypt into direct
opposition to the regent Perdikkas, who desired a good
excuse to pass with an army into Macedonia and oust
Antipater, and for this purpose announced that he intended himself to escort Alexander's body to Aegae. He
had sent two officers, Attalus and Polemo, to see that
Arrabaeus did not bring it to Egypt; but this officer's
obstinacy, and Ptolemy's armed intervention, could not be
baulked by their interference.

Seeing then that a conflict with the regent and
his forces was in prospect, it was highly desirable that
Ptolemy should strengthen his position. His first care
was to make alliance with the kings of the cities of Cyprus,
who not only manned a large fleet, but actually attacked

discovery, with magnificent reproductions, is Hamdi Bey's *Une Nécropole
royale de Sidon*, Paris, 1892, of which the three parts have appeared.

[1] Diod. xviii. 60, 61.

[2] The narrative of the complicated wars in this and the next chapter
is confined to those operations in which Ptolemy was directly concerned, or which are necessary to explain his action. Our principal
authorities are Diodorus (xviii.), Plutarch (*Eumenes, Demetrius*), and
the meagre abstracts of the history of the period in Justin and Pausanias
(i. 6). I have not thought it necessary to give references to these
authors for every statement. Stray lights from other ancient authorities
are carefully indicated. The only treatment of this perplexed period by
an English historian is that of Thirlwall, so far as it refers to the history
of Greece. In German Droysen's *Hellenismus* is still the best book,
though there is a briefer and more modern account, with occasional
new matter, in B. Niese's *Geschichte der Griechischen und Makedonischen
Staaten*, part i. Gotha, 1893; and a book of brilliant suggestiveness,
though I disagree with it in some points, Holm's *Griech. Geschichte* vol. 4.

the only town—Marea—in the island which refused to
join them. Thus he obtained a great addition to his fleet,
which from the first was vital to him. The only real danger
to Egypt was an attack by sea. Perdikkas indeed sent a
Phoenician fleet to subdue the Cypriote kings,[1] but meanwhile Antigonus, satrap of Phrygia, had been obliged to fly
for his life from Perdikkas, and take refuge in Macedonia,
where his representations to Antipater and Krateros
awakened in them a sense of their danger, and a readiness
to send ambassadors to Ptolemy, entreating an alliance
against the regent. Antigonus was at once dispatched
with a fleet, and, in conjunction with the Cypriote kings,
defeated or checked the regent's fleet. Antigonus seems
to have remained some time in Cyprus, and thus to have
at least negatively aided Ptolemy in securing him from an
invasion by sea.

§ 19. Fortune too, as usual, lent her aid to the skilful
diplomatist. The embezzled wealth of Harpalus, so
notorious in connexion with the disgrace of Demosthenes,
excited the cupidity of others besides Athenian patriots.
The wretched creature himself was murdered by his comrade the Lacedaemonian Thibron, who then hired mercenaries with the money, and was in Crete ready for an offer
of employment. It soon came to him from Cyrene, or ·
rather from the usual nemesis of Greek republics—a band
of political exiles seeking restitution. Alexander's last edict
restoring exiles throughout Hellas had indeed, as was intended, stirred up everywhere a nest of hornets. Thibron,
who seems to have intended to make himself despot over
all the Cyrenaica and the neighbouring Libyans, was at
first very successful, but by estranging his ablest lieutenant

---

[1] So far the details of this Cypriote struggle are preserved in Reitzenstein's *Fragg.* § 6.

through his parsimony he strengthened his adversaries, the aristocrats; and so we have the edifying spectacle of the two classes in Cyrene each trying to destroy the other by means of foreign help. Into the details of this savage quarrel we need not enter.[1] The aristocrats seem to have tried every other available ally—Libyans and Carthaginians—before they turned to Ptolemy. Even when he sent his general Ophelas to support this party, the whole state seemed ready to unite against so dangerous an arbitrator. But Ptolemy was too strong for them, and when he came himself to support Ophelas the Cyreneans submitted to his authority, and accepted Ophelas as governor.

The reflection of Diodorus[2] on the peaceful solution of this sanguinary internecine struggle is characteristic. It was the right thing for a respectable literary man to say, though it was unmeaning, if not mischievous: 'Thus the Cyreneans having sacrificed their freedom were ranged under the sovranty of Ptolemy.' They had already, according to the same author, offered its surrender to Alexander, whom they met on his way to the oasis of Amon. But what did their liberty mean? A long series of civil feuds, resulting in murders, exiles, and confiscations of property; nor can we doubt that the moderate tax levied by Ptolemy was but a tithe of the war requisitions and other sudden losses entailed by their perpetual discord.

§ 20. It is not stated by Diodorus at what exact time this acquisition of Cyrene was made by Egypt, but historians generally have assumed that it came (322 B.C.) shortly before the great invasion of Perdikkas, and so not only freed

---

[1] The best and fullest account of these troubles is still Thrige's *Res Cyrenensium*, a book published after the death of the author (Copenhagen, 1828). It has been fully utilised by Droysen and Niese.

[2] xviii. 21 *sub fin.*

Ptolemy from any possible diversion on his west frontier, but added a considerable contingent of Cyreneans, or mercenaries employed by them, to his army. The Petrie Papyri show that in the next generation Cyrenean veterans had received grants of land in Egypt, and if the inscriptions of their names which I found on the temple of Tothmes III. over against Wadi-Halfa date from Ptolemaic times,[1] and not earlier, we have evidence that they were employed on expeditions even as far as the second cataract.

The details of Perdikkas' invasion are preserved to us in Photius' Epitome of Arrian and by Diodorus. But unfortunately the battles which the latter describes are mere conglomerations of facts, which give us little insight into the strategy and none into the tactics of the belligerents. Perdikkas, bringing with him 'the kings,' that is to say, Philip Arridaeus and his wife Eurydike, the infant Alexander, his mother Roxane, and their suite, advanced by land to the frontier with a force which could not be resisted in the open field. There seems to have been a formal accusation brought before the assembled Macedonians against Ptolemy for having disobeyed the regent's commands.[2] Ptolemy defended himself before this assembly with ability, and convinced many that he was in the right, but surely he was not there, in Perdikkas' camp, in person, as Droysen hesitatingly,

[1] The difficulty in dating these names, Jason and Pasimenes, each styled Κυρηναιος, arises from the fact that though evidently graved at the same time, probably on the same day, in large and deep letters, one uses C, the other Σ. The round form C was commonly supposed to mark a date not earlier than the second century B.C., but its regular occurrence in the *book writing* of the Petrie Papyri, which is far more archaic in style than the cursive hands, and which reaches back to near, or even beyond, 300 B.C., makes it quite possible that any mercenary of this date might have used it. Cf. *Addit. Note* p. 487.

[2] Photius *op. cit.* § 28.

Niese[1] categorically affirm. Antigonus had recently escaped for his life from such a trial before Perdikkas, and surely Ptolemy was not such a fool as to put his head in the lion's mouth. He probably had a written defence read by a friend. But of course though the Macedonian soldiers did not decide in favour of Perdikkas, and even grumbled at the trial, mere argument was idle.[2] The fleet which accompanied this army along the coast was commanded by Attalus, and seems to have been unable to effect any independent diversion on the Egyptian coast. On the other hand the Egyptian fleet, if superior, did not take the offensive, and permitted the fleet of Attalus, even after the death of Perdikkas, to retreat with impunity to Tyre. The fleet of Antigonus, recently active off Ionia and Cyprus, is not mentioned as impeding, or even disturbing, the advance of Perdikkas.

§ 21. His military operations on the frontier seem to have been three. In the first place, he cleared out an old and disused canal, probably to the east of his position, for the purpose of drawing off the water from the canal in front of him, which protected the Camels' Fort. This engineering work seems to have been successful, for after a night march he crossed this canal without difficulty, and all but surprised the fort. On the other hand, the water broke into the old channel he had opened with such violence as to cause loss and damage to his camp, and to give an excuse to the faint-hearted and disloyal among his followers to describe the operation as a failure, and to desert. Such as he could catch were put to death with torture as traitors, and so the contrast between his haughty and cruel severity and Ptolemy's kindliness was made even more manifest than before.

[1] ii. 1, 28 ; i. 222 respectively.   [2] Photius *op. cit.* § 20.

The Egyptians came up barely in time to occupy Camels'
Fort, and in the assault which ensued, and which was
beaten off with the greatest difficulty, Ptolemy showed his
well-known personal bravery, fighting as a soldier on the
ramparts. His most brilliant feat was the disabling of the
leading elephant and his mahout, for there were no
elephants on the Egyptian side, and therefore the Indian
contingent with Perdikkas must have been his most formidable arm.[1]   After the failure of the assault, the regent,
with considerable strategic skill, abandoned his position by
night, and by a forced march reached a point of the Nile
near Memphis, where a large island in mid-stream, sufficient
to hold all his camp, offered facilities for crossing.   But,
strange to say, Perdikkas seems to have had no better
means of crossing rivers than wading at a ford.   All the
clever devices of his great master in the art of war seem
to be forgotten.   In this case the operation failed miserably.   When a part of the army had reached the island,
the ford was suddenly found to be deepening, and soon
became impassable.   Diodorus says the fine sand at the
bottom when disturbed by many feet floated down the
stream.   Presently many were lost in attempting to cross,
many more in endeavouring to recross to the east bank.
We are not told one word of what Perdikkas intended to
do, had he succeeded in bringing his whole force to the
island.   For Ptolemy was ready upon the west bank, and
could surely have starved him out on the island.   When
Diodorus says that in addition to those drowned, more
than 1000 were devoured by crocodiles,[2] we feel disposed
to lower our estimate of his authority.   Ptolemy saved all

---

[1] Diod. xviii. 34.

[2] He says, xviii. 36, οὐκ ἐλαττόνων ἢ χιλίων θηριοβρώτων γεγονότων,
but can hardly have imagined any other monsters to have been at hand.

he could, no doubt with the help of boats, and gave the rest honourable and even ostentatious burial within sight of their comrades. So it came to pass that the discontent of the generals and the rage of the soldiers against their commander proceeded to mutiny, and Perdikkas was murdered after a struggle in his tent by his cavalry.[1]

§ 22. Ptolemy now held the game in his hands. He crossed without delay into the hostile camp, bringing ample provisions, lamenting the brave soldiers that had found a wretched death in the river, deprecating the war of friends against friends to maintain the claims of one ambitious spirit. The soldiers were unanimous in offering him the regency, and the charge of the royal princes. But the cautious and far-seeing man felt all the difficulties of the situation. It would bring about him men higher in dignity and with better claims; and who could tell at what moment a military revolt, headed by one of these rivals, would not remove him as Perdikkas had been removed? Even if no such catastrophe supervened, how could he hope to maintain his place in Egypt if the young Alexander grew up in his great father's foundation at Alexandria, and claimed his hereditary rights?

Such considerations led him to decline the honour with every courtesy, but with firmness. He was at the moment so powerful that he was even able to confer the dignity on those two of his comrades who had supported him against Perdikkas—Arrabaeus in the matter of the body of Alexander, Python who had excited the recent mutiny against the regent and caused his murder. But even these men, returning with the army to Syria, found the position so difficult, that they imitated Ptolemy, and resigned the intolerable burden.[2]

[1] Photius *op. cit.* § 28.   [2] Diod. xviii. 39.

The new division of the empire at Triparadeisus (321
B.C.)—for such it practically was—left Egypt with the adjoining Libya, and 'what he could conquer towards the setting
sun,'[1] in Ptolemy's hands, 'for it was thought impossible
to oust him from Egypt which he held, as it were, by
right of conquest' (δορίκτητον) which was the best of all
titles in those days.[2]

§ 23. I incline to put the marriage of Ptolemy with
Eurydike, daughter of Antipater, as Droysen does, at this
point of our complicated history. He had indeed been
married, along with all the Macedonian grandees, on the
same day as Alexander the Great, and to Artakama,
daughter of Artabazus, satrap of Bactria. But strange to
say, besides Roxane the Queen, only two of these Persian
brides reappear in after history,[3] nor do we find even
children of the rest mentioned. Whether the ladies were
repudiated, or whether the whole affair was not considered
as a huge joke, as soon as Alexander was dead, we cannot
tell.

Within a few months after the so-called settlement at
Triparadeisus, new troubles broke out, those in Asia
Minor being specially caused by the ambition of Antigonus,
who now becomes the most active and prominent of the
Diadochi. But while he was busy in his wars with
Eumenes, Ptolemy took the opportunity (320 B.C.) of
occupying Cyprus with his fleet, and then the satrapy of
Syria, which he first tried to buy from Laomedon, but on

---

[1] Photius § 34.   [2] Diod. xviii. 39.

[3] The two were Amastris the daughter of Oxyartes, married to
Krateros ; after his death dynast of Herakleia, and married in 302 B.C.
to Lysimachus (Memnon iv. 10, in FHG iii. 530); and Apame, daughter
of the Sogdianian Spitamenes, Alexander's ablest adversary, married
to Seleukos, and mother of Antiochus Soter, and thus of the Seleukid
dynasty.

his refusal took him prisoner, and presently connived at his flight.[1] In this easy and almost bloodless campaign, we hear that Ptolemy commanded the fleet, and entrusted Nikanor with his land-army.

It is fortunately no part of our duty to unravel the complications of the wars which followed, and which rent the Hellenistic world asunder for a whole generation. It is a tedious and unedifying labour. That Ptolemy was anxiously watching, and constantly meddling by diplomacy in all these quarrels is certain. But most of the details are lost. In 319 B.C. we hear that he was approached by Casander, who upon the appointment of Polyperchon by the dying Antipater as regent, had adopted the policy of independent satrapies with a sullen determination which ruthlessly brushed aside every obstacle, and led him to the murder of all the remaining members of the royal house. Ptolemy, however, was ready to approach this very unsympathetic person for private reasons, as well as in support of his anti-imperial policy. He desired to secure the province of Syria, which he had taken, from recapture by Antigonus. In this latter object, as we shall see, he did not succeed.

§ 24. In the same year appeared the first of those misleading and mischievous proclamations of freedom to all the Greeks, which was imitated by all the rival satraps in turn, and remained a sort of political shibboleth down to the time of Nero. It was now merely a war measure on the part of the new regent Polyperchon, issued in the name of Philip Arridaeus, as ruler of Alexander's empire, and intended to cause difficulties to Casander in Greece, and to Antigonus in Asia Minor. But it must have affected Ptolemy also, inasmuch as his recent subjugation of Cyrene was the very

---

[1] Appian *Syr.* 52 says that Laomedon bribed his jailors.

latest 'enslavement of free and autonomous Hellenes,' and therefore the most notorious. Diodorus professes to give us the actual text of this famous decree.[1] The document is too long to quote, and with its details we are not concerned. But how real the proposed independence, may be inferred from one sentence near the end : 'and that all the Greeks shall pass a decree, that no one is to serve in arms, or act politically against us; and that if any one does so, he and his family shall be exiled, and their goods confiscated.'

But for the next four years the satrap of Egypt was not actively engaged in war, though the growing power of Antigonus, who had overthrown all his other rivals, and removed by execution all who could not escape as Seleukos did, showed plainly what was coming. Seleukos arrived, a fugitive to Ptolemy in 316 B.C., and his case was made a *casus belli* against Antigonus by Casander and Lysimachus, who each claimed a share of the conquests they had promoted, and by Ptolemy, who only insisted upon the retention of Syria. So a war for the possession of Syria began in 315 B.C. But before we enter upon it, let us inquire what the satrap of Egypt had been doing during these four years to consolidate his power.

§ 25. A very important event in his domestic life had taken place in 317 B.C.[2] In spite of his previous marriage

---

[1] xviii. 56. That the feeling for autonomy, whether genuine or not, was in full swing in this generation, may be inferred from the violent decree of the Ilians against oligarchy and tyranny, recently published by Brückner, which dates about 281 B.C., and was probably directed against the policy of Lysimachus towards the Asiatic cities. Cf. *Sitzber.* of Berlin Acad. for 1894, pp. 461 *sq.* Cf. also the decree of the Ionian cities discovered at Clazomenae, in which they petition Antiochus Soter to preserve their autonomy, *BCH* for 1885, p. 389.

[2] I have assumed this date with other historians because Berenike's daughter Arsinoe was married to Lysimachus not later than 300 B.C.,

to Eurydike, he now married Berenike, a grand-niece of
Antipater, who had come in Eurydike's retinue to Egypt.
She was already a widow, with a son Magas, and two
daughters, Theoxena and Antigone. But when the scholiast
on Theocritus says [1] that Lagus was her father, and she
therefore a step-sister of Ptolemy, it is likely he was misled
by the formula 'wife and sister' applied to Egyptian queens
as a mere title of honour, and which was probably used
in many documents regarding the present princess. She
seems to have been a person of amiable and yet strong
character, and to have maintained her influence over her
husband all the rest of her life. Polygamy was now the
rule among the Diadochi, but so distinctly political were
their marriages, that a new alliance did not imply even a
divorce of sentiment between the husband and his previous
wife. In the present case there is no evidence that
Eurydike was divorced, neither do we hear of any domestic
conflicts between Eurydike and Berenike. This speaks
well indeed not only for the ladies,[2] but for the diplomatic
skill of Ptolemy. The rivals for his affection might have
given him more trouble than the rivals for his power.
Berenike was, however, certainly the favourite, and was
probably a good diplomatist, seeing that her son Magas
became king of Cyrene, and her son Ptolemy, to the

and because Pausanias says (i. 6) that Ptolemy already had children by
Eurydike, whom he had married in 320 B.C. Cf. *Addit. Note* p. 487.

[1] Schol. Theocrit. xvii. 61.

[2] Koepp (*Rh. Mus.* for 1884, p. 209) adopts Hempel's theory that
two lines of Theocritus' *Encomium* (xvii. 44), which he dates as far back
as 276 B.C., allude to Eurydike viz.—

       ἀστόργου δὲ γυναικὸς ἐπ' ἀλλοτρίῳ νόος αἰεί,
       ῥηΐδιοι δὲ γοναί, τέκνα δ' οὔποτ' ἐοικότα πατρί,

and that the insinuation was justified by the career of Keraunos, and
by the fact that Cyprus seems to have been in revolt, possibly under
another son of Eurydike. These conjectures I regard as mere guesses.

exclusion of Eurydike's older son, king of Egypt. Yet is this second marriage of Ptolemy passed by in silence by the historians who weary us with their confused accounts of resultless battles. Nor do they tell us one word of his internal policy, his successes in welding the diverse population of his kingdom into an organised and definite society. The restoration of the outer shrine of the great temple at Luxor, built by Tothmes III. and ruined by the Persians, took place during the nominal sovranty of Philip Arridaeus, and therefore quite early in Ptolemy's satrapy. His restoration of the inner cella was in the name of the boy-king Alexander.[1] It is likely that even the latter restoration took place during the present interval of peace. For between the war of 315 B.C. and the young king's murder by Casander in 311 or 310 B.C., Ptolemy had but little leisure to think of temples in Upper Egypt. The statue found (I believe) in this shrine, and supposed to represent the unfortunate king, is most remarkable as one of the very rare examples of the mixture of a Greek type with Egyptian attributes. The statue is one of a grown youth, older than Alexander IV. lived to be, but we need not find any difficulty in this; for the artist, who had never seen him, would probably avoid representing the reigning king as a child. Nor can we regard it as anything more than a conventional figure, though the gentle and melancholy expression would well suit the tragic fortunes of the ill-starred boy, a martyr to his greatness.[2]

[1] Cf. Lepsius, Berlin *Abh.* for 1852, p. 463.

[2] It is much to be regretted that we have no accurate account of the finding of this statue. M. Maspero, who gives a reproduction in his *Archéologie égypt.* accepts the current story which I have followed. But in Egypt I could find no clear evidence about the whole matter. The statue, which is of speckled Aswân granite, is about nine feet high, and may be seen in the museum now at Gizeh.

§ 26. When the war of 315 B.C. began, Antigonus was somewhat in the position of the great Alexander when he first reached Syria. On land he was quite superior to any adversary, but he suffered from the weakness of his fleet. Hence as Alexander had found the subjugation of Tyre essential, so Antigonus. Ptolemy indeed did not attempt to resist him on land. He had no confidence in his genius as against Antigonus. But he garrisoned Tyre strongly, as well as Joppa and Gaza, and though the latter two were easily taken by the invader, Tyre was a more serious affair, and cost a fifteen months' siege. Had the fleet of allies, with Seleukos as its commander, been more active, or stronger, even this success would have been impossible. But their fleet did not accomplish any serious diversion, and with the fall of Tyre Antigonus could easily obtain the supremacy by sea. For he had at the same time made interest at Cyprus and Rhodes to obtain timber, ships and shipwrights. Yet the fleet under Ptolemy's brother Menelaos did succeed in ousting him from Cyprus, and by friendly letters, and a counter declaration that he would free the Greeks, Ptolemy neutralised the bid of Antigonus in the same direction. The Greeks were mainly passive, and Casander persuaded Antigonus' general in the Peloponnesus to desert his master. This set free the fleet and army of Ptolemy, which was operating on the Greek coast under Polykleitos, who crossed at once to Cilicia, and finding that two officers of Antigonus, Perilaos and Theodotos, were coming from Caria along the coast with a fleet and an army, he laid wait for them, and destroyed their force, slaying one and taking the other prisoner. This brilliant success checked Antigonus.[1] So

[1] Diodorus xix. 64. Cf. also C. Wachsmuth, in *Rh. Mus.* for 1871, p. 469.

it happened that at the end of the year Antigonus and
Ptolemy met at a place called Ekregma, on the frontier
between Palestine and Egypt, to discuss exchange or ransom
of prisoners, but no further accommodation resulted. It
must be remembered that all these rivals were old friends
and comrades, who had served together in many campaigns.
Personal hatreds among them are to be found, but they
are exceptional; their hostilities were those of conflicting
interests.

§ 27. The following year was spent in campaigns on
the coast of Asia Minor and Greece, in which Ptolemy
was not active except with his fleet at Cyprus and the
coast of Cilicia.   The complete re-conquest of Cyprus
was, however, almost contemporary with a revolt at Cyrene,
stimulated no doubt by the proclamations of Greek liberty
by Antigonus, and probably by more active propagandism.
The revolt, which went so far as to besiege the Egyptian
garrison in the Acropolis, was promptly put down by an
Egyptian force.   The ringleaders were carried in chains to
Alexandria, and the government of Ophelas restored. The
proceedings of Ptolemy at Cyprus were still more high-
handed.   He slew or deposed some of the local kings,
destroyed the city of the Maricis, and transferred the
inhabitants to Paphos.   Nikokreon, king of Salamis,
was made Strategus of the reconquered Cyprus.[1] The
position of this local king was made as dignified as
possible.   Cyprian coins of this date bear upon them
the peculiar ensigns of a helmet, an *aplustre*, and a star.
These probably indicate[2] that Nikokreon held the combined offices of strategus, admiral, and high-priest of
the island — offices held by the same person according

[1] Cf. Diod. xix. 79, both on Cyrene and Cyprus.
[2] Cf. Poole's *Coins of the Ptolemies* p. xix.

to a later Cyprian inscription.[1]   After some successful
naval raids upon the Syrian coast, Ptolemy was persuaded
by Seleukos to resume the occupation of Palestine,
especially as Antigonus had his hands full in Asia
Minor, and was only able to oppose the invasion by
sending his son Demetrius with an army not superior
to the Egyptian, except in the item of forty elephants,
of which Ptolemy had none.   As the second and third
Ptolemies procured them easily enough from the southern
coasts of the Red Sea, it is possible that the first Ptolemy
had learned from Alexander to despise this auxiliary.
Nor do we find him in any of his campaigns defeated by
them; Diodorus' authority is even most explicit in telling
us how he repulsed or obviated their attacks.

§ 28. The armies met very deliberately to try the
fortune of battle near Gaza early in 312 B.C.   Diodorus
relates the course of the conflict with great detail.[2]   To the
contemporaries of Alexander, his authorities, both strategy
and tactics had the highest interest.   Ptolemy and Seleukos
on one side, on the other the staff of the youthful
Demetrius, Nearchus, Peithon and others, were fighting
generals of great experience, brought up in continuous war
under the greatest master of the art.   Nevertheless, like
Napoleon's generals, none of them seems to have possessed
any originality, except perhaps Lysimachus and Eumenes.
They are always imitating Alexander's dispositions.   Here
at Gaza, the Egyptian army,[3] contending against an array of

---

[1] *CIG* 2622 Σελευκον Βιθυος τον συγγενη του βασιλεως τον στρατηγον
και ναυαρχον και αρχιερεα τον κατα την νησον κ.τ.λ.

[2] xix. 81 *sq.*

[3] Diod. xix. 80 says it was composed of Macedonians, mercenaries,
and a crowd of natives, partly suttlers and carriers, partly trained
soldiers.   But he does not tell us whether these latter were the caste of
Μάχιμοι.

elephants, seems to have been handled as the Macedonians had been in the battle with Porus. While the main line was directed to keep the elephants in check, the right wing of cavalry attacked those opposed to it, and when hotly engaged was supported by a reserve of cavalry which rode round farther to the right, and thus turned the left flank of Demetrius.[1] And here as elsewhere, a few initial successes determined the victory, for both armies were almost all mercenaries, not fighting for their lives and liberties, but ready to serve either side for pay. There was a good understanding among the adversaries, who did not push matters to extremities, and settled more battles by treason than by fighting. Nor can we in the least believe the large figures of the slain set down by Diodorus in his narrative of these wars. Demetrius may have lost 8000 men in this battle of Gaza, but probably three-quarters of them became more or less willing prisoners, and took service under the victor's flag. Demetrius fled, and was found at Azotus, whither Ptolemy sent him all his personal effects, which had been captured with his camp in the general rout. He also complimented him on his bravery, and there was an interchange of those courtesies which mark Hellenistic, as distinct from Hellenic culture.

The victors proceeded to occupy all Palestine and Syria; even Tyre was taken by the treachery of its defenders. Ptolemy was everywhere courteous and considerate, even forgiving Andronicus, governor of Tyre, who had treated him with insolence.[2] He laid the foundation of that popularity of the power of Egypt in Palestine which the Seleukids of Antioch were never able to attain.

[1] The account of the battle of Alexander against Porus, with plans, in Rüstow and Köchly's *Kriegswesen*, will make this plain to the reader.

[2] Diod. xix. 86.

He sent the exile Seleukos with a small force to recover
Babylon,[1] and his former satrapy. It was at the moment
a war measure, to cause a diversion against Antigonus; it
proved in the sequel a policy fraught with momentous
consequences, for Seleukos not only maintained himself
successfully, but founded a great empire. Ptolemy
further sent all the soldiers he had captured to be
distributed through the *nauarchies*,[2] or naval defences,
of Egypt. We learn also from a fragment of Hecataeus
of Abdera[3] that many Jews were now induced to settle
in Egypt, and that the high-priest Hezekias became
Ptolemy's firm friend. If the story which Josephus
repeats from Agatharchides[4] be true, that Ptolemy
seized Jerusalem on the Sabbath day, when the Jews
would not take arms, it may have happened during this
occupation, though Cless[5] puts it in his first occupation in
320. Josephus also adds two rather inconsistent statements : first, that he was a harsh ruler of Palestine ;
secondly, that he induced large numbers of Jews to settle
in Egypt, and put them in places of trust in the upper
country. The latter statement repeats precisely what had
been told of Alexander.

§ 29. But his occupation of Syria was soon cut short.
Demetrius, having reformed his army, advanced again from

---

[1] Diod. xix. 86 and 92.

[2] I take the text of Diodorus xix. 85 ἐπὶ τὰς ναυαρχίας to be correct ;
as there were ἱππαρχίαι, under which each cavalry officer was classed,
so the maritime defences were probably distributed into *nauarchies*.
At this moment Ptolemy wanted soldiers on his frontier, not up the
country.

[3] No. 14 in Müller's *Fragg. Hist. Graec.* (*FHG*) vol. ii. 393. The
extracts referred to this author by Josephus are not without grave suspicion. But the fragment just cited, which also gives the date of the
battle of Gaza from Castor, has all the appearance of being genuine.

[4] *Antiqq.* xii. 1.   [5] Pauly, Art. PTOLEMY p. 182.

Cilicia, and was lucky enough to surprise by night a whole division of troops under Killes, which were taken prisoners almost without a blow. Antigonus was not far off in Phrygia with his main army. As usual Ptolemy adopted the cautious and cowardly rather than the bold policy. After a council of war, a general retreat was ordered; all the fortresses[1] were dismantled; in the autumn of 312 Syria and Palestine were again cleared of Egyptians.

Though Antigonus at once re-occupied the territory in dispute, he was as careful in attacking Ptolemy in his 'Torres Vedras,' as Ptolemy was in avoiding the open field of battle. So he turned to subdue the Arab tribes of Nabataea,[2] in order, if possible, to obtain a line of attack from the east upon Egypt, avoiding Pelusium and the frontier defences which had been so fatal to Perdikkas. His raids against the Arabian nomads were successful as battles, but unsuccessful as conquests.[3] For he was now dealing with enemies not to be frightened, or bought over, by partial defeats. The varying fortunes and surprises of this desert fighting occupied him till the news of Seleukos' successes in the East became so alarming that he was content to make peace (311 B.C.) By the terms of this peace[4] Ptolemy did not recover Syria. It is suspected by historians that he was now involved in difficulties with Cyrene, as Ophelas was an untrustworthy lieutenant, and the cities of the district were still excited by the declaration of the freedom of all Hellenic cities, which Antigonus had recently issued, in imitation of Polyperchon, for the purpose of weakening his adversaries in Greece.

§ 30. A remarkable hieroglyphic inscription, dated

---

[1] Ake, Joppa, Samaria, Gaza; we do not find Tyre mentioned. Diod. xix. 93.

[2] Ibid. 96 *sq.*   [3] Ibid. 100.   [4] Ibid. 105.

in the seventh year of the young king Alexander, and therefore at this moment, gives us a glimpse into the internal policy of Ptolemy. It is a relief to turn to such a document, from the wearying complications of the wars with Antigonus and other hostile satraps. The whole text of this inscription I have given in another place.[1] Here I shall not repeat the elaborate formulae, but merely give the substance of the document, which is the earliest home record we have of the Ptolemaic rule: 'In the seventh year of the absent king Alexander[2] there was a great satrap, Ptolemy was his name. . . . He had brought back the images of the gods found in Asia; all the furniture of the books of all the temples of North and South Egypt, he had restored them to their place.' It is quite possible that when Ptolemy was first declared governor of Egypt at Babylon, he collected from the treasures of the Persian kings various relics of their old Egyptian conquests, and so came to Egypt with a precious gift for the priests, and a peace-offering to national sentiment.[3] 'He had made his residence at Alexandria by the sea, Rhakotis was its former name. He had assembled Ionians (Greek mer-

---

[1] From Brugsch's translation in the *Zeitschr. für Aeg.* for 1871, in *Greek Life and Thought from the Age of Alexander to the Roman Conquest*, p. 176. More recent translations and commentaries will be found noted in Wiedemann's *Gesch. Aegypten's*, p. 246. Cf. also C. Wachsmuth in *Rh. Mus.* for 1871, pp. 463 *seq.*

[2] Viz. 310 B.C. according to Lepsius, and probably after the young king's death.

[3] But it is an odd thing that the same merit is ascribed in the stele of Pithom (below § 79) to Ptolemy Philadelphus, who never, so far as we know, made conquests in Asia, and then in the inscription of Adule to Ptolemy Euergetes (§ 128), who did indeed conquer the East, but could hardly have found many Egyptian gods there, after the restitutions accomplished by his predecessors. It seems to me a mere stereotyped formula.

cenaries) and their cavalry and ships with their crews,'
and went to fight in Syria.   'He penetrated into their
land; his courage was as mighty as that of a hawk among
little birds.   He carried their princes (probably Jewish or
Phoenician nobles as hostages), cavalry, ships, works of art
to Egypt.   After this, when he had set out for Marmarica
(Cyrene), he led captive their men, women, horses in requital for what they had done to Egypt.'   The reader will
note that only the victory at Gaza is commemorated, and
no mention is made of any subsequent reverses; still it is
not asserted that he conquered Syria, but only that he
carried away from it great spoil.   As he thrice evacuated
Palestine without risking a personal defeat in the field,
we may be sure that on each occasion he sought popularity by bringing back with him not only prisoners,
but gifts from anxious cities, and other supplies, for his
country.   'When he had returned, he was glad, and celebrated a good day, and bethought him what he could do
for the gods of Egypt.   Then there spoke to him he that
was at his side '—some Egyptian adviser—'and the elders of
the sea land, called the land of Buto, alleging that it had
been granted to the gods of the cities of Pe and Tep, in
that land, by the native king Chabbas, when he was gone
to Pe Tep to examine the sea border and the marshes, to
examine every arm of the Nile that goes into the great sea,
to keep off the fleet of Asia from Egypt.'   Ptolemy then
sends for the priests of Pe Tep and makes inquiry.   They
tell him that the miscreant Xerxes had taken away this
property from the gods, and that it had been restored by
the native (insurgent) king Chabbas.   Whether this was
literally true is doubtful enough; it expresses, however, in
general, the Persian and the national policies.   Ptolemy
being satisfied has a decree drawn up giving the land of

Buto, limited by Hermopolis and Sebennytus on the north and west, to the gods of Pe and Tep as their domain. There follow imprecations against him who may venture to reverse this decree.

We thus see the new satrap taking up the policy of the priests, and identifying himself with the native religion, in contrast to the harsh and insolent Persians. There appears to me, however a hint at something more practical in this document. Chabbas had minutely examined the mouths of the Nile,[1] and given this tract of land to the priests, in connexion with the securing of these accesses to Egypt against invasions from the sea. We shall see presently how very carefully and completely these defences were organised by Ptolemy. We may therefore fairly conjecture that he got in return from the strong and friendly corporation of the priests who administered the property of the gods of Pe and Tep such assistance in defending the Sebennytic mouth of the Nile, as he could not have otherwise obtained.

§ 31. The feature of the peace of 311 B.C. to which Ptolemy probably made most objection was the clause declaring the freedom of all Greek cities, that is to say their autonomy, or right of dealing as independent states with any of the great satraps. This precluded any garrisons occupying such cities, except by invitation of the citizens, and gave the latter authority to repudiate any alliance and adopt a new one by a decision of their assembly. Such a clause was directly subversive of Ptolemy's control of the Cyrenaica.

His counter-move was one of singular success. He

---

[1] The Sebennytic mouth of the Nile, as we know from recently-found papyri, was the principal inlet to the country between the Pelusiac and the Canopic.

asserted, the following year, that this clause had not been carried out by his adversary, and manned a fleet to enter the Levant and bring the promised liberty to the pining patriots of Greece.[1] But among 'Greek cities' he chose to include those coast settlements in Caria, Cilicia, Pisidia, especially Xanthus, Kaunos, and Myndos, which were really peopled by a bold native population of hardy pirates, most useful for his navy, and a great protection to his all-important island of Cyprus. Here, with his usual severity when dealing with Cypriote kings, he ordered the death of Nikokles of Salamis, whose whole family then committed suicide.[2] Of course his 'liberation of Greek cities' was not more seriously meant than any of the like proclamations of his rivals. In his complicated operations through the Greek waters, he seems to have abstained from freeing the cities under Casander's sway, such as Athens, because Casander was now his friend and ally. But those under Casander's adversaries, especially under Antigonus, were glad to get the help of his now dominant fleet, and he secured for his dynasty a support in the Levant which was among the greatest elements of its power. He 'liberated' Kos and Andros. The citadel of Corinth was handed over to him by Kratesipolis, the strong-minded widow of Polyperchon's son Alexander, who was looking out for a new matrimonial alliance. This stronghold as well as Sikyon he kept for some time, and it must have been through Corinthian influence that he spread his sway over the islanders of Greece, who formed a coalition of which his son in after years, and probably he also, were presidents. For in the great procession with which Ptolemy Philadelphus inaugurated his accession was carried a figure of the first Ptolemy,

---

[1] Diod. xx. 19, 27, 37.   [2] Ibid. 21.

with the city of Corinth (another figure) *standing beside him.*[1]

§ 32. It would lead to no better understanding of Ptolemy to give the intricate details of his chequered campaigns. The years 310-309 were stained with the murder of the remaining members of Alexander's house—Cleopatra, the king's sister, who was in Antigonus' power, because she had designs of marrying Ptolemy;[2] Roxane and the young Alexander, in Casander's hands; Herakles, the bastard claimant, by Casander's persuasion. Thus every legitimate claimant, direct and indirect, to Alexander's succession was swept away, and the way laid open for the creation of independent sovranties.

But it was not yet settled whether there should be one—that of Antigonus, or several. We do not hear that Antigonus opposed Ptolemy actively in the Greek waters; probably he was engaged with Seleukos in the East. But he sent his very able son Demetrius to outbid Ptolemy, by liberating the cities under Casander, especially Athens, which Ptolemy had not approached.[3] Moreover, Demetrius went further, and retook Corinth and Sikyon, of which the latter had been garrisoned by Egyptian forces; the former, for some unexplained reason, had been ceded to Casander.

---

[1] Köhler (Berlin *Sitzber.* for 1891) infers from a paragraph in Suidas' article on Demetrius, that Ptolemy endeavoured to resuscitate the Corinthian Federation of Philip and Alexander. αὐτονόμους τε δὴ τὰς πλείστας τῶν Ἑλληνίδων πόλεων ἀφίησι, καὶ τὰς Ἰσθμιάδας σπονδὰς ἐπήγγειλε, κελεύων οἷα ἐπ' ἐλευθερώσει θαλλοφοροῦντας θεωρεῖν εἰς τὰ Ἴσθμια. Had he succeeded in doing so, the meaning of the figure in the procession would be plain. Possibly the influence of Corinth on the islanders was backed by commercial considerations, and intended to check the influence of Rhodes, which, curiously enough, does not appear in the Alexandrian pageant at all. Or was the alleged figure of Corinth really one of Rhodes?

[2] Diod. xx. 37. Cf. *Addit. Notes* pp. 487-8.

[3] Ibid. 46, and Suidas *sub voc.* DEMETRIUS.

The real attack on Ptolemy commenced with a counter blow of Demetrius on Cyprus, where Menelaos, the governor, was defeated, and besieged at Salamis, and when Ptolemy came to his aid with a fleet and army, he was worsted in a great battle by Demetrius.[1] Consequently though Menelaos made a successful diversion from Salamis, the island was conquered, and Ptolemy abandoned it to his foes. The sea battles, of which Diodorus describes several at great length, seem to have been as nearly as possible copied from tactics on land. The generals are also admirals, and command on their own wing.[2] There is a personage called the archpilot (ἀρχικυβερνήτης), who seems to direct the general manœuvres. It was after this signal victory that Demetrius sent his father a despatch, hailing him through his envoy as *king*, a compliment returned by Antigonus. Most of our authorities assert that the other Hellenistic sovrans — Seleukos, Lysimachus, Casander — forthwith assumed the royal title. They assert it also of Ptolemy,[3] but the era by which his dynasty dated their years does not begin till 305 B.C. Apparently therefore this great battle and the loss of Cyprus did not take place till 306, though we cannot for want of information fill the antecedent years with their events.

§ 33. If Antigonus was busy in the East, so Ptolemy, after his successful parade through Greek waters, was partly at least occupied with· the affairs of Cyrene. It seems that his viceroy Ophelas, who was not only

---

[1] Diod. xx. 47 adds a remark characteristic of the warfare of that age : τοὺς δ' ἁλόντας τὸ μὲν πρῶτον ἀπολύσας τῶν ἐγκλημάτων καταδιεῖλεν εἰς τὰς τῶν ἰδίων στρατιωτῶν τάξεις· ἀποδιδρασκόντων δ' αὐτῶν πρὸς τοὺς περὶ τὸν Μενέλαον διὰ τὸ τὰς ἀποσκευὰς ἐν Αἰγύπτῳ καταλελοιπέναι παρὰ Πτ., γνοὺς ἀμεταθέτους ὄντας ἐνεβίβασεν αὐτοὺς εἰς τὰς ναῦς καὶ πρὸς Ἀντίγονον ἀπέστειλεν.

[2] Ibid. 49 *sq.*   [3] Ibid. 53 ; Appian *Syr.* 54 ; Justin xv. 2.

a Macedonian of rank, but was married to an Athenian
lady descended from Miltiades, had thought the time
was come, in or about 312 B.C., to make himself independent, and found again the old kingdom of Cyrene.[1]
Possibly Ptolemy may have endeavoured to counteract
this revolt by policy rather than by arms, and his proclamation of freedom to all Greek cities may have been a
bid for the support of a democratic party at Cyrene against
Ophelas. He knew, of course, that he could deal with
democracy there at any moment; he could sow discord
by means of bribes, and then appear as umpire when
the sedition had become intolerable. To make an
expedition against the forces of Ophelas, who was an
experienced soldier, was another matter, and it is certain
that the revolt was tolerated by Ptolemy without any
attempt at punishing it for several years. But then,
according to the historians, fortune again plays into his
hands, and Agathocles of Syracuse, who had begun a war
against the Carthaginians in Africa, sends to solicit, with
the most tempting promises, the aid of Ophelas in subduing the Punic power. Agathocles was to claim no possessions in Africa, and after the conquest Ophelas was to
occupy all Carthage, and add it to the kingdom of Cyrene.
We are told that this prospect gathered together from
Greece a herd of adventurers, hoping to occupy new lands
in the rich and highly cultivated territory now under Carthage. After a long and very miserable march along the
deserts of the Syrtes, Ophelas reached his ally with a
diminished and disheartened force, only to find himself
betrayed, and to lose his life at the hands of Agathocles.
His army was at once absorbed into the ranks of the
victor. Thus it came to pass that Ptolemy was able

[1] Diod. xx. 40 *sq.*

to re-occupy, in 307 B.C.,[1] his outlying African province by sending a force under his stepson Magas, who remained regent or even king of Cyrene for fifty years to come.[2]

§ 34. Had this overthrow of Ophelas by the machinations of Agathocles taken place in the reign of Philadelphus, every one would have assumed that it was a deliberate stroke of policy on the part of the Egyptian diplomatists. They had ample means in their commercial relations with Agathocles to offer him inducements and rewards for his treachery, and indeed without some such negotiations his conduct seems pointless and even silly. Was it worth while to bring the veteran Ophelas with a large army into contact with his own, when any failure would have at once entailed the same results to Agathocles that overtook Ophelas? Agathocles, an upstart, but a powerful and ambitious one, was anxiously seeking to win his place as a Hellenistic sovran, and one recognised in the diplomacy of their courts. The marriage of his daughter with Pyrrhus, and his naval operations at Corcyra, show this plainly enough. His own marriage to Theoxena, Ptolemy's stepdaughter, was a far more splendid alliance, and may have been the bribe offered by the Egyptian satrap for this very service.[3] I cannot but conjecture therefore that this treacherous diversion

---

[1] Or 308; we cannot fix the date accurately. Pausanias (i. 6, 8) says after five years of revolt.

[2] Gercke (*Alex. Stud.* in *Rh. Mus.* for 1887) has shown some reasons that the royalty of Magas did not commence till 300 B.C. at earliest. If this be so, he may not have been sent at once by Ptolemy to Cyrene, or else may have only been entitled στρατηγός for some years. But Gercke's arguments are open to much question, and I prefer the ordinary chronology; cf. Thrige, p. 217.

[3] Cf. Droysen's conjectures, iv. 1, p. 243. This lady's affectionate parting from her dying husband is related by Justin xxiii. 2.

was deliberately planned by Agathocles and Ptolemy, or by their respective diplomatists, and that here we have another case of that policy of indirect counter-moves which is almost a distinctive feature in the annals of Ptolemaic Egypt.

During the interval that elapsed not only Ptolemy but the diplomatic world had had time to forget the 'liberation of all the Greeks,' and we do not hear that the appointment of a new king or royal deputy to rule over Cyrene caused any indignation throughout the Greek world.   Of course no one saw more clearly than the Greeks the hollowness of all such proclamations.   Still there were certain decencies to be observed.   Five years gave ample time and opportunity for the political situation to change ; many Greek cities had not accepted the boon ; Ptolemy may have professed a sincere desire to carry out the liberation, but pleaded his inability to overcome the difficulties it caused, and may have protested against any partial liberation affecting his own power, as compared with that of his rivals.   At all events every Hellenistic sovran who made such declarations concerning independence— and which of them did not ?—was ready to violate them, as soon as they interfered with his own interests.   The age was like that of Macchiavelli, in which principle was only asserted as a means of promoting selfish objects, and of making the want of principle more successful.   With all the courtesy and *bonhomie* which are asserted of Ptolemy, the whole course of his history shows him a true child of his age, and not superior to his fellows in morals or in uprightness, but merely in the clearness of his intellect, and the moderation of his ambition.   It was during one of his campaigns in the Aegean in 308 B.C. that his wife Berenike, who accompanied him, bore him at Kos the son who is commonly known under the title of Philadelphus.[1]

From this time onward, we know that the relations between Kos and Alexandria were very intimate, for not only was Kos the favourite retreat of Alexandrian literary men,[2] wearied with the heat and pressure of life in the great seething capital, but it was frequently chosen as a place of safety for royal exiles, and also as a place of education for royal princes. The poetical and the medical schools of this island held their own against the rivalry even of the Museum. Such being the case, we should have expected researches on the island to have unearthed for us many stray lights on Ptolemaic history. Unfortunately these hopes have not been realised. Mr. Paton's careful inquiry,[3] though he does not profess it to be final, has only been able to give us a couple of Ptolemaic inscriptions, and we can hardly hope to find much more even in the unexplored Turkish citadel.

§ 35. The defeat of Ptolemy at Cyprus, and the loss of the island, were the prelude to another attack upon Egypt, this time by Antigonus and Demetrius. The first attack by Perdikkas had ignominiously failed, but neither in power nor in popularity could he be compared with the father and son, whose combined talents seemed now likely to unite again under a single sway all the disrupted provinces of Alexander's empire. Moreover, the experience of Perdikkas' failure was there, and the obstacles which he stumbled upon could now be foreseen and avoided. The frontier tribes must be won over; the supplies along the

---

[1] Theocritus xvii. 58 *sqq.*

[2] On the poets cf. arguments, scholl. and Comm. on Theocritus, *Idyll* vii.

[3] Cf. *The Inscriptions of Cos*, Paton and Hicks, 1891, republished (1895) in N. Collitz' *Sammlung.*

route must be carried by a fleet superior to that of the
enemy and in touch with the land-army.

In all these matters Antigonus took unusual precautions.[1] The whole campaign was planned at Antigoneia,
the new capital on the Orontes, and from thence the
troops and ships were sent to assemble at Gaza, which
was the proper starting-point for the march against Egypt.
Ancient historians are utterly untrustworthy as regards
figures; I therefore only repeat the alleged numbers of
Antigonus' attacking force to show what kind of armament
Egypt was supposed able to resist. Antigonus advanced,
we are told, with more than 80,000 infantry, 8000 cavalry,
83 elephants, 150 ships of war, 100 transport ships. He
had obtained from the nomad Arabs a great convoy of
camels which he loaded with 130,000 medimni of corn
and green fodder for the beasts. His siege-train, now an
important arm of attack, was on the transport ships.

Two obvious dangers threatened the invasion. In the
first place the army was of unwieldy size and unable to
undertake quick or stealthy operations. Secondly, the
season was wrongly chosen or rather, I suppose, the expedition was accidentally delayed till the setting of the Pleiades,
early in November (306 B.C.) For not only were storms
now to be expected along the harbourless and shoaly coast,
as the seamen expressly warned Antigonus; but at this
time the Nile is still high, and the passage of any of its
mouths accordingly difficult, especially in the face of a
watchful enemy. Antigonus must have had the strongest
counter-inducements to advance in spite of these well-
known obstacles. We can only conjecture that it was
thought all-important to attack Ptolemy so rapidly after
his great defeat at Cyprus as to find his troops still dis-

[1] Diod. xx. 73 *sq.*

pirited and his fleet disorganised.   He had lost about 140
ships at Cyprus.   In a few months of dockyard activity
these might be replaced, and the supremacy at sea become
again doubtful.   An attack by land along the narrow coast-
line without a superior fleet to protect its flank, and
secure its communications with Syria, was held to be more
risky than to brave the weather.

§ 36. But the elements did their work for Ptolemy.
Demetrius, who commanded the fleet, found his task
almost hopeless by reason of the strong north-west winds
which set in, as was predicted by the seamen.[1]   He first
met a storm which drove several of his heaviest ships on
shore at Raphia, so that but for the arrival of the land-
army to succour them, and make his landing secure from
the enemy, the expedition might then and there have been
given up.   When the combined forces arrived at Pelusium,
they found it amply defended; the entrance of the river
blocked with boats, and the river above covered with
small armed cruisers to resist any attempt at crossing,
ready, moreover, to circulate among the invaders promises
of large bribes and good service if they would desert and
join Ptolemy.   As these bribes amounted to two minae

[1] The wind which blows so persistently from the sea, and up the
valley of the Nile into far Nubia, is commonly called north, but is
really north-west, as I can certify from two seasons' careful observation.
Hence it blew right on shore along the coast from Gaza to Pelusium.
The rarely visited site of Pelusium was described by Mr. Greville Chester
in the *Palestine Exploration Fund, Statement for* 1880, p. 149.   There
are two Tells or mounds, called by the natives the Mound of Gold and
the Mound of Silver, from the number of coins found in them.   These
now stand in a salt marsh which no camel can traverse, and which Mr.
Chester waded across with difficulty, sinking at times to his knees in mud.
The sea must therefore have advanced here too, as at Alexandria, and
turned the lower level of the city into a swamp.   But it must always
have been easy to defend it with canals and dykes as well as with walls.

for the private, a talent for the officer, it was with difficulty, and by punishing such deserters as he could stop
with death by torture, that Antigonus escaped an end
similar to that of Perdikkas. Demetrius, finding any
entrance at Pelusium impracticable, attempted to land
farther west, first at a so-called ψευδόστομος or sham outlet, probably from the present Lake Menzaleh, and then at
the Damietta mouth (Phatnitic). In both places he was
beaten off, and was then overtaken by another storm,
which wrecked three more of his largest ships; and with
difficulty did he make his way back to his father's camp
east of the Pelusiac entrance.

§ 37. We can imagine the feelings with which Antigonus
called a council of war to weigh the situation. The fate
of Perdikkas stared them in the face. Mercenary armies
will not tolerate ill-success and increasing want in the face
of a courteous well-supplied enemy ready to welcome
deserters. Another couple of storms would certainly
destroy any fleet, however well-handled, on this inhospitable
and harbourless coast. The nomad tribes, friendly to a
successful invader, would be certain to fall upon a dispirited
retreating army. It was determined, we may say of necessity rather than of wisdom, to retreat while retreat was a
military evolution, and not an irreparable disaster.[1]

Ptolemy seems to have made no effort to harass the
departing host. He had shown once more that Egypt in

---

[1] Modern critics have found fault with Antigonus for not fortifying
and holding a station opposite Pelusium, with Demetrius for not attacking Alexandria forthwith, and thus separating Ptolemy's troops. Such
censure should only be based upon very ample knowledge, and upon
some claim to understand the situation better than Antigonus and
Demetrius did—two men of great ability and experience in practical
war. I assume that they knew what was possible far better than any
modern professor of history can know in his study.

able hands was impregnable, and that to attack it without success was so perilous, by reason of the difficulties of retreat, as to deter any prudent commander from incurring the risk. Now therefore Ptolemy had proved himself more secure than ever, and he sent official notifications to his allies Casander, Lysimachus and Seleukos, in which I am disposed to think he first formally called himself king. As Droysen has conjectured, the official era only commenced with the opening of the next Egyptian year, and this accounts for the late date assigned to it—November 305 B.C. But the notices extant that Ptolemy assumed it along with the other satraps lead us to believe that in the acclamations of his courtiers, and in the flatteries of correspondence, the title appeared before its solemn assumption by the acclamation of the 'Macedonian' soldiers.[1] At all events, the title king belonged to him before the issue of the next great conflict, in which he was only engaged indirectly, and without great personal risk. For with the repulse of Antigonus, Ptolemy's active campaigning was over, and he was able to devote the rest of his long and useful life to the arts of peace.

[1] Cf. above § 32 note 3.

COIN OF PTOLEMY I. WITH HEAD OF SARAPIS.

COIN OF KING PTOLEMY I.

CHAPTER III

PTOLEMY I (SOTER) KING, 305-285 B.C.

§ 38. THE first event of importance after Ptolemy's assumption of royalty was the great siege of Rhodes,[1] which was attacked by Antigonus because it had refused to help him against Egypt. The Rhodians protested that they had only observed neutrality; that on Ptolemy depended a great part of their prosperity; that they were ready to make any concession short of military occupation by Antigonus. But the old king and his son were determined upon subduing Rhodes, as a stepping-stone to subdue Egypt. With the Rhodian fleet a new attack on the Delta might be successful, and the invasion had surely not been abandoned, but postponed. So Demetrius was sent by his father with 40,000 troops, 200 ships of war, 170 transports—even if the numbers be exaggerated, a veritable Armada—against the great trading city. The details of the siege, which lasted nearly a year, and was then raised by a compromise, do not concern us beyond the interference of Ptolemy. Though Rhodes had entered upon an almost hopeless struggle on his account (for

---

[1] Narrated both by Diodorus (xx. 81 *sq.*) and by Plutarch in his *Life of Demetrius.*

neutrality in a war against him was the point at issue), he did not declare war against Antigonus, and send an Egyptian army and fleet to defend that city. In fact he ran no risk of losing a battle, or even weakening his prestige against the formidable Demetrius. But both he, and the other kings opposed to Antigonus in policy, that is to say Lysimachus and Casander, sent supplies of food, war material, and Ptolemy even mercenaries, to aid the Rhodians.

§ 39. The weak point of Demetrius' attack was his inability or failure to invest the city. His first attack was upon the harbour, when the city was still supplied with men and provisions from the land side. Then he attempted to storm it from the land side, but left the harbour open so that not only could Ptolemy throw in supplies from the sea, but the Rhodian cruisers were able to cut off a portion of the supplies the besiegers derived from the mainland. They even captured the royal luxuries in robes and plate, which had been sent to Demetrius by his wife Phila, and these, as being only suitable to a royal personage, the islanders sent as a present to Ptolemy. It is quite certain that but for the active help of Egypt, Rhodes would have fallen ; yet no sooner was the success of Demetrius doubtful, than Ptolemy urged the Rhodians to accept any fair compromise. Various Greek cities had already offered arbitration ; ultimately on the intervention of the Aetolians, whose league held a far higher position in the Greek world than Polybius would allow us to suppose, the terms of an agreement were arranged. Ptolemy carried the point of importance to himself in the transaction. The Rhodians were to be allies of Antigonus against any enemy, save only against Egypt. They even gave hostages to Demetrius. So then the great siege turned out a great failure, and left the position of Egypt untouched.

The anxiety of so many neutral cities to end the conflict was of course owing to commercial reasons. The whole trade of the Levant, and that of Egypt too, suffered terribly from the closing of the great mart and banking centre, upon which all their correspondences depended. In the next century we hear that the stopping of payment at Rhodian banks meant a collapse of credit all through the Hellenistic world.[1] Hence the protracted siege was a commercial disaster of the gravest kind, and to business men it mattered little under what conditions Rhodes made peace, provided she could resume her trading business. These reasons may have weighed even upon Antigonus, who was building his brilliant capital Antigoneia, on the Orontes, and could hardly obtain all the appliances required, when the sea was being swept by Rhodian cruisers and quasi-Rhodian pirates, and when commercial credit was shaken everywhere. But far more serious to the old king was the threatened combination of Seleukos, Lysimachus and Casander, a thundercloud which burst upon him at Ipsus, and laid his ambitions to rest with his life.

§ 40. Meanwhile the Rhodians showed themselves extravagantly grateful for the active succour afforded them by Ptolemy, even though he had risked nothing but some of his wealth to save them from subjugation. They had already set up statues to Antigonus and Demetrius, in the hope of averting the attack ; and they were too prudent to disturb them, even during the siege. Of course therefore they were bound to set up statues of the friendly kings, Lysimachus and Casander, who had helped them with

[1] Cf. § 148.

supplies. But this was not enough to represent their gratitude to Ptolemy. They sent to the oracle of Amon to ask whether it were lawful to honour him as a god, and receiving an affirmative answer, set up a shrine in a sacred enclosure surrounded by four colonnades, each a stadion long, which they called the *Ptolemaeion*.[1] Athenaeus[2] refers to the hymn sung in his honour at this shrine which had the form of a Paean. These events seem to have taken place in 304 B.C. and the result to Ptolemy was not only the confirmation of his royal dignity, but the additional sanction of that quasi-divinity which was so easily accorded in those days, that its absence may have been considered a deficiency in the attributes of a king.

The form of worship established in this case points to his being regarded a second founder of the city. Pausanias adds that now the title of σωτήρ was given him by the Rhodians, by which he was known in Egypt, as we learn from coins and the documents of his son's reign.[3]

---

[1] Diod. xx. 100.   [2] xv. 52, pp. 696 f.

[3] We have now ample evidence of this not only in the Petrie Papyri from the Fayyum but in the Revenue Papyrus, parts of which are dated in the twenty-third year, others in the twenty-seventh of Philadelphus' reign, and in which *in the reign of Ptolemy, son of Ptolemy Soter*, is the opening formula. The origin of this title is however more than doubtful. Fränkel (*die Quellen der Alexander-Hist.* pp. 51 *sq.*), struck by the fact that our worst authority, Pausanias (i. 8, 6), whose chronology is particularly loose, is the only one to mention the fact, while Diodorus, in his full account of the Rhodian honours, omits it, is of opinion that Ptolemy must have obtained the title much earlier and in Egypt, probably at the very opening of his satrapy. It is of course absurd that a title adopted from a foreign people should appear upon his coins. The coins with σωτῆρος upon them have dates running from 25 to 39; those with βασιλέως have none. But that fact refers exclusively to the Phoenician coinage of the second Ptolemy, who seems to have established the worship of his father as Soter in the twenty-fifth year of his reign, and issued these coins

§ 41. But as his years advanced, we see an increase of that caution, which marred his greatness. He makes no attempt to recover Cyprus, now a secure residence even for the Antigonid princesses; he attempts no more to dispute Demetrius' supremacy at sea, and when that prince carries his baffled fleet from Rhodes into Greek waters, and begins to press sore upon Ptolemy's old ally Casander, the king of Egypt does nothing till an alliance of Casander and Lysimachus with Seleukos promises him the result that he may again re-occupy Palestine, and perhaps Syria.

The operations of the allies commenced in the spring of 302 B.C.[1] While Casander strove to maintain himself against Demetrius, Lysimachus, by a sudden invasion, took possession of almost all Asia Minor. His arrangements must have been prompt and secret, for they came upon Antigonus as a surprise, while he was organising a great feast at his newly-built capital on the Orontes. But this is not the only case in these wars where we find a great want of proper information and prompt transmission of news from one land to another. We should have thought it impossible for Lysimachus to mass troops and provisions on the northern frontier of Antigonus' dominions, without ample notice reaching his adversary. Antigonus, however, stopped his Founder's feast, dismissed all the theatrical

accordingly (cf. Mr. R. S. Poole's *Coins of the Ptolemies*, p. xxxv. and below § 88). But I still think that Fränkel is so far right, that the official title Soter did not originate with the Rhodians, and that it was given to Ptolemy during his life. The moment most likely is after the defeat of Antigonus' attack upon Egypt, if the Alexandrians did not invent it as a sarcasm regarding the cautious salvation of Rhodes by their king in 305. The title θεοὶ σωτῆρες was used by the Athenians of Antigonus and Demetrius in an inscription of 306 B.C., and therefore shortly before these events. The titles σωτήρ and εὐεργέτης had been applied to Gelon according to Diod. xi. 26.

[1] Diod. xx. 106 *sq.*

artists there assembled with ample gifts, and set out to
fight his old comrade.

And here we see at once how much greater the capacity
of Lysimachus was than that of Ptolemy, in resisting
a superior force.   Instead of forthwith evacuating Asia
Minor, and carrying off his spoil and captives to Thrace,
Lysimachus occupied a fortified camp, at which Antigonus was checked for a long time and could not force
a battle.   When he managed to cut off Lysimachus'
supplies, the latter abandoned this camp with such skill
as to make his retreat safely and without loss to another
position, forty miles north, where the same tactics were
renewed.   In vain did Antigonus offer battle, or endeavour
to starve out his enemy.   His only resource was to storm
the works, and when he had brought up with delay and
trouble his siege-train, Lysimachus again outwitted him
one stormy night, and carried off his own army to winter
quarters, whither Antigonus essayed in vain to pursue him,
foreseeing that his enemy was sure of a junction in the
spring with the host of Seleukos advancing from the east
along the northern highway by Armenia and Paphlagonia.

By this masterly campaign, Lysimachus had not only
enjoyed the revenues of Asia Minor and the prestige of
occupying his adversary's country, but he had secured the
unmolested advent of his allies.   Towards the end of the
season he was in considerable difficulties as to his northern
communications, for the fleet of Demetrius, summoned by
Antigonus, controlled the coast along the Dardanelles, and
threatened his rear.   Nevertheless he did what Ptolemy
never ventured to do, and to him was due the successful
issue of the war.   For Ptolemy, advancing into Palestine
according to the terms of his alliance, and busy with the
siege of Sidon, was frightened away by the mere false

rumour that Antigonus had met and defeated the allies.
He left indeed some garrisons behind, but lost his great
chance of extending his territory northward, for when the
issue came at Ipsus (301 B.C.), those who had borne the
brunt of the conflict, made their settlement without even
consulting him.

§ 42. It was indeed a great battle, like that of Leipzig
in our century, where the kings of the earth met together
to settle a momentous question. Antigonus, now eighty-
one years old, and for more than thirty years dominant in
Asia Minor and Syria, was supported by his son Demetrius,
the most successful captain of the younger generation, and
with him was the youthful Pyrrhus, presently to become
the most brilliant soldier of his age. On the other side
were Lysimachus, now over sixty, the best strategist
among Alexander's generals, who had carved himself out,
amid successes and reverses, a noble kingdom in the
northern provinces ; Seleukos, the most successful, and
perhaps the ablest of the Diadochi, and now also the
most powerful with his army of Indian elephants; Casander,
whose cruel consistency and stubborn determination had
influenced the course of this history more than the superior
tactics of his rivals.

In this famous array, Ptolemy was absent, hiding
himself in the security of his far-off Egypt, and waiting
to take advantage of the result. The fact that Demetrius
commanded the sea could hardly have hindered his
effecting a landing on the south coast of Asia Minor,
especially while Demetrius was operating on the Hellespont against Lysimachus and his communications.

§ 43. Most unfortunately our only full authority for
the period, Diodorus, is not preserved, except in needy
excerpts, beyond his twentieth book, which ends just before

the great battle. We are consequently unable to discover what were the exact terms of the division of Antigonus' empire among the victors. Seleukos certainly got the lion's share; though most of the sea coast of Asia Minor, as far as Cilicia, seems to have been ceded to Lysimachus. Syria was certainly from henceforth a part, and a very vital part, of the kingdom of Seleukos. He intended no longer to be a king of the far East, ruling at Babylon, but a Hellenistic sovran, in contact with the culture, the trade, the politics of the Greek world. A quotation from the lost twenty-first book of Diodorus tells us: 'After his victory over Antigonus, Seleukos marched back to Phoenicia, in order to occupy Coele-Syria in accordance with the terms of the partition. But Ptolemy had already occupied the cities and complained that Seleukos, his ally, should have agreed to accept the territory already occupied by the king of Egypt, and, moreover, that the other kings had not allotted to Egypt, in spite of its participation in the war, any part of the conquered territory. To this Seleukos replied: that it was only fair for those who had actually overthrown the enemy in fight to control what they had conquered; yet for old friendship's sake he would not for the present insist upon the matter of Coele-Syria, but in due time would consider his position towards allies who were too grasping.'[1] Thus the question was left open, and the discussion was so indefinite that in after days both Seleukids and Lagids appealed to it as giving them a right to occupy the disputed country.[2] As a matter of fact, when Seleukos and Ptolemy met and discussed the possession of Syria, the coast from Tyre to Gaza belonged to neither of

[1] Stark *Gaza* p. 362 thinks that this fragment does not apply to Ptolemy in 301 B.C., but to Demetrius some years later, when Seleukos found him difficult to manage. [2] Polybius v. 67, 7.

them, but to Demetrius and his garrisons. Hence the country claimed by Seleukos could only be inner Syria, which we know to have been the country settled with independent cities under Seleukid influence. All the Decapolis was a Syrian creation. Ptolemy on the other hand, having the only fleet which could cope with that of Demetrius, must have contended with him not only for Cyprus, but for the coast cities of Philistia and Phoenicia. In the end Ptolemy prevailed, and it is likely that he put garrisons into these cities after Demetrius fell, while Seleukos occupied the Cilician and Pisidian forts. This seems to be the general outline of the wars from 301 to 294 B.C.[1]

§ 44. But, of course, new jealousies led to new complications. Ptolemy took care to fortify himself against the threatened advances of Seleukos, by drawing closer to Lysimachus, who though now living at Sardis in perfect harmony with his noble Persian wife Amastris, sent her home to her city Herakleia, and married (probably in 300 B.C.) Ptolemy's daughter Arsinoe,[2] whose half-sister · Lysandra also married Lysimachus' eldest son and heir Agathocles.[3] On the other hand Seleukos, who at once set about founding his new capital Antioch, with the materials of the dismantled Antigoneia, drew near in policy to Demetrius, who, though a fugitive without a kingdom, commanded the sea, and hence Cyprus, and many Cilician

---

[1] The facts have been ably discussed and arranged in Stark's *Gaza* pp. 361 *sq.*

[2] This was Berenike's eldest child by her second marriage, and born not later than 316 B.C., perhaps a year or two earlier. So a girl of eighteen or less, was given away for political purposes to a man of over sixty.

[3] Plut. *Dem.* 31 ; Paus. i. 10. The great difficulties as to the date of this second marriage are stated by Niese i. 354.

coast towns and lesser islands. It is at this moment that historians suppose Ptolemy to have sought the friendship of the upstart Agathocles, and obtained a diversion against Casander at Corcyra, by marrying to Agathocles his step-daughter Theoxena, sister of Magas of Cyrene.[1]

The complicated wars, alliances, counter-alliances of the next five years are not to be extricated from the confusion in which we have them, till we discover some further information. Plutarch, who covers the period in his *Life of Demetrius*, seems to have no clear idea of the sequence of events. The action of Ptolemy is perhaps more obscure than the rest. He had to maintain himself against the fleet of Demetrius, and we even hear from one source (Eusebius) that the latter took from him Samaria, which had been settled with a new population, perhaps of veterans, by Perdikkas. On the other hand, it is certain that during this period the two kings came to some agreement, according to which at one moment Demetrius offered hostages, and his brother-in-law Pyrrhus voluntarily undertook the agreeable bondage. At another, Ptolemy betrothed his daughter Ptolemais to his rival. Pyrrhus so ingratiated himself with Ptolemy and his favourite wife Berenike, that they gave him her daughter Antigone to wife, and so established Egyptian connexions with Epirus, which the young man soon made his kingdom.[2]

But where did Ptolemy not form these matrimonial alliances? He now had daughters or stepdaughters married: Theoxena to Agathocles of Syracuse, Antigone to Pyrrhus, Lysandra to Casander's son Alexander, Lysandra (probably a second of the name) to Agathocles son of Lysimachus of Thrace, Arsinoe to Lysimachus himself;

---

[1] I have placed this marriage earlier, but without any confidence; cf. above § 34.   [2] Plut. *Pyrrhus* 4.

Eirene to Eunostos king of Soli in Cyprus, ultimately (in 287 B.C.) even Ptolemais to Demetrius.

§ 45. We hear from a decree in honour of Demochares (preserved in pseudo-Plutarch's *Life* of the orator) that Ptolemy contributed fifty talents to help the Athenians in their struggles against Demetrius. He also succeeded in recovering (in 295 B.C.) Cyprus, held for eleven years by Demetrius. But now the strange power and fascination of the Besieger were on the wane; his vast plans terrified all the reigning kings, and he ended his life a state prisoner in the hands of Seleukos. On the other hand, the deliberate foundation of the new capital of Seleukos in Syria must have convinced Ptolemy that any permanent hold on Coele-Syria was for Egypt impossible. He did not cease, however, to assert his claims upon Palestine, and it is probable that such towns as Gaza, Jerusalem, Joppa were permanently under his influence.

But according as the king grows older, he retires from the wearisome conflicts to liberate the Greeks, to hold cities on the Cilician coast, to maintain the balance of power among his warring rivals, and devotes himself to the internal organisation of his kingdom, which was the wealthiest in the Hellenistic world, not excepting the vast domain of Seleukos. Here it is that the history of Ptolemaic Egypt truly begins, and here we indeed long for larger and better materials to tell us of so important a step in the world's civilisation. But alas! inscriptions and papyri, which multiply in the reigns of the later kings, are here but few and trifling. The old historians have left us nothing. The development of Alexandria, and even the foundation of the world-famed Museum are left in obscurity and in doubt. The time will come when further discoveries will disclose to us these secrets; at present we can only enumerate the few facts that are known, and 'wait for the day.'

§ 46. Mention has already been made of the grant of lands to the gods of the cities of Pe and Tep by Ptolemy, acting for the youthful Alexander IV., as well as the restorations at Thebes in the names of Philip Arridaeus and the boy Alexander. There is also a shrine cut in the rock at Beni Hassan, near the *Speos Artemidos*, which is dated in this Alexander's reign, Ptolemy being satrap of Egypt. In the centre of the cornice are the well-known globe and asps which mark all the Ptolemaic temples, and on the architrave beneath, the king is kneeling to present the figure of Truth to the goddess Pasht. Behind him stands Hathor. On one side of the door the figure of the king is represented standing in the presence of Amon and Horus, on the other, in presence of Thoth and Chem.[1] There is no Greek flavour in any of these representations. They are purely Egyptian. It would be difficult to find a bolder or more complete assumption of a strange cult by any conqueror. Ptolemy and his staff can hardly have understood what these symbols meant in detail. But his policy was clear-sighted enough. So thoroughly did he and his successors adopt as an official religion the old faith or faiths of the Egyptians, that modern scholars were long at fault concerning the temples the Ptolemies erected all over the country. Until the reading of the hieroglyphics was assured, and the Greek inscriptions were shown by Letronne to agree with what the hieroglyphics said, no one suspected that the great temples of Edfu, Esneh, and Dendera could be other than old Egyptian. It was imagined that the Ptolemies had left no mark on the land. We know better now. The great majority of the

[1] Cf. Murray's *Egypt* ii. p. 413.

surviving Egyptian temples is either partly or wholly of Ptolemaic construction. And here it is of importance to note that this whole policy was inaugurated by the first king.

§ 47. It is, however, most remarkable that the actual buildings which can now be ascribed to him of this Egyptian character all date from his satrapy, not from his royalty. Is this an accident, or does it indicate a modification of his policy? The destruction of so large a proportion of the temples by Arabs and Turks may have hidden from us buildings in the upper country dating from his later days. Still the silence in our authorities agrees with the absence of archaeological evidence, and makes it probable that as soon as he had pacified the priests with endowments, and shown the people, by some signal restorations of what the Persians had destroyed, his friendliness to national traditions, he turned to the Greek or Macedonian element in his realm, and spent his later liberalities upon Alexandria. Tacitus says it was he who built the fortifications of the city.[1] But even here we do not learn of his doing as the older Greek settlers at Naukratis had done—introducing the gods of their respective cities and building them a dwelling-place, just as English settlers in any part of the world are wont to carry their religion with them, and build a church. As he designed the population of his new capital to be composite—or may I use the word mongrel—so we hear that he was at pains to introduce a mongrel god into the city, and make his shrine the principal sanctuary of Alexandria.

§ 48. He had already, at the opening of his rule, contributed fifty talents of silver (nearly £12,000) to the obsequies of the Apis bull that died at that time, and it is likely that this peculiar form of the worship of Osir-

[1] *Hist.* iv. 83.

hapi [1]—Osiris Ptah, two distinct deities jumbled together, in a manner only possible among the Egyptians—was the most prominent at that period. The excesses of Cambyses had reached their culmination by his attack on this particular god in his animal manifestation.

It seems that a further fusion of this vague personage with the Greek Zeus, or Hades, as the god of the dead, was considered by the priests and politicians of the day a valuable aid to the fusing of the nationalities. The story told us by Plutarch [2] and by Tacitus [3] has not the least the air of naïve enthusiasm, but rather of a calculated and prepared appeal to popular superstition on the part of those who regarded religion as an engine for civil administration. Unfortunately the details given by the authors just named, and by Clemens from Athenodorus of Tarsus, [4] show considerable discrepancies. This would seem strange if their only source was the book on Egyptian religion by Manetho, a contemporary priest, who enjoyed the confidence of this and the next Ptolemy, and who did so much to expound Egyptian history and cult in the Greek tongue. Possibly Tacitus, who cites *Aegyptiorum antistites*, got his account from the cicerone-priests who showed Roman tourists round the temples, and who had embellished the narrative of Manetho.

[1] In the *Imprecation of Artemisia*, a very old papyrus now at Vienna, which probably dates from the days of the first Ptolemy, the form Osirapis, and not Sarapis, occurs. The Greeks afterwards assumed Sarapis to be the name of a special Egyptian god, which it was not. There was an oracle of Osiris at Abydos in Upper Egypt, consulted from early times by Greeks, as Mr. Sayce has shown from the graffiti on the walls of the temple of Seti. The inscriptions go back apparently to the sixth century B.C. Cf. *Soc. Bibl. Arch.* for 1888, p. 377. There can be little doubt that here Osiris passed into Sarapis and then into Bes.

[2] *De Iside et Osiride* § 28.   [3] *Hist.* iv. 84.   [4] *FHG* iii. 487.

At all events the king had a dream, in which a divine figure ordered him to seek the statue of the god, and make a home for it in Alexandria.   Tacitus says that Pontus was specified as the residence of the god, Plutarch that the figure gave no details, and that the king had to ascertain by description of his vision to experienced persons where the image was to be found.   At all events, by the help of Greek theologians the right statue was found at Sinope, in a temple of Pluto, or Dis, and then was obtained either by theft, as Plutarch most improbably relates, or by long persuasion of the tyrant of Sinope and his unwilling people, aided by large gifts, and of course apparitions of the same figure to the ruler of Sinope, as soon as he felt it prudent to give way.   So the statue was brought with pomp to Alexandria, and set up in a special temple built on the spot called Rhakotis, now the centre of the new city of Alexandria.

I learned, when at Alexandria in 1894, from M. Lumbroso, the architect and contractor who was building the new bank in that city, that in making the foundations he came upon the basement of an old structure, and that on removing a large stone, he found the under surface hollowed out so as to form a cup with a corresponding cavity on the upper surface of the nether stone.   In the cavity there had been deposited four plaques—one of gold, one of silver, one of bronze, and one of stone.   The gold plaque had its inscription still quite legible, and was assumed to contain the dedication of the temple to Sarapis by the first Ptolemy.[1]   But this inference of M.

[1] My attempts to see this plaque, which is now, I hear, in Paris, or to obtain a photograph of it, have been ineffectual, so I quote it from a copy sent me by M. Wilbour, viz. Σαραπιδος και Ισιδος θεων σωτηρων και βασιλεως Πτολεμαιου και βασιλισσης Αρσινοης θεων Φιλοπατορων.

Maspero, who first published the text in No. vii. of his *Recueil*, was erroneous. It is really a dedication by Ptolemy (IV.) Philopator, who was indeed very zealous in promoting the cult of his great grandfather, but in the present case calls Isis and Sarapis the Saviour Gods. It is likely, however, that this shrine was connected with the first temple of Sarapis at Alexandria, for the depth of the foundations of the modern building is so much less than that at which we find the remains of ancient Alexandria at other points, that we can well believe our authorities who call this site, once named Rhakotis, a citadel, or ἄκρα, though it was not the main (artificial) hill now known as Kom-el-Dick.

§ 49. The naturalisation of the Pluto of Sinope as Sarapis was, however, of wide religious import. Many other shrines were set up to him, first in Egypt, then throughout the Hellenistic world. At Sakkara Mariette even found a Greek Serapeum, a regular temple *in antis*, in conjunction with the old Egyptian Serapeum, with its pylons and its courts. In the Egyptian temple, but beneath the surface, were the famous vaults of the Apis bulls, buried there ever since the eighteenth dynasty.

It will be noticed that in the legends of the foundation the king plays the principal part. To him comes the dream, and he sets the learned in theology at work to find the solution. We know so little of his character that we cannot tell whether the ingenious idea of fusing a Greek god with an Egyptian was his own, or whether it was suggested by the priests, such as Manetho, who had learned Greek, and could advise him on the religious requirements of the new state. The Greek historians were always ready enough to identify foreign gods with their own, and in Egypt the hopeless confusion of persons had

certainly arisen from unsystematic attempts of the priests
to incorporate the worship of the several ancient cities of
Egypt into some sort of unity.[1] If we are to believe
Arrian, who is generally trustworthy, the temple of Isis
at Alexandria, a goddess afterwards so popular in the
Graeco-Roman world, was founded by the orders of Alexander himself.[2]

It is remarked by both Tacitus and Clemens that
isolated authors referred the affair of Sarapis to the second
or even to the third Ptolemy, and in the last case that the
statue was said to have come from Seleukeia (on the
Orontes).   Both these variations of the story are to be
rejected.   The former arose from the habit of the flatterers
of the second king, who loved to ascribe to him all the
great founder's ideas, as we shall show in other cases.   The
latter arose from the pompous inscriptions of Euergetes,
which told of his having brought back the gods of Egypt
from abroad.   Probably, as we shall see, he did no such
thing.   But in any case those who believed him, and
wished to show an example of the restitution, could find no
better than that of the god Sarapis, who had certainly
come from abroad.

§ 50. Though Ptolemy adorned his new capital with
palaces and temples, with parks and colonnades, and
with the other splendours of Hellenistic cities, though he
paid special attention to the official promotion of religion
and, as we shall see, of letters, he seems not to have
favoured political or even communal liberties.   According

---

[1] Cf. Erman's *Aegypten* cap. xii.

[2] Cf. Arrian iii. 1.   The coins of Alexandria under the Roman Empire
show that there existed in the Ptolemaic city at least one temple in
Egyptian style among the many Hellenistic structures which appear
on these coins.   This was the temple of Isis.   Cf. Poole *Coins of
Alexandria* Nos. 542, 879, and the text p. xci.

to all theorists and critics, the one great source of Hellenic superiority in civilisation was the autonomous *polis*, or polity which might embrace a mere town and its suburbs, and yet give it the privilege of treating as an independent community with great kings or federations. It was essential to a *polis* to have its own assembly of citizens, who passed laws for its management, and elected the magistrates who were to carry out these laws. It possessed the exclusive right of taxing its inhabitants, and even issued coinage from its own mint. We feel surprise, though we have no evidence of this feeling among the men of that day, that Alexander's greatest foundation possessed none of these privileges.[1] Alexandria was from the outset the royal residence of the satrap-king, never a foundation of Graeco-Macedonians with city-privileges in a foreign land. Such foundations were very common, especially in the Seleukid empire. We have the coins of

---

[1] From the fact that there were φυλαί and δῆμοι, Droysen (iii. i. 34) seems to infer that it was a πόλις in the Greek sense. But he confesses that there was no βουλή, and no deliberations of the assembly, the town being ruled by royal officials. Thus his facts controvert his theory. Dion (in speaking of the settlement of Egypt by Augustus, li. 17) says definitely τοῖς δ' Ἀλεξανδρεῦσιν ἄνευ βουλευτῶν πολιτεύεσθαι ἐκέλευσε, owing to their turbulence, but mentions neither their previous condition nor any ἐκκλησία of citizens. We have no evidence that either ever existed there up to the time of the Emperor Severus. Niebuhr (*Vorträge* iii. p. 360, note) thought it absurd that Ptolemais in Upper Egypt should have a Greek city-constitution, yet the capital not so. He held that the first Ptolemy, who established φυλαί, etc., had granted it, but that in Physkon's persecutions of the Greek inhabitants this part of the population with its privileges had disappeared, so that the Romans only found natives and Jews, with the soldatesca, still residing there. The fact remains that we have found more than one decree of the βουλή of Ptolemais. We have not a word concerning its existence at Alexandria. Concerning the δῆμοι, see the important information of the Pet. Pap. utilised by Wilcken in his review of my book, Göttingen *GA* for 1895, pp. 136 *sqq.*

many such independent cities in Syria and Palestine, with the date of their own era, which meant the starting-point of their existence, or the declaration of their independence. Alexandria was not set up on this model. Her inhabitants had many privileges, so much so that in after days it was the necessary step for a native, who desired the Roman franchise, first to acquire the status of an Alexandrian.[1] Unfortunately we have no details beyond the triviality that while the rest of the population could be beaten with the whip, the Alexandrian only with a stick.[2] The whip was probably nothing else than the *kurbash* used till yesterday to keep the natives in order.

§ 51. We may, however, be certain that Alexandria was free from most of the taxes that weighed upon the country population. Just as the Turks made Stamboul free of taxes, so it is more than probable that the poll-tax was not levied in the capital, and also that some indirect taxes were not there enforced.[3] Thus we find that veterans settled in the Fayyum, under the next Ptolemy, speak in their wills of their furnished house in Alexandria, 100 miles distant. No doubt this enabled them to retain the privileges of that sort of citizenship.

[1] Pliny (*Letters* x. 5, 6) had asked for the Roman franchise for his trainer, Harpocrates. *Sed admonitus sum a peritioribus debuisse me ante ei Alexandrinam civitatem inpetrare, deinde Romanam, quoniam esset Aegyptius.* Trajan, in his reply, makes a special compliment of giving the Roman franchise, but issues a letter (tantamount to an order) to the prefect of Egypt, to grant the Alexandrian conditions.

[2] Philo *in Flacc.* 10. In modern Egypt the distinction would be by no means trivial, as it marks a difference of race. To strike an European with a *kurbash* would be a horrible insult.

[3] We have now in the Revenue Papyrus, cols. 61 *seq.*, the frequent formula και ωστε εις την εν Αλεξανδρειαι διαθεσιν (stores, or wholesale market) ου τελος ουθεν πραξεται, applying to the amount of oil (sesame and croton) which each nome should furnish yearly. But Mr. Grenfell interprets this passage differently.

But the only assembly recognised there was that of the 'Macedonian' soldiers, who proclaimed a new king, or could try a state-prisoner, as they had done under the old home kings. This occasional and not strictly organised assembly was generally backed up by a great mob, whose influence under a weak ruler might increase into a veritable despotism.[1] The early Ptolemies saw the danger, and kept the city submissive with the aid of a large mercenary force, so well paid and appointed that service in Egypt was the promised land of the Greek soldier of fortune.

We shall return again to the details of government at the opening of the next reign. What here concerns us is only the general principle adopted by Ptolemy in contrast to that of Seleukos, and indeed to that of Alexander. But both Alexander and Seleukos proposed to themselves to rule as emperors over a conglomerate of widely varying nationalities or states, in each of which the free cities would form a nucleus of civilisation, and a moral support to the imperial crown. Ptolemy, as far as Egypt went, had a different task before him, or rather, he chose to solve his task in a different way. He possessed indeed a homogeneous, isolated kingdom, which he could control personally and completely from his capital. But did it not require real genius for any one of the Diadochi to abandon the great idea framed and partly carried out by their matchless master, who was the very ideal to them of imperial monarchy? This is the great historic claim to honour of the first Ptolemy,[2] and how thoroughly Aristotle would have agreed with him !

[1] This is what Julius Caesar tells us, *Bell. Civ.* iii. *sub fin.*

[2] Mommsen (*RG* v. 559-62), while perfectly appreciating the facts, and comparing the Ptolemaic monarchy to that of Frederick the Great, where an able king, labouring incessantly at the administration, is the personal benefactor of all his people (εὐεργέτης), fails to see this great merit.

§ 52. It was remarked that, while founding cities in
outlying dependencies, the Ptolemies avoided doing so in
Egypt. The first Ptolemy only founded two that we can
name, Ptolemais[1] (now the site of Menshieh), which succeeded to the prosperity of Thebes, and Menelaos, the
principal place in the Nitriotic nome south-west of Alexandria, which was called, says Strabo, after the king's
brother. About the man Menelaos we know nothing
beyond his military command in Cyprus, and about the
city nothing but the name.[2] Ptolemais is specially reported to have been founded on the Greek model, and
the few inscriptions which have as yet been discovered
there corroborate the statement of Strabo. There was
a guild of Dionysiac artists settled there, which shows
that even Greek amusements had to be supplied for its
population.[3] It is certain that the settlement dates from
the first king, but (as Niebuhr argued) if it was his principle not to allow civic liberties in Alexandria, why should
he set up another city with greater privileges? My reply
is, that we now know from the Revenue Papyrus, which
agrees very well with Strabo,[4] that the list of Ptolemaic

[1] The evidence of this is an epigram of a certain Celsus, given in
CIG 4925 και πατρης γλυκερης Πτολεμαιδος ην επο[λι]σσεν Σωτηρ,
and the fact that special priests of Soter, established in this city, are
mentioned in many papyri ; cf. also Strabo p. 813.

[2] Strange to say, the νομος Μενελαιτης is not placed by the geo-
graphers around this town, but on the coast adjoining Alexandria to
the east.

[3] There are two resolutions passed by the ' artists attached to
Dionysus and the Brother gods '—a guild resident in the city of
Ptolemais—preserved in the Museum of Gizeh (room 40), and numbered
301 and 307 in the Catalogue of 1893. Cf. Addit. Note p. 488.

[4] Some critics had assumed a gap in Strabo's text (xvii. I. 41-42)
because he stops suddenly in his enumeration of the nomes when he
reaches the Thebais. We may now be sure that he was copying from a
document such as that we have recovered.

nomes ended with Kynopolis, and that the whole south country was called the Thebaid. It is quite likely that Ptolemy found it difficult to persuade Hellenic settlers to go so far up the river, and only persuaded them to do so by establishing them in a sort of southern capital with special privileges.[1]

It was now that Thebes and its wonders were opened to ordinary Greek travellers, and we can still see, in the transcript of Diodorus, the astonishment of Hecataeus of Abdera, and other Greek tourists, who ascended the river from Ptolemais, and visited the splendours of the Tombs of the Kings. Stray Greek mercenaries had of course penetrated farther. Inscriptions at Abu-Simbel, and even at Wadi Halfa of far older date tell us that. But now first was Thebes open to the tourist, as Syene was opened to him by the expedition of the next king.[2] We may assume that the populations of decaying Thebes and of Abydos, once great centres of wealth, came to swell the new city.

But what happened at Naukratis, an old Hellenic settlement certainly possessing its own communal constitution, and proving it to us by the occurrence of two coins, which seem to date from this very period?[3] It is not unlikely that Cleomenes, a citizen of Naukratis, whom Ptolemy found controlling the country, may have pro-

[1] Mommsen (*RG* v. 557 note) expresses his opinion that the so-called privileges of Ptolemais were only those granted to Alexandria. Whether Naukratis was allowed to preserve her old constitution he thinks doubtful.

[2] It has been already stated that Alexander, when in Egypt, ordered certain Chian politicians, who had made disturbances in Asia Minor, and were brought to him as prisoners, to be sent to Elephantine, there to be kept in strict internment (Arrian iii. 2). It would appear from this that the island had been a penal settlement under the Persian domination.

[3] Cf. W. F. Petrie *Naukratis* i. p. 66.

moted this assertion of liberty, and it may have been one of the reasons why Ptolemy so promptly got rid of him. The majority of the important people at Naukratis could be bribed or coerced into the greater and more brilliant Alexandria; the rest were too insignificant to make them-selves heard. At all events Naukratis sinks henceforward into a mere Egyptian town, ruled, we may assume, as all the rest were, by officers of the crown.[1]

§ 53. It is sometimes stated that the new foundation of Crocodilopolis[2] in the Fayyum was also a city on the Greek model. Neither the many documents recovered from the papers of that city nor the statements of Strabo support this view. It appears to me that the position of capital in a nome precluded in some way the existence of Hellenic political rights; Ptolemais, being beyond or out-side the Ptolemaic nomes, though the chief town of the whole Thebaid, stands on a different footing. Even Naukratis is mentioned as a distinct item in the Saitic nome.[3]

[1] This may have been the case, even though old traditions were maintained. We now know that Philadelphus was at pains to restore and enlarge the Hellenion there, and G. Lumbroso (*Econ. pol.* p. 222) infers from the mention of τιμοῦχοι in the papyrus 60² of the Louvre col-lection, in relation to this very Hellenion, that the old magistracies of the city still survived in Ptolemaic days. But in the present case (cf. Athenaeus, p. 149 f. to which he refers) they were religious officers regu-lating religious feasts, which is exactly what we should expect, even if all those of political importance were abolished. An οικονομος των κατα N. is mentioned (under Philopator) in an inscription (below, § 158 note). This seems quite Egyptian, not Greek. The governors of provinces in the Syrian empire were called *satraps*, even in Cilicia (*Pet. Pap.* II. xlv.), those of the Ptolemies were *strategi*. ἡγεμόνες was a military title common to both.

[2] It is frequently spoken of as the city of Arsinoe, which was a name it did not possess till long after. In all the early papyri it is *the city of the Crocodiles in the Arsinoite nome* (to distinguish it from that in the Pathyrite nome).

[3] In the enumeration of nomes in the Revenue Papyrus col. 60.

But in addition to Egypt, which was to a great extent literally crown property, there were outlying possessions or dependencies of the crown of Egypt which required very different treatment. There was Cyrene, most valuable for the production of silphium, and for its breed of horses, not to say for its very pure and distinguished Greek population. There was Cyprus, which supplied Egypt with timber and with copper; there was Palestine, the highway to Syria and to Babylon, not only the great source of produce most important to Egypt, such as balm and asphalt, but the home of a stirring mercantile population, invaluable as friends, dangerous as enemies. There was, moreover, the whole series of islands through the Aegean, which, from the moment that Demetrius' sea-power was broken (in 294 B.C.), and he himself interned by Seleukos, became the subject in some sense of the Egyptian naval power, which ruled the waters for several generations. These various dependencies, often mutinous, often occupied by his enemies with a superior force, offered great difficulties, both military and diplomatic, and left ample scope for the king to show his resources as a statesman.

§ 54. Cyrene was the easiest to control, so far as the population was concerned. For here, beyond the reach of the great armies which had intimidated most Hellenic cities under Alexander and his generals, the old feud of aristocrat and populace was in full vigour. The whole territory was occupied by a group of independent communities always jealous, and often at variance. Within each city the majority of votes in the assembly was set against the preponderance of wealth, and so we have those desperate wars of city factions, in which either side is ready to call in a foreign force, in order to subdue, or massacre, or exile, its opponents. And then there are always exiles, seeking to be restored to property and power by foreign intervention. But as soon as they are restored, there is the usual impatience of foreign control, especially of the control of that sentimental bugbear, a king, who prevents the restored from wreaking their vengeance, and insists on preserving peace. Thus it was very easy for Ptolemy to obtain a pretext for interference, but not so easy to maintain permanent order and obedience in this remote appanage of his empire. He could only rule it by keeping a military force there under a viceroy.

The course of events showed that these viceroys themselves were not trustworthy. Whenever they were able to reconcile the cities to harmony under their sway, they too were ready to throw off their allegiance, and become monarchs for themselves. This ambition was of course promoted by all the inducements which the rivals of Egypt, especially the Macedonian monarchy, could offer.

The policy of Ptolemy was consistent under all these difficulties. He never trusted the Cyrenaica to rule itself, which would mean that it must fall into the hands of some military adventurer; but he left to his lieutenant, and under him to the cities, great liberty. That he ruled in the interests of the richer classes is obvious. That he drew subsidies from the taxes upon exports, and regulated the external policy of the Cyrenaica, may be assumed as certain. But their internal arrangements did not concern him; probably he knew it to be his interest to keep both factions, the aristocratic and popular, alive, and at variance. His only danger lay in a loyal combination of all the cities, either as a federation, or under a popular viceroy.

§ 55. His control of Cyprus was much more high-handed. He had to deal here not with free Greek communities, but with local 'kings' or dynasts, who ruled the various cities of the island after the manner of the tyrants in Greece, except that they seem to have possessed hereditary power, which the Greek tyrant very seldom established.   Ptolemy was ready to attach them to his house even by alliance with his family, though we may note that it was only a bastard daughter whom he gave away to Eunostos, king of Soli.   But when these kings played him false, and joined his opponents, they did so at the risk not only of their thrones but of their lives.   This we know from the case of Nicocles, tyrant of Paphos, whom he compelled to commit suicide (which his whole family also did) on the plea of suspected treason.[1]   Ptolemy's brother Menelaos was for some time viceroy of Cyprus; in after days it was usual for a royal prince to be sent there; he collected and forwarded the taxes of the island to his sovran.   It is remarkable that, while this was the simple form of government, the cities under the kings were still counted free cities, which retained their right of local coinage, like the cities of Cyrene, and were even allowed to use a local era—*e.g.* the era of the people of Kition —to mark the date of their independence.   They had, according to inscriptions, their council ($\beta o v \lambda \acute{\eta}$), and consequently their assembly.[2]   But these must have been a mere shadow, like the constitution of the Greek cities long afterwards under Roman sway; the practical power

[1] This tragic story is told by Diodorus xx. 21.

[2] According to M. Ph. Berger (Acad. des Inscriptions, etc., *Comptes rendus* for December 1893) the traces of Phoenician worship and of hereditary priesthoods in the north of the island show a strong Semitic influence, and he even infers that the Ptolemaic rule was marked by a revival of the national spirit which had been suffering from Hellenic influences.   I do not know any evidence sufficient for this conclusion. In whatever cases the cities had cast out despots who opposed Ptolemy, he would naturally favour their local autonomies.

lay with the kings, and through them Ptolemy conquered, lost, and ultimately recovered the island.[1]

§ 56. His relations to Palestine are more difficult to understand, or at least, are not explained by the historians who tell us the facts. It was noticed as remarkable with what favour Alexander had treated the Jews. In contrast to Tyre and Gaza, Jerusalem, which offered no resistance to his conquest, received every consideration. In another place I have pointed out that to Alexander the friendship of this people was a military advantage of the highest importance. The Jewish *diaspora*, scattered through all the cities of inner Asia as far at least as Rhagae,[2] were in frequent contact with Jerusalem, and made regular voyages to its temple. Hence to an invader of Asia, who had no maps, no full information as to the routes and resources for feeding his army, no organised system of interpreters, these Jews were the natural intelligence department.[3]

[1] I disagree with Droysen who is led by the numismatists to assert that the Cyprian cities were of the strict Greek type. Diodorus is express on the other side, viz. xvi. 42 ἐν γὰρ τῇ νήσῳ ταύτῃ πόλεις ἦσαν ἀξιόλογοι μὲν θ', ὑπὸ δὲ ταύτας ὑπῆρχε τεταγμένα μικρὰ πολίσματα τὰ προσκυροῦντα τοῖς θ' πόλεσιν. ἑκάστη δὲ τούτων εἶχε βασιλέα τῆς μὲν πόλεως ἄρχοντα, τῷ δὲ βασιλεῖ τῶν Περσῶν ὑποτεταγμένον. As soon as these people revolt against the Persians, αὐτοκράτορας τὰς ἰδίας βασιλείας ἐποίησαν. Is this compatible with Greek polities?

[2] Cf. *Tobit* i. 6, 14. Tobit, dwelling with his deported tribesmen near Nineveh, goes regularly to Jerusalem, and also to Rhagae, where he deposits money with a friend.

[3] A hint of the truth is contained in the answer put by Josephus (*Antt.* xi. 8, § 5) into the king's mouth, when he was asked why he specially venerated the high-priest. Alexander replies: when I was reflecting how I could conquer Asia, a figure dressed like the high-priest appeared to me in a dream, and told me not to delay, for that he would himself *lead my army* and make over to me the Persian empire. Here are the actual words : καὶ πρὸς ἐμαυτὸν διασκεπτομένῳ μοι, πῶς ἂν κρατήσαιμι τῆς Ἀσίας, παρεκελεύετο μὴ μέλλειν ἀλλὰ θαρσοῦντα

They knew all the roads, stations, towns, fords in the interior, and could communicate through the Jewish residents of the *diaspora* with all the foreign nations of the far provinces. Hence it was, as Arrian tells us, that a large number of Jews took military service under Alexander, and went with him, first to Egypt, and then to Asia.

It is added by Josephus that the king settled a great number of them in his new Alexandria, a statement which can hardly be false. When a large new population, especially of trading people, was required, the Jews were at hand, friendly to the king, and ready to seize the all-important moment. He further states [1] that Alexander gave the Jews rights equal to those of the Macedonians and Greeks in that city. Seeing that it was not a Greek *polis*, and that these rights were rather privileges over the aborigines, or immunities from taxes, I am disposed to believe this also. [2] Moreover in the settlement of the Fayyum they (or the Samaritans) were allowed to found villages, and there are allusions which point to their being on a par with the Greeks. [3] But surely the so-called Macedonians must

διαβαίνειν· αὐτὸς γὰρ ἡγήσεσθαί μοι τῆς στρατιᾶς καὶ τὴν II. παραδώσειν ἀρχήν.

[1] *Cont. Apion.* 2, 4.

[2] Mommsen (*RG* v. 491), in a very instructive note, discusses the question, and by the way contradicts the view he had adopted earlier (*op. cit.* iii. 442). As, however, he does not express himself clearly concerning the privileges of the Macedonians and Greeks, he does not decide the matter.

[3] Especially the fragment published in the *Pet. Pap.* I. p. 43 :

εις τα αποδοχια της κωμης
παρα των Ιουδαιων και των
Ελληνων εκαστου σωματος S

(viz. for each slave which they had, a tax of half a drachma),

και τουτο λογευεται δια
Δι . . . ιου του επιστατου.

Mr. Grenfell, among the papyri he acquired in 1895, has shown me

always have had that right of meeting as free men in arms, which they brought with them from their homes, and which no other Alexandrian could claim.

The Jews, then, under Alexander were made at home in Egypt, and were friendly to the Macedonian conquest. For if they had met with some violence at his hands, they had also received unusual favours. When Ptolemy had succeeded to the throne of Egypt, and had beaten off the attack of Perdikkas, he forthwith made an invasion into Palestine and Syria, and annexed all the country.[1] When driven out of it by Antigonus, we hear that he carried off to Egypt a large number of the inhabitants either as slaves, or as compulsory settlers. And this happened apparently four times. He always retreated in time to carry his booty with him. But in spite of these repeated raids, or temporary occupations, and this repeated carrying off of plunder from Palestine, we are persistently informed that the house of Ptolemy was most popular with the Jews, in contrast to those of the other Diadochi, Antigonus, and afterwards Seleukos. Whenever the Seleukids did occupy Palestine, they took it by force, and held it by force.

§ 57. Whence did the lasting popularity of the Lagidae arise? Diodorus lays great stress on the pleasant manners and courtesy of the first Ptolemy, and contrasts it with the harshness of Perdikkas, and the overbearing roughness of Antigonus. But this is not sufficient. There must have

one (K) from the Fayyum speaking of the σαββαθιον (synagogue) of Aristippus, son of Jakoub, no doubt in Samaria there. In another (O) from Luxor, a Jew called Danooul is accused of cheating a man in the sale of a horse. Both these are of the second century B.C.

[1] Agatharchides of Knidos, as quoted by Josephus (xii. 1), says that he seized and occupied Jerusalem by fraud, making a sudden attack on the Sabbath day.

been far larger causes to outbalance the considerable disturbance, if not suffering, caused to the people of Palestine by the repeated armed incursions and occupations of the Egyptians.[1]

Two such causes present themselves, one sentimental, the other real.

In the long duel between Mesopotamia and Egypt, when Palestine lay between the hammer and the anvil, and was the prey alternately of Assyrian and Egyptian conquerors, the feeling of the people had turned to Egypt as the lesser evil, if conquest there must be. There was something harsher and fiercer about the Assyrians or the Babylonians. Captives were treated better in Egypt, and the land was so near Palestine that they knew its comforts and its luxuries, and could expect to make a home there. We learn this feeling from the angry objurgations of the later Hebrew prophets, who oppose its influence with all their might. They know the cruelties and hardships of Babylonian dominion, the miseries of Babylonish exile; but these are far better for the people of Jehovah than the fleshpots of idolatrous Egypt, where the captive will be well fed and happy, and forget his God. Thus Jeremiah and Ezekiel are always contending against the desire of the wealthier Jews to go and settle in Egypt.[2] But they were unable to prevent it. The ultimate violent deportation by Nebuchadnezzar to inner Asia must have burnt this hatred for Babylonia (in comparison with Egypt) deep into the popular mind.

---

[1] These hardships are emphasised by Josephus xii. 1 : πολέμους τε συνεχεῖς καὶ μακροὺς συνέβαινε γένεσθαι, καὶ τὰς πόλεις κακοπαθεῖν, καὶ πολλοὺς ἐν τοῖς ἀγῶσιν ἀποβάλλειν τῶν οἰκητόρων, ὡς καὶ τὴν Συρίαν ἅπασαν ὑπὸ Πτολεμαίου τοῦ Λάγου, Σωτῆρος τότε χρηματίζοντος, τὰ ἐναντία παθεῖν αὐτοῦ τῇ ἐπικλήσει.

[2] Cf. Jeremiah xlix.-li. ; Ezechiel xxix., xxx., xxxii., etc.

When the Persians succeeded to the empire of
Mesopotamia, it was only the founder Cyrus who treated
the Jews with consideration ; he alone was broad-minded
enough to respect their religion. The succeeding kings
were either bigoted, or cruel, or both ; and the inhabitants
of Palestine could not congratulate themselves upon the
change of dynasty. The Persians in their wars against
Greece and against Egypt had compelled many Jews
and Phoenicians to serve. The conquest of their country by Ochus (350 B.C.), on his way to Egypt, had been
marked by great cruelties,[1] and was still fresh in Jewish
memories.

None of these extreme misfortunes had ever resulted
from Egyptian occupation. Many Jews had found a friendly
reception there in recent times. Thus there must have
been a strong sentiment, produced by long experience, in
favour of Egypt, and against the inland powers of the
North East.

§ 58. The policy adopted by Seleukos in his Empire
must have greatly strengthened this feeling. He undertook to found a great number of cities on the Hellenic
model through all his various provinces, not the least in
Coele-Syria, and along the course of the Jordan. We do
not know what arrangements were made with the surrounding inhabitants of each city : how the territory of each city
was acquired, and what indemnity, if any, was granted to
the old possessors. But we may be sure there were many
cases of positive hardship and injustice, not to speak of
the theological objections which the Jews would have to
Greek cities, with Greek manners and gods, settled through
their country.

Ptolemy avoided this policy. During his long occupa-

---

[1] Diod. xvi. 45.

tion of the country, we are not aware of any new foundation in Palestine.   Ptolemais (Ake) on the sea-coast
could hardly count, as the fortresses along the Philistian
coast were inhabited by people hostile to the Jews, whose
subjection to Ptolemy and subsequent quietness would
benefit their unfriendly neighbours.   Thus while Ptolemy
would provide for any number of Jewish emigrants in
Egypt, and make room in their homes for the rest,
Seleukos would crowd the country with heathen settlers,
privileged in their cities, offering a bad example, and
much inducement to follow it, to the ambitious youth of
Judaea.   Such considerations account for the comparative
popularity of Ptolemy, though a foreign conqueror.

§ 59. We come now to the relations subsisting between
Ptolemy and the islands of the Aegean.   I have already
narrated his interference on behalf of Rhodes, and the
extraordinary gratitude of that community for the supplies
of men and provisions which he sent them.[1]   The position
of Rhodes was too independent to admit of any political interference with its constitution ; yet the religious
honours conferred upon the king amounted to those of a
second founder.   But more than once he passed through the
Aegean, not only to Athens, but either he or his admirals
swept the sea up to the Hellespont, declaring the freedom
and autonomy of these little communities.   About 289-8
B.C. he was approached by a begging embassy from Athens,
organised by Demochares, and contributed 50 talents to
the demes of Athens.[2]   But the fact that stingy Lysimachos gave 130, only shows how much more important

---

[1] § 40.

[2] Ps.-Plut. Decree in *vita Democharis*.   It is with a passage of
indignant eloquence on this beggarly patriotism that Grote closes his
immortal history (ch. xcvi. *fin.* ; ch. xcvii. is a mere appendix).

the good will of Athens was to the king of Thrace in his impending struggle with Seleukos. Possibly Lysimachos was paying the Athenians for the possession of Lemnos, which served him to check the Egyptian naval supremacy, for we now know that Seleukos gave back the island to the Athenians, who complained of the tyranny of Lysimachos.[1] It appears from the inscriptions found by M. Homolle at Delos, that there was a confederation of the islanders— κοινὸν τῶν νησιωτῶν—of which the king of Egypt was formal president, and which celebrated, probably at Tenos, a festival called Πτολεμαῖα.[2] Unfortunately none of the inscriptions as yet found specify the particular king of the series, and it has usually been assumed by historians that the League was formed by the diplomacy of Philadelphus. In the absence of positive evidence I incline to think that the first Ptolemy is more probably the author of this important adjunct to the naval power of Egypt. He was for a long time contending with Demetrius for the supremacy by sea and, though sometimes defeated, succeeded ultimately in consolidating his power. We may be certain that the Rhodians lent all their influence to aid this combination. It seems to me more likely that the active and stirring Soter effected it, than the somewhat easy-going Philadelphus. Moreover, had the latter really been the author, some of his many flatterers would probably have told us all about it.

§ 60. I have reserved till now any mention of the famous Museum at Alexandria, which has also been ascribed by many to the second king, but which was certainly the work of Soter, aided by the advice of

---

[1] Cf. Athenaeus vi. pp. 254 f., and the inscription from Lemnos discussed by Wilhelm in *Hermes* xxiii. pp. 454 *sqq.*

[2] *BCH* viii. p. 242.

Demetrius of Phaleron,[1] who migrated to Egypt a short time after his expulsion (307 B.C.) by Demetrius the Besieger from Athens, which he had governed for Casander during at least ten years. This Demetrius the philosopher is known to have been against the succession of Philadelphus to the throne, and in favour of the elder Ptolemy Keraunos, in consequence of which the new king disliked him and sent him into exile.[2]

It is indeed strange that so famous a seat of learning should not have left us some account of its foundation, its constitution, and its early fortunes. No other school of such moment among the Greeks is so obscure to us now. And yet it was founded in the broad daylight of history, by a famous king, in one of the most frequented cities of the world. The whole modern literature on the subject is a literature of conjectures. If it were possible to examine the site, which now lies twenty feet deep under the modern city, many questions which we ask in vain might be answered. The real outcome of the great school is fortunately preserved. In literary criticism, in exact science, in geography and kindred studies, the Museum made advances in knowledge which

[1] I find that Wilamowitz in his *Antigonus von Karystos* holds the same view, which is supported with good arguments by K. Kuiper in the *Proceedings* of the Utrecht Society of Letters for 1894. He shows that the current statement that Demetrius Phalereus and Philadelphus together founded it *must* be false, as the two men were opposed, and the rise of one produced the fall of the other. The whole structure of the Museum is so distinctly what we might expect from the Peripatetic philosopher, that we are compelled to maintain his claim, and reject that of Philadelphus. As Ptolemy and his fleet were on the Greek coast during 307 B.C., Demetrius may have accompanied the king back to Egypt.

[2] Cf. Plutarch *de Exil.* p. 602; Diog. L. v. 78; Cicero *pro Rabir. Post.* 9, and many more references in Susemihl's *GAL* i. 138-42.

were among the most important in the progress of
human civilisation. If the produce in poetry and in
philosophy was poor, we must attribute such failure to
the decadence of that century, in comparison with the
classical days of Ionia and of Athens. But in preserving
the great masters of the golden age, the Library, which
was part of the same foundation, did more than we can
estimate. It is, therefore, well worth while to tell what
is known, and to weigh what has been conjectured, concerning the origin of this, the greatest glory of Ptolemaic
Alexandria.[1]

§ 61. The idea of making Alexandria a centre, not only of
commerce but of letters, seems to have matured gradually in
the mind of the king. The date of the foundation is nearly
determined by the arrival of the philosopher Demetrius in Egypt,
where he helped the king's idea to take shape by his experience
of the academies of Athens. The very name *museum*, which
is still in Germany applied to literary clubs, points to an Attic
origin. It is well known that a nominal religious cult gave
security to the property of each school, and that each society of
the kind at Athens gradually became an independent corporation, endowed by the founder and by his disciples. The state
stood aloof, except at a few stray moments, when it interfered

---

[1] The literature worth reading on the subject is Clinton *Fasti* iii.
380 *sq.*; Ritschl *Opuscula* vol. i.; Bernhardy *Greek Literature* i.
pp. 527-42; Weniger *das Alex. Museum* Berlin 1875; Holm *G. G.*
iv. cap. 14, with his many valuable references. In the following
short sketch of the literary Alexandria of Ptolemy Soter, it would be
absurd to crowd my pages with the authorities for each statement,
as the critical reader will find them all in the Index of Susemihl's
Geschichte der Griech. Litt. in der Alexandrinerzeit (*GAL*) 2 vols. 1892,
a perfect thesaurus of knowledge on the subject. Nor will I trouble
him with the uncertainties and controversies which cloud almost every
assertion which we can make on the subject; fortunately this book is
only concerned with literature, so far as it affects Egyptian history.
The following extract is taken from my *Greek Life and Thought, etc.*,
where the literary aspects of this age are more fully considered.

to repress or persecute. It was clearly out of the question for the military bureaucracy of Egypt to tolerate a powerful intellectual force of this kind beyond government control and patronage. Hence from the first the endowment of the new Museum was a state allowance, given directly by the king to each member. But for what?

Ptolemy was by no means interested in the spread of any special doctrine; he probably knew little, and cared less, about the differences of the Athenian schools. What he wanted was to have celebrated men thinking and writing at Alexandria, and he left it at first to the superior judgment of Demetrius, and perhaps to his own son, the crown prince, what the complexion of the school—if such we can call it—should be. It seems, therefore, that the king and his minister of education founded an institution more like an old college at Oxford or Cambridge than anything else of the kind. It was a foundation supported by the king, and adjoining the royal buildings, in which there was a Commons' Hall, courts, cloisters, and gardens, where dwelt men selected for their literary and scientific eminence.[1] They were under a provost or principal, who was a priest, and who was nominated by the king, but whose religious services in the college were apparently confined to the formal cult of the Muses, a feature borrowed from the Academy at Athens. It may serve to show the contrast of spirit between the republican academics of Athens and the Royal University of Alexandria, that the priest of the Muses, who had the charge of the religious services of the Peripatetic Academy, and was for the time president in the Commons' Hall, was elected by the members for thirty days, on the last of which he gave an entertainment, partly by subscription and partly at his own cost. The ecclesiastical head of the Museum was nominated by the king, apparently for no short or fixed period, but no doubt during royal pleasure. If this provost was also the high priest of Sarapis, we come to something like the Episcopal Visitors in some of our old colleges. It is certain that he was not an Egyptian. We hear the names of no Egyptians mentioned as members of the Museum, and the Egyptian reaction upon Greek and Jewish philosophy certainly did not work through the Museum. This college, on the con-

---

[1] Strabo xvii. 1, 8.

trary, like our own ancient colleges, was rather a home of critical research and of erudition than of new ideas and of the advancement of knowledge. Its provost was probably no more important intellectually than the heads of houses are now at our universities. The endowed fellows were no doubt men of learning, still more men of critical habit, and sometimes great men of science. But they seem rather to have· taught accurately what was known than to have ventured into new paths in philosophy or religion.

§ 62. It is moreover tolerably certain that teaching and tutorial work were not among the early conditions of their appointment, just as in the foundation of old Oxford colleges there was sometimes a provision that the fellows should not be required to spend their energy in teaching, but should devote it to their own studies.[1]   Yet, just as at Oxford this admirable provision gradually went out of fashion, and was discarded for the lower view of making the colleges advanced boarding-schools, so at Alexandria young men naturally gathered about the Museum, and the Fellows of that college were gradually persuaded to undertake tutorial or professorial work.   And this too determined more clearly than ever their function to be that of promoting erudition and not knowledge.   In pure mathematics, starting from Euclid, in medicine and allied researches, in natural history, we may make exception, and say that the University of Alexandria did original work ; but, on the whole, we can conceive thinking men in later classical days saying what they now say of our richly-endowed colleges—that the outcome has not been worth the cost.

The Museum of Alexandria can certainly vindicate itself before the world.   Apart from the scientific side, which requires special knowledge to discuss, and for which I therefore refer to Mr. Gow's *History of Greek Mathematics*, the Fellows of the Museum, when brought together into a society by their intercourse with the second Ptolemy, developed that critical spirit which sifted the wheat from the chaff in Greek literature, and preserved for us the great masterpieces in carefully edited texts.

It also became the model to men who wished to found

---

[1] This is so, for example, in the foundation of Queen's College, and appears in the modern history of All Souls, Oxford.

colleges. There were several more such houses founded at Alexandria, one for example by the Emperor Claudius, with the condition that his own historical works should be read through there publicly once a year. So the Jews had a school there, and presently the Christians—all separate centres for study.

It seems therefore quite legitimate to compare this condition of things with the old English universities and their colleges. Foreign scholars writing about it are not familiar with these colleges, and therefore the analogy does not strike them. But though there were many points of difference—notably the very questionable advantage of the Museum being situated in a great capital, the adjunct to a royal palace, directly supported by annual royal gifts—the likeness is too strong to be evaded, and makes the history of this establishment of the deepest interest to English students.

§ 63. So it came to pass that Ptolemy Soter gathered into his capital every kind of splendour. He had secured for it the most important monument of its kind in the world—the tomb of the great Alexander, which commanded the veneration of centuries, down to the debased age of Caracalla. He established the most brilliant palace and court, with festivals which were the wonder of the world. He gathered all that he could command of learning and literary fame. And for this the city was adequate by the largeness and splendour of its external appearance. We have it described in later times as astonishing the beholder not only with its vastness — to wander through its streets, says Achilles Tatius, is an ἔνδημος ἀποδημία, taking a tour without leaving home—but with the splendour of the colonnades which lined the streets for miles,[1]

---

[1] The colonnades were a distinct feature of Hellenistic cities, notably Alexandria and Antioch, in the latter of which they are especially described. The modern reader who desires to feel the effect of this will find it in the city of Bologna, where most of the streets are built in this way. The result is a great development of *echoes*, which sound very strangely through the quiet hours. This peculiar sound must be appreciated to understand Polybius's famous narrative of the riot at Alexandria (xv. 25 *sq.*), and seems to me also implied in Apollonius Rhodius's description of night (iii. 749), οὐδὲ κυνῶν ὑλακὴ ἔτ᾿ ἀνὰ πτόλιν, οὐ θρόος ἦεν ἠχήεις.

and kept the ways cool for passengers ; with the din and
bustle of the thoroughfares, of which the principal were horse
and carriage ways, contrary to the usual Greek practice ; with
the number and richness of its public buildings, and with the
holiday and happy air of its vast population, who rested not
day and night, but had their streets so well lighted that the
author just named says the sun did not set, but was distributed
in small change—ἥλιος κατακερματίζων—to illumine the gay
night.   The palaces and other royal buildings and parks were
walled off, like the Palace at Pekin, and had their own port
and seashore, but all the rest of the town had water near it
and ship traffic in all directions.   Every costume and language
must have been met in its streets and quays.   It had its
fashionable suburbs too, and its bathing resorts to the east,
Canopus, Eleusis, and Nicopolis ; to the west its Necropolis.
But of all this splendour no eye-witness has left[1] us any
detail.

I can find but few recent studies upon this great subject.[2]   Even Lumbroso, so learned and so thorough on
other Graeco-Egyptian questions, has barely touched the
Museum and the Library in either of his excellent books.[3]
No doubt he found that there was no new material at
hand.   We do not know how many Fellows were appointed on his Foundation by Soter, and can only infer
from the bitter jibe of Timon that there were a good
many, and that he thought them occupied about idle
controversies, under royal control—

[1] It did not enter into Strabo's plan to give more than a very general
account of Alexandria, and he has done it badly enough.   The coronation scene in Polybius (xv. 25 *sq.*), to which we shall return in due time,
is far more living and suggestive, cf. below, §§ 165-9.

[2] In addition to Holm's recent vol. iv. of his History there are two
important articles on Alexandria by Puchstein, and on Alexandrian
literature by Knaack, in Pauly-Wissowa's *Encyclop.* (1895), but neither
describes the Museum or the Library.

[3] Cf. especially his *Egitto*, etc. (2nd ed. 1895), with the elaborate
bibliographical appendix on the literature of the last twenty-five years.

πολλοὶ μὲν βόσκονται ἐν Αἰγύπτῳ πολυφύλῳ
βιβλιακοὶ χαρακῖται, ἀπείριτα δηριοῶντες
Μουσέων ἐν ταλάρῳ—

but we also know that the literary men with whom the king associated, as well as those whom he invited to come and who declined, were the most eminent of the day.

§ 64. Concerning the great Library, we are not better informed. Was it part of the Museum, or separate? Was the chief librarian, who was a great literary personage, as such a Fellow of the Museum? It is difficult to suppose he was not, or that the primary use of the Library should not have been to supply materials for the researches of the Museum. We only hear vaguely of the Libraries of the Museum, and that the first was built in the Bruchium.[1] Diodorus[2] says he used the Court Journals at Alexandria (βασιλικὰ ὑπομνήματα), but so does Appian,[3] writing long after the supposed conflagration of 48 B.C. Strabo, visiting Alexandria in the days of Augustus, makes no mention whatever of the Library, or of its alleged destruction. The only reasonable inference is that he regarded it as part of the Museum. But he says not a word about consulting books or archives. The story that the physician Memnon borrowed a book from the great Library, to read, and added notes of his own, is as late as Galen.[4] This curious state of our evidence leads me to give some weight to the remark of Seneca[5]: *quadringenta millia librorum Alexandriae arserunt. pulcherrimum regiae opulentiae monumentum alius laudaverit, sicut et Livius, qui elegantiae regum curaeque id opus ait fuisse. non fuit elegantia illud aut cura sed studiosa luxuria ; immo ne studiosa quidem, quoniam non in studium sed in spectaculum comparaverant.*

---

[1] Cf. the texts in Susemihl i. 336.   [2] iii. 38.
[3] *Praef.* 10.   [4] xvii. 603.   [5] *de tranquil. an.* 9.

*sicut plerisque ignaris etiam servilium literarum libri non studi-
orum instrumenta sed coenationum ornamenta sunt.* If this
were indeed so, it would be comparable to such English
libraries as the Sunderland and Spencer, gathered by rich
dilettanti in the same way that they gather china and
pictures. This too might possibly account for the extraordinary apathy with which the destruction of it in Julius
Caesar's day is mentioned, or not mentioned, by those
whom we should expect to lament over it.[1]

§ 65. Under these circumstances it is not easy to form
an idea of the literary life at Alexandria under the first
Ptolemy. The recorded facts are very few, and concerning the leading men it is generally uncertain whether
they worked under the latter half of the first or the
opening of the second reign. Utilising, however, the
researches of the Germans chronicled in Susemihl's inde-
fatigable book, we may state as probable that Ptolemy
Soter, in spite of his active life and his many other occupations, did spend both time and treasure on the pursuit
and patronage of learning. He had his views, too, based
upon what was good for the state, for though he did not
scruple to employ in confidential missions Theodorus of
Cyrene, an atheist so decided that the people of Athens
would not tolerate him, no such patronage was extended
to Hegesias, who taught practical pessimism so cogently,
as to produce a public tendency to suicide, and who was
therefore silenced. We hear of Ptolemy associating with
Diodorus (the dialectician) and with Stilpo, both of whom
he met at Megara, apparently in 307-6 B.C. If it be true
that Ptolemy nicknamed the former Kronos, because he
long delayed to answer some subtle question of Stilpo's,

---

[1] But the very fact of this destruction seems doubtful, cf. below,
§ 267.

he must have had some wit, for in Homer *subtle* (ἀγκυ-λομήτης) is the standing epithet of Saturn, but this god is nevertheless dethroned by a younger rival.[1] His relations to Demetrius the Phalerean have already been mentioned, and there is no doubt that this man was as competent as any then living to advise about the literary projects of the king. Philetas of Kos was chosen as tutor for the crown prince—Philetas not only honoured as the greatest master of the modern elegy, but as a skilled grammarian and the compiler of the first lexicon of strange terms. This grammatical side of philology was further prosecuted by Zenodotus, the first Librarian and author of a recension of Homer. That Ptolemy built a theatre in Alexandria is very probable; if he invited Menander to come from Athens, it may have been to produce a play; it may have been to honour the Museum with his company. The exploring of the southern Red Sea and its coasts was entrusted to his admiral Philon; the exploring of the no less remote mysteries of Egyptian theology to Hecataeus of Abdera,[2] who with Manetho and Timotheos began that fusion of creeds so essential to the new empire.

But all these various literary or quasi-literary developments at Alexandria were as nothing compared to the momentous studies and teaching of Euclid in geometry, of Herophilos in surgery. Euclid was probably not so much a discoverer as a teacher, unsurpassed in establishing once for all the conditions of scientific demonstration. For his immortal *Elements* are perhaps more distinctively exercises in Logic than they are in Mathematics. He

---

[1] Cf. the authorities in Susemihl i. 15.

[2] Susemihl i. 313. This man's book supplied Diodorus (Siculus) with the fanciful view of ancient Egypt contained in the first book of his History.

omits no step in his reasoning, and yet with all his explicitness modern attempts to abbreviate him have shown that, logically, nothing is redundant. This man, therefore, alone makes the reign of his patron an epoch in the scientific development of the human mind.

Not less important was Herophilos, the first great teacher of anatomy, and the father of surgery, as Hippocrates may be called the father of medicine. We might have guessed that the process of embalming would make Egypt the best country for beginning the study of the viscera, and ascertaining the causes of death from autopsy.[1] But we are told that the king's influence did far more than that for Herophilos. He was permitted to dissect the human body, and even to vivisect not only the lower animals, but criminal men abandoned to him for the purpose. We have no evidence how far he made use of this terrible license. There can be no doubt, however, that he too founded a truly scientific method of investigating facts, and so added his vast influence to make Alexandria the centre of the highest Hellenistic civilisation. While the schools of Athens—Stoics, Epicureans, Peripatetics—were discussing abstract questions of metaphysics and morals, these men were the pioneers of that positive science, which is the most fruitful legacy left us by the Graeco-Roman world, for this alone is directly applicable to every new form of civilisation.

§ 66. From the time that Ptolemy recovered Cyprus, and with it the supremacy at sea, from Demetrius, he was no longer engaged in any serious conflict. The gigantic armaments of the Besieger in 288 B.C. evidently foreboded an attack on Seleukos rather than on Egypt, and though

---

[1] Cf. also Pliny *NH* xix. 27 *in Aegypto regibus corpora mortuorum ad scrutandos morbos insecantibus.*

Ptolemy joined the coalition against this desperate knight-errant, the prudent king probably saw clearly that the great army of Demetrius was not a reality.   The numbers of his troops—98,000 infantry and 12,000 cavalry with 500 ships [1]—were probably at the time grossly and intentionally exaggerated, and, whatever the quantity was, the quality was bad, for such bands and their condottieri could always be bribed with superior pay to abandon a needy cause. Our astonishment is that Demetrius should have been able even to enlist a large force with the financial resources at his command.   Promises of plunder must have served him for actual payments, so that the solid wealth of Ptolemy or of Seleukos was certain to overcome him, unless his initial successes were rapid and complete.   The king of Egypt was, moreover, an old man, disinclined to enter upon foreign conflicts and, like his brother Diadochi, desirous to increase the beauty and establish the importance of his capital.

If, as we have seen, he founded the Museum and Library, it is most unlikely that he allowed the body of Alexander to lie at Memphis till the reign of his son,[2] though that prince may have been formally charged with the guard of honour and the pompous ceremonies with which this solemn transference of the great relics in their coffin of gold must have been performed.   Thus it would happen that Philadelphus was credited with this act by his courtiers.   For all through Soter's life, we find him not concerned with claiming originality or greatness, provided his kingdom reaped the fruits of his wisdom.   He was one of those rare rulers, like Victor Emmanuel in our own century, who choose and utilise brilliant men, casting them aside when they prove dangerous, but allowing them to

---

[1] Plutarch *Dem.* 44.   [2] Paus. i. 6, § 3.

obtain credit with the world for all the steady and consistent background of government whereby a nation makes solid growth. But to ascribe to the transient minister or agitator the work of the permanent ruler, is to assert that the ship of the state is guided by the brilliant planets which wander across the heavens, not by the modest polestar, whose sleepless eye never sets in the northern sky.

§ 67. It was probably in connexion with the founding of the Library, and the transference of the body of Alexander to the *Sema* in the capital,[1] that Ptolemy in his old days, or in his comparative leisure, was persuaded to turn author, and perhaps inaugurate the collecting of books by an authentic account of the great wars of Alexander, in which he had taken so prominent a part. Arrian cites this book as the best and safest authority for his history, though for the silly reason that it was written by a king, who would naturally have less cause than other men to tell falsehoods, and, moreover, would be less likely to violate his dignity by doing so. If, however, the impression produced by the work had not been that of a sober and honest writer, we may be sure Arrian would have been compelled to admit that even a king may lie.[2]

The analysis of the fragments by Fränkel[3] leads him to hold that the narrative of Ptolemy was shorter and plainer than those of Aristobulus and the rest, that he dealt less

---

[1] In this monument the conqueror's body was preserved, and visible when Octavian came to Egypt to war against Antony and Cleopatra. Dion (li. 17) tells us that Octavian not only saw, but handled it, so that the nose of the mummy was injured. He would not look at the Ptolemies in their tombs, saying: ' I want to see not dead men but a king.'

[2] By far the greatest sovran in our own century, the first Napoleon, was also the most infamous and incorrigible liar.

[3] *Alexander-Hist.* §§ 13, 14.

in the marvellous, and made it his principal object to narrate accurately the military operations which he was so competent to explain. One ingenious German even goes so far as to think that he wrote his book specially to contradict the exaggerations of Kleitarchos. Our evidence is insufficient to establish any such conclusions, though we are naturally attracted by the view that a real general would write without pomp or exaggeration, as Julius Caesar has done in his *Gallic War*. We have furthermore references made to a collection of his *Letters*, apparently on public affairs, published by Dionysodorus, a pupil of Aristarchus.[1] There seems no reason to doubt that this work was genuine, but alas! we only know it by name.[2]

It seems inconsistent with the temperate character of his life that he should have held such a feast as to be specially described by the contemporary Lynceus of Samos among the most luxurious banquets of his time. It stands, too, in direct contradiction to the note preserved in Plutarch's *Apophthegms* to the effect that Ptolemy, son of Lagus, frequently dined and slept at his friends' houses; and when he did give a feast, he used their appointments, sending for cups, and carpets and tables; as he himself possessed only what was necessary for his own use. He used to say that making rich was more royal than being rich. Perhaps, however, the description of Lynceus was only to illustrate the thesis of this gastronomic author,

---

[1] Luc. *pro lapsu* 10.

[2] Cf. Susemihl ii. 161, 596. The story told by Lucian of the quarrel of Ptolemy with Apelles, and the revenge of the latter by painting his famous allegorical picture of *Calumny*, does not appear to me even possibly true. The Ptolemy described as a foolish tyrant, in whose reign Pelusium was lost by treachery, cannot be earlier than the fourth, while on the other hand Apelles was a contemporary of Alexander, and so of the first.

that cooking was an art far more advanced in Egypt than elsewhere.[1]

§ 68. Yet it might be said, and was said by ancient historians, that his relations with women showed a pleasure-loving nature. He had at least twelve children by various wives, as well as the courtezan Thais, and as he grew near the term of his life, the question of the succession to his throne must have long and anxiously concerned the prudent king. On the one hand his eldest son, whose mother Eurydike was now of royal race, being sister of Casander, was a youth of fiery temper and unsteady life. The epithet Keraunos, by which he was designated, is said to refer to his gloomy violence.[2] Yet the safest rule for founding a hereditary sovranty was to observe primogeniture, and this was doubtless the substance of the advice of Demetrius of Phaleron. On the other hand, Berenike was the favourite wife of the old king, and her son a youth of gentle and popular manners. His sister Arsinoe was the young queen of Lysimachus, and not unlikely to control the policy of that king. Wilamowitz[3] holds that grave political considerations

[1] Cf. Müller *FHG* ii. p. 466, note.

[2] I have a suspicion, which I dare not set forth as more than possibly true, that as ' the thunderbolt, which is constant in the field of the reverse of this king's coins, may be regarded as Ptolemy's badge' (Poole, p. xvii.), the first issue of this type may have been coincident with the birth of this son, and therefore the nickname may have been then given him by the Alexandrians, who saw the thunderbolt added to the eagle. I do not think it suits what we know of his character, and is not like a *personal* nickname so much as one of *circumstance*. The usual account is taken from Memnon (*FHG* iii. 532) in his account of the conspiracies at Lysimachus' court : ὁ δὲ Πτ. ὃς αὐτόχειρ τοῦ μιάσματος ἐγεγόνει, ἀδελφὸς ἦν 'Αρσ., καὶ ἐπώνυμον διὰ τὴν σκαιότητα καὶ ἀπόνοιαν τὸν κεραυνὸν ἔφερεν. The former quality does not apply to thunder, the latter not to this Ptolemy, who was a wily miscreant, carefully preparing his plans.

[3] *Weihgesch. des Eratosth.* p. 15.

may also have been dominant. Keraunos and his supporter
Demetrius may have been the advocates of a trenchant
Macedonian policy, which would grant nothing to Egyptian
tastes. Philadelphus may have represented the more
liberal policy of fusing the two cultures, and promoting
the compromise of creeds and of cults inaugurated by
Soter. At all events Ptolemy determined to settle the
question during his life, and abdicated in 285 B.C. in
favour of his second son. The coronation of the new
king was received, we are told, with great enthusiasm by
the people, and Ptolemy Keraunos went into exile, whether
voluntary or not, to his relatives at Lysimacheia. His
life was certainly not safe within the realm of the new
king. Thus Ptolemy Soter had the satisfaction of be-
queathing his kingdom to a popular successor without civil
war or assassinations, and we are told that for two years
longer the old man used to appear at the court of his son
in the new character of a subject.[1]

§ 69. In 283 B.C. he died, in the eighty-fifth year of
his age, leaving a record to posterity which few men in
the world have surpassed. Equally efficient whether as
servant or as master, he made up for the absence of genius
in war or diplomacy by his persistent good sense, the
moderation of his demands, the courtesy of his manners
to friend and foe alike. While the old crown of Macedon
was still the unsettled prize for which rival kings staked
their fortunes, he and his fellow-in-arms, Seleukos, founded

---

[1] Porphyry however, who includes these two years in Ptolemy's 40
years of sovranty, evidently thinks the abdication not to have been
absolute, but a public association of the son in the royalty, and this
gives point to the anecdote told in Diogenes L. (*Life of Demetrius*) that
when the king consulted the philosopher on this point the latter replied :
'if you give it away, you won't have it yourself'—a mere truism,
unless a partial abdication was in question. Cf. *Addit. Note* p. 488.

dynasties which resisted the disintegrations of the Hellenistic world for centuries.

We have no portrait of him, either literary or artistic, except upon his coins, and therefore miss almost completely throughout his life those small touches of character, those semi-historical anecdotes, which give us the impression made by his personality on those around him.[1] Pausanias saw portrait-statues of him at Athens, Delphi, and Olympia, but does not describe them, nor have modern excavations been as yet fortunate enough to recover them. His portraits on Ptolemaic coins[2] are probably somewhat idealised and therefore not trustworthy in giving us an accurate reproduction of his countenance. Yet the face, even so, is not handsome, in the sense that the Alexander-type on the coins of the same king are, which is more like a god or hero than an actual man. Ptolemy's features on coins are very marked, and the face is not classical in its features. The forehead is remarkably fleshy over the eyes, and not high; the eyebrows arched; the nose is too short, but thick and with very wide nostrils. The mouth is firm and the chin rather prominent. If asked to guess his character from these coins, I should say that

[1] The very few anecdotes scattered through Aelian suggest as his chief characteristics astuteness and courtesy. Köhler (Berlin *Sitzb.* for 1891) shows from scraps in Suidas, *sub voce.* ἔγκαρπον and ἄκρατον, that certain Alexandrian fables about his birth, his being exposed on a shield, and protected by an eagle, are simply constructed from the suggestions of his coins. Lucian tells a story (*Prometh.* 4) of his exhibiting at Alexandria a black Bactrian camel, and a man half white and half black. The Alexandrians were frightened at the one, and disgusted at the other, and Ptolemy disappointed at the result.

[2] The reader should be here cautioned that his head appears on the coins of most of his successors, whose portraits are even in some cases assimilated to his type. Hence I speak of *Ptolemaic* coins including those of various reigns.

energy and kindliness are the most prominently indicated qualities.

§ 70. There is but one more point concerning which researches upon the site of Alexandria may yet enlighten us. While we have shown it to be more than probable that Ptolemy bestowed special care upon the domesticating of science, philosophy, and literature in his capital, we can only infer from the beauty of his coinage that he was a patron of art. Yet it is most unlikely that, as he controlled the architectural features of the new city, he could have avoided an intimate connexion with the sister arts of sculpture, painting and music. Many great temples and palaces, not to speak of the Sema, grew up in his day, and in a land where he had to rival the massive and gorgeous architecture of the Pharaohs. All the resources of the best Greek art were not too great for this mighty competition, and it might be assumed by many that this art being now in its decadence, would hardly prove equal to the trial. This very impression—that Greek art was now decaying—has probably been the cause of the lukewarm spirit with which the antiquities of Alexandria have been regarded by classical scholars.

Yet now we can prove that this impression is false, and that the Alexandria of the Ptolemies may still contain wonders of artistic taste, as it certainly did of learning. The marble sarcophagus of a nameless king of Sidon, with its matchless coloured reliefs, dating certainly from this generation, stands in the museum of Constantinople, convicting us of the narrowness and folly of placing limits to the Protean manifestations of Greek genius. These battles of the Macedonians and Persians, these hunting-scenes of Persians and Macedonians, wherein the artist has celebrated the marriage of Europe and of Asia in grace, in dignity, in manly sport, as well as in heroic combat, are rendered to us in marble and in colours with a perfection second only to that of the frieze of the Parthenon. If such was the work done by an unnamed sculptor, for an unknown king at Sidon, what must have been the work done for the early Ptolemies at Alexandria by the most distinguished artists of the same generation? That they can have exceeded in perfection the tomb of the king at Sidon is well-nigh impossible, but how much larger may have been the scale, how much greater the variety of the work done upon the Sema to honour the tomb of Alexander? Let no one, therefore, think of the decoration of the city of Ptolemy Soter as of some Roman, or Roman-Greek city. We know that there were transcendent artists living in his day; we may be sure they helped him to make his capital the fairest in the world.

It is but yesterday that a new mass of evidence for the artistic culture of Alexandria has been brought together by M. Schreiber.[1] In a masterly essay he has shown that *Toreutic*, or the working of small gold and silver household vessels, which has usually been regarded as a development of artistic handicraft chiefly Roman, is really the production of Alexandria. He enters with great detail into the spirit and the exquisite execution of this work, of which many beautiful specimens are still extant. He shows how the ideas of the artists—the forerunners of Benvenuto Cellini and his school—were analogous to those of the best Alexandrian poets, with this addition, that there is more distinctly an Egyptian flavour in many of the accessories.

It would be unfair in this place to give a mere summary

---

[1] *Abh. der sächs. Gesell.* for 1894, pp. 272-479 (to be concluded in a future volume).

of his fascinating essay, but any one who reads it and examines his many illustrations will perceive the peculiarly romantic colouring of this art. A deep sense of the beauty of landscape, a delight in flowers, garlands, and arabesques is peculiar to it. We see in it plainly the problem set before the artists—to invent decorations for the feasts of a stately court. It is but another brilliant manifestation of that hybrid civilisation, in which science and art, the east and the west, old creeds and new dogmas are woven into a gorgeous texture like the Byzantine robe, with an intricate design like the splendid surfaces of the marble tombs in the first bloom of the Italian Renaissance.

APPENDIX

The date and particular cause of the assumption of the title *Soter* by Ptolemy is still under dispute. Our only extant ancient authority, Pausanias, refers it to the flattery of the Rhodians in commemorating his assistance during the great siege of 306 B.C. But no modern critic will accept this account, seeing that no king is likely to assume a formal title given him by a people outside his own kingdom. Arrian indeed and Curtius give a refutation of historians (Kleitarchos and Timagenes) who asserted that Ptolemy received the name from having, along with Peukestas, saved Alexander when set upon by the Malli in their city. Fränkel (*die Quellen der Alex.-Hist.* p. 53) further cites Josephus (*Antt.* xii. 1) to the effect that Ptolemy, invading Syria, showed qualities the very opposite of the title he then used (Σωτῆρος τότε χρηματίζοντος) and infers that he must have received it early in his life, and from the Egyptians, when he saved them from the extortions of Cleomenes (323-2 B.C.) But when he supports his argument by the many coins bearing the title Πτολ. σωτηρος, with year-dates (Ｌ 30-39) whereas the coins Πτολ. βασιλεως have none, and infers that these coins mark the years of Soter's rule from the beginning of his satrapy, he is refuted by the later researches of Revillout, Feuardent, and Poole, specialists in numismatics, who tell us that the mint-marks of all these Soter-coins are Phoenician, and issued by Tyre, Sidon, Gaza, etc., with the permission of Ptolemy Philadelphus, when he established in his twenty-fifth year (271-0 B.C.) the worship of his father with the title Soter. Thus the title need not have been borne by the first Ptolemy at all during his life.

I cannot accept this last conclusion, though Revillout may be probably right about the date of the establishment of the formal cult. The general impression of all our sources that the title was assumed during Ptolemy's life is too strong to be set aside. I have already suggested one likely occasion when his people gave it to him. The repulse of Antigonus (309 B.C.) was a far more serious reason for it than the execution of Cleomenes. But I will here add a further conjecture. It is repeatedly told us that the epithets of the Ptolemies, Philopator, Philometor, etc. were *Alexandrian nicknames*, given by the populace by the way of satirical comment on real facts. Modern historians justly reject any such explanation of solemn titles, adopted in the most serious documents by these kings. Yet if the title was long in use among the people, whatever its origin was, its formal adoption might not be unreasonable. I therefore suggest that Pausanias was more nearly right than we have supposed, and that the title *Soter* may have been given at the time of the siege of Rhodes, not by the Rhodians, but by the Alexandrians to their king. They knew perfectly that he had risked but very little to help the island-city, and was now receiving extravagant thanks. They may have called him Soter satirically, owing to the great fuss made about a very lukewarm support. When the name became current, it would soon lose the associations connected with its origin, and in forty years' time Philadelphus might very seriously adopt it as the solemn epithet wherein he celebrated his father's divinity. This hypothesis (1) adheres more closely than the rest to Pausanias' report; (2) gives us an instance of what is positively asserted about the origin of other royal epithets among the Ptolemies; (3) accounts for the trivial invention of the name not being inconsistent with its solemn use.

CHAPTER IV

PTOLEMY II. (PHILADELPHUS), KING 285-47 B.C.

§ 71. In spite of the splendour with which Philadelphus [1] entered upon his reign, there were dangers and complica-

PTOLEMY II.

tions connected with his numerous brothers and sisters which all the prudence of Soter could not avert. The elder queen of Soter, Eurydike, daughter of Antipater, seems to have left the Egyptian court with her children, when her rival was declared successful. Her daughter she married to Demetrius the Besieger, who only cohabited with this latest of his wives long enough to beget a son that became a dangerous enemy to the Ptolemies. [2]

Her sons, Ptolemy Keraunos, Meleagros, and one or more stepsons, all left Egypt with her to seek their fortunes abroad.

[1] So I call him for discrimination's sake, as do ancient historians. But during his lifetime only Arsinoe II. was called Philadelphus. Syncellus (p. 40 B) indeed professes to quote Manetho's personal dedication of his history to this king: βασιλεῖ μεγάλῳ Πτολ. Φιλαδέλφῳ σεβαστῷ κτλ. : but I do not think this can be genuine ; neither Φιλαδέλφῳ nor σεβαστῷ occurring elsewhere at this period.

[2] Plutarch *Demet.* 47. The issue was Demetrius the Fair.

At this moment the ties of Egypt and the kingdom of Thrace were very intimate. Probably the old king of Egypt had watched the growing power of Seleukos, and knew that with Lysimachus for an ally he could cope with any foe. For at this time the kingdom of Thrace included large parts of Asia Minor, and of Macedonia, and reached northwards into the barbarous regions near the Danube. Accordingly not only was the Egyptian crown-prince's sister Arsinoe given to Lysimachus to wife, but her step-sister Lysandra was married to the Thracian crown-prince Agathocles, an able soldier and much beloved by the peoples of Asia Minor where he acted as regent for his father. It even came about shortly after the young Philadelphus' accession, and in consequence of the disturbances which I am about to relate, that Lysimachus' daughter (half-sister to Agathocles) was sent in marriage to the new Egyptian king.

§ 72. But the arrival of Ptolemy Keraunos at the Thracian court upset all the prosperity of the new dynasty. The youthful Arsinoe, though she had her old husband under her influence, and had obtained from him the formal cession of Casandrea in Thessaly, also of the Pontic Heraclea and some neighbouring towns, was still discontented.[1] She desired the succession for her young children to the exclusion of her stepson and step-brother-in-law Agathocles. It appears that Keraunos upon his arrival took up the policy not of his full sister Lysandra, the wife of Agathocles, but of his half-sister Arsinoe. They made plots against Agathocles, calumniated him to

---

[1] To judge from Strabo's statement that she calumniated Philetaerus, governor of the treasure-fort of Pergamum, to her husband, and so drove him to abandon his allegiance to Lysimachus, and take the side of Seleukos, I suspect that she also intended to obtain Pergamum as a gift from the king. Cf. Memnon vii. viii. (*FHG* iii. 531).

Lysimachus, and caused him to be put to death. Thus one claimant to the crown of Thrace was removed. But the brother, widow, and children of Agathocles fled to Seleukos,[1] and urged him to take the occasion of enlarging his kingdom at the expense of a murderous and godless tyrant. Many subordinates of Lysimachus, amongst others the commandant of the treasure-fort of Pergamum, declared for Seleukos[2]; it seems to have been at this crisis that the Thracian princess Arsinoe went to Egypt to cement that alliance as queen. At all events the ruffian Keraunos was discredited; his schemes were discovered, and he too fled to Seleukos, who received him kindly, as a claimant to the Egyptian crown who might prove convenient.

Such were the events which darkened the political sky during the last days of the Ptolemy Soter. No actual war broke out till after his death, but then Seleukos advanced into Phrygia, drew over to him forts and garrisons, and finally forced Lysimachus to the decisive battle at Korupedion, where the latter lost his crown with his life. Keraunos accompanied Seleukos as an ally, and as the lawful heir to the crown of Egypt, to which the Syrian king is said to have promised to restore him. This great crisis, the last battle between the two surviving companions of Alexander, took place in 281 B.C., and left Seleukos for the moment arbiter of the world.[3]

§ 73. What had the young king of Egypt been doing during these years, the first four of his reign? It was not only according to the old man's advice, but in con-

---

[1] Pausanias says (i. 10, 3 *sq.*) to Babylon, and he has been copied by several modern historians. But of course this is one of Pausanias' many errors, as Seleukos was long since residing at Antioch.

[2] Strabo xiii. 4, § 1.

[3] Cf. Memnon viii. (*FHG* iii. 532); Appian *Syr.* 62 *sq.*; Justin xvii. 2.

formity with his own character, that he took no active part in the threatened collision of his two great neighbours. Of course he must have watched the progress of events with much anxiety. No sooner was his father gone than he put to death his elder step-brother Argaeus, whom he charged with fomenting a revolt in Cyprus. Or it may be, as Pausanias says,[1] that Argaeus was put to death in Egypt, and another whose name we know not in Cyprus. At all events the policy of the new king is plain enough; within his dominions he will tolerate no rival claimants. This, as Polybius says, was an axiom as strict as those assumed by the geometers, and the murder of brothers under such circumstances was hardly considered a crime. But even the adviser who had spoken in favour of Keraunos suffered. We are told that Demetrius the Phalerean was sent into exile in Upper Egypt where he soon died, let us hope by an accidental death.[2] These were the dark corners of Philadelphus' policy, while to the world he was all smiles and courtesy. He is said to have complained in after life that one of the hardships in a despot's life was the necessity of putting people to death who had done no harm, merely for the sake of expediency.[3] And, indeed, while his brothers were to be murdered, there was nothing but respect and attention for his sister Philotera, a princess who seems never to have married, but to have lived at his court in perfect harmony with her brother and his successive wives. She shared with his mother Berenike and his second wife the honour of having new cities named after her, there being three such known to Strabo, to

[1] i. 7, 1. Cf. *Addit. Note* p. 488.

[2] Cicero *pro Rab. Post.* 9. 23 says : *aspide ad corpus admota vita esse privatum*, which seems to be suicide, though Susemihl (i. 139, note) denies that the words mean any such thing !

[3] Stobaeus ii. p. 287 (ed. Teubner).

which we may now add a village in the Fayyum.[1] But
to Philotera he gave the additional honour of a shrine
at Memphis, where she was worshipped as a goddess.[2]
I believe the third granite statue (of a princess) which
stands beside those of Philadelphus and Arsinoe II. in the
Egyptian museum of the Vatican, to be the conventional
portrait of Philotera. Unfortunately the name and titles,
which were on a smooth band down the back of the
statue, are polished away.

The pomp of Philadelphus' coronation-ceremony which,
by the way, was purely Hellenistic, so dazzled the world,
that they ignored and forgot his domestic murders.

§ 74. The first thing that strikes us is the ostentation of
the whole affair, and how prominently costly materials were
displayed. A great part of the royal treasure at all courts
in those days consisted not of coin but of precious gold and
silver vessels, and it seems as if all these were carried in the
procession by regiments of richly dressed people. And
although so much plate was in the streets there was a great
sideboard in the banqueting hall covered with vessels of gold
studded with gems. People had not, indeed, sunk so low in
artistic feeling as to carry pots full of gold and silver coin,
which was done in the triumph of Paullus Aemilius at Rome,
but still a great part of the display was essentially the ostentation of wealth. How different must have been a Panathe-
naic festival in the days of Pericles! I notice further that

[1] Letronne (*Recherches* p. 183) maintained that Philadelphus used
no other names but these (and Philadelphia) for his new foundations.
This limitation cannot now be maintained, as there were several other
royal names applied in the Fayyum.

[2] Cf. Lepsius in Berlin *Abh.* for 1852, p. 500, who thinks that this
cult, together with that of Ptolemy II. and Arsinoe at Memphis, was
first established by Euergetes. I do not believe that this king had any
reason for honouring his aunt Philotera, who was probably dead before
he ascended the throne, and who was not one of his royal ancestors.
Philadelphus' attentions to her seem to have been purely personal.

sculpture and painting of the best kind—the paintings of
Sicyonian artists are specially named—were used for the
mere purpose of decoration.   Thus in describing the appearance of the great chamber [1] specially built for the banquet,
Callixenus tell us that on the pilasters round the hall were one
hundred marble reliefs by the first artists, in the spaces
between them were paintings, and about them precious
hangings with embroideries representing mythical subjects or
portraits of kings.   We feel ourselves in a sort of glorified
Holborn Restaurant, where the resources of art are lavished
on the walls of an eating-room.   In addition to scarlet and
purple, gold and silver, and skins of various wild beasts upon
the walls, the pillars of the room represented palm-trees and
Bacchic Thyrsi alternately, a design which distinctly points to
Egyptian rather than Greek taste.   The whole floor, we are
told, was strewn with all manner of flowers, like a celestial
garden, and then follows this interesting detail; 'For Egypt,
on account of its good climate, and the care of those who
grow what is rare and in blow at special seasons elsewhere,
has flowers in abundance all the year, and neither rose nor
white lily nor any flower is wont to fail them at any time.'
This festival was held in winter,[2] and yet there was abundance
of fresh grapes to afford a vintage-scene on one of the great
vehicles of the procession, where sixty satyrs trod the wine-
press to the sound of the flute and song, with Silenus super-
intending, and the streets were flooded with the foaming
must.

Among other wonders the Royal Zoological Gardens seem
to have been put under requisition, and we have a list of the
various strange animals which joined in the parade.   This is
very interesting, as showing us what could be done in the
way of transporting wild beasts, and how far that traffic had

---

[1] He calls it σκηνή, but it was all of marble, gold, and other solid
materials.

[2] Niese (i. p. 389) says that the presence of these grapes proves the
feast to have been *in autumn*, which betrays a curious ignorance both
of the climate of Egypt and of the habits of the Nile.   The grapes
which are ripe in Niese's country in September would be gathered in
June or July (early in *Payni* according to a letter from the year 240 B.C.
in the *Petrie Papyri* ii. [136]).

reached. There were 24 huge lions—the epithet points no doubt to the African or maned lion—26 snow-white Indian oxen, 8 Aethiopic oxen, 14 leopards, 16 panthers, 4 lynxes, 3 'young panthers,' a great white bear, a camelopard, and an Aethiopic rhinoceros. The tiger and the hippopotamus seem to have missed this opportunity of showing themselves, for they are not mentioned. There were besides 24 chariots drawn by elephants, 14 by various antelopes, 60 by goats, 8 by wild asses. There were droves of camels bearing all the spices of Arabia-Felix; Nubians bearing 600 ivory tusks and 2000 stems of ebony, with endless gold dust (not coin) in gold and silver vessels. Then came 150 men bearing shrubs peopled with all manner of birds, and besides, in cages, peacocks, pheasants, guinea-fowls, and the like. Among them were 2 hunters, with 2400 dogs of Indian, Molossian, Hyrcanian, and other breeds. This zoological exhibition was, however, artistically introduced in that part of the show which represented the victorious return of the god Dionysus from his Indian conquests—a splendid gold and ivory figure attended by crowds of Sileni and satyrs with ivy and pine cones, carrying home all this spoil, and among it Indian and other foreign women, in the guise of captives, under tents in chariots. It reminds us of the triumphal progress of Alexander after he had escaped the deserts of Gedrosia.

But this great Bacchic show was only one of a large number of mummeries or allegories which paraded the streets; for example, Alexander attended by Nike and Athene; the first Ptolemy escorted and crowned by the Greek cities of Asia Minor, and with Corinth standing beside him.[1] Both gods and kings were there in statues of gold and ivory, and for the most part escorted by living attendants—a curious incongruity all through the show. But to represent either a god or a king by a living actor was perhaps thought even then unseemly. There came, however, in the beginning of the procession, an allegorical representation of *the Year*, given by a very tall man dressed in tragic costume and mask, with a golden horn of Amalthea in his hand. He was accompanied by an equally splendid female figure, surnamed the *Five-year Feast*, escorted by four Seasons carrying their

---

[1] Cf. above, §§ 31 and 59.

fruits. There were attendant satyrs, and after them Philiscus the priest of Dionysus, and all the Company of the Tragic Theatre. This was what we should call legitimate or living mummery.

The procession lasted the whole day, being opened by a figure of the Morning Star, and closed by Hesperus. 80,000 troops, cavalry and infantry, in splendid uniforms, marched past. The whole cost of the feast was over half a million of our money. But the mere gold crowns offered by friendly towns and people to the first Ptolemy and his queen had amounted to that sum.[1]

§ 75. While the new king was thus exhibiting his wealth and the power which it implied to the world, external events were developing with considerable rapidity. Magas of Cyrene, not his step-brother, though son of Eurydike the discarded queen-mother, seems to have soon renounced his allegiance to Egypt. We are not told that this revolt was in connexion with the intrigues of Keraunos, but we may infer it with great probability. Magas would argue that as the natural heir had been ousted of his succession, no allegiance was due to Philadelphus. Yet he can hardly have broken out into open revolt till the great war which ended in the battle of Korupedion, that is to say, after the death of the old king in 283 B.C.[2] Otherwise it is inconceivable that Philadelphus with his hands free should not have overcome the rebellion with the great army which paraded at Alexandria during the coronation. But when Seleukos invaded the dominion of Lysimachus in Asia Minor, and

---

[1] Athenaeus v. 196 *sqq.* The whole passage is from *Greek Life and Thought* pp. 201 *sq.*

[2] If the old king remained nominal sovran till his death, we can understand that Magas had no formal ground for rebellion till Philadelphus was sole ruler.

brought with him Ptolemy Keraunos with a promise to help him to his throne in Egypt,[1] Philadelphus must have felt himself in a critical position. As soon as Lysimachus was overpowered, an attack on Egypt was to be expected; Keraunos must have been urging· the old Syrian king to fulfil his vague promises. That was the opportune moment for Magas; for Philadelphus would not risk a division of his army and fleet in the face of the formidable Seleukos.

§ 76. All these hopes and fears were checked by the sentimental resolution of the old king, when he had ordered the affairs of Asia Minor, to return to his ancient home in Macedonia, and abandon the splendours of Antioch to his son. It was more than fifty years since he had seen his home. The rugged glens and harsh climate of Macedonia may have appeared to his mind's eye softened by the mists of childish memories and across the distance of so many eventful years.

To Keraunos it must have been on the contrary a bitter disappointment. He saw his hopes of the throne of Egypt, when they were at their highest, changed into nought by this strange vagary of his so-called benefactor. Cold indifference or even opposition to a demand does not excite such fierce disappointment as the non-fulfilment of fair promises; nor is there any ingratitude more bitter than that shown to a partial benefactor. These reasons, though not stated by the historians, are surely sufficient to account for the murder of Seleukos when he had crossed the Hellespont, and was approaching Lysimacheia. For the murderer Keraunos was a wild and lawless person who recoiled from no crime.

It is far more difficult to make modern readers under-

[1] Memnon xii.

stand how the astonished army should have allowed him
to assume the diadem and proclaim himself king in
Seleukos' place.[1] He must have had many partners in the
plot, people who were likewise disgusted with the prospect
of a campaign in Macedonia, instead of luxurious quarters
in the cities of Asia Minor, and a speedy return to their
homes in Syria. If, as was usual, a large part of the troops
were mercenaries, such as were regularly transferred from
the standard of the vanquished to that of the victor[2]
after each decisive battle, they looked in the first instance
for a paymaster, and how could they wait till Antiochus
the son of Seleukos arrived from the inner provinces of
Asia which he was governing for his father? At all events,
they acquiesced in his crime, and in his assumption of
royalty. Keraunos, on his side, could no longer think of
attacking Egypt. For instead of his patron Seleukos with
all the power of Syria to help him, he had Antiochus
hurrying to avenge his father's death ; any attempt to pass
through Asia Minor and Syria to Egypt would have
brought him through the heart of Seleukos' kingdom,
where the population would be eager to punish the
murderer of their king, and by sea Philadelphus was
master. So Keraunos naturally seized the throne of
Thrace now vacant; and instead of venturing back to Asia
Minor, turned to Macedonia, which was in dispute between Pyrrhus and Antigonus, to carve out for himself an
European kingdom.

§ 77. The most dangerous competitor, Pyrrhus, was
disposed of in a singular and characteristic way. He had
just received an invitation to Tarentum, and was hesitat-

---

[1] We have only the brief account of Memnon and the rhetorical talk
of Justin to enlighten us.

[2] Cf. above, § 32 note.

ing to accept it for want of sufficient equipment. The warring kings Antigonus, Keraunos, and even Antiochus agreed to contribute troops, elephants, money, and buy off this very dangerous rival. Of these Keraunos made the largest contribution, and even undertook to hold Epirus quiet during its king's absence.[1] It was no large attempt to gain Italy for Hellenistic civilisation, but merely a bribe to occupy the brilliant knight-errant, while the eastern kings settled their own quarrels. When he applied again from Italy in 274 B.C. and asked for more help, they turned to him a deaf ear.[2]

We do not hear that Pyrrhus obtained help from Egypt even in the first instance. For Philadelphus desired to keep Europe embroiled in war; nor did he regard with disfavour the successes of Keraunos, so far as they drew the latter away from any attack upon Egypt. He is even said to have sent a fleet to aid Keraunos and to thwart Antigonus Gonatas' efforts to regain the crown of Macedonia.[3]

The career of Keraunos was one of singular activity. He maintained himself successfully against Antiochus; against a son of Lysimachus who claimed his father's throne; against Antigonus; nay more, he induced his half-sister Arsinoe, the widow of Lysimachus, to marry him, which she did with many misgivings, and no sooner had he got her and her younger children[4] into his power, than he murdered the children as being possible heirs to the throne of Thrace, and banished Arsinoe with contumely to Samothrace. But the end came soon. He had not been two years in possession of his throne,

[1] Justin xvii. 2.

[2] Ibid. xxv. 3, and R. Schubert's *Gesch. des Pyrrhus* p. 163.

[3] Cf. *Addit. Note* p. 489.

[4] The eldest son seems to have escaped, and actually to have set up as a claimant to his father's throne. But we hear nothing of him afterwards.

when the great tempest of the Gallic invasion burst upon
Macedonia. In the first battle with the Gauls he was
thrown from his elephant, seized alive, and then hacked
in pieces by the barbarians. Justin[1] preserves to us, or
invents, picturesque features in the setting of this stormy
life. While other kings were buying off the dreaded
invaders, Ptolemy alone heard of the approach of the
Gauls without fear, and went out to meet them with few
and ill-disciplined troops, as if wars were as easily managed
as murders, urged, as it were, by the avenging furies of
his domestic crimes. He even rejected the offer of the
Dardanians, to send 20,000 soldiers to his assistance, with
the insulting words, that it was indeed 'all up' with the
Macedonians, if after conquering all the East single-handed,
they now required Dardanians to protect their frontier; that·
his soldiers were the sons of the men who had served
under Alexander as victors all over the world. When this
answer was brought the Dardanian king, he observed that
the famous Macedonian kingdom would presently fall by
the rashness of a youth. The proposals of the Gauls for a
treaty were rejected with similar insolence.

The wild career of this prince is so intimately connected both with the royal family and with the policy
of Egypt that it can hardly be called a digression to
have devoted so much space to it. And now for several
years all the northern portions of Hellenism are so terrified
at this strange invasion that they have but little inclination
for private quarrels. Ptolemy alone, in his southern home
with his commanding fleet, is secure and at peace, even
though he has occupied most of that Syria which was so
often won and lost by his father. But the new king of
Syria, Antiochus, was at war with the Gauls, and, though

[1] xxiv. 3, 4, and Memnon's scrap xiv.

he gained his title Soter from a victory over them, had no means of resisting the Egyptian aggression.

§ 78. It is quite hopeless, with our present materials, to give any connected or orderly history of Philadelphus' reign. The stray documents which we possess are either panegyrics, which are sure to be misleading, or they tell us isolated facts which we cannot fit together. Thus we hear that in hiring an army to fight against Magas who had advanced from Cyrene to the western borders of Egypt,[1] Ptolemy obtained by means of his recruiting officer Antigonus 4000 Gallic mercenaries,[2] and that when these were discovered plotting to seize Egypt for themselves, they were isolated in an island and all drowned, probably by the rising Nile.[3] It is this shabby triumph which the panegyrists of the court magnify into a victory over the barbarians, such as those signal battles which gave Antigonus his throne, Antiochus his title, Attalus his right to found a kingdom. We know it only from a fulsome digression in Callimachus' Hymn to Delos, with a valuable scholion.[4] Though the exact date of this Hymn is not

[1] The evidence of Cyrenean coins led Mr. R. S. Poole to place this revolt about 279 B.C. or shortly after. It fits better with the probable date of Antiochus Soter's simultaneous attack, and with the events of the Gallic invasion, to put it a little later, say 277 B.C.

[2] Lumbroso *Egitto* ed. 2, p. 82, refutes the idea of Droysen that this Ἀντίγονός τις φίλος τοῦ Πτολ. could be the king of Macedon. He also calls attention to the frequent occurrence of the figure 4000 in such forces, apparently the normal force of a Hellenistic legion. Koepp (*Rh. Mus.* for 1884, p. 212) assumes that Gonatas must be intended, and quotes with approval C. Wachsmuth's emendation αντιγονοσγονατασ-φιλος, the scribe having omitted the second γον(α), and so τας being changed to τις.

[3] According to the scholiast to Callimachus (*Hymn Del.* 175). Pausanias says that they died either of hunger, or at one another's hands.

[4] The unborn Apollo objects to be born at Kos for prophetical reasons, as follows (vv. 162 *sqq.*) :—

known, it evidently alludes to this Celtic affair as recent, and the terror of their invasion must still have been quite fresh to make such an allusion anything but ridiculous.

§ 79. I shall revert presently to the Greek panegyrics,

μὴ σύ γε μῆτερ
τῇ με τέκοις. οὐ τὴν ἐπιμέμφομαι, οὐδὲ μεγαίρω
νῆσον, ἐπεὶ λιπαρή τε καὶ εὔβοτος, εἴ νύ τις ἀλλή.
ἀλλά οἱ ἐκ Μοιρέων τις ὀφειλόμενος θεὸς ἄλλος   165
ἔστι, σαωτήρων ὕπατον γένος· ᾧ ὑπὸ μίτρην
ἵξεται οὐκ ἀέκουσα Μακηδόνι κοιρανέεσθαι
ἀμφοτέρῃ μεσόγεια, καὶ αἱ πελάγεσσι κάθηνται,
μεχρὶς ὅπου περάτη τε, καὶ ὁππόθεν ὥκεες ἵπποι
ἠέλιον φορέουσιν· ὁ δ' εἴσεται ἤθεα πατρός.   170
καὶ νύ ποτε ξυνός τις ἐλεύσεται ἄμμιν ἄεθλος
ὕστερον, ὁππότ' ἂν οἱ μὲν ἐφ' Ἑλλήνεσσι μάχαιραν
βαρβαρικὴν καὶ Κελτὸν ἀναστήσαντες Ἄρηα
ὀψίγονοι τιτῆνες ἀφ' ἑσπέρου ἐσχατόωντος
ῥώσωνται, νιφάδεσσιν ἐοικότες, ἢ ἰσάριθμοι   175
τείρεσι, ἡνίκα πλεῖστα κατ' ἠέρα βουκολέονται.

He then prophesies the attack on Delphi, and the dedication of swords, corslets, and shields at his shrine there, after the Gallic defeat as regards these spoils :—

τέων αἱ μὲν ἐμοὶ γέρας, αἱ δ' ἐπὶ Νείλῳ
ἐν πυρὶ τοὺς φορέοντας ἀποπνεύσαντας ἰδοῦσαι
κείσονται, βασιλῆος ἀέθλια πολλὰ καμόντος
ἐσσομέναι· Πτολεμαῖε, τά τοι μαντήια φαίνω.

It would be hard indeed to interpret this effusion were it not for the scholion, which tells us that after the defeat at Delphi : ὀλίγων οὖν περιλειφθέντων, Ἀντίγονός τις φίλος Φιλ. Πτολ. προξενεῖ αὐτοὺς αὐτῷ ὥστε ἐπὶ μισθῷ στρατεύεσθαι. καὶ γὰρ ἔχρηζεν ὁ Πτολ. τούτου στρα- τεύματος, οἱ δὲ ὁμοίως ἠβουλήθησαν καὶ τοῦ Πτολ. διαρπάσαι τὰ χρήματα. γνοὺς οὖν συλλαμβάνει αὐτούς, καὶ ἀπάγει πρὸς τὸ στόμιον τοῦ Νείλου τὸ λεγόμενον Σεβεννυτικὸν καὶ κατέκλυσεν αὐτοὺς ἔκεισε. ταῦτα οὖν φησιν Ξυνὸν ἀγῶνα ἔσεσθαι. (v. 166) We know already how fond the Ptole- mies were of calling themselves Macedonians. Soter must already have been worshipped as a god. (v. 168) The two continents mean Europe and Asia, into which the world was then commonly divided. (v. 169) περάτη is used for the West. If these Gauls were the captives taken by Antigonus at his victory over them in 278 B.C., then the title Soter Gods is twenty years older than is commonly supposed.

but must first quote an Egyptian one, which is among
the recent additions to our knowledge. M. Naville in
his excavations at Pithom in 1883 found a stele giving
an account of three visits paid by the king to Pithom
(Heroopolis) for the purpose of founding and endowing
a temple there, and also for the purpose of inaugurating
the re-opening of the canal of Necho and of Darius, which
made a water-way from the Nile to the Red Sea.[1]

The stele of Pithom was not set up till after the twentieth
year of his reign, and mentions other facts to which we
shall recur; the first visit was in the sixth year of his
reign, and in the usual fulsome and wordy preamble of the
document, while there is much about his general destroying of his enemies, there is nothing yet deciphered which
seems to have any direct allusion to the Celtic affair.[2] But
the rest of the preamble distinctly places the chief glory of
the king in his fleet. If this is not done to please the
natives, who did (I believe) more work as sailors than as
soldiers, it would imply some early naval successes of
Philadelphus not elsewhere definitely recorded. The text
proceeds to say that he went on a voyage to Persia,
and brought back, by way of the new canal, the gods taken
away from Egypt by former enemies. M. Naville, in his
Commentary, exercises himself to determine what foreign
expedition of Philadelphus this can record. It seems
much more likely that it is one more instance of the senseless copying out of older documents with facts applying
to a previous king, of which Wiedemann has cited such

[1] We can now use the amended version of the late H. Brugsch, just
published from his papers by A. Erman *Z. für Aeg.* for March 1895, pp.
74 *sqq.*

[2] As this preamble was not composed till long after, such an allusion
would then have been quite stale. Cf. below, § 86.

curious examples.[1] The opening of the canal was however
a real step in advance, and one which facilitated the
eastern and southern trade-routes of Egypt for some time.[2]

§ 80. I have already mentioned how Thebes was a
place strange to the Greeks, though we know that Ptolemy
Soter as satrap had rebuilt a shrine at Karnak (in purely
Egyptian style). We have no evidence that his sway was
more than nominal higher up the river. Philadelphus was
an important builder at Philae, but probably in his later
years.[3] Nevertheless the trade of Arabia and of Aethiopia
was of great importance to the king in two respects:
because the gold-mines of Nubia added greatly to the
king's wealth, and because of the elephants, in which
the armaments of Egypt hitherto had been strangely
deficient. We read in Diodorus what careful provision
the first Ptolemy and Seleukos had to make against the
elephants of Demetrius at the battle of Gaza, and though
as the result of that battle most of the Indian elephants
were wounded and taken, we hear not a word about them
in the later annals of Soter. In the great pomp of Philadelphus' coronation, there is indeed a decked-out elephant

[1] *Gesch. Aegypten's* pp. 29 *sq.*

[2] The geography of the Red-Sea coast was explored, and the sites of
most of the Ptolemaic settlements identified, by Richard Burton and
Gardiner Wilkinson, and the results published in the second volume of
the *Geograph. Society's Journal* as far back as 1832. Recently we have
the admirable studies of Mr. E. A. Floyer, head of the Telegraph department in Egypt, on the Eastern desert. These stations of Philadelphus
may be regarded merely as trading-places, whereas his Syrian towns must
have been intended as important military outposts. We know of Ptolemais on the coast, Philadelphia (Hamath), two Arsinoes, one near
Damascus, and one to the south in the gorge (αὐλῶν) of Syria. Lastly
a Philoteria mentioned by Polybius (v. 70, 3) near the lake of Tiberias.
So far and so completely did his influence reach into Syria. He
founded, so far as we know, four Berenikes, eighteen Arsinoes, and
three Philoteras.   [3] Cf. *Addit. Notes* pp. 489-90.

to carry Dionysus, and there are twenty-four 'elephant-
chariots,' along with chariots drawn by other strange beasts,
but not a word about war-elephants in the enumeration of
all the military forces (ἱππικαὶ καὶ πεζικαί) which were displayed in the streets: whereas at this time Seleukos kept a
herd of 500 at Apamea, higher up than Antioch on the
Orontes, a city where their Syrian kings had their arsenal.[1]
Nor was it an easy task, even if elephants were still to be
caught in Nubia, to bring them down the cataracts to
Egypt. A way was now found by sea and canal, and this
at once became the high road of the Ptolemies to the south
country. I have myself searched in Nubia along the Nile
in vain for traces of Philadelphus or Euergetes higher up
than Philae.[2] There are none anywhere extant. On the
other hand Strabo tells of the foundation of a number of
settlements on the Somali coast by the officers sent to
catch elephants for the second and third Ptolemies.
These animals were brought to Alexandria by means of
transport ships called ἐλεφαντηγοί, up the Red Sea and
along the canal of Pithom.[3] The same ships, as those of
Queen Hatasu had done long before, brought other strange
creatures to nourish the king's taste for zoology, and supply
his beast-gardens at Alexandria.

§ 81. Strabo and Diodorus note the scientific interest
in exploration, and in the curiosities of natural history,

---

[1] There is a like absence of mention of elephants in Theocritus'
Encomium, which is strange, unless it was composed early in Philadelphus' reign, for later on he must have had many. This agrees with
the views of Koepp (*Rhein. Mus.* vol. 39), who thinks both this and
Callimachus' encomium were written before 270, and gives several good
reasons for his opinion.   [2] Cf. below, § 95.

[3] These ships are specially mentioned by Agatharchides (Phot. 83)
as being wrecked frequently in the shoals of the Red Sea. The word
does not appear in the Lexica. Diodorus, in paraphrasing the passage,
avoids the term, cf. *Geog. Graec.* i. 171; also *Pet. Pap.* II. xl. (a) 26.

shown by all the Ptolemies, especially the second, and the
consequent ardour of their subjects to please them in this
respect.   Diodorus (iii. 36) tells us a wonderful tale of the
huge serpent which was caught by private enterprise to
please the king, by a whole army of people, 'horse, foot,
and dragoons,' in a sort of giant lobsterpot, and brought
to Alexandria, where Philadelphus was fond of showing it
to his visitors.   The story is far too long to quote, and
contains the most amusing exaggerations.   This taste for
natural history, and for the collecting of foreign fauna and
flora, was no doubt stimulated by Demetrius of Phaleron
and the other Peripatetic philosophers at Alexandria ; but I
should not wonder if the brilliant and lifelike reliefs on the
tomb-temple of Queen Hatasu, in the gorge of the kings'
tombs over against Thebes, with her ships bringing from
the Somali coast apes, ebony, strange trees in pots, and
other wonders, had a more direct effect upon his imagination, when he went to see the wonders of Thebes.

§ 82. Whether he worked the Nubian gold-mines from
the sea is more than doubtful.[1] We can hardly suppose
that during the recent decadence of the native kingdom
of Egypt the Nubian mines had been maintained.   They
were the penal settlement of the old Egyptian kings, as
they afterwards were of the Ptolemies and Romans, and
we have a terrible picture of the sufferings of the miners

[1] The old Pharaonic roads to the gold-mines went into the desert from
the fortress of Kubban in Nubia, perhaps from Korosko.   Plin. *HN*
vi. 34 says that the far-off Berenike was called the golden, on account
of the gold found in the neighbourhood.   If so, even the mines were
worked from the Red-Sea route.   But I doubt this.   The earlier and
later history of the Red-Sea Canal, from the first attempts of the old
Egyptians and Persians down to the Roman Empire, when it was of
great value for the transporting of porphyry from the quarries of Ham-
mamat to Rome, and lastly the causes of its silting up and disuse, are
all treated fully in Letronne's essay on the subject, *Recueil* i. pp. 189 *sq.*

(convicts) in this tropical 'Siberia' preserved to us by Diodorus.[1] But the income derived from trade, and from the minute and severe taxation of all farming in Egypt, was quite sufficient to make Philadelphus the richest king in the world. This is the purport of the *Encomium* of Theocritus,[2] who celebrates the extraordinary wealth

[1] iii. 12.

[2] xiv. 60 and Herondas i. 30 celebrate his generosity as a patron. His empire is described in Theocr. xvii. 82 :—

> τρεῖς μέν οἱ πολίων ἑκατοντάδες ἐνδέδμηνται,
> τρεῖς δ' ἄρα χιλιάδες τρισσαῖς ἐπὶ μυριάδεσσι,
> δοιαὶ δὲ τριάδες, μετὰ δέ σφισιν ἐννεάδες τρεῖς.
> τῶν πάντων Πτολεμαῖος ἀγάνωρ ἐμβασιλεύει.
> καὶ μὴν Φοινίκας ἀποτέμνεται 'Αρραβίας τε
> καὶ Συρίας Λιβύας τε κελαίνων τ' Αἰθιοπήων·
> Παμφύλοισί τε πᾶσι καὶ αἰχμηταῖς Κιλίκεσσι
> σαμαίνει Λυκίοις τε φιλοπτολέμοισί τε Κᾶρσι
> καὶ νάσοις Κυκλάδεσσιν, ἐπεί οἱ νᾶες ἄρισται
> πόντον ἐπιπλώοντι· θάλασσα δὲ πᾶσα καὶ αἶα
> καὶ ποταμοὶ κελάδοντες ἀνάσσονται Πτολεμαίῳ.

ἀποτέμνεσθαι is used in the same sense by Plutarch *Demetrius* 36, and in Memnon περὶ 'Ηρ. c. xix., so also in the Megarian inscription on Orsippus (*CIG* 1050) which seems to go back at least to classical times, and in an epigram of Chaeremon, κάτθανες ἀμφίλογον γᾶν ἀποτεμνόμενος (*Anthol. Graec.* vii. 720).

As regards the actual money-value of Philadelphus' income, or of the treasure which he collected at Alexandria, we have several divergent notices. Regarding the coin alone, S. Jerome (*ad Dan.* xi.) puts the revenue at 14,800 silver talents yearly, Appian (*prooem.* 10) says the treasure accumulated in the treasury was 740,000 talents. Cicero says (ap. Strabon. xvii. p. 798) the income of the broken-down Auletes was 12,500. That figure agrees very well with that of S. Jerome; for the reign of Philadelphus was the climax of Ptolemaic splendour. But what sense is there in Appian's statement? Boeckh supposed the 740,000 to be copper talents, but now that we hold the ratio of silver to copper to have been 1 : 120, this would not be a year's income. Until however this ratio is certain, we cannot dogmatise, nor do I think it at all likely that Appian meant copper. Ancient authors are so loose about their figures, and copyists so often mistook them, that I refrain from any decision on this question. Cf. Ruehl in *Jahrbb.* for 1879, pp. 621 *sq.*

of Ptolemy, and his liberality in dispensing it to the priests, the poets, and his 'friends.' Here again we are at a loss to date the poem, in which the absence of Cyrene and Cyprus from the list of his possessions has perplexed modern historians. Even had these provinces been in revolt at the moment, or temporarily out of the king's power, I do not think the court poet would have scrupled to add them to the list, which is surely more comprehensive than sober truth would admit. Nor can we see why he should not have also included those towns about the Hellespont, which Ptolemy's second wife claimed as her private property. Though these omissions are not easily accounted for, I cannot accept the conclusion that Philadelphus had lost Cyprus, and surrendered all claims upon Cyrene.

We know that the invasion of Magas was met by raising up enemies against him in his own territory; his claims to a separate kingdom were settled by betrothing the crown-prince of Egypt to his infant daughter. The so-called first Syrian war, which Antiochus probably began as soon as his hands were free in Asia Minor, seems to have been indecisive, and if it resulted in any loss to Philadelphus, it was not such a loss as that of Cyprus. The evidence of the coins struck and dated by Philadelphus at Tyre from 266 B.C. to his death, together with the existence of a prior undated Egyptian coinage of this king at Tyre and Sidon, have convinced Mr. R. S. Poole [1] that the Egyptian king won the province from Antiochus as early as 270 B.C. On the other hand Koepp, in his able article on the Syrian wars of the early Ptolemies, holds that Palestine and Coele-Syria had been practically an Egyptian province ever since the battle of Ipsus, and that Philadelphus inherited it from his father. He explains the

[1] *Coins of the Ptolemies* p. xxix.

first Syrian war as an invasion of Antiochus Soter, only so far successful that he took Damascus,[1] just as Demetrius years before had raided Samaria.   But by the same policy of raising up difficulties in far provinces of the Syrian empire, especially in Pontus, Philadelphus thwarted the attack. Koepp even imagines that Philadelphus' second marriage was part of his policy in this Syrian war, to gain influence with the old subjects of the house of Lysimachus.   The many struggles between Syria and Egypt, known as the Syrian wars, in which Judaea was necessarily involved, form the subject of the eleventh chapter of Daniel.   But the author is so vague, and omits so many important occurrences, that not even the intelligent commentary of S. Jerome, who derives his facts chiefly from the sceptical Porphyry, can make it a proper source of history for us. Whether this vagueness is intentional or not, I leave to theologians to decide.

§ 83. Theocritus' statement that the king spent great sums of money on temples and priests can still be verified from the ruins marked with his name.   In addition to the temple and endowment in the east of the Delta near Pithom, there are in the centre of the Delta, near the ancient Sebennytus, the remains of one of the most costly buildings in Egypt, a temple to the Isis of Hebt, of great size, constructed altogether of grey and of pink granite, which must have come from Syene, 700 miles up the river.   The whole structure has tumbled down, and has been ransacked for curiosities, or treated most ruthlessly as a quarry, little attention or care being hitherto paid to any antiquities in the Delta.   There are elaborate sculptures and inscriptions on this very hard material, but none of those as yet uncovered contain more than the usual barren

---

[1] If we may trust Polyaenus iv. 15.

formulae of this epoch, which tell us that this king dedicated the temple to Isis.   Unfortunately we have found no date.

So likewise in the west of the Delta, Mr. Petrie, when excavating the site of Naukratis, found that Philadelphus had patronised the Hellenion, a common temple to the Greek gods at that ancient settlement of Greek traders, thus showing that his devotions and offerings were not confined to Egyptian gods.[1]   At a spot where the great wall of the temenos may have been broken down, he set up pylons, and an entrance gate, with a building behind them covering the line of the wall.   Under the foundations were found models of the tools employed, and the vessels, in materials ranging from an ordinary mud-brick to fragments of agate and lapis lazuli, together with gems containing the cartouche of the king.   He may possibly have restored the temple of Aphrodite inside the enclosure. But unfortunately no inscription beyond the mere cartouche of his name has been found.

Thus we learn that at three points of the Delta he built temples to the gods both Greek and Egyptian, and the stone of Pithom, to which we shall revert, tells us of large endowments whereby he added to the value of his restorations.   Many dedications throughout the Greek world show his liberality abroad, perhaps the same politic desire to conciliate the priesthood throughout the Hellenistic world.[2]   But before we pass to these, we may note the evidences of his donations in Upper Egypt.

[1] Cf. W. F. Petrie *Naukratis* part i. pp. 26 *sqq.*

[2] There would appear to have been a careful impartiality in his worship of Greek and of Egyptian gods.   All the statues of the king and queen in Egypt were probably strictly Egyptian; *e.g.* those preserved in the Vatican Museum, on the back of one of which are this king's titles, on the second those of his second queen (above, § 73). Where these statues were found in Egypt I could not ascertain.

§ 84. I do not believe that a single Ptolemaic temple, in the whole series up the Nile, now shows traces of his work, except the great temple of Isis at Philae, and here we see it so overlaid by that of his successors, that we can easily understand how his foundations in other places may have been completely obscured by the additions of later kings. It is most unlikely that he built freely in the Delta, and again on the southern limit of his kingdom, without doing something for the many holy places which lay along the 700 miles between his splendid granite temple and his picturesque structure at Philae. The island had not been the original holy island; inscriptions at the neighbouring Biggeh show its more ancient sanctity. It was apparently Nectanebo II. who began the buildings at Philae, and he had done but little, when Philadelphus determined to erect here also a shrine to his favourite Isis. This temple was probably later than those of the Delta; at all events his second queen figures upon the sculptures. The fact too that this island was beyond the limits of Egypt, above the cataract, shows that he must have stood in peaceful relations with the Nubians. We are told by Diodorus[1] that the founder of the Nubian dynasty of independent kings, Ergamenes, was contemporary with Philadelphus. I shall show in due time that this is very improbable, and that Ergamenes' extant cartouches are evidently copied from that of the fourth Ptolemy.

Enough remains then to show that Philadelphus had either pacified or humoured the inhabitants of lower Nubia, so that they did not molest the temple of Isis built upon their territory. What temples he may have founded on sites along the Red Sea cannot be known till that country is better explored. Letronne[2] thinks that the sites of two

[1] iii. 6.   [2] *Recueil* ii. pp. 175 *sq.*

Arsinoes, two Philoteras, and of Myos Hormos are identified, and shown to have been military and naval stations. He proceeds to argue that all his other colonies were named after his second wife, or his sister Philotera. But there were exceptions such as Philadelphia (Rabbat Amon) known even to him, and the list of village-names which I found in the Petrie Papyri,[1] and which are formed on the same principles, with Arsinoes and Philoteras, afford us several more, such as Lagis, Theadelphia, Philagris, Lysimachis, etc. and a Berenikis, long after Berenike's death, all founded under this king. I add with pleasure the following paragraph from Mr. Floyer's brilliant essay[2]: 'The violent north-winds that prevail in the Red Sea made the navigation so difficult and slow for the poor ships of the ancients that Ptolemy Philadelphus established the port of Berenike. This is 200 miles south of the ancient ports at or near Kosseir, and consequently saved that distance and its attendant delays and dangers to the mariners from Southern Arabia and India. I suppose the best camels[3] and the worst ships would choose Berenike, while the best ships and the worst camels would carry the Kosseir traffic. For it is interesting to note that Phil-

---

[1] Cf. the list in vol. ii. p. 98 of that publication.

[2] *Proceedings* of the Geograph. Soc. for 1887, p. 665; cf. also two texts of Strabo i. 4, 7 μεθ' ἦν ἡ Πτολέμαις πρὸς τῇ θήρᾳ τῶν ἐλεφάντων, κτίσμα Εὐμήδους τοῦ πεμφθέντος ἐπὶ τὴν θήραν ὑπὸ Φιλαδέλφου: and a few sentences earlier: εἶθ' ὁ τῆς Σωτείρας λιμὴν ὃν ἐκ κινδύνων μεγάλων σωθέντες τινες τῶν ἡγεμόνων ἀπὸ τοῦ συμβεβηκότος οὕτως ἐκάλεσαν, coupled with the inscription from Koptos which I copied in the Gizeh Museum (1894), θεοις μεγαλοις Σαμοθραξι | Απολλωνιος Σωσιβιου | θηραιος ηγεμων των | εξω ταξεων σωθεις | εγ μεγαλων κινδυνων εκ | πλευσας εκ της ερυθρας | θαλασσης ευχην. It is wrongly interpreted by Maspero *Catalogue* p. 359.

[3] Though the Ptolemies used no camels in Egypt, they were probably long naturalised in this desert, and we have Camels' Fort already mentioned (§ 21) as a place near Pelusium.

adelphus at the same time that he built Berenike also rebuilt the old Kosseir port, and Myos Hormos was still kept in repair. In former days it is probable that many a sea-sick traveller, buffetted by contrary winds, landed joyfully at Berenike, and took the twelve days' camel journey sooner than continue in his cramped ship, just as now they disembark at Brindisi rather than Venice [on their way from India].'

I think it more than probable that the worship of the Samothracian gods, which we can prove from inscriptions during this century, was introduced by him or by his second wife. For on the island of Samothrace have been found remarkable remains of a building set up in honour of these mysterious divinities by this queen Arsinoe. We hear that in her great troubles, especially after the murder of her children, she found a refuge in the holy island. But it may have been from some earlier gratitude to the local gods that she not only built them a temple, but afterwards introduced their worship into Egypt. The temple was a Rotunda, with Corinthian pillars, and not unlike in design to the monument set up by Philip of Macedon at Olympia to commemorate his victory at Chaeronea. It was a fine structure, built of the most solid materials. The inscription over the entrance appears to have been—

βασΙΛΙΣΣΑ ΑΡσινοη βασιλεως πτολεμΑΙΟΥ ΟΥΓΑτηρ
ΒΑΣΙΛΕΩΣ [πτολεμαιου] γυνη ευχην ΘΕΟΙΣ ΜΕΓΑΛοις.[1]

Other *anathemata* of hers, simply inscribed αρσινοης φιλ-αδελφου, have been found at Amorgos, which she probably visited during her misfortunes.[2]

---

[1] The name bracketed may have been Λυσιμαχου. Cf. Conze *Samothrake* pp. 17 *sqq.*, who further notes that we know of three Alexandrian writers of this period who wrote about the Samothracian deities. [2] Cf. *Mitth.* i. 336.

§ 85. These dedications bring us face to face with an important turning-point in Philadelphus' life—his second marriage, to his own full sister Arsinoe, who first assumed the title Philadelphus, *loving her brother*, by which the king came to be known in later generations.[1] His first wife Arsinoe is reported to have been detected plotting against his life, and to have been banished to Koptos,[2] while her children were adopted by the new queen, who was now a childless widow, of middle age, and not likely to have any more heirs. After her misfortunes in Macedonia she returned to Egypt, and used her passion for intrigue to good account ; she ousted the existing queen[3] and rose to her place, which she raised to an extraordinary position of dignity. It is now generally agreed that this marriage took

[1] Contemporary documents never call the king by this title ; but most historians have adopted it for convenience sake.

[2] Mr. Petrie has found at Koptos, in 1894, an interesting corroboration of this account. On a stele, an Egyptian (whose name is uncertain) in giving an account of his life, mentions that he was steward of a queen Arsinoe, and was employed by her to rebuild and beautify a shrine to the god. As the Arsinoe in question is not further described, we may be pretty certain that it was not Arsinoe Philadelphus, and so it probably refers to the first queen of the name, who accordingly may have lived in some state in her exile in Upper Egypt. This agrees with the interpretation given by Krall (*Studien* ii. p. 40) to a stele found at Koptos which runs : ' Goddess of Ascher, give life to Lysimachos, brother of the royalties, the Strategos, year vii.' ; viz. year 7 of Euergetes, or 240 B.C. He was the king's younger brother and strategos of Koptos. So his mother had lived with him.

[3] Though the first and second Arsinoes were respectively daughter and wife of King Lysimachus, it is most unlikely that they were actually daughter and mother. Not only do the dates make it difficult (though not impossible) but the silence of all gossip on such an interesting affair as a mother supplanting her daughter in the affections of the king, and taking her place upon the throne, is to me a conclusive objection. To the gibes about the incest of the union would have been added the scandal of a mother invading her daughter's rights. The scholion to Theocritus xvii. 128 is our best and most distinct authority for the crisis which

place within the years 278-277 B.C. Droysen, by various ingenious combinations,[1] tried to fix it at the year 267, or the eighteenth of his reign. This decision seems clearly refuted by the stele of Pithom. At the head of this stele the second queen Arsinoe is represented as a deity conferring favours on the king, her husband. But then the stele was not set up till during or after his twenty-first year. The text, however, contains an account of three visits of the king to Pithom, the first in his sixth year, with the opening of the canal, a visit to Persia, and the alleged recovery of the gods of Egypt. In this there is no mention whatever of his queen, and of course he could not as yet have been married to this second Arsinoe. But then the text proceeds to say that in his twelfth year—that is in 273 B.C.—he paid another visit in company with his queen and sister, and not only endowed the gods of Pithom, but founded a city called after a daughter of Ptolemy,[2] at the junction of his new canal with the Red Sea, from which the royal pair sent out a commander to go to the land of the negroes, from which he brought back not only a large number of elephants, but also many other curiosities to please the king and queen.

§ 86. Let me cite this curious text.[3] l. 21 : At the first month His Majesty called for transports, ships . . . laden with troops and all the good things of Egypt [entrusted] to the first general of His Majesty [Eumedes]. They replaced the first Arsinoe by the second. The difficult question of the appearance of Philadelphus' son in some dates during his reign I shall postpone till we come to consider Euergetes' youth.

[1] *Hell.* iii. 266 note.

[2] This is odd, for surely the city was known as Arsinoe. Whereas it seems intended to mean Philotera, and Satyrus, the other general sent out by him to the Trogodyte country, did found cities called Philotera and Berenike (Strabo xvi. 4, 5).

[3] Naville's *Pithom* p. 21. There is a corrected version by Erman in the *Z. für Aegypt.* for 1895 (March).

sailed to the Kemuer-sea . . . he navigated from the harbour of the Red Sea [?]; he arrived at Khatit [?]. He reached the land of the negroes [and returned to the Lake of the Scorpion]. He brought all the things which are agreeable to the king and to his sister, his royal wife, who loves him, and he built a great city to the king with the illustrious name of the king, the lord of Egypt, Ptolemais.[1] And he took possession of it, with the soldiers of His Majesty and all the workmen of Egypt and the land of Punt. He made these fields and cultivated them with ploughs and cattle; he did not come back before it was done.[2] He caught elephants in great number for the king, and he brought them on his ships to the king, on his transports on the sea. No such thing had ever been seen by any of the kings of the land. There came ships and ships to Kemuer-sea.' And at this place the king had 'founded a large city to his sister [l. 21], with the illustrious name of the daughter of king Ptolemy [Philotera].[3] A sanctuary was built there to the princess Philadelphus; the statues of the gods Adelphi were there erected,' etc., etc.

§ 87. There were so many dedications in Egypt to this queen Arsinoe that we can hardly infer from this text that her marriage and deification were quite recent.[4] But

---

[1] M. Naville reads *Ptolemy*, which does not give a different sense.

[2] Strabo says he unexpectedly seized a promontory, and fortified it on the land side with a ditch, but then made friends of the natives who at first had tried to hinder him.

[3] It appears that court poets like Callimachus not only wrote in praise of queen Arsinoe, but addressed poems to Philotera. Cf. the citations in Gercke *Alex. Stud.*, *Rh. Mus.* for 1887, p. 604.

[4] Droysen has gathered evidence (Berlin *Sitzb.* for 1882) that her deifications were gradual. In the fifteenth year of the king's reign she was made goddess of Mendes (H. Brugsch in *Zeitsch. für Aegypt.* for March 1875). In the year 19 she was goddess at Thebes. It appears from another text that she was made goddess (Isis-Arsinoe) at Sais in

they may have been so. At all events we have attained a minor limit for the former, which may even have been as early as 278 B.C.[1] This marriage, which was quite in accordance with Egyptian notions, where for ages past the queen had been called sister of the king, whether she was so or not,[2] and which was compared by the court poets with the marriage of Zeus and Hera, scandalized Greek feeling. The poet Sotades reflected upon it in a very outspoken line, and is said to have consequently lost his life, when caught by an Egyptian admiral Patrokles, in the Cilician town of Kaunos, whither he had fled to avoid the king's resentment.[3]

Droysen thinks the proprietary claims which the queen had upon Cassandrea as well as Pontic Heraclea and its

the twentieth year. I infer that the whole process was complete in the king's twenty-first year, when he claimed for her the ἀπόμοιρα paid to all the temples in Egypt.

[1] Koepp (*Rh. Mus.* vol. 39) is disposed to date the marriage as far back as 276 B.C.

[2] Erman shows (*Aegypten* pp. 222 *sq.*) that it was a term of endearment, that brother often meant lover, and so the use of the terms was not confined to royalty. There is evidence even in the *Song of Solomon* (v. 2) and in the LXX of the book of *Esther* (v. 1. 16 τί ἐστιν Ἐσθήρ ; ἐγὼ ὁ ἀδελφός σου, θάρσει, says the king) for the same curious identification of sister and wife.

[3] Bergk (*Rh. Mus.* 35, p. 259) says that the joke on the subject preserved from Alexis' Ὑποβολιμαῖος must have been inserted after that poet's death, and in a reproduction of his drama, which I greatly doubt. The line of Sotades was—

εἰς οὐχ ὁσίην τρυμαλιὴν τὸ κέντρον ὠθεῖς :

those of Alexis—

ἐγὼ Πτολ. τοῦ βασιλέως τέτταρα
χυτρίδι' ἀκράτου τῆς τ' ἀδελφῆς προσλαβὼν
τῆς τοῦ βασιλέως, ταῦτ' ἀπνευστί τ' ἐκπιὼν κτλ.
καὶ τῆς ὁμονοίας κτλ.

But there is great difficulty in prolonging Alexis' life till the date of Arsinoe's marriage.

dependent cities, bestowed upon her by her first husband, made the match politically important and desirable to Ptolemy. Personal attraction is a more obvious and a better reason. I give no credit to the epigrams of flatterers declaring her beauty to be incomparable. Her head on the many coins still extant is not ugly, but not remarkable for beauty. There is ample evidence that Philadelphus loved intellectual pleasures no less than those of sense. This able woman made life easy for him; she adopted his children; she connived at, perhaps encouraged his mistresses;[1] she took part in his politics, perhaps even more in the financial administration of the country; she saved him from the desire, and from the peril, of making any other matrimonial alliances.

§ 88. In the year 273, that is to say some years after his second marriage, and when Pyrrhus' campaigns had acquainted the Hellenistic world with the Roman power, Philadelphus showed his far-seeing political sense by sending an embassy to Rome, to offer friendship (not alliance). The Romans answered with a ceremony and respect quite unusual; their return-embassy of three senators included the *princeps senatus*, Q. Fabius Gurges. The king honoured them with golden crowns, which they placed on his statues; his other precious gifts they laid before the senate, who commanded them to keep them as heir-looms.[2] Thus commenced a commercial inter-

---

[1] Polybius (xiv. 11, 2) speaks of Kleino, his cup-bearer, whose statues, dressed in her chemise only (μονοχίτωνας) with a pitcher in her hand, were to be seen all over Alexandria. The finest houses in the city were known as those of Myrtium, and Mnesis, and Potheine, low fluteplayers or actresses in farces. He compares them with Philopator's Agathokleia, but the latter upset the monarchy, while the former only amused the king.

[2] The evidence for this interchange of courtesies has been stated and sifted by Bandelin in his excellent *Inaug. Diss.* (Halle, 1893), pp.

course with Italy, which lasted into the days of the Empire. Politically, it is regarded by Mommsen as the first official recognition that Rome was one of the great powers in the Mediterranean system.[1]   The cornships of Alexandria were awaited as anxiously at Puteoli as the Pontic cornships had of old been at Athens in the summit of her might. It was this move of Ptolemy that enabled him to refuse the Carthaginians when, towards the close of the first Punic war, they desired to borrow from him 2000 talents. He asserted a strict neutrality.[2]

We also hear [3] that he carried on war by means of his fleet with the cities on the Euxine which refused to admit Arsinoe's jurisdiction ; and if he had been able to command that sea, and close the Dardanelles, he might have raised the price of his exported corn as much as he pleased, for he would have closed the only other avenue for providing Europe with bread.   But then he would have set against him all the trading interests of the Levant, especially Rhodes, and this would have been contrary to all his policy.

The next date which we can now fix in Philadelphus'

6-8. We have the fact only mentioned in Livy's Epitome (xiv.), but Val. Max. iv. 3, 9, Dionys. Hal. xx. 14, Dio Cass. fr. 41, and other second-rate authorities agree very well, probably all deriving their information from Hieronymus of Kardia.   Two of these senators, three years after, issued the first consular silver coinage at Rome (Pliny xxxiii. 3), thus indicating that Rome borrowed the practice directly from Alexandria.   But this borrowing extended afterwards to many other Hellenistic arts.   Cuneiform astronomical texts are cited to prove that at this very date there was an Egyptian garrison east of the Euphrates (Epping und Strassmeier *Zeitsch. f. Assyriol.* vii. 200 *sq.*, according to Holm's citation, *Gr. Gesch.* iv. 202), and Philadelphus coined in Phoenicia from 268 B.C. onward, though we find Aradus commencing its era of freedom (under the Seleukids) in 259 B.C.

[1] *RG* i. p. 429.   [2] Appian *Sic.* 1.
[3] Cf. the doubtful evidence discussed by Droysen iii. 272.

reign for an important internal reform was the year 264 B.C.
(his twenty-first year), when according to M. Naville's
version of the stone of Pithom he again visited his foundations in the eastern Delta, and fixed the amount of his
religious endowments in money value. In any case the
king's great liberality in giving this endowment to the
Egyptian temples is there specially lauded. But in the
new document brought by Mr. Petrie from Egypt in 1894,
the Tax-farming (Revenue) Papyrus, as I have called it,
quite another face is put upon this affair. Columns 36
and 37 of that document contain royal rescripts, dated
in his twenty-third year, wherein the official secretaries
(βασιλικοι γραμματεις) of each nome are required to furnish
a list of the gardens and vineyards which in the official
budget of taxes (εν τηι φορολογιαι) were charged with the
dues (απομοιρα) of one-sixth for the temples, also a list of
the temples and what amount they received yearly up to the
twenty-first year. This was done in order to farm out the
collection of this tax, not for the temples, but as dues for
Arsinoe Philadelphus. In other words that lady had been
deified, and to her were to be paid all the dues which the
temples had received on vineyards and wine throughout all
Egypt up to the twenty-first year.[1] In the text referred to
only vineyards and gardens are mentioned, and only wine
as a produce. In the gardens were primarily fruit-trees,
but in that climate vines could be grown climbing on
trees,[2] so that we need not assume the monstrous charge
of one-sixth upon the whole fruit produce of Egypt.

However, the large sums paid to the priests mentioned

---

[1] Possibly she was regarded as a sort of mediating deity, who could
offer sacrifices (σπονδην και θυσιαν) to the invisible gods for the people.
But this is only a hypothesis.

[2] The αναδενδρας mentioned in *Petrie Papyri* I. xxx.

on the Pithom stone are evidently the *quid pro quo* granted by the king. We may also suppose that for two years the Government collected the tax, in order to find out approximately its value, and the proper price at which to farm it in succeeding years. We may be sure that the king did not make a bad bargain. The prosperity of Egypt was rising. The introduction of many Greeks would increase the cultivation of wine, and it is more than probable that he had already received reports from his engineers concerning the important reclaiming of lands at the lake near Crocodilopolis.

§ 89. This great agricultural reform, and presently the settlement of a population of veterans [1] in the now-called Fayyum, was in some way directly attributed to the benevolence of Arsinoe. The whole district was renamed, after her, the Arsinoite nome. We are told [2] that the fish of the great lake had of old been given to the queen of Egypt for her pin-money. By some large draining or dyking operations—Ἀρσινόης χῶμα was the name of one of the new villages—a tract of land was reclaimed, and made fit for cultivation. In the twenty-ninth and thirtieth we know

---

[1] By veterans I do not mean necessarily soldiers released from the standards and in retirement, but a reserve force, which could be called upon, if necessary, though such cases must have been rare. For most of the men whose wills are preserved to us in the P.P. are 60-70 years old. Diodorus indeed (xix. 41) speaks of this advanced age being the great reason why the Argyraspides under Eumenes were invincible, but I do not believe anything so absurd. From the constant mention (in the P.P.) of the regiment to which the Fayyum settlers belong being that of one of the explorers of the elephant country—Lichas, Pythangelos, etc.—I think it possible that these veterans were those who had served in this dangerous and distinguished service.

[2] τὴν δ᾽ ἐκ τῆς λίμνης ἀπὸ τῶν ἰχθύων γινομένην πρόσοδον ἔδωκε τῇ γυναικὶ πρὸς μύρα καὶ τὸν ἄλλον καλλωπισμόν, φερούσης τῆς θήρας ἀργ. τάλαντον ἑκάστης ἡμέρας. Diod. i. 52.

from the papers of Kleon the chief engineer (ἀρχιτέκτων) of the district that it was being reclaimed (though not yet renamed), and most of his work seems to have been the management of the dykes in the new province. Thus we are at last able to fix the date of this large reform. Probably Arsinoe had found the ἑκτή collected from the vineyards so profitable, that she was ready to resign her rights upon the fish of the lake, and of the canals passing in and out of it.

From this time onward the Arsinoite nome, lying as an oasis away from the Nile, with its salt lake fed by deep water coming from inner Africa, its higher lands irrigated by the well-known canal (now Bahr Yusuf) which comes from Assiût far up the Nile, became the most wealthy and populous nome in Egypt. Very probably the priests were now sorry they had accepted, or even been obliged to accept, the king's great liberality lauded on the Pithom-stele. Moreover by the progress of this policy, the priests became the direct pensioners of the state, and only thus could they ever have been trusted to support the foreign throne. But the memories of their old corporate rights and their separate property were too strong for their loyalty, and we shall find that more than once again they stimulated national revolts.

§ 90. The same papyrus which tells us of the transference of the ἀπόμοιρα of the gods to the deified Queen, also gives details, dated in the twenty-seventh year of the king, concerning the farming of the State monopoly in oil to the companies of *publicani*, as we should call them in Roman days, who bought the right of selling the oil to the retailers, and so making their profit. It is indeed hard to make out where and how this profit could be made. For just as the husbandmen were not allowed to have their vintage or make their wine, without the presence of a government officer, and an officer of the farmers of the tax, so in the case of oil, even the seed was to be served out by the state sixty days before the harvest, the quantity of acres in each nome to be planted in oil was determined, so was the special kind of the oil. The retail price was fixed; a list of all the retailers and of the amount each of them could dispose of—all is fixed by state-regulation. There are careful instructions protecting the tax-farmers from the dishonesty of the husbandmen, protecting the husbandmen from the extortion of the tax-farmers, special regulations prohibiting the importing of Syrian oil by way of Pelusium, beyond what was requisite for three days' use. The very cooks are prohibited from melting down suet, and passing it for oil.

These minute provisions also make clear to us that up to the twenty-seventh year of this king, there was no olive-oil in Egypt. Four sorts are specified—sesame-oil, the most valuable, and used for cooking; kiki-oil, made from the croton-plant, which, being like our castor-oil, was hardly fit for food, but used for lamps; and then three other kinds, of which we do not hear in other papyri, κνηκινον, made from the head of some sort of artichoke, κολοκυνθινον or pumpkin-oil, and linseed oil.[1] Had there been olive-trees, or olive-oil, in the country, such could not but have been mentioned in these state-regulations, which affect all the provinces or nomes of Egypt. It was not till the new nome was filled with veterans, many of whom brought wives from Greek lands, that the olive was settled in Egypt, and

---

[1] Pliny (xix. 26) speaks of oil made of radishes, *hoc maxime cupiunt serere, si liceat, quoniam et quaestus plus quam e frumento et minus tributi*, and elsewhere of many varieties of oil, as if the natives had endeavoured to ease the burden of the monopoly by these various inventions.

made a distinct impression upon Strabo, when he visited the Lake and Labyrinth two centuries later.

§ 91. We may take it for granted that all this minute and complicated legislation was adapted from that of the old Pharaohs. It was unlike anything that would be tolerated either in Greece or Macedonia. But the Pharaohs and the Ptolemies (in this matter copied by Augustus and his successors) regarded the land of Egypt as little more than a crown-estate, to be managed with a view to the interests of the sovran only.

This view has been strongly put forward in the brilliant Greek history of A. Holm,[1] who can see nothing good in any Ptolemy but the first, and thinks all the Hellenistic kings a mere damage to that Hellenic civilisation, which could not thrive beyond the pale of the free Greek polity. On the other side we have not only Droysen, but Wila-mowitz-Möllendorff, who see in the Greek *polis* of these days but a useless survival, if not a mischievous parody.

If we compare the best of either form of government with the worst of the others, or the good moments of either with the bad moments of the other, we can find sufficient reasons for the very strong judgments of these eminent men, though they stand in direct conflict. In Egypt at all events, the introduction of the Greek *polis* among the natives would have been ridiculous, if not impossible.

§ 92. The first and the great thing to do was to put down with a firm hand the extortions of local magistrates.[2]

---

[1] iv. 176.

[2] This has remained the great desideratum in Egypt up to the present day ; and the recognition that it is so, together with some vigorous dismissals of dishonest officials, is both one good justification of the English occupation, and also the reason why that occupation is hateful to the dishonest classes, both inside Egypt and in such other countries as stand in close relation to its finances.

This the Ptolemies attempted, not only by subjecting the whole control of local magistrates to a complete system of central regulations, but also by establishing those travelling or assize judges, who were appointed to hear complaints, and adjudicate them, for the husbandmen who could not easily find redress on the spot, and were unable to appeal to the central government far away in Alexandria. This is the well-known institution of the χρηματισταί, attributed by pseudo-Aristeas to Philadelphus, and corroborated both by the Petrie Papyri and by an inscription as a current institution in Egypt. According to the inscription[1] it consisted of three members—Greeks—with an εἰσαγωγεύς or secretary, and an apparitor, and extended not only over Upper Egypt, but also to the Delta, where the group of nomes round the Prosopitan formed one circuit. There was, however, in the Fayyum as early as the third Ptolemy a distinct local Greek court, with at least four judges sitting under a president (πρόεδρος), appointed to adjudicate suits between the settlers.[2]

It is remarkable that among the many complaints of injustice found in the Petrie and Serapeum Papyri, made by poor people who seek redress from the law, there is not a single tale of horror. There is assault and battery, there is the common sort of violence, but torture, rape, and even murder do not occur among these complaints. We also find many cases among natives, who had their own native courts, brought up by preference before the Greek magistrates, and pleaded in Greek. The effect which these papers produce upon the careful student of them, is that they

---

[1] Cf. Krebs in Göttingen *Nachrichten* for December 1892.

[2] Cf. *Petrie Papyri* I. xxvii.-xxviii., and this did not exclude the action of the χρηματισταί, cf. ibid. II. viii. 2 ; xxxviii. (c). According to Wilcken's restoration (*Gött. G. Anz.* for 1895, p. 143) the court consisted of ten judges and a president.

belong to an orderly and well-managed society, where there is but little actual want, and but little lawlessness. There are complaints of violence against natives committed by Greeks in the earlier documents; in those of the next century there are complaints of violence against Greeks, committed by natives; in neither case is there any approach to the horrors which we read in the memoirs of Simplicissimus, or in the legal records of France before the Revolution.

The great burden of the peasants' life must have been the luxuriance of officialdom. Every new papyrus brings us new names of officials, whose functions we can hardly distinguish from those of their colleagues; there is no end of red tape, and therefore of delay in obtaining justice, and there are times when such delay may amount to positive cruelty. There are prisoners who talk of themselves as likely to rot in jail unless their case is decided, but there is no actual case known to us where such consequences resulted. There was a current opinion that imprisonment for debt was not permitted in Ptolemaic law. The recent discoveries of papyri in the Fayyum contradict that opinion. We have several cases of applications from jail made by prisoners on account of default. But the very fact that they do appeal and that their complaints are set on paper, and sent out, show that the imprisonment was not a rigid one, or anything like the dreadful confinement in mediaeval dungeons.

§ 93. These important financial arrangements seem to have been contemporaneous with the so-called Chremonidean War, in which Athens sought to shake off the bondage of Macedonia, and though assisted by the fleet of Ptolemy, failed in the attempt, surrendered, and was obliged to submit to the very gentle and intelligent despotism of Antigonus Gonatas—about 260-58 B.C. We now know[1] that Athens with her allies, and Sparta with her allies made a treaty with Philadelphus to protect the Greeks from those who were plotting against their liberty. The pompous enumeration of all the allies, and the primacy ceded to the king of Egypt, must have promised great things, and Pausanias tells us that the Egyptian admiral Patrokles occupied and fortified the island afterwards called by his name near Sunium. The delays and then the defeat of Areus king of Sparta are regarded as sufficient cause for the failure of the whole scheme by Holm.[2]   The result rather shows the weakness of the Greeks, and perhaps the lukewarm support of Egypt, which did not risk any great outlay upon these treacherous and unstable allies.

But we are not here concerned with this war further than to note that the fleet of Ptolemy, far from maintaining the mastery of the sea, was signally defeated by Antigonus at Kos, in consequence of which Egypt actually lost that branch of her power for some fourteen years, when it was recovered by the victory at Andros, over the same Antigonus. All the facts are very hazy; we only know of the battle off Kos by stray allusions, but the appearance at Delos of votive offerings of Antigonus, who seems to replace Philadelphus as president of the islanders' Confederacy, and some other stray evidences such as the adventures of Aratus on his way to Egypt in 250 B.C., make the combination of facts very probable.[3]

§ 94. Into the same period, but a year or two later, Droysen and others put the second Syrian war, apparently so called because the second Antiochus waged it against

---

[1] *CIA* ii. No. 332.   Cf. *Addit. Note* p. 490.

[2] *Griech. Gesch.* iv. 251.

[3] See the summary of the conjectures on this matter ibid. 265.

Philadelphus. We know nothing about it, save that the
Egyptian fleet, which is supposed to have been driven from
the sea by the victory of Kos, still commands the coast of
Asia Minor, even round to the Black Sea, and not only
occupies many settlements in Cilicia, but also seizes
Ephesus, and wars with Heraclea in Pontus. Where was
Antigonus' victorious fleet, which probably would help the
Syrian power? If Antigonus did make a diversion, it was
to send his step-brother Demetrius the Fair to Cyrene, to
accept the invitation of the Syrian wife of Magas, Apama,
and to secure a marriage with the still infant Berenike,
the heiress of that throne. But the jumble made by our
stray authorities, and the mass of conjectures wherewith
modern scholars have essayed to correct them and make
them consistent, forbid any clear or acceptable account of
this once so brilliant, now so obscure period.

§ 95. As regards Philadelphus we notice his modern
conception that the office of king does not include that
of military commander. He sends expeditions to
Aethiopia and to Pontus, but I do not believe the statement that he led them himself. He was a delicate and
pleasure-loving man, fond of foreign curiosities, but not
of adventures. Diodorus indeed gives him the credit
of being the first explorer of Aethiopia.[1] This statement is manifestly false, because we know that Greek·
mercenaries went up to Nubia under Psammetichus, and
they went up by the Nile. Diodorus does not seem to
know whether Philadelphus explored Nubia as well as

[1] i. 37 ἀπὸ γὰρ τῶν ἀρχαίων χρόνων ἄχρι Πτ. τοῦ Φιλ. προσαγορευ-
θέντος, οὐχ ὅπως τινες τῶν Ἑλλήνων ὑπερέβαλον εἰς Αἰθιοπίαν, ἀλλ' οὐδὲ
μέχρι τῶν ὅρων τῆς Αἰγύπτου προσανέβησαν· οὕτως ἄξενα πάντα ἦν τὰ περὶ
τοὺς τόπους καὶ παντελῶς ἐπικίνδυνα. τοῦ δὲ προειρημένου βασιλέως μεθ'
Ἑλληνικῆς δυνάμεως εἰς Αἰθιοπίαν πρώτου στρατεύσαντος ἐπεγνώσθη τὰ
κατὰ τὴν χώραν ταύτην κτλ.

Aethiopia, but the information concerning the summer rains in the Aethiopian Alps, which caused the inundation of the Nile, was probably discovered by land expeditions from the Somali coast. Strabo, too, often speaks of Philadelphus having *sent* officers to the south country to catch elephants, never of his having gone there himself. Strabo adds (xvii. 1, 5) that if old Egyptian kings like Sesostris, and Persian like Cambyses, went up to Meroe, and left monuments detailing their visit, the secret of the inundation should have been long before discovered. If Philadelphus himself had gone to Nubia, and seen there the inscriptions of ancient kings, is it likely he would have left no trace of his presence in the country? And yet we can find nothing on any monument which can be referred to him, unless it be the names of the two Cyreneans, which are inscribed on a pillar of the temple of Tothmes III. over against Wadi Halfa. There are also traces of older Greek inscriptions, and some Carian on the same temple.[1] From Ptolemy III. we have the inscription of Adule ; from Ptolemy IV., the inscriptions at Debot and Dakkeh. There is no probability that those of Philadelphus, had he cared to set them up, should have vanished. All the stories of the capture of strange beasts speak of their being brought to the king at Alexandria. I conclude, therefore, that he probably made a triumphal progress in a state barge as far as Elephantine, and visited Philae, but nothing more.

§ 96. These are the facts, or the absence of facts, which make me ascribe to Philadelphus a considerable interest in the land and produce of the far south, but not the energy to explore them personally. A like tendency to ease, and to avoid trouble, is apparent in his wars with his Mediterranean neighbours.

[1] Above, § 20. Cf. *Addit. Note* p. 490.

It is a very curious point about these conflicts that one
victory seems to settle the naval supremacy of the Aegean.
Is this our notion of a naval supremacy? How often have
the fleets of modern nations who claimed that supremacy
survived a single defeat? And yet it is not in this case
to be set down wholly to any unwarlike sloth on the part
of Philadelphus. For when the prudent and tenacious
Soter lost one great battle off Cyprus against Demetrius,
we have already seen that his naval supremacy departs,
nor does he recover it for ten years, and even then not
until his adversary's sea-power falls to pieces before a combination of his enemies. No modern historian seems to
have felt the smallest difficulty here, far less to have offered
any explanation. And yet some large causes must have
operated upon naval affairs in those days, of which the
ancients have left us no record. The scantiness of our
information is, however, such that we need not be surprised at any gap in our knowledge, even affecting so
large a question as the naval supremacy of the Eastern
Mediterranean.

If we endeavour to supply this strange deficiency by
conjecture, we shall seek it in the action of the neutral
powers who used these seas as their highway—the islands
of the Aegean, and especially Rhodes, whose cruisers kept
down the swarm of pirates which have infested the Levant
from the beginning of history till the invention of steam.
A protracted naval war meant, as we know, the flourishing
of piracy, and with it the ruin of trade. There may, therefore, have been some definite understanding between the
naval powers of that day that as the neutral lesser states
would not tolerate a protracted struggle, even the great
powers must abide by the result of one fair stand-up fight.
What would be the result if either Macedon or Egypt—

Syria had now no naval power of any account—refused to acquiesce? In the first place the Rhodians might refuse to guard the seas, since their patrols of three small cruisers might meet any day large armaments raiding the coasts, and disposed to plunder any ships they encountered. In the second place, the pirates, whom they kept in control, could at a word be let loose on the side of the victor, thus giving his fleet an enormous addition of strength, and so crippling the remaining power of the defeated side. It is doubted by historians whether Antigonus, owing to the victory of Kos, occupied Karia and Cilicia or not. Probably the meaning of the phrase is that the victor at sea controlled the pirates, whose principal homes were in the fortresses of this wild country.

§ 97. How far this reverse checked the external policy of Egypt we cannot tell. There is no clue to the date of the mission of a certain Dionysius, whom Philadelphus sent to India. The object of such a mission, which Pliny[1] alone reports to us, is easily guessed. The main route to the West still lay through Mesopotamia and Syria to the Mediterranean. Some of the wealth of the East had been tapped by the Red-Sea route, and the Canal into the Nile. But the trade from central India still came by caravan to Babylon, Thapsacus, and Antioch. If Ptolemy's ships held the Black Sea, then the old and well-known northern trade-route might also be gained to Egyptian influence. And in those days, when free trade was unknown, the control of a trade-route meant a large increase of revenue to the controlling government. I speak with hesitation of the inferences drawn from

---

[1] *HN* vi. 17, 21. Gutschmid (Sharpe p. 195) inclines to put it in the reign of Açoka, who mentions Ptolemy in his inscriptions, and therefore after 263 B.C.

Ptolemaic coins—a very intricate and unsatisfactory study. But here the conclusions of E. Revillout from the dating of demotic papyri agree with Mr. Poole's researches[1] that in the twenty-fifth year of this reign the title Soter first appears on the Phoenician coinage as a title of the first Ptolemy, whose head is reproduced throughout every reign in the series. 'It is obvious,' says Mr. Poole, 'that the issue of the [new] Phoenician coinage of the year 25 [261-0 B.C.] seems to indicate a more complete organisation of the country than does the earlier money. It may be conjectured that the king of Egypt allowed his new subjects, wrested from the Syrian dominion, some degree of autonomy, and by this commemoration coinage indicated his favour, and the final success of his father's efforts to subdue them under cover of deliverance.' For Tyre, Sidon, Joppa, Ptolemais and Gaza all put their initials on these coins.

[1] *Coins of the Ptolemies* xxv., xxxv. We now have further evidence from the Revenue Papyrus that it was the year 27, in which the earlier formula : 'In the reign of Ptolemy, son of Ptolemy, and of his son Ptolemy,' was exchanged for : 'In the reign of Ptolemy, son of Ptolemy Soter'; the former seems to have been corrected into the latter in the first lines of the Papyrus. Hence some have imagined an unknown son of Ptolemy II. and Arsinoe II., who was associated in the throne to the exclusion of Euergetes, but who died in this year. The schol. on Theocritus xvii. is express that she was childless when she was queen of Egypt, and that she also adopted the children of Arsinoe I. This together with the statement (Suidas) that Euergetes' reign began in 271, and the silence of all our authorities on this other child, make me reject such an assumption. But why was the prince royal dissociated to make room for the deified father? I am now disposed to think that he was in that year (258-7 B.C.) declared king of Cyrene upon the death of Demetrius the Fair, and that the change may have been out of compliment to the Cyreneans. If Soter was indeed not deified till this year, it explains the rest.

CHAPTER V

PTOLEMY II. (*continued*)

§ 98. THE next great event which we can approximately date is the bringing of the large Greek colony into the newly reclaimed, and therefore greatly enlarged, oasis of lake Moeris, now known as the Fayyum. The reclaiming was in process, and partly completed, in the twenty-ninth year of the king. The first problem in regard to this foundation not yet raised is this : Did the queen surrender her rights to the district during her life, or was it a bequest? The year of her death is unknown, and her deification certainly took place during her life, some years before the settlement of the re-named nome. But we also know that she died before her husband. What can we gather from the newest papyri on the subject?

In the first place we have in the Revenue Papyrus two royal rescripts[1] (262 B.C.) quoted in the ordinances of the year 27 of the king's reign, in which the ἀπομοιρα of the temples is directed to be paid to Arsinoe Philadelphus. At first one is led to suppose that she was already dead, for there is no title, no mention of her royalty, no personal expression of loyalty. She appears simply as a deity like

[1] Called προγραμματα, not προσταγματα.

Aphrodite or Demeter. But the express date of these rescripts, in the twenty-third year of the king's reign, makes it most unlikely that this was so, especially as we know she had been deified, and had a yearly *canephorus* since the year 19.[1] When we further examine the documents of the year 27, we find that in them the Arsinoite nome is not yet known by that name, but by the older appellation of *the lake*—η λιμνη.[2] This occurs in both the enumerations of the nomes in that text.[3] So then the gift of the queen, if it was such, was not yet completed at that date, and in any case she must have been alive.

§ 99. By the light of these facts we can even find further evidence in the published Petrie Papyri, which was overlooked for want of this help. There are in that collection numerous texts of the next reign, in which the Arsinoite nome is mentioned. But when we search for it in the few specimens from the reign of Philadelphus, we find that in those of the years 35 and 36 it does not chance to be required; in the two earliest texts the older name seems still in use. The date of the first,[4] which seems to be the year 28, is not quite certain, but in it the words *along the lake*—παρα την λιμνην—occur in a way that suggests a technical use. The second case[5] is far clearer. The date is quite certain, the year 29 of Philadelphus, and so is the employment of the old name—'If you do not assist us, we shall be obliged to write to Apollonius,

---

[1] This we have on the evidence of dated demotic papyri. Cf. Revillout *RE* i. 13.

[2] We have apparently found ο λιμνιτης (*sc. νομος*), col. 71. For the formula of the date cf. above, p. 155, note. It is βασιλευοντος Πτολ. του Πτολ. και του υιου Πτολεμαιου L ΚΖ according to our restoration of the gaps, changed into βασ. Πτολ. του Πτολ. σωτηρος.

[3] Cols. 31, 71.

[4] *Pet. Pap.* I. xxii. [2].   [5] II. xiii. [5].

and tell him that his farm is the only one *in the lake* not irrigated.' Here, then, we have the very phrase of the Papyrus of the year 27 repeated in a Papyrus of the year 29.

It is of course not at all out of the question that the old appellation should have been sometimes employed in familiar use, even after the official declaration of the new title.[1] People can hardly avoid making mistakes like that. But in this formal letter to the chief architect of the nome, and in this ceremonious age, such an use seems to me not likely, and I infer from it that though Kleon the Chief Commissioner of Works was already carrying out engineering plans to reclaim and to irrigate the new province, it had not yet received its new name. This then would not have been done till at least the year 30. As there are several allusions in the Petrie Papyri to an impending visit of the king to the province in (or about) the year 30,[2] it is quite likely that this visit was the very occasion when, with much solemnity, the province received its new name, and the queen was co-ordinated or identified with the local gods, as at Pithom and Mendes.

But whenever it was done, the queen, if she was not still alive, must have been lately deceased. For we can imagine the title given as a mark of respect and affection to one who had bestowed so great a gift or left such a bequest when the facts were fresh; not after some years had passed away. She was therefore probably alive in 255 B.C. and died, as we know, before 247 B.C. From the fact that the disconsolate king was planning wonderful

---

[1] From the fact that the present name Fayyum is the Coptic for *the sea*, or lake, I suppose that the old designation never went out of use among the natives.

[2] *Pet. Pap.* II. xiii. [18 a], xi. [1], and perhaps xiv. [16].

temples in her honour, which were not finished at the time of his death, we may infer that she predeceased him three or four years.

§ 100. She must have been a most remarkable woman, for though most Egyptian queens were officially deified, not one, till we reach the last, Cleopatra, ever wielded greater political influence. She took her place beside the king not only on coins, but among those statues at the entrance of the Odeum at Athens where the series of the Egyptian kings was set up. She was the only queen among them.[1] At Olympia, where there were three statues of the king, she had her place.[2] Pausanias also saw at Helicon a statue of her riding upon an ostrich in bronze.[3] It is very likely that this statue, or a *replica*, was present to the mind of Callimachus, when he spoke, in the *Coma Berenices*, of the winged horse, brother of the Aethiopian Memnon, who is the messenger of Queen Arsinoe. She is also in that poem called *Venus* and *Zephyritis*, owing to her temple on the promontory Zephyrion. But why she is called *Locris*, if indeed that be the true reading, is not explained.[4] No doubt there were many other statues of her at such places as Samothrace, where she founded a temple, at Ptolemais in Cyrene, and at Arsinoe in Aetolia, if indeed she there founded a new city.[5] It is unfortunate that we cannot com-

---

[1] Paus. i. 8, 6.   [2] Bötticher *Olympia* p. 385.   [3] ix. 31.

[4] The best commentary on Catullus' version of this once famous poem is Vahlen's article in the *Sitzber.* of the Vienna Academy for December 1888. There may be some connexion with Epizephyrian Locris in Sicily.

[5] Strabo (x. 2, 22) is quite explicit that the village of Konopa was refounded by Arsinoe Philadelphus, and I have elsewhere attempted to account for such foundations by a desire of the Egyptian king to have a city voting for him in the various leagues. But Mr. Woodhouse, in his forthcoming book on Aetolia, questions both Strabo's statement and my hypothesis. He thinks that the town

pare some of these Greek portraits of her with the purely conventional Egyptian figure already mentioned, or with her cold and dull face upon her coins. For though some of these coins, of which Mr. Poole has reproduced a large number,[1] may represent her as handsome, none of them suggests the fascination or the astuteness manifested in her eventful life.

Athenaeus[2] tells us that she was generally represented with a *rhyton*, or double horn of Amalthea, in her left hand, and quotes flattering allusions of the court poets concerning her. Her coins constantly show this emblem. Pliny[3] tells us that the disconsolate king, after her death, lent an ear to the wild scheme of an architect to build her a temple with a loadstone roof, which might sustain in mid-air an iron statuette of the deified lady, who was identified with Isis (especially at Philae) and with Aphrodite. She had an Arsinoeion over her tomb at Alexandria, another apparently in the Fayyum,[4] and probably many elsewhere. Her temple on the promontory between Alexandria and the Canopic mouth, dedicated to her by Kallikrates, where she was known as Aphrodite Zephyritis, is mentioned by Strabo, and celebrated in many epigrams.[5] He also men-

---

Arsinoe, as well as the neighbouring Lysimacheia in Boeotia, was probably founded as an outpost of his power by Lysimachus of Thrace, when this Arsinoe was his wife. Mr. Woodhouse has been kind enough to send me his criticisms, which are very well worth careful study.

[1] Cf. that at the head of this chapter.　　　　[2] xi. 97, p. 497.
[3] xxxiv. 14.　　　　[4] *Pet. Pap.* II. xi. [1].
[5] Strabo xvii. 1, 16. Athenaeus p. 318 B quotes two epigrams; a third was recently found on a papyrus in the Fayyum, which I quote from Blass' text *Rh. Mus.* vol. 35, as it is not yet in ordinary text books:—

μεσσον εγω Φαριης ακτης στοματος τε Κανωπου
εμ περιφαινομενωι κλιματι χωρον εχω

tions two towns in Aetolia and Crete, two in Cilicia, two in
Cyprus, one in Cyrene, besides those in Egypt, called after
her. She seems to us to have only wanted a Plutarch and
a Roman lover to make her into another *Cleopatra*. Even
as early as the opening of the Chremonidean War (before
265 B.C.) we find on an Attic inscription a distinct assertion of her political influence.[1] M. Homolle has found at
Delos a dedication to Arsinoe Philadelphus, Apollo, and
Artemis.[2] All over Egypt we find dedications in her
honour more numerous than to any of the queens her
successors, a clear evidence of her widespread popularity.[3]
We have no definite description of her; we have but a
single remark of hers recorded. Athenaeus reports[4] from
a book called *Arsinoe* written by the famous Eratosthenes:
that Ptolemy having established many new feasts and sacrifices, especially in honour of Dionysus, Arsinoe asked a
bearer of the olive branches what the day was and the feast.
When he answered the λαγυνοφόρια, in which they all
assemble and dine on couches upon the food they have
brought, and each man supplies his own *lagynos* of wine,
she turned to us, when he was gone, and said: 'this is
a shabby consorting together, for the company must be a

τησδε πολυρρηνου Λιβυης ανεμωδεα χηλην
την ανατεινομενην εις Ιταλον Ζεφυρον
ενθα με Καλλικρατης ιδρυσατο και βασιλισσης
ιερον Αρσινοης Κυπριδος ωνομασεν
αλλ επι την Ζεφυριτιν ακουσομενην Αφροδιτην
Ελληνων αγναι βαινετε θυγατερες
οι θ αλος εργαται ανδρες ο γαρ ναυαρχος ετευξεν
του δ ιερον παντος κυματος ευλιμενον.

[1] *CIA* ii. 332 ο τε βασιλευς Πτ. ακολουθως τει των προγονων και τε
της αδελφης προαιρεσει φανερος εστιν σπουδαζων υπερ της κοινης τω
Ελληνων ελευθεριας κτλ.   [2] *Archives de Délos* p. 59.

[3] Strack in *Mitth.* for 1894, p. 235, enumerates twelve.

[4] p. 276.

mixed crowd of all sorts, the food stale, and not decently served.' It seems that she changed the arrangement and had the feast served at her expense in private, and by private hosts. As Eratosthenes only knew the queen in her later years, the anecdote points to a contemptuous neglect on her part of the masses in Alexandria, and at the same time to a perhaps equally contemptuous liberality. The picture of her betrayal and the murder of her children by Keraunos at Cassandrea[1] does not agree with her character, such as we know it, and is probably a mere rhetorical flourish. We only know her as a woman whose early intrigues brought upon her tremendous punishment, and yet when she seemed to have played at high stakes, and to have lost everything, she recovers herself, and becomes the leading person in the most brilliant court in the world.

§ 101. The figure of Philadelphus is much clearer to us. His coins represent him (generally with Arsinoe) as of a weaker type than his father, with a strong resemblance to him, but with more regular features, and the peculiar thick neck which indicates the tendency to obesity notorious in several members of the dynasty. We also know that he was fair-haired and delicate in health. Such details very seldom reach us from this period so wretchedly recorded in extant Greek literature. We hear of him as a noble patron of science, literature, and art, as well as a man of pleasure, first shocking the sensibilities even of the loose Greeks of Alexandria by what they considered an incestuous marriage, then seeking new excitements by raising one mistress after another into public notoriety, probably for the sake of a passing fancy, or for the sake of a new experience. His philosophy was that of the Cyrenaic school, which held that

[1] Justin xxiv. 3.

to seize and enjoy the passing pleasure, the brief acme of each delight, the μονόχρονος ἡδονή, was the only thing worth living for, and the only brief, though intermittent happiness attainable.[1] We have from Phylarchus[2] a curious passage which asserts that 'though the most august of all the sovrans of the world, and highly educated, if ever there was one, he was so deceived and corrupted by unseasonable luxury, as to expect he could live for ever, and to say that he alone had discovered immortality; and yet being tortured many days by gout, when at last he got better and saw from his windows the natives on the river bank making their breakfast of common fare, and lying stretched anyhow upon the sand, he sighed: "Alas, that I was not born one of these!"'

I am not sure that Athenaeus understood or properly reported his authority, and that the king's real meaning may not have been that he alone discovered immortality (ὅτι μόνος εὕροι τὴν ἀθανασίαν) by living every hour of his life. Moreover, we know from other sources that he and his wife, probably in their later years, turned to the mysteries of the Cabeiri, which sought to still the longings of the soul with spiritual food, and with dim revelations of the unseen. We hear also from the inscriptions of Açoka, that the first great Buddhist king of India sent his missionaries with healing herbs, and with yet more healing

---

[1] Strange to say, this theory found a recent advocate, and a most sober and serious one, in the late Mr. Walter Pater, who not only held that the Epicurean attained to an *anima naturaliter Christiana*, but that our greatest vice was the formation of habits, which so shackled us that we were unfit to seize the passing pleasure as it presented itself. This doctrine he preached in an Epilogue to the first edition of his *Studies on the Renaissance*. Possibly to a mind so refined as his no theory of life was dangerous.

[2] Athenaeus p. 536 E.

doctrine to this Ptolemy, to Magas, and to Antiochus, and that they received his missionaries with courtesy.[1] Who knows then that the report of Phylarchus, which I have above interpreted in its Epicurean sense, may not have been the outburst of hope in the weary sovran, when the solemn missionaries of the remote king brought him balm for his tortured limbs, and the promise of eternal rest for his world-sick soul? We are told of the great impression the Indian ascetic philosophers had produced upon Alexander the Great and his companions.[2] Here was a new mission from this land of fable and of gold, brought by living men who promised to seekers after God eternal communion with His very essence, to the weary pessimist eternal forgetfulness.

§ 102. However this may be, the king did not discard the pleasures of the mind, and alternated the company of his mistresses with that of his philosophers, poets, and men of science. The members of the Museum, all supported by his royal bounty, and not by any independent endowment, were always ready to instruct and amuse him, and not the smallest amusement must have been the literary quarrels

---

[1] Vahlen, in discussing the probable date of this mission (Vienna *Sitzber.* for 1888, p. 1383) cites from a specialist, Oldenburg, a passage in the thirteenth chapter of Açoka's great edict 'in contrast to warlike deeds, it is the victory of right which he (Açoka) seeks above all, peace and safety among all creatures. In this the king finds his delight, both in his own kingdom and in those of his neighbours. Such are Amtiyoka the king of the Yomas (Ionians), and beyond him these four : Tulamaya, Amtikina (Antigonus), Maga, Alikasadara (Alexander of Epirus); to the south the Codas and Ceylon.'   In chapter ii. Antiochus and his neighbours are also mentioned. Of course Syria was the kingdom best known to Açoka. This edict was issued in the thirteenth year of his reign, but the date is uncertain, and may reach as far back as 258 B.C., as the beginning of the reign is not established by any comparative chronology.

[2] Arrian vii. 1-3.

which abounded in this critical and jealous society. Two of the greatest of them, Callimachus and Apollonius, were at open war,[1] and we may be sure that among the rest there were many who only met at the royal table as bitter rivals for royal favour, and ready to turn the feast into an arena, the smart repartee into the libellous retort.

A catalogue of the literary men and their work at the court of Philadelphus is the proper duty of a historian of Greek literature, and recently this thorny subject has been handled with marvellous learning and great acuteness by Susemihl. I must here content myself with giving such sketches as are needful for a picture of the times, and for an estimate of those aspects of a nation's civilisation which are reflected in literature. But we must always remember that this literature was merely that of the dominant minority; it was like the writings of Spenser, of Jer. Taylor, of Swift, of Berkeley, who composed masterpieces in English, and for the English public, in a country (Ireland) where all the lower classes spoke a wholly different language, and though they might learn enough English for daily use, were far apart from any touch of English literature. So the native Egyptians neither had the knowledge nor the inclination to approach the many Greek books written for the court at Alexandria, and for the Greek-speaking population of all the ancient world. But unlike the English writers named, whose works are still recognised as masterpieces, these Alexandrian literati, in the critical atmosphere of their Museum, lapsed into self-consciousness, captious criticism, querulous pedantry, ostentatious learning. The majority did at all events; though of course here as elsewhere, in the midst of so blasted a growth, some beautiful

[1] This famous feud has given rise to quite a literature. Cf. the account in Susemihl i. 354, and the references there given.

bloom, like the Idylls of Theocritus, or the best of the epigrams in the *Anthology*, surprises and delights us.

§ 103. The beginnings of a brilliant epoch had been manifest under Soter. As I have said already, both Museum and Library, and learned men to grace and direct them, were there before Philadelphus assumed the crown. Even the seeds of those jealousies afterwards so notorious among the court, or would-be court, poets were bearing fruit, for we note with some surprise that Philetas and Straton, the educators of Philadelphus in literature and in philosophy, did not remain at his court, but retired to Kos and to Athens, while Aratus composed his famous *Phenomena* after, and Lycophron his *Alexandra* before, their Alexandrian residence.[1]

There can be no doubt, however, that the literary and scientific policy of the second king carried on, or carried out, the ideas of the first. If there be less mathematics noticeable under Philadelphus, there is its proper consequence, the advance of mechanics under the first Ktesibios.[2] If Soter had founded the first great Library, adjoining the Museum, and close to his palace, it was one of the earliest acts of Philadelphus to appoint Zenodotus, already there and active, to the formal office of chief librarian, while he gave him for assistants or colleagues Alexander the Aetolian, to catalogue and classify the tragedies, while Lycophron undertook the comedies. Zenodotus himself was occupied, as we know, with the epic and lyric poets.

Such a step became necessary, not at the founding of

---

[1] Cf. Susemihl *sub voce.* for the details.

[2] There were two scientific men of the name. The first invented machines for artillery, and for scaling walls ; the other, who lived later, a water-organ. Susemihl i. 734.

the Library, but when it was discovered after some years' collecting that the ordering of the accumulating treasures was beyond the capacities of any one man.[1] Philadelphus even went further, and founded a second library in the Sarapieion of Rhakotis, which was called the daughter-library.[2] We do not know whether this smaller library consisted merely of duplicates, as would naturally suggest itself, or whether it was intended for the use of people dwelling in this part of the city, as Bernhardy and Susemihl suppose. I am not the least disposed to assume in any Ptolemy a regard for the education of the people beyond the precincts of the court.

At all events, this official ordering and cataloguing of the old master-pieces, which was continued with great zeal and learning by the succeeding librarian, Kallimachos (Callimachus), has been of inestimable service to every generation of Hellenists down to our own times. For these eminent men were not satisfied with mere recensions of the texts, they made grammatical and biographical studies upon the authors, and furnished later ages with almost all the safe *external* knowledge we have concerning old Greek poets and their works.

§ 104. To have accomplished so much was enough for lasting glory, but the Alexandrian scholars of this genera-tion were not of that opinion. They all were authors as well as critics,[3] but, as might well be expected, the critical tone of their minds, and those of their audiences, affected very seriously their poetic gifts. An age of science and of criticism is seldom an age of poetry, unless society be

[1] This consideration by itself should decide the question of the foundation as the work of Soter.

[2] Epiphanius, quoted by Susemihl i. 336.

[3] The first great exception was Aristarchus, who confined himself to criticism. But this was one hundred years later.

divided into lesser societies which have little mutual contact. It was not so at Alexandria, though the literary
men seemed to have used Kos as a sort of retreat, where
they could have quiet moments, far from the madding
crowd. Most unfortunately, their criticism has only
reached us at second hand, through the copies and notes
of later students. Not a single grammatical work or commentary from these pioneers has survived. But of their
poems we have a large assortment. We have Apollonius
Rhodius' elaborate epic, Aratus' didactic poem on astronomy and weather, Callimachus' pompous hymns to gods
and Ptolemies, Theocritus' idylls, bucolic, epic, comic,
the character-sketches of Herondas, and in the *Anthology*
epigrams from them and many other contemporaries, not
to speak of considerable fragments of the elegiac poetry,
then perhaps most fashionable and successful of all. There
is, in fact, hardly a generation in Greek history which has
left us so much in quantity, and which has more deeply
moulded Roman poetry, whereas its influence upon modern
literature is confined to its bucolic idylls. Of all these
writers, once so highly esteemed by themselves and others,
only Theocritus survives in himself as well as in Virgil.
Callimachus and Aratus, not to speak of the lost Philetas,
speak to us chiefly through the great Roman poets. Their
extant texts seldom appear even upon the shelves of Greek
scholars in our universities.

§ 105. The causes of this curious obsoleteness in men
so able and so famous are not far to seek. In the first
place there was no national or home flavour in this society.
They were men brought from the four winds of heaven,
and set down in the midst of a multitude of mongrel
breed and mongrel tastes. Their epics and hymns were
therefore no natural growth, but a literature of learned

and careful reproduction, to be judged by antique standards, or by the critical taste of grammarians and pedants. Moreover, the influence of the court was paramount; the favour of the king far more vital than the favour of the muse ; the royal patron must be flattered by the insistance upon agreeable topics, and the avoidance of all that might offend. The result was that these court effusions, these laudations of gods in whom the poet did not believe, these elaborations of myths that woke no response in the popular imagination, suffered the just consequences of their unreality.

If some of these poets sought to indemnify themselves by drawing life-sketches of the lower classes, they generally erred in the opposite extreme. It was only the coarse and repulsive features which seemed to them to have sufficient contrast to the lying flatteries which gave the sovran every imaginable virtue. Hence their character-poems, especially as we have them in Herondas, err in the opposite direction. If the former have idealised so absurdly as to spoil their ideal, the latter have been so realistic as to distort what was real—an error not unknown to us in the realistic schools of the present day. The only artist among them who succeeded in concealing his art, and in restraining his realism within the limits of general human sympathy, was Theocritus. In his bucolic idylls, which he framed with the uplands, the meadows, the woods of far-off and picturesque Sicily, he created a new *genre*, drawn, though remotely, from popular song, fascinating to the Alexandrian liver in dust, glare, and noise, elaborated with all the skill and care of a consummate workman.[1]

---

[1] Cf. the interesting essay of Gercke on Theocritus' genius, and his relations to his younger contemporary Callimachus, and a chronology of their works, in his *Alex. Stud., Rh. Mus.* for 1887, pp. 592-626.

§ 106. But we have no reason to think that the critical society of the Museum were of this opinion. To them the learned and versatile Callimachus, with his hymns and elegies on mythical subjects, with his myriad learned allusions, was a far greater man. The love - stories of Hermesianax, classical in form, even though one of them made the court of Nikokles of Cyprus and his daughter Arsinoe—almost contemporaries—the scene of such a domestic tragedy, were probably far more elegant and refined, in Alexandrian opinion, than the clumsy crudeness of Theocritus' Menalcas or Polyphemus. And it is with the fashion of the day that we are here mainly concerned.

§ 107. The king seems to have moved in this atmosphere of pedantry and flattery much as Louis XIV. moved in his court at Versailles.[1] There was no doubt the same eagerness in the ladies of the court to attract his favour, and though the mistresses of whom we hear were by no means noble ladies, we probably only know of those which excited scandal because they were ignoble. If he had any special scientific taste, it was for natural history, for the fauna and flora of remote lands, for the wonders of unknown countries. Of this, and of his exploring admirals, we have already spoken. What he did in collecting and producing in Greek form the learning and the literature of foreign tongues seems to have been confined to Egyptian and possibly Jewish books. He commissioned Manetho to render the history of ancient Egypt into Greek, and he may possibly have begun the publication of the sacred books of the Jews in the form now known as the LXX. The work of Manetho produced no effect upon the Greek world. It is only cited long after, by Jewish and by Christian writers, for

---

[1] Niebuhr compares him to Solomon profiting by the abilities and conquests of his father David.

controversial purposes. The question of the LXX is too vexed to detain us here, and must be postponed to a more suitable place.

§ 108. If, as Droysen supposes, the decisive Egyptian victory at Andros, which recovered the supremacy of the sea, did not take place till 245 B.C., we may assume that Philadelphus made no further wars towards the end of his life.[1] His differences with the Syrian king Antiochus II. he sought to settle by his usual policy. He offered him in marriage his daughter Berenike with a great dowry, but with the intention of obtaining further claims on Syria, and also in the hope that her children might succeed to the throne, instead of the growing boys of the first queen Laodike, who was divorced to make way for her rival. We hear of it as a special piece of Egyptian luxury,[2] that the young princess had water sent for her use from the Nile to Antioch, which was indeed 'carrying coals to Newcastle,' seeing that the clear springs of Daphne even gave to the city its distinctive name ; it was the Antioch near Daphne.[3] The significance of sending the muddy Nile water with the princess was not understood by those who recorded the fact. This water had an extraordinary reputation for fertilising whatever it touched. The whole object of marrying Ptolemy's daughter to the sickly king was to raise up Egyptian claimants to the Syrian throne. Hence this unusual precaution.

But there were other and greater obstacles in the way— the very natural hatred on the part of the discarded queen, and the weakness of the king, who seems to have gone to visit her at Ephesos, after his new queen had borne him her first child. In order to secure the succession Laodike poisoned her husband, and set her friends at Antioch or

[1] Cf. *Add. Note* pp. 490-1.   [2] Athenaeus ii. 25.   [3] Strabo xv. 1, 73.

Daphne to murder the young queen and her infant. Berenike's adherents resisted, and she was besieged at her villa or palace in Daphne, but was unable to hold out till succour should come from Egypt, and so perished miserably by the command of her rival.[1] The aged Egyptian king, aged from living too fast rather than from years, for he was now only sixty-two years old, seems to have lived to hear of this catastrophe, but not to avenge it. That duty was the first that fell to his successor.

§ 109. From this failure in external policy we turn again with pleasure to consider the details of the most permanent benefit conferred upon Egypt by this Ptolemy and his queen—I mean the extension and better irrigation of the province called the Lake, which took place, as I have shown, in the concluding years of her life. The condition of this nome has received so much illustration from recent discoveries that I may well be excused for giving it an ample space in this chapter. The problem of what and where Lake Moeris was, has occupied the learned for a long time. Mr Cope Whitehouse still insists that it filled the depression called Wadi Rayan, south of the present Fayyum. Linant Bey discovered on a far higher level than the present lake great mounds or dykes, which he concluded to have been intended to enclose a sufficient water-area along the highest eastern side of the district where the water of the Nile runs in. Major Brown and the English engineers now controlling the irrigation think this impossible, and that the present lake, with a far higher level than at present, covered most of the area now under cultivation.[2]

[1] Justin xxvii. 1.
[2] Cf. *The Fayyûm and Lake Moeris* by R. H. Brown (Stanford, 1892).

What are the causes of this great difference of opinion ? The ordinary maps do not give the reader, unless he be a trained geographer, a correct idea of the place.

§ 110. When the train leaving Wasta on the Nile has passed a long cutting in the desert, through the saddle of high ground separating the oasis of Arsinoe from the Nile valley, the traveller suddenly looks down upon a band of the richest green—orchards, gardens, farms—which extends north and south as far as the eye can reach ; from its east border he looks downward about five or six miles, till the gradual slope reaches a long very blue lake, stretched out as the western boundary of the oasis, and beyond it the amber mountains of the Libyan desert rising abruptly from its shores. The scene is one of strange and unexpected beauty, and probably the most fascinating in all Egypt. There is now little doubt that the lake at the bottom of this oasis, which lies far deeper than the level of the sea—not to say the low Nile —is fed by the same sort of supply that fertilises the other oases—a deep underground drainage from the mountains far south in Africa. But at present this lake is brackish, its banks far round the eastern shore are salt marshes,[1] not fit for cultivation, and only inhabited here and there by wild fishermen, who reap the harvest of the well-stocked water.

This lake, as it now stands, is of course useless to the irrigation of the district, except to hold surplus water sent down to it. There is no possible escape but evaporation, as it, like the Dead Sea in Palestine, is far below the level of the Mediterranean. But along the upper rim of the eastern side, the traveller coming in from Wasta finds the ample supply of the so-called Bahr Yusuf, a natural canal which leaves the

---

[1] This is the αλμυρις αφορος in the curious fragment *Pet. Pap*. 11. xxx. [6].

Nile far away south, and runs like an independent river in its own channel. As soon as it arrives over against the Fayyum, it is diverted into channels running south-west, west, north-west, in curved lines, so that on the map the district seems to have a hollow cup shape. All these various arteries amply irrigate a large area, and finally make their way, sometimes through ravines, and even by water-falls, to the lake. But yet most of the downward slope is very gradual, and the whole aspect from the desert near the Nile is, not that of a cup, but of a crescent-shaped salad-plate, deepening very gradually as it reaches the outer rim, and holding in the bottom of this curved depression the water of the lake. At present, all the water which comes in from the Bahr Yusuf is employed for the irrigation of the Fayyum, and none returns to the Nile.[1]

Such is the condition of the district, which, as I saw it in spring, is so intersected by rivulets and rivers coming round and downwards from the Bahr Yusuf, that one can only cross the country with difficulty, and either by wading pretty deep, or by making long digressions to find means of passage by bridges.

§ 111. Now the ancients who describe the place, Herodotus, Diodorus, Strabo, give a wholly different account.[2] Though the two latter speak of the great fertility of the province (which Herodotus does not), they all agree that the lake, which they describe as one of enormous size, was designed or applied not to make a fertile province here, but to hold surplus water from the

---

[1] Cf. the description in Mr. Petrie's *Illahun* p. xxx. and his map, or Major Brown's monograph.

[2] Herod. ii. 148-50; on which cf. Wiedemann's excellent Comm. pp. 524-41; Diod. i. 52; Strabo xvii. 1, § 37.

Nile, and give it back again when the inundation fell, thus irrigating middle and lower Egypt, below the point of exit (somewhere near the present Wasta). The old lake Moeris therefore, which they saw, or may have seen, must have been very much higher than the present lake.[1] Instead of being far below the level, even of the sea, it must have been above the level of the low Nile. Either therefore the lake Moeris of antiquity was an artificial lake, made at the high level, where the Bahr Yusuf enters the oasis, and separated by a large declining slope of land from the present lake, or the present lake must then have covered almost the whole of the Fayyum. The former is the French theory set forth by Linant Bey; the latter that of the English, supported in Major Brown's recent book.

Linant's great artificial reservoir would of course do the work of holding a surplus of Nile water, and returning it to the low Nile; it would satisfy the story told to Herodotus that the lake was artificial; above all it would leave a considerable amount of the present province, between the two lakes, to account for the great reputation of the nome for fertility.

§ 112. On the other hand, Major Brown insists that the engineering difficulties of such a scheme must be insuperable; not only would the area which Linant assumes cover all the richest land, especially that fertilised by the deposits of the inflowing river, but the inhabitants of the rest would be in daily danger of being swept away by a bursting of the reservoir over their heads. Into the errors

---

[1] Schweinfurt found clear evidences of the level being 40 metres higher than the present in Roman times. Mr. Petrie found similar evidences (at Dimeh) of a shore on a far higher level; so that this part of the question seems decided.

of detail as to levels and contours exposed by Major Brown, I need not enter. The French theory does not any more than the others agree with the figures given by Herodotus. The statement that the great lake was artificial is passed over in silent scorn by Strabo, who evidently thinks that it once formed part of the sea.

According to the English theory, when the income and outcome of water had been regulated by the great kings of the twelfth dynasty, it was observed that by building dykes or causeways a great deal (comparatively speaking) of land could be reclaimed along the borders of the great lake without injuring its usefulness to the rest of Egypt. Hence the huge mounds, the remains of which are still extant, were not to hold up water on the high level, but to hold it back from a certain portion of its old area. Thus the ground about the labyrinth and about Crocodilopolis would be reclaimed, and a very rich estate obtained. Major Brown suggests that by successive enterprises this operation may have been repeated, and so a considerable tract, though nothing like the present province, obtained for cultivation. Unfortunately, all the stately edifices once marking the king's palace, tomb,[1] etc. have vanished. Of the labyrinth only the site seems at last identified. Whether the pyramids and colossal figures were indeed what Herodotus describes, seems to me very doubtful. I am not even sure that he ever had seen the place. Diodorus apparently had not. Strabo who had, describes the labyrinth, and a square pyramid[2] at the corner of it; concerning the rest of Herodotus' wonders he is silent.

§ 113. What weighs very strongly against Linant and in favour of the English theory, is the total absence in all

[1] Herod. ii. 149.
[2] Apparently that of Hawara, cf. Petrie's *Hawara*, etc.

our older authorities of any allusion to two lakes, or the country between the lakes. The great lake of Moeris is always one. There is indeed in the Petrie Papyri[1] one mention of 'the little lake,' but in no case could Linant's lake be so called, and I think we may identify it with the small lake (or reservoir) in which Strabo saw the sacred crocodiles fed by his host.[2] It was small enough for the priests to run round and feed the animal at the opposite side while Strabo was looking on.

But Diodorus adds one detail which falls in very well with the action of Queen Arsinoe. He says (i. 52) that the king who made the lake gave the revenue from the fishing to his queen for her unguents and other adorn-ments, the catch of fish being worth a talent of silver per day. 'For they say that there are twenty-two kinds of fish in the lake, and so many are taken that the great number of people employed in curing them can hardly get through their work.' At the present day the govern-ment farms out this revenue.[3]

Now if we adopt Major Brown's theory, that the province was won from the great lake by successive reclaiming of shallow tracts, the history of the present reign becomes clear enough. If Arsinoe resigned her claim on part of the lake, which was her perquisite, and so gained a considerable area for cultivation, we can account for the settlement of the colony of veterans who appear in the Petrie Papyri, without forcible expulsion of the natives ; we can also account for the fact that the nome was named the Arsinoite (it had no previous name but *the lake*), while no change was made in the name of the

---

[1] *Petrie Papyri* II. [36].   [2] xvii. 1, § 38.
[3] At 50 per cent of the fish caught. Wilkinson states it to have been in his day £210 per annum. I was told that it is now £2500 (?).

chief city.   In Strabo's day indeed the latter had come
to be called Arsinoe, but in the papyri of the third
Ptolemy's reign it is uniformly Crocodilopolis, or rather
the city of the crocodiles (κροκοδίλων πόλις) in the
Arsinoite nome.

§ 114. In the nome, and in connexion with the sale
of oil, we find the names of at least fifty-five towns or
villages,[1] which implies a very considerable population.
Crocodilopolis remains the chief town of the nome, but
though called a πόλις, shows no traces of being 'settled
in the Hellenic fashion.'   Among the names of the
villages, there are many Egyptian, but the majority
have names of the Ptolemaic time, and were therefore
then first settled.[2]   That called Samaria betrays its origin
plainly enough.[3]   So too does the Ἀρσινόης χῶμα, which
is in accordance with the theory that her works of reclaiming were her main achievement in the province.   Lagis,
Berenikis, Ptolemais, Philadelphia, Philoteris, are called
after members of the royal family.   It would be strange
anywhere else, but is not so in Egypt, that such names as
Pelusium, Bubastis, Sebennytos, possibly even Memphis
seem to have been freely adopted for obscure villages in the
district.   In a country where we know that people named
two brothers in the same family by the same name, no
repetition of proper names, however confusing, need surprise us.   As regards the nationality of the settlers, we
find of course that they come from the four winds of
heaven, from Persia to Campania, from Thrace to Cyrene.

[1] *Pet. Pap.* II. xxvii. p. [98].

[2] Or re-named, which I consider most improbable.

[3] The village was known by this name down to 290 A.D., in which
a papyrus (Berlin *Urkunden* iv. 94) speaks of Σ. της και Κερκεσηφεως,
showing that an indigenous name had either survived, or had been
invented to replace it ; probably the former.

But there is distinct evidence that Macedonians were specially privileged. There was a class called κληρού-χοι, some of whom had as much as 100 arourae (hence ἑκατοντάρουροι); there was another called τῆς ἐπιγονῆς, and the two appear to be quite distinct. Wherever a Macedonian is mentioned, he appears to be of the former; I also notice that these κληροῦχοι appear to have been on the average older than the rest, from which we may even infer a double settlement, though the great engineering works of which we know seem not to have been begun till the twenty-seventh year of the king's reign.[1] Some of them certainly brought wives (who are described πατρόθεν καὶ πατρίδος) from their own homes. They must have had good schools, for they spoke and wrote correct Greek, with no admixture of Egyptian words. There is no evidence that Jews or Samaritans held land among them; those whose names occur being distinctly shopkeepers or retail traders. Neither do the μισθοφόροι, who are mentioned as a distinct class, appear to have been landowners, or to have made wills, though one παρεπίδημος does.[2]

[1] These facts are derived from a comparison of the names and ages of the κληρουχοι with the rest in the wills of the *Pet. Pap.* I. pp. [34] *sq.* That the two classes were distinct appears from entries like the following: *Pet. Pap.* II. xxxviii. (a) παρα Σωσιου του Σωσου Κρητος και Ηρακλειτου του Θοινου Απολλωνιατου των δυο της επιγονης και Σωσιβιου Μακεδονος των υπο Φυλεα τριακονταρουρου κληρουχου. In witnessing the wills we find groups of Macedonian κληρουχοι, and again groups of members of the επιγονη—they are never called επιγονοι—so that there was evidently some social distinction attached. In a demotic document published in Revillout's *Chrestom. dém.*, a man is described as an *Ionian born in Egypt.* This I take to be the meaning of the *Epigone.* Lumbroso has discussed the Greek texts on the subject, *Egitto* pp. 83 *sq.*

[2] These mercenary soldiers were occupied not only as land troops, but as guards on the river, for the Papyrus cvi. of the British Museum contains (according to my own decipherment) the following complaint to the king, probably the second Ptolemy: Αρευ[s της του] Πολεμωνος

§ 115. The Greek spoken by the colony is accordingly far superior to that of the LXX, even in its best books. At the same time there are such similarities of vocabulary as to give linguistic support to the tradition of 'Aristeas,' copied by Josephus, that among other literary enterprises Philadelphus had the Law of Moses translated by a Commission of learned Jewish elders.   In the Fayyum colony we have found early and precious fragments of Homer (of course), Plato (of the *Phaedo* and the *Laches*), Euripides (*Antiope*), scraps of collections of elegant extracts from the New Comedy, and of epigrams, as well as from several prose works, which we cannot identify.[1]   All these indications when put together prove to us that a settlement of soldiers, in these early Hellenistic days, could be a settlement of educated and cultivated people.

There must have been many more such settlements throughout the East, especially in the Syrian kingdom. We have in Josephus a threat of the third Ptolemy that if the Jews will not pay their tribute to him regularly he will seize their land and distribute it to κληροῦχοι.[2]   We even know that in the Fayyum 'prisoners from Asia' had been given land to cultivate.[3]   We might therefore take it as a specimen of such settlements, about which we hitherto have learned so few details, were it not plainly a country settlement, and not a city.   The colonists with their farms are citizens not of Crocodilopolis, but of Alexandria. They reserve for themselves houses there, and consequently the privileges granted to its inhabitants.   They bequeath

τριημιολιας μισθοφορου ερετης αδικουμαι υπο Κεφαλωνος.   σταθμοδοτηθεντος γαρ μου υπο Μοσχιωνος, Κεφαλων [made a raid] εις τον σταθμον, τα τε σκευη μου εξερριψεν εις την οδον etc., showing that there was a naval force of marines, etc. on the river.

[1] *Pet. Pap. passim.*   [2] *Antt.* xii. 4.
[3] *Pet. Pap.* II. p. [99].

these houses to their heirs; there is not a word of any
assembly, or council, or elected magistrates in the nome.
Everything is managed by crown officials.

§ 116. The number and variety of these officials
were prodigious. There is seldom a single new business
papyrus discovered that does not give us the names of new
offices. In the Revenue Papyrus we have the οἰκονόμος
always associated with an ἀντιγραφεύς, who is no mere
reporter or short-hand writer, but can act as a deputy to
the οἰκονόμος. In the Petrie Papyri this antigrapheus is
unknown. There is besides in a formal list in the same
papyrus, with the usual local officers, a class called *Libyarchs*,
apparently to manage the nome called Libya, according to
some peculiar arrangement. These had never been heard
of in this sense before, though we knew of an Arabarches
for the nome of Arabia. In the published Petrie Papyri
there is not only the ἐπιμελητής and the ἀρχιτέκτων, or
Chief Commissioner of Works, mentioned by Diodorus
(though not in such a way as to make us suspect his official
importance), but a συγγραφοφύλαξ, a δοκιμαστής, a γεωμέτρης
and a χωματοφύλαξ. There are also in the Revenue
Papyrus λογευταί and ἐπιλογευταί, ἔφοδοι (inspectors), not
to speak of the ὑπηρέται and πραγματευόμενοι under these
officials. All these are local people, even the διοικητής
must be regarded as under the control of the chief man of
the name, the Chancellor of the Exchequer at Alexandria.[1]
As was known long ago, the στρατηγός, though of military
origin, had become a purely civil officer. The chief of the
police—ἀρχιφυλακίτης—looked after the criminal classes,
if such there were. There was certainly imprisonment for

---

[1] In the papyri of the next century, even the chief financial magistrate
of the important nome about Thebes is a ὑπο-διοικητής. In the Petrie
Papyri we find no such officer, but a διοικητής. Cf. *Add. Note* p. 491.

debt, though this had been against the old Egyptian custom. The whole management of the kingdom, if we can judge from the details in this nome, was a complicated bureaucracy, leaving no political interests to any of its subjects, and exploiting all the country for the benefit of the royal exchequer.

In the Revenue Papyrus we get an insight into the method of making government profits out of the oil and wine of the country. We do not know how many other imposts there were. No mention is made in the Petrie Papyri of a poll-tax upon the natives, but then most of the papers refer not to them but to the settlers. There is, however, a salt-tax, a police-tax (φυλακιτικόν), or tax for watching the crops. There is a dyke-tax, a tax on orphans,[1] and probably the next papyrus we find will tell us of more.

Nevertheless we do not hear of any misery among the farmers, such as we hear of in the gold-mines where condemned criminals worked. The Egyptian fellah then as now was patient and uncomplaining, probably he was very hardly used, but we have no protests left, even on the part of the priesthood, that he was cruelly treated. All the revolts seem to have arisen from national or religious sentiment, not from the burden of intolerable oppression.

§ 117. I think a very instructive parallel regarding the imposts demanded by Hellenistic kings from their subjects may be found in the letters[2] which Josephus inserts into his thirteenth book of *Antiquities*,[3] where he tells of the bidding for the favour of the Jews on the part of rival claimants for the throne of Antioch. These were Alexander Bala, and Demetrius Soter, and the events happened 153-146 B.C.

---

[1] *Pet. Pap.* II. xxxix. e, f.   [2] Given in I Macc. xi.

[3] 2, §§ 2 and 3.

But though a century later, the state of things assumed
was evidently well established and normal, and Josephus
gives us the same account (substantially) in a later letter
from Demetrius' son.[1] The former letter, however, is the
most explicit. The king, desiring the support of the
Jews, says: 'I will remit you most of the taxes and
contributions (φόρους καὶ συντάξεις) which ye paid to my
predecessors and myself,' and proceeding to details: 'I
give you as a favour the value of the salt-tax and the (golden)
crowns which ye did bring to me, and my share, even
one-third of ground crops, and one-half of the fruit trees,
I surrender from to-day. Also the poll-tax paid by every
inhabitant of Judaea, and the taxes of the three toparchies
adjoining Judaea, viz. Samaria, Galilee, Peraea, I grant you
in perpetuity.' Jerusalem is to be free from tithes and taxes
(τῆς δεκάτης καὶ τῶν τελῶν), and the citadel in the hands of
the high-priest. The draught-cattle of the Jews are not
to be pressed into the post-service (ἀγγαρεύεσθαι), and the
feasts and fasts of the nation are to be respected. The
Jews are to have the *privilege* of military service, and the
king will pay and maintain up to 3000 of them, and put
them into positions of trust and honour, such as guarding
forts, and serving, as household troops. Moreover the
king offers a large sum to support the temple expenses,
and remits the 10,000 drachmae which he had received
yearly as a tax paid by those who came to sacrifice at
Jerusalem.

There is no reason to reject the statements of this
document, drawn from the very trustworthy first book of
Maccabees, and it shows us clearly what the burdens of a
Hellenistic monarchy were. Probably the Egyptians were
used even more hardly than the Jews, but these oppres-

---

[1] xiii. 4, § 9.

sions were now so traditional and well-established that they were not regarded as unjust. Within our own memory, and by a sovran who survived his deposition till 1895, the Egyptian fellahs were taxed not only as severely as the Jews under Syria, but with a high-handed injustice and cruelty probably exceeding the oppression of Lagidae or of Seleukidae.

§ 118. The whole country was not more carefully administered, as regards agriculture, than as regards trade. Philadelphus' works of irrigation, his canal into the Red Sea, have been already discussed. But not content with this sea-route to the south, he engineered a highway for caravans to cross from Berenike to Koptos (now Suakim to Kench), so that precious things from the Red Sea, and also the yield of precious stones in the Arabian desert of Egypt, might more easily reach the river. Strabo seems not very clear as to the two distinct routes, one from the nearest point of the Red Sea (Kosseir), the other much longer, and intended to evade as far as possible Red Sea navigation.[1] The king was led by disasters on the shoals, and amid the currents and storms of the Red Sea, such as the sinking of the elephant

---

[1] Strabo xvii. 1, § 42 ἐντεῦθέν ἐστιν ἰσθμὸς εἰς τὴν ἐρυθρὰν (θάλασσαν) κατὰ πόλιν Βερενίκην, ἀλίμενον μέν, τῇ δ' εὐκαιρίᾳ τοῦ ἰσθμοῦ καταγωγὰς ἐπιτηδείους ἔχουσαν. λέγεται δ' ὁ Φιλάδελφος πρῶτος στρατοπέδῳ τεμεῖν τὴν ὁδὸν ταύτην, ἄνυδρον οὖσαν, καὶ κατασκευάσαι σταθμούς, . . . τοῖς ἐμπόροις ὑδρεύματα καὶ αὔλια τοῖς καμήλοις (the text is here corrupt, and is emended according to the necessary sense), τοῦτο δὲ πρᾶξαι διὰ τὸ τὴν ἐρυθρὰν δύσπλουν εἶναι, καὶ μάλιστα τοῖς ἐκ τοῦ μυχοῦ πλωιζομένοις. ἐφάνη δὲ τῇ πείρᾳ πολὺ τὸ χρήσιμον, καὶ νῦν ὁ Ἰνδικὸς φόρτος ἅπας κ.τ.λ. ἐς Κοπτὸν φέρεται. A demotic inscription first published in vol. i. of the Revue archéol. by l'Hôte, and afterwards more correctly in Lepsius Denkmäler (vi. plate 69), is interpreted by Krall to be the dedication of statues of Philadelphus and of Arsinoe by an Egyptian named Psiamon, in the twenty-sixth year of the king's reign. This is I believe the only epigraphic evidence of the king's engineering of the road, cf. Krall Studien ii. p. 33.

transport mentioned in the Petrie Papyri,[1] to secure for himself a second route to Arabia and India. Is it not strange that at the present moment the English power in Egypt is preparing the very same duplication of routes to provide against any disaster to the Suez Canal by a railway from Kench to Kosseir?

There are not wanting in Ptolemaic and Roman times evidences of the importance of this route. On a stele at Alexandria[2] there is a record in the year 51 of the ninth Ptolemy how Soterichos of Gortyn, sent by the strategus of the Thebais for the collecting of precious stone, and to afford safety for those that carried valuable cargoes across the desert at Koptos, offers a dedication to Pan the god of successful voyages and the other gods. And again from Hadrian's time we have a record upon a stone in the Gizeh Museum found on the site of Antinoopolis, how that emperor cut a new 'Hadrian road' from Berenike to his new foundation of Antinoopolis through level and safe places along the Rea Sea, and disposed along it ample watering-places, stations, and guards.[3]

§ 119. On the other side of his kingdom Philadelphus took similar care to make the entrance to his great harbour safe and easy. By his orders Sostratos the Knidian built the great Pharos, dedicated to the Saving Gods (the king's parents), which has given its type and name to all the lighthouses in the world.[4]

---

[1] ii. p. [135].   [2] No. 2461 in the Catalogue of 1893.

[3] αυτοκρατωρ καισαρ Αδριανος (I omit a series of titles) οδον καινην Αδριανην απο Βερενικης εις Αντινοου δια τοπων ασφαλων και ομαλων παρα την ερυθραν θαλασσαν υδρευμασιν αφθονοις και σταθμοις και φρουριοις διειλημμενην ετεμεν ετους ΚΑ φαμενωθ Α.

[4] The epigram of Posidippus found a few years ago on a papyrus of the second century B.C. is worth quoting:—

Ελληνων σωτηρα Φαρου σκοπον, ω ανα Πρωτευ,
Σωστρατος εστησεν Δεξιφανους Κνιδιος

In the most recent and perhaps the most brilliant sketch of these times—that of Holm—this king as well as his successors are set down as mere men of pleasure, if not bloodthirsty miscreants, who did no service to Egypt or to the world except by accident, and in pursuit of purely selfish or passionate pleasure. That the kings of that day were men of pleasure is clear enough; that they were also enlightened men, to whom the civilisation of their kingdoms was no less distinctly an object than material wealth, is so plainly shown by the facts, that it requires a man of theory to avoid seeing it. There are indeed few kings, Hellenistic or other, who have left more enduring evidences of useful administration to posterity than the second Ptolemy. But we must resume our history.

§ 120. We know very little indeed about the later years of Magas, which seem to have been peaceable enough, after his quarrel with Philadelphus had been settled. Nor is even the chronology of his fifty years' reign very certain.[1]   It was either in direct connexion with the now mysterious and unintelligible second Syrian war, or in prosecution of the general policy which governed

ου γαρ εν Αιγυπτωι σκοποι ου ριον οι' επι νησων
αλλα χαμαι χηλη ναυλοχος εκτεταται,
του χαριν ευθειαν τε και ορθιαν αιθερα τεμνων
πυργος οδ' απλατων φαινετ απο σταδιων
ηματι, παννυχιος δε θεων συν κυματι ναυτης
οψεται εκ κορυφης πυρ μεγα καιομενον
και κεν επ αυτου δραμοι Ταυρος κερας ουδ αν αμαρτοι
σωτηρος, Πρωτευ, Ζηνος ο τηλε πλεων.

I give the text as established by Bergk and Blass in vol. 35 of the *Rhein. Museum.*   The name Pharos was old.   Thucydides speaks (i. 104) of Inaros beginning his insurrection from Marea above the city Pharos (459 B.C.)

[1] Gercke (*Alex. Studien* in *Rh. Mus.* for 1887, p. 266) thinks that he cannot have died till shortly before Philadelphus, not earlier than 251, so that the affair of Demetrius and the marriage of Berenike would all

all the rival Hellenistic kingdoms—to keep their neighbours occupied with domestic disturbances—that Antigonus of Macedon, when Magas was dead, sent his own half-brother Demetrius the Fair[1] as an aspirant to the throne of Cyrene, to charm by his presence the heart of Berenike, the growing child of Magas, who had been betrothed to the prince of Egypt. The plot showed a fair chance of success, had not the charms of Demetrius proved too strong for the queen-mother of Cyrene, the Syrian Apama. We are told that the young princess discovered the intrigue, and with a courage beyond her sex and her years had Demetrius put to death in her mother's chamber, and hastened her own marriage to the son of Philadelphus.

Our authorities upon this transaction are singularly untrustworthy. Eusebius[2] says that Demetrius had already obtained royal power over all Libya and Cyrene; we have a highly rhetorical passage in Justin[3] on the catastrophe; we have the encomium of Theocritus on Philadelphus, in which Droysen seeks to discover several allusions to it, and Catullus' translation of the hymn (*Coma Berenices*) which the court-poet Callimachus wrote in honour of the rising queen. Such evidence is very unsatisfactory to

be crowded inside two years, and this agrees with the first view of the facts we take, for a delay of nine years between the death of Magas and the marriage of Berenike seems strange. Nevertheless Vahlen, in his discussion of the *Coma Berenices*, as we have it in Catullus, holds fast to the older view that Magas reigned 308-258 B.C., while it is certain that Berenike was a bride in 247 B.C. If then the poet says he knew her pluck from her youth, she was a mere child, say six or seven years old, when Demetrius came to Cyrene; had she been older, why was her marriage with the crown prince of Egypt delayed for nine years?

[1] Justin (xxvi. 3), who calls the widow of Magas Arsinoe, says that she sent for Demetrius, in order to break off the Egyptian marriage of her daughter, which had been forced upon her.

[2] *Arm.* vi. p. 237.   [3] xxvi. 3.

the historian.   It has been inferred that the crisis in Cyrene
took place about 250 B.C., and that the princess Berenike
was then not fourteen years old, as she would not otherwise have delayed her marriage, and according to Callimachus she was the bride of Ptolemy in 247 B.C., the year
of Philadelphus' death.[1]

§ 121. Almost contemporary with this attempt of
Antigonus to unsettle the relations of Egypt and Cyrene,
came the momentous freeing of Greek cities from their
tyrants, begun by the murder of the respectable and able
Aristodemus of Megalopolis by two philosophic enthu-
siasts, the pupils of Arcesilaus.   One of them, Ekdemos,
was the confidant of Aratus, whose liberation of his native
Sikyon is the most picturesque page in all Plutarch's very
picturesque writings.   But this Aratus was no philosophic
theorist; he was a rich young man (though an exile at
Argos), an athlete and a judge of pictures, who loved
royal courts on a large scale, and was the great friend of
both Antigonus and Ptolemy.

He wished, however, to be restored to his native Sikyon,
and Plutarch says he sought this end through the influence
of Antigonus or of Ptolemy.   Antigonus made him promises—of course he did, he was a hereditary guest-
friend; but he took care not to fulfil them; for restoring
Aratus meant upsetting the reigning tyrant of Sikyon, and
we know it was the policy of Antigonus rather to plant
tyrants than to root them up.   He could manage a single
ruler far more easily than a turbulent popular assembly.

---

[1] It is worth noticing that the language of this hymn, as well as the
solitary anecdote told above of Arsinoe Philadelphus (§ 100), indicate
a sort of familiarity between the Ptolemies and their subjects quite
foreign to old Egyptian or Oriental etiquette.   This is a Hellenistic
feature, coming down by tradition from the Macedonian and military
habits of Alexander's household and court.   Cf. *Add. Note* p. 491.

Ptolemy's tardiness may be accounted for quite as easily. He was never a man to play a bold game; he found it safer to watch events, and spend his money to aid success already partly assured. If the overthrow of a tyrant was set before him as a desirable object, his sympathies were probably against it, nor would he favour democracies even for the purpose of weakening rival kings. We may be sure that he told Aratus he would give him ample help as soon as he had struck the blow, and shown that there was something in the game. Therefore although Aratus pretended in his *Memoirs* that he undertook the liberation of his city quite independently, subsequent events show that he had a distinct prospect of subsidies from Philadelphus. For he had courted the king's favour long since by 'picking up' paintings for him in Greece, especially those of the fashionable Pamphilos and Melanthos, and sending them to Egypt. Aratus professed to be a judge and a critic, but the anecdote which Plutarch adds about his long hesitation whether he could tolerate in the liberated Sikyon a portrait of Aristratos, a long-departed tyrant, standing by his chariot, though it was partly the work of Apelles, shows what he knew about art. He, as a great concession, allowed the chariot and horses to remain, with the figure painted out, and a palm tree replacing it. Under the chariot, the tyrant's feet were left by mistake![1] How generally unscrupulous Aratus and his friends were appears from his hiring men, from bandit chiefs who roamed the country, and moreover passing off his preparations as intended for a raid to steal mares from the royal domains at Sikyon[2]— I presume those owned or rented by Antigonus.

---

[1] These anecdotes show how Alexandria collected its art-treasures.
[2] Plutarch *Aratus* 6, 13.

§ 122. No sooner had Aratus succeeded, and persuaded his city to join the Achaean League, than Philadelphus sent him a present of twenty-five talents, which he applied to public purposes at Sikyon, thus strengthening his position, and founding his popularity. But then came the great difficulty of providing for the restored exiles, some of whom had been many years dispossessed, and of disturbing the owners who had taken up the vacant houses or lands by purchase. We are most fortunate in having an ancient instance of this perpetually recurring difficulty brought before us, with its solution, in the life of Aratus. We have had the same sort of thing discussed recently in the British Parliament under the title of the Irish Evicted Tenants Restitution Bill.

In Aratus' case at Sikyon it was settled in the only way it ever can be honestly settled, by finding a large foreign fund of money wherewith to pay off the actual owners, or bribe off the claims of the old ones.[1] But Aratus was obliged to set sail for Egypt himself, now a dangerous expedition, seeing that Ptolemy no longer swayed the sea. A storm drove him to Andros, where he narrowly escaped the Macedonian Governor, who seems to have had orders to arrest him. Then he has the luck to find a Roman ship, therefore neutral, going to Syria, which lands him on the coast of Caria, which we may therefore assume was now (250 B.C.) Egyptian. At last he reaches Alexandria, and obtains 150 talents as a royal gift, of which he brings home forty himself, while the rest follows.[2]

[1] The facts are well stated by Cicero *de off.* ii. 24.

[2] I do not understand Plutarch's words (c. 13 *sub fin.*) τὰ δὲ λοιπὰ διελὼν εἰς δόσεις ὁ βασιλεὺς ὕστερον κατὰ μέρος ἀπέστειλεν, for it was all a gift. Either this must be the medical meaning of δόσις, our *dose*, or it may be εἰς δ' δόσεις, into four donations, one δ having dropped out.

§ 123. Aratus must have found the king aged and failing, and very probably did not form a favourable judgment of any future chances of Egyptian money, for he began to make overtures to Antigonus Gonatas, so much so that he was in danger of falling between two stools, as the flatterers of each king hastened to proclaim the waverings in the loyalty of Aratus. On this point Plutarch quotes a curious remark of Antigonus, made, he says, with a view of discrediting the Sikyonian hero.[1] 'I thought this youth was merely frank in spirit, and patriotic, but now he seems to me a competent critic of the lives and affairs of kings. For formerly he despised me, looking abroad in his hopes, through admiration of the Egyptian wealth, hearing of elephants and processions and palaces ; but now having seen behind the curtain that the whole business there is tragic pomp and scenic effect, he has come over body and bones to us. I accept the youth and am minded to make him generally useful, and desire you to consider him a friend.' This was said at a feast held in Corinth.

The position therefore of the rival sovrans in general was clear enough. In each kingdom it was the Greek spirit of independence, perhaps of mere turbulence, which neighbouring kings utilised. While Ptolemy is manœuvring to loosen the hold of Macedonia upon the cities of Hellas, Antigonus is manœuvring to loosen the hold of Egypt on Cyrene, its only purely Greek dependency. And we may assume that both powers attempted a similar policy with Syria, and were met by counter-moves of the same kind. Indeed the Syrian Queen of Magas is directly credited with the disturbance at Cyrene.

But all this generation of the Diadochi were now growing old and passing from the stage. Ptolemy died in 247 B.C.,

---

[1] *Aratus* c. 15.

his neighbour Antiochus Theos, evidently a broken-down though not an elderly man, being poisoned in the same year by Laodike.[1] Antigonus Gonatas lasted till 239 B.C. but was already over seventy, and fully occupied with the complicated interests of the Leagues, the cities, the tyrants in Greece.

It was the crisis in the royal house of Syria that stirred up the eastern world, and gave rise to a series of events of vast importance in the history of the Ptolemies.

[1] Clinton sets down his whole life at forty years. But there are reports that he was a drunkard (Athenaeus x. p. 438, and Aelian *VH* ii. 41), and so may have aged prematurely. Upon his character, cf. Droysen iii. 310.

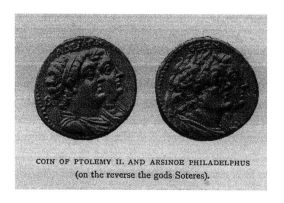

COIN OF PTOLEMY II. AND ARSINOE PHILADELPHUS
(on the reverse the gods Soteres).

CHAPTER VI

§ 124. WHEN Ptolemy III. succeeded to the throne, at his father's death, he was a man in the prime of life, probably between thirty-three and thirty-six years of age, so that we are surprised not to hear of any earlier marriage than that with the youthful Berenike, which took place close to the time of his accession. He had long been associated[1] in public acts with his father's name, and in the years immediately preceding his accession may have managed a considerable part of the royal administration by controlling the affairs of Cyrene. But strange to

PTOLEMY III.

say, I am not aware that we hear one trait of his character during all his youth at the most public court in the world. The statement that he was called *Tryphon*[2] is no evidence whatever of luxurious habits. Even upon his love affairs, if he had any, the poets and epigrammatists

---

[1] Assuming that Arsinoe II. had no child by Philadelphus.

[2] Eusebius *Armen.* i. p. 251, whose evidence I here disbelieve.

are silent; he never seems to have commanded armies or
fleets for his father, beyond perhaps proceeding on the part
of Egypt to occupy Cyrene as king after the murder of
Demetrius the Fair.   What was he doing during the first
thirty years of his life?   Can we imagine that the activity
he showed immediately upon his accession to power was
the outburst of his pent-up energy, and that hitherto he had
been compelled to do nothing?   Yet in all the gossip about
Philadelphus' court, and there is not a little surviving—in
the panegyrics upon his father, in the anecdotes of the
learned in the Museum and Library, there is a strange
silence concerning him.

   This will give the reader some idea of the scantiness of
our miserable sources when we attempt to write a human
history of Egypt, and draw a living picture of the men who
swayed this wealthy kingdom so long.   This third king is
perhaps the most enigmatic figure in all the series.   He
shows strange fits of activity and sloth, of greatness and
insignificance.   He dies at no advanced age, and yet his
vigour is gone, and he seems like an old and worn-out
man.   How shall we account for all these anomalies?
When shall we unearth some anecdotist in that age of
anecdotes, who will give some life and colour to this
shadowy outline, as unmeaning as the representations of
him which we see on his Egyptian temples?   The very last
and newest fragment upon his great war does not tell us one
word about the king himself, or what personal part he took
in a campaign that was only exceeded in importance by
those of Alexander.   Of all the Ptolemies he is the only great
conqueror, and yet at the moment of victory he seems to surrender his conquests, and abandon the fruits of all his labour.

   § 125. I can only suggest two considerations, mutually
consistent, to account for this strange silence concerning

the early life of the third Ptolemy. We know that he was
nominally regent with his father. That fact the Petrie
and Revenue Papyri have shown us in plain Greek.[1]
But at the same time the persistent mention of his step-
mother in every public act, her great importance in the
state, show that she asserted to the utmost her rights as
queen. The young prince may have been regarded by
her with some jealousy, so that he, and his father also,
may have thought it both safe for his life, and for the
peace of the house, to keep him away from Alexandria.
The Adulitan inscription comes to our help, for it speaks
of the Aethiopic and Trogodyte elephants which he and
his father had procured there, as accompanying him in
his first campaign into Asia. He may have been occupied
in these adventures during Philadelphus' life, after he was
grown to man's estate. It was an old tradition with the

---

[1] Cf. on this question Krall *Studien* ii. 23, who states and criticises the
theory of Revillout, and the refutation of it by Wiedemann, as to the
import of the formula βασιλευοντος Πτολ. του Πτολ. και του υιου Πτολ.
It certainly refers to Ptolemy II. and his son, and occurs in demotic
papyri of his years 19, 21, 24, besides its occurrence in Greek (*Petrie
Papyri* II. xxvi. and in the Revenue Papyrus) in 27. Strange to say it
occurs twice in the latter document, in one case corrected into βασιλ. Πτολ.
του σωτηρος, or του Πτολ. σωτηρος, and this latter is the only one found
in the Petrie Papyri of years 33 and 36. We also know that from the
year 25 onward, the Phoenician cities under the influence of Egypt coined
with the head of Ptolemy I. and his title σωτηρ. Thus it would seem
that about the year 27 the former formula was replaced by the latter.
The earlier occurrence (demotic) of Ptolemy and his son Ptolemy is
understood by Krall and Wilcken to refer to an otherwise unknown son
of Ptolemy and Arsinoe II., and that it was only some years after his death
that Euergetes was so associated. But this, a pure hypothesis, does not
account for the change so late in Philadelphus' reign, when Euergetes
was older and more clearly the heir. I hold that this του υιου Πτολ.
always means Euergetes, and account for its disappearance from the
formula by his mission to Cyrene, where he became king for nine years.
Hence he omits it (below, p. 199, note 3) from his *inheritances*.

Pharaohs that the heir-apparent should be prince of Kush ;
this may even have suggested a practical resumption of the
title, though I can show no epigraphic support for it.
'The generals whom Philadelphus sent' to far Aethiopia
are often named, never the royal prince. I take this to refer
to the first explorations. The very fact of the marble throne
and inscription being found at Adule indicates that the new
king had some special interest in that remote province.

§ 126. The events of his opening reign, so far as we know
them, are as follows : whether Philadelphus lived long enough
to hear of the murder of his daughter, the young Queen of
Syria, is uncertain. The first act of the new reign, was that
Ptolemy III., recently married to the Cyrenean Berenike,[1]
started in great haste, possibly to save his sister's life—for she
seems to have been besieged in her palace at Daphne for some
short time—at all events, to avenge her death, and restore the
Egyptian influence in Syria. It was on this occasion that
his bride dedicated the lock of hair which has been im-
mortalised in the *Coma Berenices* of our heavens.[2] The elder
Syrian queen, Laodike, who was either the sister of Antiochus
II., her husband, whom she had just murdered, or the sister
of Achaeus a grandee in Asia Minor,[3] had evidently her
stronghold at Sardis, or at Ephesus. Having obtained the
murder of her rival by means of her own adherents in
Antioch, she of course proclaimed her elder son Seleukos,

[1] Cf. *Addit. Note* p. 491.

[2] Cf. Catullus' well-known poem and the Comm. for the details. A
courtier, however, might call her a bride long after her marriage.

[3] This question has been much discussed. Cf. the inscription in which
the king speaks of her as his 'sister' in *BCH* 1885, p. 326, and the
commentary there of MM. Paris and Holleaux. A priestess is mentioned
in that text called Berenike, daughter of Ptolemy son of Lysimachus,
and said to be the king's συγγενής. But perhaps this too was but a title.
I incline to think that Laodike was sister of Achaeus, and not of the
king. Cf. C. Müller's note, *FHG* iii. 707.

now a growing lad, king, and was preparing to return from
Ephesos with an armament, to place him on the throne
of Antioch.[1] But an Egyptian fleet intervened, occupied
the Cilician cities, secured the passes, and ultimately
sailed for Seleukeia on the Orontes, the port of Antioch,
where the adherents of the Egyptian queen had meanwhile
overcome their at first successful opponents, and were
able to open both the great harbour fortress of Seleukeia,
and the gates of Antioch, to the invading Egyptians.
The king seems not to have taken part in this campaign,
but must have led his army by land through Palestine, so
as to reinforce his fleet, and secure its successes. The
prompt action of the fleet had cut off Laodike and her
adherents from the Syrian capital, and her delay in
advancing from Ephesos seems to have been caused by
loss of time in gathering treasure from the hill fortresses in
Caria and Cilicia (where the Syrian kings were wont to
keep reserve funds for war), and in organising with this
money an adequate army.

§ 127. These opening events in the great campaign
called the Third Syrian War have only quite recently come
to light from fragments of a report by a soldier in the
fleet, found among the Petrie Papyri. They tell us how
the king of Egypt got the capital of his enemies into
his hands, apparently without a struggle. Concerning the
interpretation of the fragments, there is but one great
difficulty, which is that all the place-names occurring in it
are to be found not only in Syria, but in Cilicia. There
was an Antioch, a Seleukeia, even a fort Poseidion in each.
Thus the stupid Hellenistic habit of repeating a few names

---

[1] Cf. all the details and citations in Droysen iii. 378. According
to Justin the young king was proclaimed at Antioch, and it was he that
ordered the murder of his stepmother.

everywhere, as if their imagination was unable to compass a larger variety, has left us in some doubt whether the whole of this campaign, so far as the fragments go, may not have taken place on the Cilician coast. But the balance of opinion, to which I subscribe, is in favour of the interpretation I have given.[1]

The abstract in Justin,[2] though vague and inaccurate, points to some of the facts in this contemporary record, when he says that many states (does he mean satrapies or free Greek towns?) being outraged at the cruelty of Berenike's murder, declared for Ptolemy. The anecdotes told of the murders perpetrated by Laodike at Ephesus corroborate the report of her harsh character.[3]

Meanwhile she was powerless, while the King of Egypt took possession of the capital, and advanced into the

---

[1] Cf. *Petrie Papyri* II. xlv. with the autotype plates of the text printed in the appendix of 1894. Von Wilamowitz-Möllendorff has pointed out to me, in connexion with the new sketch-map of the Cilician coast published by Heberden (Vienna, 1890) that all the facts can fit themselves to the places in this district. U. Köhler (Berlin *Sitzber.* for 1894), in a very able and learned article, has corrected some of my mistakes, and got over the difficulty which I felt, that the Syrian Poseidion was out of the direct line from Cilicia to Antioch (it lies two hours' sail *south* of the mouth of the Orontes) by assuming that the writer was the admiral commanding the main fleet at Salamis in Cyprus, and that upon news of the successes at Soli and probably Tarsus, he set sail with the main fleet, stopping at Poseidion, in order to run into Seleukeia on the Orontes by daylight. U. Wilcken agrees that the fleet started not from Cilicia, but from Cyprus, and that there is a break in the middle of the narrative. The real obstacle in the way of the prevailing interpretation is that it requires two Seleukeias, that in Cilicia, and that in Syria to be mentioned, without further specification. Even among people who habitually used ambiguous names, this seems not a little remarkable, and is the mainstay of Wilamowitz' view. The text can now be read in Köhler's article as well as in my original publication.

[2] xxvii. 1.

[3] Athenaeus xiii. p. 593.

eastern provinces, occupying Babylon, and even Persia and Susiana, as far as the new kingdom of Bactria.

§ 128. Unfortunately the limits of his conquests are only known to us from the panegyrical inscription found in the fifth century by the monk Cosmas (Indicopleustes) on a marble throne at Adule, far down the African coast of the Red Sea. The monk copied what he saw faithfully— that we can tell at once from the formulae, the style, the tenor of the document [1]—but did the composers of it show the same fidelity?

In the first place the pedigree of the king from the Greek gods is set down, as it was under his successor by Satyrus,[2] and then his conquests are enumerated. We may feel somewhat more confidence in an official Greek enumeration than if it had been in hieroglyphics, as a mere senseless copying of earlier texts would hardly have been permitted by the Macedonian officials, who could read and understand it. Nor have we any proof that direct falsehoods ·have been told in it.[3] Nay, rather, we have direct confirmation

---

[1] There were really two, which Cosmas thought were parts of the same text, whereas the latter passage, in the first person, is from a different king, and probably of much later date. It is in this portion that the year 27 is mentioned, which long puzzled historians as regards the reign of Euergetes, which certainly did not exceed twenty-five years. But the date does not concern Euergetes, as is made clear by the Commentary in Boeckh's *CIG* iii. 5127.

[2] Müller *FHG* iii. 165.

[3] The text of the inscription is as follows (*CIG* 5127):—

Βασιλευς μεγας Πτολεμαιος, υιος βασιλεως Πτ. και βασιλισσης Αρσινοης, θεων αδελφων, των βασιλεων Πτ. και βασιλισσης Βερενικης, θεων Σωτηρων, απογονος τα μεν απο πατρος Ηρακλεους του Διος, τα δε απο μητρος Διονυσου του Διος, παραλαβων παρα του πατρος την βασιλειαν Αιγυπτου και Λιβυης και Συριας και Φοινικης και Κυπρου και Λυκιας και Καριας και των Κυκλαδων νησων εξεστρατευσεν εις την Ασιαν μετα δυναμεων πεζικων και ιππικων και ναυτικου στολου και ελεφαντων Τρωγλοδυτικων και Αιθιοπικων ους ο τε πατηρ αυτου και αυτος πρωτος εκ των χωρων τουτων εθηρευσαν και

from S. Jerome's very capable Commentary on Daniel (xi. 8), *in tantum ut Syriam caperet et Ciliciam, superioresque partes trans Euphratem, et propemodum universam Asiam. cumque audisset in Aegypto seditionem moveri, diripiens regnum Seleuci* 40,000 *talenta argenti etc. et simulacra deorum* 2,500 *tulit.* Lepsius [1] cites from Rosellini the list of conquered nations, which that scholar saw and copied on the (now destroyed) small temple of Esneh, and among them Persians, Susians, Thracians, and Macedonians are enumerated. So all our evidence seems too consistent to be false. Yet what we desire to know is not what Euergetes conquered, but what he refrained from conquering, and what he ceded to the young Seleukos. We should have expected that an Egyptian aggressor would rather turn westwards from Antioch, as the inscription declares, and lay hold of Asia Minor, than turn, as I believe he did, eastward, and occupy the trans-Euphratesian provinces, far from the sea, and difficult of access for his government. Here we are told he left as satrap of Persia Xanthippus, apparently the famous mercenary general who had just defeated Regulus and his victorious Roman army at Carthage.[2]

καταγαγοντες εις Αιγυπτον κατεσκευασαν προς την πολεμικην χρειαν. κυριευσας δε της τε εντος Ευφρατου χωρας πασης και Κιλικιας και Παμφυλιας και Ιωνιας και του Ελλησποντου και Θρακης και των δυναμεων των εν ταις χωραις ταυταις πασων και ελεφαντων Ινδικων και τους μοναρχους τους εν τοις τοποις παντας υπηκοους καταστησας διεβη τον Ευφρατην ποταμον, και την Μεσοποταμιαν και Βαβυλωνιαν και Σουσιανην και Περσιδα και Μηδιαν και την λοιπην πασαν εως Βακτριανης υφ εαυτωι ποιησαμενος και αναζητησας οσα υπο των Περσων ιερα εξ Αιγυπτου εξηχθη και ανακομισας μετα της αλλης γαζης της απο των τοπων εις Αιγυπτον δυναμεις απεστειλεν δια των ορυχθεντων ποταμων.   Here it breaks off.

[1] *Dekret von Kanopus* p. 5.

[2] S. Jerome *ad Dan.* xi. 8, and Droysen's note, iii. (1) 384. Jerome constantly cites Porphyry as his authority, but consulted many others (*Pref.* in Dan. *sub fin.*)

I suppose the solution is to be found in the attitude of Rhodes and the Greek cities of Asia Minor, for whom the only practical foreign policy was to preserve the balance of power between the great kingdoms. We may assume that they all promised him sympathy and aid if he would conquer in the East; opposition if he attempted to add Asia Minor to his kingdom. Indeed we hear that even so when he came to attack Ephesus, the Rhodians fought against him.[1] We now know from a Samothracian inscription published by Kern,[2] that in accordance with the statements of Plutarch and Teles, a Spartan grandee, Hippomedon, son of Agesilaos, escaped. with difficulty from the fate of the revolutionary leaders, and took his father with him to Egypt. Teles mentions him in his tract *on Exile*, as being one of the fugitives, like Chremonides, who had been promoted to honour by King Ptolemy—Hippomedon by being appointed military governor of Thrace. He earned the gratitude of the Samothracians by honouring their mysteries, by paying up arrears due to local troops, by restoring and completing the fortifications on the island, which were necessary owing to the attacks of pirates.

§ 129. Historians have not brought the alleged victory at Andros, placed in 247 B.C., into close enough connexion with this matter.[3] If by this victory Euergetes (or his father) crushed the naval power of Antigonus in the Aegean, and recovered the presidency of the island confederation, it was

---

[1] Teles in Stob. *Flor.* ii. p. 72.

[2] *Mitth.* for 1893, p. 348, revised and improved by Fränkel *ibid.* for 1894, p. 133. Here are the most important parts of this text : επειδη [Ιππομεδων] Αγησιλαου Λακεδαι[μονιος ο καταστασθεις υπο τ]ου βασιλεως Πτολεμαιου σ[τρ]ατ[ηγος του Ελ]λησποντου και των επι Θραικης τοπων ε[υσεβω]s διακειμενος προς τους θεους, etc., etc. ακο]λουθα πραττων τηι του βασιλεως αιρεσει, etc. Honours are granted by the civic authorities to him, and sacrifices for the king and queen.   [3] Above, § 93.

still more pressing for the lesser powers—Rhodes, Pergamum, Byzantium, and the Pontic cities, to act vigorously on
behalf of the Syrian heirs to the throne, and prevent the
Levant from becoming an Egyptian lake.[1] On the other
hand the presence of a strong Egyptian army in the East
would put a limit to the invasion of oriental forces, which
were now seriously limiting Hellenism in the far East. It
is true indeed that the Bactrian kingdom was professedly
Greek, that even the Arsacids came to adopt Hellenistic
fashions, but all historians have justly regarded the rise of
the latter Empire as a reaction of the East against the
conquering West.

These may have been the circumstances which set
the Greeks of Asia Minor against Egyptian supremacy
in the Aegean, and in favour of its extension to the East.
Ptolemy seems to have left Xanthippus to do as he pleased
in the far East; he seems to have given the control of
Cilicia to one Antiochus, probably no other than Hierax,
the younger brother of Seleukos, who presently endeavoured
to oust his brother from the succession, and waged a long
war with him in Asia Minor.

§ 130. The Syrian kingdom seemed hopelessly dislocated.
Seleukos Kallinikos, though able to regain his kingdom so
far as to found Kallinikon beyond the Euphrates in 242 B.C.,
naming it after his own title, and to add a new quarter
to his capital, did nothing that we now know worthy
of that name. He lived all his life in struggles with the
Galatians, with his brother Hierax, and with Hellenic
cities which humoured the various pretendants, so as to

[1] Cf. Droysen's *Hellenismus* iii. 419 *sq*. Thus the Telmessians
(Lycia) thank a Ptolemy, son of Lysimachus, for reducing the heavy
taxes charged by Ptolemy II. when their city had been wasted with
war. This man had apparently got the town *in gift* from the king.
The date is $L7$ of Ptolemy III. Cf. *BCH* xiv. 162.

preserve for themselves a considerable amount of independence. Holm compares the Asia Minor of that day to the Germany of the Thirty Years' War. Happily we have no need to tell of these vicissitudes, nor to add to the various hypotheses by which learned men have endeavoured to set in order our vague and sometimes absurd sources.

As regards Greece, both Athens and the Achaean League preferred Ptolemy as a dominant ally to the nearer and therefore more dangerous king of Macedon, and accordingly Aratus, shortly after his capture of Corinth, appointed the King of Egypt Generalissimo of the Achaean League by land and sea.[1] Thus the whole external condition of the Hellenistic world was eminently favourable to Egypt. The established alliance of Egypt with Rome made it of little importance that Seleukos sent there to ask for alliance and support, and that the Romans answered him in a Greek letter assuring him their alliance provided he left the cradle of their race—Ilium—in peace and independence.[2] It must have afforded the Hellenistic world a moment's amusement, perhaps a moment's pride, but no more.

§ 131. Nevertheless we are told (by Justin and by S. Jerome) that Ptolemy was recalled from Asia by *domestic revolution*. This strange and enigmatical statement has been referred by Droysen[3] to the spiritual commotion excited by the theorists Eudemos and Ekphantides who had put down tyrants in Greece, and went to preach their inflammatory doctrine at Cyrene. The passage which he

---

[1] Plutarch *Aratus* 24.

[2] Suetonius *Claudius* 25. On the other hand Eutropius iii. 1 says the Romans offered help to Ptolemy against Syria, which he did not accept as the war was over. This was *finito bello Punico*, therefore about 240 or 239. But Eutropius calls the Syrian king Antiochus, which must be wrong.   [3] iii. 402.

quotes from Polybius [1] only speaks of them as arranging the laws of that city.   It seems to me certain that our authorities meant something quite different.   They are pointing to the first of those home disturbances which marked the reigns of almost every Ptolemy who succeeded Euergetes. I suppose that the priests were discovering the difference between a direct property in the taxes, and a subsidy from the king.   The people also may have found the burdens of a foreign war very great, and producing no advantage. For we know that this king brought a number of prisoners home with him, to some of whom he gave farms, or at least made them tenants, while the prisons seem occupied by others who cannot be malefactors [2] from the home population.   I think a careful study of the passage in the Canopus decree [3] referring to the sudden danger of a famine, and the prompt measures taken by the king and queen to obviate it, will persuade the reader that this was also the moment of the domestic disturbance.   Had there been a civil war, it is probable that there would have been some direct mention of it, as we find is the case in the very analogous Rosetta inscription.   But there seems to have been a refusal to pay taxes, and a large remission of them by the king, in addition to the importation of corn from provinces which were under his control, though the corn was paid for.   But mark the consequence : it is on account of this that the gods have given him (l. 20) *well-established monarchy*.   Probably the domestic complaint was that a king employed in foreign conquests did not protect the

[1] x. 25, 3.
[2] Cp. *Pet. Pap.* II. pp. [99, 101] : where they are called αἰχμάλωτοι from Asia, and one of them is concerned with the working of a farm.   These papers come from the second and the fourth years of the king's reign, in the former of which he was probably still absent at his wars.
[3] Line 15.   The text is subjoined in the Appendix to this chapter.

interests of his own land in a crisis, and so Ptolemy was urged to hurry back from Asia, and avert an impending revolution. These causes, and more generally the oppression of natives by Greeks, seem to have brought about some internal disturbance, of which we have no details, though they not only recalled the king to his home, but probably affected many subsequent acts in his domestic policy.

§ 132. The earliest great official (Greek) document, now happily recovered from the sand at Tanis, is the decree of Canopus, passed by the synod of assembled priests in Canopus in the ninth year of this reign. The substantial benefits enumerated are the recovery of all the Egyptian gods (S. Jerome says 2500) carried away by the Persians as spoil; the prompt averting of a famine threatened by a low Nile, and this by importing at great cost corn from Phoenicia, Cyprus and Cyrene; favours bestowed upon sacred animals, especially Apis and Mnevis, and upon the priests as well as the people of the country; lastly, the maintenance of order and peace throughout the empire. An important reform in the calendar is also ordained.

This decree, full of pompous phrases, and conferring formally upon the king and queen the title of Bene-factors, together with divine honours to their child Berenike, then suddenly deceased, appears to me more than formal praise.[1] It is so far like the very similar Rosetta inscription—a treaty of peace between the nationalists and the Macedonian dynasty. There seems

---

[1] We notice that in the two earliest texts known of this king's reign, the Adulitan inscription and the gold plaque found under the founda-tions of his temple to Sarapis and Isis at Canopus (*CIG* 4694), he is not called Euergetes, because that title had not yet been conferred upon him.

to follow a distinct increase in the building of Egyptian temples, especially at Thebes, and certainly a diminution of offerings to temples throughout the Greek world. Pausanias, who saw so many statues and dedications of the first and second Ptolemies throughout Greece, does not mention a single statue, or benefaction of this king, and yet he was a king who ruled over the Aegean far more undisputedly than his predecessors. We now know that the most splendid of all Ptolemaic temples, that of Edfu, was founded anew in the tenth year of the king, that is to say in the year following the decree of Canopus, and the inscription on the temple which gives us the chronicle of its gradual completion, tells us that the king went in person to this remote city in Upper Egypt, with great pomp, to lay the foundation. How perfectly this accords with the inferences I have drawn, need not be insisted upon.[1] In fact the indigenous forces were beginning to react with their usual obstinacy upon the intruding Hellenism. The Egyptian calendar, at first set aside for the Macedonian, begins to assert itself—the Egyptian day and month being placed after the Macedonian—and before the close of the king's reign frequently supplants it. It is commonly said that the figure of this king on his great pylon at Thebes is in Hellenic, not Egyptian dress. It is really a mongrel costume between the two. His small temple at Esneh, destroyed by a local pasha in this century, contained, as Champollion and Rosellini report, a full account of his wars in purely Egyptian style.

§ 133. In Alexandria of course he is a Hellenistic king speaking Greek, and educating his son under the

---

[1] For the substance of the Edfu inscription cf. the second Appendix to this chapter.

best Greek tutors. At no time was the Museum more
flourishing and famous. This forms the principal feature
of the Alexandria of his day. It has been pointed
out by Susemihl[1] that if Philadelphus was zoologically,
Philopator aesthetically disposed, the leading tastes of
Euergetes seem to have been for pure science. He
deserves great credit for summoning the celebrated
Eratosthenes from Athens, not only to be Chief Librarian,
probably upon the death of Callimachus, but also to
educate the crown prince. We still possess a dedication
to the king, containing a practical solution of the problem
of finding two mean proportionals between any two
lines, which Eratosthenes set up in the temple of the
Ptolemies (probably adjoining the *Sema*) with an epigram,
of which Wilamowitz has recently established the genuineness.[2] Compliments to the king and prince are combined
with the object of asserting for the *savant* an important
discovery. We need not delay over the mathematical
part, but the concluding lines are worth quoting from so
famous an author:—

εὐαίων Πτολεμαῖε, πατὴρ ὅτι παιδὶ συνηβῶν
πάνθ' ὅσα καὶ Μούσαις, καὶ βασιλεῦσι φίλα
αὐτὸς ἐδωρήσω· ὃ δ' ἐς ὕστερον, οὐράνιε Ζεῦ,
καὶ σκήπτρων ἐκ σῆς ἀντιάσειε χερός.
καὶ τὰ μὲν ὡς τελέοιτο· λέγοι δέ τις ἄνθεμα λεύσσων
τοῦ Κυρηναίου τοῦτ' Ἐρατοσθένεος.

We indeed wish he had told us more, even in epigrams,
of his scientific researches, which not only embraced
astronomy, but even the foundation of physical geography.
If at the king's solicitation Sphaerus brought him
Stoicism, Chremonides the newest tactics, Eratosthenes
was his pioneer in more exact and therefore more

___

[1] i. p. 8.   [2] Göttingen *Nachrichten* for 1894.

permanent science, and in constant personal intercourse with the great Archimedes who came from Syracuse to study at Alexandria.   Dositheos, Konon, and others enlarged the sphere, and extended the applications, of pure mathematics.   There were not wanting lesser features to the picture.   A series of books of marvels, of which that of Antigonus of Karystos is the least obscure, the treatise of Philo on the seven wonders of the world, and many epigrams date from this period.   Even the desire of collecting old books became so widespread that people began the artificial dyeing and spoiling of manuscripts to ape antiquity and deceive the collectors.   Every indication we have points to literary activity at Alexandria, and to the full maintenance of the glories both of the Museum and of the Library.

§ 134. If such were the Hellenistic aspects of the king's rule in Egypt, the fortunate discovery at Tanis in 1865 by Lepsius has recovered for us the official recognition of the king's action in favour of the native population in a decree drawn up by the Synod of Canopus in the ninth year of his reign (238 B.C.)   It seems to have been the custom to set up a decree of this kind in many temples throughout Egypt by way of a publication of the contents,[1] and of this very text the demotic version has been found separately, so that there is some means of controlling our previous copy.   At such a holy place, for example, as Philae, a great number of these documents must have been set up, and it is to be hoped that the examination of the whole site, recently ordered by the Egyptian Government and entrusted (1895) to the

---

[1] The same fashion prevailed in Greece, where in many decrees the various temples in which it shall be set up are specified, generally Delphi and Delos.   Cf. for an example Dittenberger *Sylloge* No. 215.

competent hands of Captain Lyons, R.E., may result in
fresh discoveries.   Several fragments of other texts, set
up on granite steles, will be quoted in the course of this
work.

§ 135. The present text, which the reader will find in
the appendix to the present chapter, has not been reprinted
as frequently as was to be expected.   Coming too late for
insertion in the *CIG*, it was discussed in some periodicals
at the time of the discovery—half of it given by Wescher
in the *Revue archéologique*—but I am not aware that it is
accessible in a separate shape except in Lepsius' monograph with German translation, and with a copy of the hieroglyphic text, an expensive folio published in 1866.   It
therefore needs no apology on my part that I should repro-
duce in this book both the decree of Canopus and that of
Memphis, known as the Rosetta stone—this too, though
much commented on in the beginning of the century,
now rather neglected.   Yet they contain what may well
be called first-hand information, which is far the most
important we possess on this period, and which has cleared
up many points which the historians had omitted to explain.

§ 136. With regard to the internal condition of the
land, and in connexion with the alleged disturbances, it
is well to turn to the strange batch of documents recently
recovered from the coffins of Gurob, and learn what we
can from their analysis.   It has already been described how
Ptolemy II. and Arsinoe Philadelphus increased the available
land by engineering in the Fayyum, and how the papers
of Cleon the Commissioner of Works in the twenty-ninth
and thirtieth years of that reign show him busily occupied
in the constructing of dykes, economising of reservoirs,
providing for new and wider irrigation.   The documents
dating from the days of Ptolemy Euergetes, as we are now

entitled to call him, are not of the same character. They chance to be papers referring to the police regulations of the nome, complaints of individuals against injustice or assault, taxing accounts, and from the tenth year onward the disposition of properties by testament.

The very dating of these wills of the tenth year is most interesting. The formula is precisely that of the Canopus decree, even to the very names of the eponymous priest and priestess — Apollonides, son of Moschion, and Menekrateia, daughter of Philammon—for these officials of the ninth year were reappointed, most exceptionally, for the tenth, owing apparently to the exaltation and variation of their functions as servants of the Benefactor gods.

§ 137. The description, πατρόθεν καὶ πατρίδος, of the testators is most instructive. They are men from every corner of the Hellenistic world, and even from Campania, Persia, Thrace, and Libya, who are settled with wife and family in this military colony. The grants of land seem to have been various not only in size but in tenure. We have the farms stated to be from 100 arourae down to thirty. This latter seems to be an 'infantry lot' as distinguished from a 'cavalry' lot. The term lot-owner (κληροῦχος) is only applied to a small number of persons, chiefly, though by no means exclusively, Macedonians, and all either officers of one of four *hipparchies*, or τακτόμισθοι, whatever that may mean, and often citizens of Alexandria, which seems to be indicated not only by the obvious Ἀλεξανδρεύς, but by the name of one of the *demes* Ἀνδρομάχειος, Φιλαδέλφειος, etc. of that city.[1] They also specify houses and property there in their wills. These people formed the aristocracy of the nome,

[1] This is Professor Wilcken's suggestion.

and in one case at least we find a testator of this rank choosing for his witnesses men of the same rank. Besides these we have the class called τῆς ἐπιγονῆς (never ἐπίγονοι) evidently important people, sometimes even Macedonians, but holding a title in contrast with that of *cleruch*.[1]

§ 138. The impression produced on me by these facts is that these people 'of the Epigone' were a second foundation in the Arsinoite nome, probably by Ptolemy Euergetes. They were Macedonian Greeks born in Egypt, the sons of settlers who had come from Hellenistic lands. They were distinctly not landholders in the sense that the

---

[1] In the extant specimens (cf. *Pet. Pap.* I. index *sub vocc.*), της επιγονης takes exactly the place in the description of a man that κληρουχος or εκατονταρουρος does, the latter of these two being merely a more dignified subdivision of the *cleruchs*. We never find κληρουχος and της επιγονης attached to the same name. Moreover the κληρουχος generally states his military rank, ιλαρχης etc., the other never. The clearest example, however, of an intended contrast is the preamble published in the *Pet. Pap.* II. xxxviii : παρα Σωσιου του Σωσου Κρητος και Ηρακλειτου του Θοινου Απολλωνιατου των δυο της επιγονης και Σωσιβιου Μακεδονος των υπο φυλεα λ α̅ (viz. τριακονταρουρου) κληρουχου (the two are seldom used together) του ενος ημων Σωσιβιου κεκληρουχημενου περι Λυσιμαχιδα του Αρσινοιτου νομου και μεμισθωκοτος εις το Λ̅γ τον κληρον κατα δυο μερη Σ. και Η., και αυτου etc. συνγεωργουντος. The former evidence on this interesting question was gathered by G. Lumbroso *Egitto* etc., chap. ix., with his usual learning and acuteness. In the papyri under the seventh Ptolemy, the term κληροῦχος is never applied to the Greek cavalry soldiers settled about Memphis, but κάτοικος, and apparently with the same contrast to the men τῆς ἐπιγονῆς. We shall revert to the ἱππεῖς κάτοικοι in due time. Diodorus (i. 32) speaks of settling the companions of the king in war on the best of the land as an old Egyptian habit. To these people, 1700 in number, says he, κατεκληρούχησε τὴν ἀρίστην τῆς χώρας, ὅπως ἔχοντες ἱκανὰς προσόδους καὶ μηδενὸς ἐνδεεῖς ὄντες ἀσκῶσι τὰ περὶ τοὺς πολέμους. This makes these landholders active soldiers, as Wilcken thinks the κληροῦχοι of the Fayyum were intended to be. I do not believe in a set of men mostly over sixty (as we know from their wills) being more than veterans, perhaps liable to keep horses for the state, and to be called out upon a great emergency.

older settlers were. All the vacant land may have been taken up. But they may have held crown land ἐν δωρεᾷ, an expression which occurs in the Revenue Papyrus, and in contrast to absolute ownership.

These upper classes, who, in some cases which we know, and probably in many more which we do not, imported wives from their old homes, were surrounded by sojourners (παρεπίδημοι), traders, among whom were certainly Jews and Samaritans, and by a vast body of natives, settled all through the sixty or seventy villages of the nome, of which Crocodilopolis and 'Ptolemais at the harbour' were the chief towns. In the latter was the βασιλικὴ κατάλυσις, the king's lodge, when he visited the district,[1] and also the principal bank of the province. The harbour, of course, means the widening of the canal so as to hold the shipping which came to and fro from Memphis, or down the Bahr Yusuf from Upper Egypt. Hence public proclamations were made at these two centres.[2] The province was quite self-supporting, and was even required from its surplus to supply Memphis with oil.[3]

Amid the various forms of farm industry was the breeding of horses, which may have been one of the conditions of holding land in gift.[4] The state elephants on the other hand, if not in Alexandria, were kept at Memphis.[5] Travelling in carriages drawn by (from two to five) horses, under

---

[1] Preparations for a visit of Philadelphus probably in the thirtieth year of his reign (255 B.C.) are mentioned in surviving fragments (*Pet. Pap.* II. pp. [27, 43, 48-9]). The βασιλικὴ κατάλυσις was apparently restored for his reception, which suggests that royal visits to the Fayyum were not frequent.

[2] *Pet. Pap.* II. p. [44].

[3] Revenue Pap. col. 72.

[4] Cf. ιπποσκοπος, etc., mentioned in the *Petrie Papyri* I. 42, and the curious list in II. [115-7].   [5] *Op. cit.* II. [64].

a contract with *vetturini*, can be proved from the accounts sent in by these people.[1] There were high-roads, called the king's way, but it is likely that this travelling in carriages was confined to government officials. While there are Egyptian civil servants who correspond concerning the control of local affairs in good Greek, there are donkey boys with Greek names who cannot write Greek and have their receipts drawn up by an amanuensis.[2]

§ 139. What makes it certain that the Hellenistic settlers did not intermarry with native women, is the frequent occurrence in the wills of the formula 'I leave all that I have to my wife X., and nothing to anybody else, and I choose the king and queen and their children as my executors.' It does not appear that the κλῆρος was included in such bequests ; it may have been entailed on the eldest son ; unfortunately we are without evidence on this point yet, but the policy of the Crown could not have been to enrich native women even with personal property in this free way. There is no appearance of any death-duties on these wills, nor could there well be, as there is in them no accurate statement or probate of the testator's property, and as he makes his will while in good health, and probably long before his decease.

But the Crown might well excuse a dead man his dues, when it taxed each item of his property during all his life. There are sixths and tenths and twentieths in dozens of documents. Every field, and its produce, we might almost say every plant, was catalogued. Consequently the civil service, and the service of the new State religion, seem to absorb all other professions. How far the old superstitions prevailed, we cannot tell. There are ἰβιοβοσκοί and ἱερακοβοσκοί mentioned, but seldom priests, and seldom

---

[1] *Op. cit.* II. xxv. [2] *Op. cit.* II. pp. [72] *sqq.*

any worship but that of the Ptolemies.   The wills contain
no religious imprecations; the universal oath in contracts
was now the royal oath, of which specimens are preserved.[1]
It adds Sarapis and Isis and all the other gods, as an
appendix to the enumeration of the Ptolemies, past and
present.

One point justly astonished the students of previous
Ptolemaic papyri. The wealth of honorific titles, such as First
Friends of the King, his Cousins, Chief of his Staff, A.D.C.,
or whatever we may translate the titles so freely bestowed
on officials in the next century, are here wholly absent.   One
solitary occurrence of the title ἀρχισωματοφύλαξ on a small
scrap is the only exception I have found, and that scrap may
possibly belong to those very few documents of Ptolemy V.'s
reign which were found in the coffins of Gurob; but on this
point our evidence fails us.[2]   Nor is the king addressed
with any pomp.   Very likely the simple and practical Soter,

---

[1] *Pet. Pap.* ii. xlvi. (a) and Wilcken's *Aktenstücke* No. xi.

[2] In connexion with the troubles of Epiphanes, I had conjectured
(below, § 182) that these titles may have been devised to gain popularity.   But an original suggestion of Mr. J. E. Healy, a pupil
attending my class, deserves careful mention.   He asked whether the
case might not be parallel to that of James I. in England, who invented
and sold titles to raise money.   Such a solution of the apparently
sudden appearance of these titles is by no means improbable, and
would give a new and telling point to the story about the death
of Epiphanes (below, § 183) who when asked where he could find
funds for a foreign war, answered *that his wealth consisted in the
number of his Friends.*   As the term φίλος, like συγγενής, was purely
ceremonial, and no doubt conferred upon the holder precedence at
court and elsewhere, it is not at all unlikely that the device of James I.
found its prototype in that of Ptolemy Epiphanes.   That the φίλοι, etc.,
were limited in number, and so an aristocracy, appears to follow from
the title τῶν ὁμοτίμων τοῖς συγγενέσι, which must have been a sort of
expectant peerage, pending the co-option into the proper συγγενεῖς.
The title *Friends* was imitated by Augustus, as is well known, at the
court of the early Roman empire.

when he came to learn the absurd luxury of titles which encumbered the hieroglyphic texts, and the fulsome praises of the king, determined that while he adopted from the Egyptian court its administration and general management of the country, he would repudiate all such nonsense, and thus it was only gradually, and with the reassertion of national habits, that even those titles which were customary at the Macedonian court began to be applied to officials throughout the country, while the kings themselves became deified, and so gradually acquired the style and titles of the native sovrans.

§ 140. Though we can thus give some details concerning a single isolated province in the reign of Euergetes, we are still left in darkness concerning the king himself. As the foundations of the great temple of Edfu were laid in the year after the synod of Canopus, it may be that the great temple of Esneh, so similar to it in character, was then also founded, but even the former temple, together with his great pylon at Karnak, shows clearly how differently this king regarded the Egyptian cult, as compared with the views of his predecessors. To this time of peace also we may ascribe researches in the far south, which (as I have conjectured) he began while he was only crown prince. Diodorus says [1] that the third Ptolemy, being very zealous about the taking of elephants, sent out one of his officers, Simmias, to explore the country of the Ichthyophagi, apparently beyond the Straits of Aden. We do not hear of this man having founded any settlement, as the several agents of the second Ptolemy did, according to Strabo, nor does this author say a word concerning Euergetes' activity. But the marble throne at Adule shows that Diodorus was right, and it is possible that Euergetes' apparent neglect of European

[1] iii. 8.

affairs, is owing to the fact of his having spent much of his life in this out-of-the-way exploration.[1]

It must be, I think, to this king also that the story in Agatharchides[2] is to be referred, who describes how the savages of the Trogodyte country killed the elephant, either by hamstringing him or by shooting at him with great bows worked by three men. They destroyed so many recklessly, as all savages are wont to act in similar circumstances, that Ptolemy feared the supply of these animals required for Egypt would fall short, and offered the people, through his generals, large rewards to preserve them. They replied that they would not take his whole sovranty as compensation for their sport. There is so little mention of elephant-hunting under any king later than Ptolemy IV. that I set this anecdote in the present reign.

§ 141. The long story told by Josephus[3] concerning the astuteness of a young Jew named Josephus, nephew of the high-priest Onias, who managed to avert the anger of Ptolemy, and secure for himself the lucrative appointment of tax-farmer for the whole tribute paid by the Jews to Egypt—this long story, even if it be not genuine, and only one of the many falsifications of history by the Jews, gives us a curious picture of the ways and manners at Alexandria during this great king's reign. Anecdotes concerning Euergetes are so scarce—not even Athenaeus has any to tell us—that we linger over this doubtful piece of history, and interrogate it more closely than it probably deserves.

In the first place it is tolerably clear that the narrative, which Josephus does not introduce in its chronological

---

[1] Cf. above, § 100. Athenaeus says that Kallikrates, no doubt the man who dedicated the temple to Arsinoe as Aphrodite Zephyritis, was also the flatterer of Euergetes, but how or in what respect, he does not specify.   [2] *apud* Phot. 14.   [3] *Antiqq.* xii. 4.

order, is to be referred to the reign not only of Euergetes, but of his son. For the Jew held his office and his importance for twenty-two years, and towards the end, when he is now old, he sends his son Hyrcanus to the birth-feast of a son in the royal house, that is to the birth-feast of the future Ptolemy Epiphanes. The control therefore of the Jewish and Syrian taxes by Josephus possibly extended from 229 to 207 B.C.[1]

The historian tells us that the uncle of his hero, Onias the high-priest, being a stingy man, refused to add to the usual tribute sent from Palestine the twenty talents contributed habitually by the high-priest—a sort of half present half bribe—to have things left in his hands.[2] For the danger of a strange tax-farmer was very serious Then the Egyptian king, or his finance bureau, writing in his name, threatens Onias that unless the usual sum is paid, the king will seize the land for a military colony, and send his veterans to settle in it.[3]

This then was the procedure, if the taxes of the subject lands were not paid ; and in this way cities were settled in foreign provinces which became permanent garrisons to support the power of Egypt.

§ 142. However, when this threat comes by an ambassador, the young Josephus, nephew to the high-priest, takes the matter in hand, entertains and pleases the envoy, and gets himself appointed to go to Egypt with the excuses of the Jewish people. On his way he meets all the chief men of Syria and Phoenicia going down to Egypt to bid for the farming of the taxes, and is held in contempt because he

---

[1] Stark *Gaza* pp. 412 *sq.*

[2] This sort of present was usually, I think, called a στέφανος.

[3] Jos. *Antiqq.* xii. 4, § 1 καὶ ἠπείλει κληρουχήσειν αὐτῶν τὴν γῆν, οὐκ ἀπολαβών, καὶ πέμψειν τοὺς ἐνοικήσοντας στρατιώτας.

could spend no more than 20,000 drachmae upon his out-
fit and voyage.   This then was too little for a person of
importance.   We hear in the sequel, however, that 10,000
drachmae was a fair sum for a private individual to expend
for the same purpose.   Hearing that the king has gone up
to Memphis, Josephus does not wait at Alexandria, like the
rest, but forthwith goes up the river, knowing that he will
there be introduced by his friend the recent ambassador to
Judaea.   This actually happens, and he is asked to take a
seat in the king's chariot with the Queen and Athenion the
ambassador !   He then excuses his uncle's misdeeds on the
ground that he is silly with age, and makes himself so agreeable to the king, that when they return to Alexandria, the
clever young man is invited to the palace, and entertained
at the royal table, to the disgust of the Syrian grandees.

§ 143.   When the day of auction came on, the intending
farmers were disposed to bid 8000 talents for all the taxes
of Coele-Syria, Phoenicia, Samaria, and Judaea, this being
the usual sum, but Josephus cries out upon them, saying that
they have combined to cheat the king.   He offers double
the money, and moreover that he will hand over the confiscated property of recusants to the king, this being
hitherto an item of profit left to the tax-farmer with the
collecting of the tax.   The king is delighted, but asks for
the usual sureties, when Josephus offers, by way of joke,
the king and queen as sureties to themselves on his part.
This additional piece of impudence is also successful, but
he does not leave Alexandria without a force of 2000 men
to carry out his extortions.   He begins with Ascalon,
where he puts twenty leading citizens to death and sends
their property, 1000 talents in money, to the king.   He does
the same at Skythopolis, a non-Semitic town, to show that he
will treat natives and settlers in the same fashion, and so,

having full powers from the king, has it all his own way for twenty-two years, making great profit out of the business. His further adventures will recur to us under the reign of the next king.

§ 144. We can now see another reason for the great popularity of the Egyptian rule in Palestine. Eight thousand talents had been accepted for a long time as sufficient tribute, whereas it is not said to have been at all ruinous to the country to pay 16,000, and as much more as made a great fortune for Josephus. The burdens therefore of Egyptian rule were comparatively light. It is also likely that the threat of founding military settlements was not carried out by the Ptolemies with anything like the frequency of similar colonisations from Antioch.

As the Revenue Papyrus now gives us a close insight into the methods of farming the home taxes in wine and oil, so this story shows us how the foreign taxes were farmed, and how closely in this, as in so many other respects, the Roman system with its *publicani* was copied from the Hellenistic precedents.

Another point strikes us in the story, which is probably in accordance with the popular tradition of Alexandria, and therefore credible. It is the familiarity with which the king calls up a young stranger, recommended by a high official to be amusing, into the state carriage, when driving with his queen, and not only talks to him, but bandies jokes with him.[1] Yet this king was surrounded by all the old Egyptian pomp, and moreover claims descent from Herakles and Dionysus. The remarkable absence of

---

[1] This makes Stark reject the whole story as fabulous. We may add to the text the fact that in the ordinances (Rev. Pap.) settling the duties on wine formerly given to all the gods, upon the deified queen, she is simply called Arsinoe Philadelphus, or even ἡ Φιλαδελφος.

honorific titles in the early papyri as well as the plain language used by the court-poets, and the rude jokes (sometimes indeed severely punished) which were made at the expense of the sovrans, corroborate this.

Josephus so jumbles together two kings, and gives them but one queen, whom he calls by a wrong name in both cases, that we can hardly cite his anecdote as evidence for the character of Euergetes. But other stray indications, and the king's political inactivity in later years, agree with it, and lead us to imagine him as an easy-going, good-tempered, perhaps slothful man in the autumn of his life. It seems to be proved[1] by the evidence of coins, coupled with the allusions of Polybius[2] and Plutarch,[3] that the legislation of the philosophic reformers Ekdemos and Demophanes asserted for the province of Cyrene considerable independence—certainly more than a vigorous king and queen of Egypt would allow. The money issued by the κοινόν of these cities seems to date from the closing years (*circa* 230 B.C.) of the reign. These facts are in harmony with the conception we draw from the other sources.

§ 145. Yet the condition to which his great campaign had reduced the Syrian kingdom, the prolonged conflicts of the two Seleukid brothers, the rise of the power of Pergamum—all these confusions among his Asiatic rivals had made it easy for him to hold his possessions towards the East. But the rise of any strong power in the West was likely to impair his influence over Greece and the Aegean. And it so happened that several remarkable men arose in that part of the Hellenistic world, fortunately for Ptolemy at war with one another, but all of them rivals or foes to be carefully reckoned with. Concerning some of these

---

[1] Cf. Poole *Coins of the Ptolemies* p. xlviii. [2] x. 25.

[3] *Philopoemen* 1.

men and their views we are well informed. Whenever
Plutarch undertakes to illustrate a period through its
principal men, we are sure to have an effective picture,
which at all events gives us material for historical criticism.
When he has touched Egyptian history in his *Antony*, how
precious is every line he has written !

In the epoch before us he has chosen the lives of three
men — King Agis, a visionary reformer, of transparent
honesty, who fell a victim to his singleness of heart; Aratus,
a shifty opportunist, to whom a successful compromise was
the highest diplomacy, a hero of secrets and nightly surprises, that grew pale at the flash of arms in the light of day ;
Cleomenes, he too a socialist king, but who carried out
his reforms within, and his diplomacies without, neither by
preaching theories, nor by securing rich friends, but at the
sword's point, by political murder, as well as by victorious
campaign.

§ 146. It is in relation to these remarkable figures,
and these only, that we know anything of the great
kings of the world. These Greeks were justly thought,
in their day, three mere pawns in the game, and yet
they have not only fascinated the world, but have preserved from oblivion the kings and queens for whose sake
they were moved. Even the vigorous and successful
Demetrius, surnamed the Aetolian, the son and successor
of Antigonus Gonatas, who recovered the whole kingdom
which his rapacious neighbours thought to divide, who
humbled Aetolians, Achaeans, and fairly dominated the
other Greek powers, has disappeared altogether from among
the historic portraits of the day. We know nothing of
him save that he fought, and won, and at last (229 B.C.)
was killed in battle against the barbarians of the north.

But his successor Antigonus Doson is known, because

the policy of his life connected him with Aratus and Cleomenes ; and the subject of this chapter, Euergetes, is only spoken of as the paymaster of both these men.   It is almost openly confessed that he is master of the situation ; his money supports Aratus and the League, till Cleomenes starts the idea of a democratic royalty, wherein the sovran shall side with the poor and against the rich.   This popular idea, supported by the great personal qualities of the Spartan, completely overthrew the aristocratic policy of Aratus, whose defeats both in the field and in diplomacy led him to betray his old paymaster Ptolemy,[1] and call in the armed power of Antigonus.   Even then Cleomenes would have held his own, had he obtained sufficient money from Egypt. But Euergetes seems to have been tired of paying Greek politicians who turned against him after he had supported them for years, and when Antigonus entered into negotiations with him, it is clear from Plutarch's account that it was for the purpose of settling the war by arrangement, rather than by arms.   The long postponement of the deciding battle (Sellasia) was due to these negotiations. We do not know what advantages Antigonus offered his Egyptian rival.   That he ceded to him the coast of Caria, as Droysen conjectures, seems most improbable.   At all events Ptolemy cut the sinews of war, and Cleomenes was at last obliged to fight or disband his army.[2]

---

[1] Polybius, probably led by Aratus' Memoirs, implies that Ptolemy abandoned the Achaeans, because he thought Cleomenes an abler and more serviceable tool against Antigonus (cf. Polybius ii. 51), thus relieving Aratus of the charge of treason against his country.   But it is more likely that Aratus took the first step in this disgraceful policy.

[2] For this Polybius is also our authority (ii. 63) but in a polemical passage, where he uses this statement in Phylarchus to discredit the subsequent account of the capture of Megalopolis.   Nevertheless the historian does not express any doubt of the facts in my text.

§ 147. Plutarch gives us pathetic details of Cleomenes' flight and embarkation, and how a friend endeavoured to persuade him that if he must go to a master, how much better to serve a representative of Philip and Alexander and a Macedonian, than an Egyptian. Ptolemy had indeed shown his distrust of Cleomenes, by taking as hostages the king's mother and son, and possibly this may have been the deciding motive which brought Cleomenes to Egypt, though his panegyrists labour to show that neither his mother nor he were swayed by such considerations. But Plutarch does show us the old Egyptian king finding out that Cleomenes was no ordinary Greek adventurer, but a noble spirit, full of high thoughts, and worthy of restoration to a sphere of activity. Probably the contrast he found in him to the polished, artistic, shifty Aratus was impressive enough. At all events it is declared to have been the Egyptian king's intention to fit him out with a fleet and army, and send him back to reconquer Greece for Egyptian interests —a matter become easy, since Antigonus Doson had died suddenly within a few days of his victory at Sellasia—when death overtook Euergetes also. We are told by Polybius that he died of disease.[1] He was not, like Antigonus, an active man in the prime of life, but over sixty years of age, and evidently declining for some years in vigour. Within the same year apparently the Syrian king Seleukos (III.) Soter also ended his short life and reign, so that we have that singular set of coincidences, upon which Polybius has made such striking comments.[2]

§ 148. It is fruitless to search the fragments of the literature of Alexandria during the days of Euergetes, and so endeavour to raise some of the thick mist of oblivion

---

[1] Polybius ii. 71 νόσῳ τὸν βίον μεταλλάξαντος, not murdered by his son and heir, as Justin says twice over.   [2] iv. 28, 37.

which hides from us the character and policy of this once-famous monarch. Is it not strange that while we know not only Agis, whose life was nothing but a failure, and Cleomenes, whose life was but a brief success, nay even their mothers and wives and sisters, with all their virtues, their uncles and cousins, with their vices ; of Euergetes and his Berenike, there is no personal image save that upon their coins ?[1] And yet it is the one reign in which neither rival wives nor harlots agitated the court. But when we consult the coins, there is here too a curious lack of individuality. The king, except for his spiked or radiate crown, is hardly distinguishable from Philadelphus—the same short, full, handsome face, with evident signs of corpulency. The queen, except for her emblems, is almost identical in type with Arsinoe Philadelphus, perhaps a little handsomer, so that even here we are baulked in our hopes.

Probably the last act of Euergetes' life was to lead the way in contributing princely gifts to the Rhodians, when their city was almost destroyed, and their commercial credit was shaken, by a disastrous earthquake. The date of this event is not certain, and Polybius, narrating it[2] after the campaign of Raphia, would lead us to believe that it did not occur till Philopator's reign. But the fact that the other contributing kings were Antigonus (Doson) and Seleukos (Soter) force us to put it before the death of Euergetes, since he must surely have outlived Doson, who died very shortly after the battle of Sellasia, while Cleomenes was living in exile with Euergetes. The whole

---

[1] Athenaeus (xv. p. 689) says that Berenike was a great patroness of various aromatic oils. Aelian (xiv. 43) tells of her gentle interference, when the king, while playing dice, had a list of criminals read out to him for condemnation. The queen took the list from the officer, and would not suffer the king to dispose of lives with such levity. In this he at once acquiesced.   [2] v. 88 *sq.*

chapter in Polybius indicates that the solvency of Rhodes
implied the solvency of all the neighbouring powers, and
that bankruptcy there would produce a commercial crisis
all over the civilised world.   Most of these subsidies
were sent off almost immediately, but much more was
only guaranteed, and it is therefore likely that Euergetes
did not live to carry out his promises.   These must
have been loyally executed by his successor, and perhaps
because the promised subsidies were being paid for some
years, Polybius thinks fit to tell us the facts under the
reign of Philopator.   This is all the more reasonable as
demotic scholars tell us that Philopator was formally associated with his father in the sovranty, and probably did
some of the official work during his father's decaying
activity.   But Polybius justly reflects upon the solidarity
of the Hellenistic world, and how not only wealthy kings,
but petty dynasts and free cities saw clearly that the
damage of one great centre of commerce must imply
the impairing of all the rest.   He speaks also of the public
spirit or generosity of those days, as compared with his
own.   We should gladly believe him, but cannot put much
confidence in the generosity which only manifests itself in
accordance with enlightened self-interest.

COIN OF PTOLEMY EUERGETES I.

Q

APPENDIX I

THE INSCRIPTION OF SÂN

The discovery of this trilingual[1] inscription among the ruins of Tanis (Sân) has done much not only to illustrate the history of the third Ptolemy, but to explain difficulties in the long known decree of Memphis (Rosetta stone) which is of a kindred character.   In the first place we may deliberately call it trilingual, though two of the scripts represent Egyptian language; for it is now certain that hieroglyphic writing was a thing foreign and artificial, even to the Egyptian priests of that age, and by most of them imperfectly understood.   The variations undergone by the language since the days when hieroglyphics were the only script, and the manifest efforts at what is subtle and recondite in this form of writing under the Ptolemies, show clearly enough that the 'sacred script' was no mere transcript from the demotic, but a distinct version almost in the sense that the Greek was.   This consideration is of great importance in settling a controversy which Letronne raised, and determined without sufficient consideration.   Assuming that the hieroglyphic was the *bona fide* Egyptian version, and very imperfectly informed regarding the demotic, he was urged by various small points of difference to maintain that on the Rosetta stone (the only one then accessible) the Greek was the original, afterwards translated into Egyptian.   Revillout, coming long after him, and with the Sân stone also before him, armed moreover with a knowledge of demotic, asserted that he was wrong.   For, finding great contrasts in the style of the two documents, of which the later is very much more contorted and verbose, he asserted that while in the Rosetta stone the Egyptian was certainly the leading language, it was not so in the Sân stone, and that here the original text had been Greek.

It seems very difficult to maintain this distinction.   The circumstances of both decrees make it quite certain that the

---

[1] The demotic version was in this case round the edge of the stone, and not at first observed.   Another version of this kind has since been found.   The bibliography relating to the inscription is given by Groff *Rev. Eg.* vi. 13.

conclave of Egyptian priests, meeting for the transaction of their own business, with no foreigner present, discussed this business in the native tongue, and had their resolutions taken down by their secretaries in demotic script. Then they had recourse to interpreters on the one hand, with whom they concocted a Greek version for the Ptolemaic court ; on the other, to the department of their own body that understood hieroglyphics—probably the ἱερογραμματεῖς—to compose the version which would give a sacred and dignified character to their proclamation. But as the hieroglyphic was not understanded of the people, and probably not intended to be read, this artificial text should not have been compared by Letronne with the Greek, and its variations assumed to have any real import in the question. For according to Revillout's studies, there are considerable variations between it and the demotic, which was certainly the text understood, and therefore drawn up by the whole sacerdotal conclave.

M. Revillout has therefore done the right thing for the proper understanding of both texts when he published a literal translation of the demotic text, giving in parallel lines the Greek version.[1] Though there are still disputes and doubts regarding his decipherment, it is certainly the foundation from which all future considerations of these texts must start.

The facts which made him assert the priority of the Greek in the earlier of these decrees are mainly I think concerned with the dating, which here follows the usual formulae now known to us in many early papyri, while the dating of the decree of Memphis, which the Greek strives to copy, is quite foreign, not only to that tongue and its grammar, but to the practice of the Greek population in Egypt. But this striking contrast is to be easily explained by the character of the Greeks who were entrusted with the translation. In the days of the third Ptolemy, the foreign population was still dominant, and had taken little care to accommodate itself to the prejudices of the natives. Thus when the native scribes began with their ' year 9,' with which both demotic texts open, the officials of Euergetes exclaimed ' Nonsense, that won't do ; we must at least date the thing according to our practice,' and so they adopted their usual formula, advising the Egyptians to accommo-

[1] Cf. his *Chrestomathie démotique.*

date the demotic as best they could.   Hence a whole group of inflated praises, which in the Memphis decree come between βασιλεύοντος and Πτολεμαίου do not appear here.   It seems also to be true that the Greek and demotic of the earlier text are in much closer harmony than those of the later.   M. Revillout has indeed published a special Essay in which he calls attention to discrepancies between the two extant demotic copies of the text, inferring from them that they were independent versions of the hieroglyphic and Greek originals. The differences alleged are, however, so unimportant, and the vagaries of demotic writing such, that he probably lays too much stress upon them.   Variations are much more likely to occur in the ordinary script of the day, and with writers who perfectly apprehended the sense, than in copies of obsolete or foreign writing.

But to imagine that Greek scribes composed as the original such passages as those describing the honours to the princess Berenike, is to me absurd.[1]   No Greeks would have the necessary knowledge of these ceremonies, and even if they had, could they have ventured to dictate them to the Egyptian priests. The whole therefore even of the earlier document is distinctly and essentially Egyptian, though from ignorance or insolence the Greek officials may have departed in some cases from the demotic version as explained to them.   I have set down the date, according to Lepsius' determination, in the year 238 B.C. When the month comes to be fixed, there is considerable difference of opinion.   Lepsius decides for March and this was generally accepted, but recently Ed. Mahler has endeavoured to establish with much learning that the real date was 3rd December.[2]   Fortunately this controversy does not affect the history of the period.

I now proceed to comment upon the text of the decree of Canopus, chiefly with a view to illustrate the likenesses and unlikenesses it shows to the sister decree.

Superfluous words and syllables, written by mistake of the scribe, are enclosed in square brackets.   Necessary additions or corrections in round brackets.

---

[1] I am glad to find that Mommsen (*RG* v. 564) implies that he holds the same view as mine.

[2] Cf. *Congress of Orientalists for* 1893, vol. ii. p. 327.

The Decree of Canopus (Sân Stone) 238 b.c.

§ 149. Βασιλευοντος Πτολεμαιου του Πτολεμαιου και
Αρσινοης θεων Αδελφων, ετους ενατου, εφ ιερεως Απολλωνιδου
του | Μοσχιωνος Αλεξανδρου και θεων Αδελφων και θεων
Ευεργετων, κανηφορου Αρσινοης Φιλαδελφου Μενεκρατειας |
της Φιλαμμονος, μηνος Απελλαιου εβδομηι, Αιγυπτιων δε Τυβι
επτακαιδεκατηι. ΨΗΦΙΣΜΑ. οι αρχιερεις | και προφηται
και οι εις το αδυτον εισπορευομενοι προς τον στολισμον των
θεων και πτεροφοραι και ιερογραμματεις και | οι αλλοι ιερεις οι
συναντησαντες εκ των κατα την χωραν ιερων εις την πεμπτην
του Διου, εν ηι αγεται τα γενεθλια του | βασιλεως, και εις την 5

ll. 1, 2. I found this very formula repeatedly in the wills now
published in the *Petrie Papyri* vol. i., and the same eponymous
officers, with this difference only, that they are noted as serving
their *second* year of office in the *tenth* of the king's reign. That
such officials should be re-appointed was unusual—I doubt
whether another case is known—and may have been in connexion with these very ceremonies, and with the reform of the
calendar instituted below. The priest of Alexander etc. and the
Canephoros of Arsinoe Philadelphus always bear Greek names,
and the former need not at all be identified with the *priest of
all Egypt*, as Letronne imagined. That priest must rather
have been the Chairman of the Board to be discussed below.

l. 3. The demotic version (DV) which begins with *year* 9,
in the native style, omits to add the date in Tybi, thus only
giving the Macedonian month. This, if correctly deciphered,
must be a mere oversight of the copyist.

l. 4. The form πτεροφοραι (not οι) which appears also on
the Rosetta stone (R), and was there suspected by Letronne, is
by this case supported, and points to a form πτεροφορας.
Diodoros (i. 87) identifies these *feather-bearers* with the *hiero-
grammateis*, but there was evidently some difference.

l. 5. We find the Macedonian calendar, so inferior in precision
to the Egyptian, still dominant. The greater convenience,
however, of the native system gradually asserted itself, as
may be seen from a comparison of these with later documents.

πεμπτην και εικαδα του αυτου μηνος, εν ηι παρελαβεν την
βασιλειαν παρα του πατρος, συνεδρευσαντες | ταυτηι τηι
ημεραι εν τωι εν Κανωπωι ιερωι των Ευεργετων θεων ειπαν·
ΕΠΕΙΔΗ βασιλευς Πτολεμαιος Πτολεμαιου και Αρσινοης,
θεων Αδελφων, | και βασιλισσα Βερενικη η αδελφη αυτου
και γυνη, θεοι Ευεργεται, διατελουσιν πολλα και μεγαλα
ευεργετουντες τα κατα την χωραν ιερα και | τας τιμας των
θεων επι πλεον αυξοντες· του τε Απιος και του Μνηυιος και
των λοιπων ενλογιμων ιερων ζωιων των εν τηι χωραι την |
επιμελειαν δια παντος ποιουνται μετα μεγαλης δαπανης και
χορηγιας· και τα εξενεγχθεντα εκ της χωρας ιερα αγαλματα
10 υπο | των Περσων εξστρατευσας ο βασιλευς ανεσωισεν εις
Αιγυπτον και απεδωκεν εις τα ιερα, οθεν εκαστον εξ αρχης
εξηχθη· την τε | χωραν εν ειρηνηι διατετηρηκεν, προπολεμων
υπερ αυτης προς πολλα εθνη και τους εν αυτοις δυναστευοντας·

l. 6. It has been questioned whether the second feast
celebrates Euergetes' actual accession to the crown, or his
association in the crown with his father, during the lifetime of
the latter. The DV is in favour of the former : *il prit la
puissance suprême après son père.* The phrase occurs in
R(osetta stone) 1. So also does the formula describing all
the priests in ll. 6, 7 of that text.

l. 7. It thus appears that already (1) the king and queen
had been formally deified as *Benefactor Gods ;* (2) a temple
had been erected to them at Canopus. This had been the old
western port of Egypt, and no doubt a considerable trading
city. Its business population had been transferred to Alexandria (above, § 12), but its religious dignities remained. The
gold plaque found here (*CIG* 4694) shows that this king had
built a new temple to Isis and Sarapis.

l. 8. Of course *sister* is here a mere formal title. Cf.
§ 87.

l. 9. The terms αὔξειν and ἐπαύξειν occur in a like connexion, R 38, 53.

ll. 9, 10. Apis and Mnevis are mentioned below, 54, and also
R 31, as the representative sacred animals of Egypt. For
the other facts alluded to cf. § 128.

και τοις εν τηι χωραι | πασιν και τοις αλλοις τοις υπο την
αυτων βασιλειαν τασσομενοις την ευνομιαν παρεχουσιν· ΤΟΥ
ΤΕ ποταμου ποτε ελλιπεστερον ανα-|βαντος και παντων των
εν τηι χωραι καταπεπληγμενων επι τωι συμβεβηκοτι και
ενθυμουμενων την γεγενημενην καταφθοραν | επι τινων των
προτερον βεβασιλευκοτων, εφ ων συνεβη αβροχιαις περιπεπ-
τωκεναι τους την χωραν κατοικουντας, προσταντες κηδεμο- | 15
νικως των τε εν τοις ιεροις και των αλλων των την χωραν
κατοικουντων, πολλα μεν προνοηθεντες, ουκ ολιγας δε των
προσοδων υπερ-|ιδοντες ενεκα της των ανθρωπων σωτηριας,
εκ τε Συριας και Φοινικης και Κυπρου και εξ αλλων πλειονων
τοπων σιτον μεταπεμ-|ψαμενοι εις την χωραν τιμων μειζονων,
διεσωισαν τους την Αιγυπτον κατοικουντας, αθανατον ευεργεσιαν

ll. 12, 13. Similar commendation is given to Ptolemy Epiphanes, and in analogous terms, R 20, 21, but with far less
reason.

ll. 13 *sq.* The peculiar case of the low Nile and the king's
efforts to feed the population are without parallel in the sister
inscription. Unfortunately there is no date given, though
we may confine it to some season between his third and
seventh year, probably near the former date, as ποτε can
hardly mean *recently.* My conjecture is that it took place at
latest in his third year, and recalled him from his Asiatic conquests, cf. § 131. The DV for ποτε is lost or illegible.

ll. 16, 17. The topic barely mentioned here 'neglecting
(the levying of) no small amount of his revenues' is that amplified in great detail by the priests in R 13 and 59, who enumerate
with satisfaction all the special imposts remitted by Epiphanes.
It is remarkable that they state Euergetes to have *bought* the
corn in his outlying provinces, not to have obtained it by
requisition, for so we must interpret τιμων μειζόνων. The
expression οἱ τὴν χώραν κατοικοῦντες here means the natives,
but in many other occurrences of the phrase is merely those
dwelling in a country. Hence Revillout has no right to
translate ἱππεῖς κάτοικοι, *native* cavalry. He might have
found the proper meaning in *Turin Pap.* viii. l. 13 των παρ-
επιδημοῦντων και κατοικουντων εν ταυταις ξενων, with Peyron's
instructive note (*Turin Pap.* part ii. p. 50).

και της αυτων αρετης | μεγιστον υπομνημα καταλειποντες τοις
τε νυν ουσιν και τοις επιγινομενοις, ανθ ων οι θεοι δεδωκασιν
αυτοις ευσταθουσαν την βασιλει-|αν και δωσουσιν ταλλ αγαθα
παντα εις τον αει χρονον· ΑΓΑΘΗΙ ΤΥΧΗΙ. ΔΕΔΟΧΘΑΙ
20 τοις κατα την χωραν ιερευσιν· τας τε προυπαρχουσας | τιμας εν
τοις ιεροις βασιλει Πτολεμαιωι και βασιλισσηι Βερενικηι θεοις
Ευεργεταις και τοις γονευσιν αυτων θεοις Αδελφοις και τοις
προγονοις | θεοις Σωτηρσιν αυξειν· και τους ιερεις τους εν
εκαστωι των κατα την χωραν ιερων προσονομαζεσθαι ιερεις
και των Ευεργετων θεων· και ενγραφε-|σθαι εν πασιν τοις
χρηματισμοις, και εν τοις δακτυλιοις οις φορουσιν προσεγκολαπτεσθαι και την ιερωσυνην των Ευεργετων θεων· προσ-
αποδειχθη-|ναι δε προ[ι]ς ταις νυν υπαρχουσαις τεσσαρσι
φυλαις του πληθους των ιερεων των εν εκαστωι ιερωι και

l. 20. The assertion of the king's future prosperity, on account of his merits, is repeated with a little variation in R 35-6. The formula there is ἔδοξεν, which affords a simpler construction, and τὰ ὑπάρχοντα τίμια πάντα etc., which is only worth citing to show that the Greek scribes did not copy these formulae from one decree into another. Such small differences e.g. ἴς τὸν ἅπαντα χρόνον for εἰς τὸν ἀεὶ χ. are to be found all through the parallel passages of the two texts.

ll. 22, 23. ἐπαύξειν μεγάλως R 38, αὔξουσι ibid. 53. προσ-ον. is in R 50 προσαγορεύεσθαι: ἐνγράφεσθαι is in R 51 καταχώρισαι εἰς, a verb which also occurs below, 29. The following words δακτ. etc. can now be used to supply the gap in R 51. It is to be noticed that while the honours here voted to the reigning king and queen stop short of images, to be set up beside those of the gods, and carried in sacred processions —a distinction accorded presently (ll. 59 sq.) to the princess Berenike, who is dead—the priests in the Memphis decree, forty years later, do not hesitate to vote all these forms of adoration to the living Epiphanes. Such a progress in flattery, and degradation in the dignity of the priests, we might naturally expect.

Still by the present decree the reigning king and queen were declared σύνναοι θεοί with all the gods in Egypt.

l. 24. πλῆθος, which usually in these texts means merely a

αλλην, η προσονομασθησεται πεμ-|πτη φυλη των Ευ(ε)ργετων
θεων. επει [και] συν τηι αγαθηι τυχηι και την γενεσιν βασιλεως
Πτολεμαιου του των θεων Αδελφων συμβεβηκεν | γενεσθαι 25
τηι πεμπτηι του Διου, η και πολλων αγαθων αρχη γεγονεν
πασιν ανθρωποις· εις [δε] την φυλην ταυτην καταλεχθηναι τους
απο | του πρωτου ετους γεγενημενους ιερεις και τους προσ-
καταταγησομενους εως μηνος Μεσορη του εν τωι ενατωι ετει,
και τους τουτων εκγονους εις τον αει | χρονον, τους δε
προυπαρχοντας ιερεις εως του πρωτου ετους ειναι ωσαυτως
εν ταις αυταις φυλαις εν αις προτερον ησαν, ομοιως δε και
τους | εκγονους αυτων απο του νυν καταχωριζεσθαι εις τας
αυτας φυλας εν αις οι πατερες εισιν· αντι δε των εικοσι
βουλευτων ιερεων των αιρουμενων | κατ ενιαυτον εκ των
προυπαρχουσων τεσσαρων φυλων, εξ ων πεντε αφ εκαστης
φυλης λαμβανονται, εικοσι και πεντε τους βουλευτας | ιερεις 30
ειναι, προσλαμβανομενων εκ της πεμπτης φυλης των Ευεργετων
θεων αλλων πεντε· μετεχειν δε και τους εκ της πεμπτης | φυλης
των Ευεργετων θεων των αγνειων και των αλλων απαντων των

number, seems to mean the whole caste of the priests (as below
l. 71), who were represented by councils chosen from, and
probably by, the πλῆθος.

ll. 25, 26. Both the first καί (as Lepsius noted) and below
δέ are superfluous. All those born, and all those appointed
priests for the previous nine years, were to form the new φυλή.
The creation of this fifth guild has since been used to determine
the major limit of the dates of documents in which they are
mentioned.

l. 29. The βουλευταὶ ἱερεῖς are evidently a governing council,
and in each section of them there was a φύλαρχος : they are
mentioned again l. 72. If these twenty (or twenty-five) were
elected from all the body of the priests, and themselves selected
their President, we have a very early instance of a representative democracy, such as has existed among the monks of Mt.
Athos for many centuries. Revillout translates the demotic
equivalent as *prêtres accomplissant parole*, and notes that the
adjective is singular, not plural.

l. 32. The ἀγνεῖαι here mentioned are certainly some sort

εν τοις ιεροις· και φυλαρχον αυτης ειναι, καθα και επι των
αλλων τεσ- | σαρων φυλων υπαρχει· ΚΑΙ ΕΠΕΙΔΗ καθ
εκαστον μηνα αγονται εν τοις ιεροις εορται των Ευεργετων
θεων κατα το προτερον γραφεν ψηφισμα | η τε πεμπτη και η
ενατη και η πεμπτη επ εικαδι, τοις τε αλλοις μεγιστοις θεοις
κατ ενιαυτον συντελουνται εορται και πανηγυρεις δημοτε-|λεις,
αγεσθαι κατ ενιαυτον πανηγυριν δημοτελη εν τε τοις ιεροις και
... καθ ολην την [την] χωραν βασιλει Πτολεμαιωι και βασιλισσηι
35 Βερενικηι | θεοις Ευεργεταις τηι ημεραι, εν ηι επιτελλει το
αστρον το της Ισιος, η νομιζεται δια των ιερων γραμματων
νεον ετος ειναι, αγεται δε νυν εν τωι | ενατωι ετει νουμηνιαι
του Παυνι μηνος, εν ωι και τα μικρα Βουβαστια και τα μεγαλα

of priestly emoluments, and seem to correspond to the mutilated word in R 48, variously restored προθέσεις or προθεσμία.
Revillout asserts this positively from the evidence of the
hieroglyphic and demotic versions of both passages, but here
merely transcribes ἀγνεία in his version.

l. 33. 'The previous decree,' so called also in the DV, was
probably drawn up at the coronation ceremony, which may
have been necessarily postponed till the king returned from
Asia.

ll. 35 *sq.* There is added to the feasts already appointed
another of great importance, on the 1st of Payni, with which
the solar year now commenced. The priests having observed
for many centuries that twelve months of thirty days, and five
intercalary days at the end of each year, still fell short by a
quarter day of the true solar year, so that the feasts of the
summer months moved gradually earlier till they occurred
in the winter, now ordain that every four years a special day
(our Leap-year day) shall be added to the calendar, and
celebrated as a special feast to the gods Euergetes. This
reform, though it seems not to have been accepted by subsequent Ptolemies, was recognised as scientifically correct, and
passed from Egypt first into the Julian calendar, and then
into ours. The fact that the priests had long noted a cycle
of 1461 years (the Sothiac cycle), which is equal to 1460
solar years, shows the enormous age, and the accuracy, of their
observations.

Βουβαστια αγεται και η συναγωγη των καρπων και η του |
ποταμου αναβασις γινεται· εαν δε και συμβαινηι την επιτολην
του αστρου μεταβαινειν εις ετεραν ημεραν δια τεσσαρων ετων,
μη μετατι- | θεσθαι την πανηγυριν, αλλ αγεσθαι τηι νουμηνιαι
του Παυνι, εν ηι και εξ αρχης ηχθη εν τωι ενατωι ετει· και
συντελειν αυτην επι ημερας | πεντε μετα στεφανηφοριας και
θυσιων και σπονδων και των αλλων των προσηκοντων· ΟΠΩΣ
ΔΕ και αι ωραι το καθηκον ποιωσιν δια παντος κατα την νυν
| ουσαν κα[τασ]ταστασιν του κοσμου και μη συμβαινηι τινας 40
των δημοτελων εορτων των αγομενων εν τωι χειμωνι αγεσθαι
ποτε εν τωι θερει, του αστρου | μεταβαινοντος μιαν ημεραν
δια τεσσαρων ετων, ετερας δε των νυν αγομενων εν τωι θερει
αγεσθαι εν τωι χειμωνι εν τοις μετα ταυτα καιροις, καθαπερ
προ- | τερον τε συμβεβηκεν γενεσθαι, κα(ι) νυν αν εγινετο
της συνταξεως του ενιαυτου μενουσης εκ των τριακοσιων και
εξηκοντα ημερων και των υστερον προσ- | νομισθεισων επαγε-
σθαι πεντε ημερων, ΑΠΟ ΤΟΥ ΝΥΝ μιαν ημεραν εορτην των
Ευεργετων θεων επαγεσθαι δια τεσσαρων ετων επι ταις πεντε
ταις | επαγομεναις προ του νεου ετους, οπως απαντες ειδωσιν,
διοτι το ελλειπον προτερον περι την συνταξιν των ωρων και
του ενιαυτου και των νομιζο- | μενων περι την ολην διακοσμη- 45
σιν του πολου διωρθωσθαι και αναπεπληρωσθαι συμβεβηκεν
δια των Ευεργετων θεων· ΚΑΙ ΕΠΕΙΔΗ την εγ βασιλεως
Πτολεμαιου | και βασιλισσης Βερενικης, θεων Ευεργετων,
γεγεννημενην θυγατερα και ονομασθεισαν Βερενικην, η και
βασιλισσα ευθεως απεδειχθη, συνεβη ταυτην παρθενον | ουσαν

l. 40. The words are almost repeated in R 48-50. προση-
κόντων is there καθηκ.

l. 47. This is one of the many royal children, of whom we
only hear in Ptolemaic history by a solitary accident. Revillout
says that the DV of the words η και βασ. ευθεως απεδ. are
qu'on allait manifester comme reine, which gives quite a different
sense, and would require εὐθέως ἂν ἀπεδείχθη. But we
know that it was a usual compliment in this hieratic style to
declare a prince to be born a king, or declared a king from his
birth.

εξαιφνης μετελθειν εις τον αεναον κοσμον, ετι ενδημουντων
παρα τωι βασιλει των εκ της χωρας παραγινομενων προς αυτον
κατ ενιαυτον ιερεων, | οι μεγα πενθος επι τωι συμβεβηκοτι
ευθεως συνετελεσαν, αξιωσαντες δε τον βασιλεα και την
βασιλισσαν επεισαν καθιδρυσαι την θεαν μετα του Οσιριος
εν τωι | εν Κανωπωι ιερωι, ο ου μονον εν τοις πρωτοις (ι)εροις
εστιν, αλλα και υπο του βασιλεως και των κατα την χωραν
50 παντων εν τοις μαλιστα τιμωμενοις υπαρχει,— | και η αναγωγη
του ιερου πλοιου του Οσειριος εις τουτο το ιερον κατ ενιαυτον
γινεται εκ του εν τωι Ηρακλειωι ιερου τηι ενατηι και εικαδι
του Χοιαχ, των εκ των πρω- | των ιερων παντων θυσιας
συντελουντων επι των ιδρυμενων υπ αυτων βωμων υπερ
εκαστου ιερου των πρωτων εξ αμφοτερων των μερων του
δρομου—| μετα δε ταυτα (τα) προς την εκθεωσιν αυτης νομιμα
και την του πενθους απολυσιν απεδωκαν μεγαλοπρεπως και
κηδεμονικως, καθαπερ και επι τωι Α[πει | και Μνηνει ειθισμενον
εστιν γινεσθαι, ΔΕΔΟΧΘΑΙ συντελειν τηι εκ των Ευεργετων
θεων γεγενημενηι βασιλισσηι Βερενικηι τιμας αιδιους εν απασι
τοι[ς | κατα την χωραν ιεροις· και επει εις θεους μετηλθεν εν
τωι Τυβι μηνι, εν ωιπερ και η του Ηλιου θυγατηρ εν αρχηι
55 μετηλλαξεν τον βιον, ην ο πατηρ στερξας ω[νο- | μασεν οτε μεν
βασιλειαν οτε (δε) ορασιν αυτου, και αγουσιν αυτηι εορτην και
περιπλουν εν πλειοσιν ιεροις των πρωτων εν τουτωι τωι μηνι,
εν ωι η αποθεωσις αυ[της | εν αρχηι εγενηθη, συντελειν και
βασιλισσηι Βερενικηι τηι εκ των Ευεργετων θεων εν απασι
τοις κατα την χωραν ιεροις εν τωι Τυβι μηνι εορτην και

l. 49. ἀξιώσαντες is the technical word in dozens of papyri for
making a formal request. The Attic form ἡ θεός (cf. l. 66)
seems to have given way to θεά. We find a second temple in
Canopus, that of Osiris, probably ancient and celebrated, besides
the temple to the Ptolemies.

l. 54. In this and three following lines, a few letters are lost
at the right edge of the stone, which are easily supplied.

l. 56. We expect ὅτε μὲν βασιλείαν ὅτε δὲ ὅρασιν, and the
DV has : 'sometimes his crown, sometimes the apple of his
eye.'

πε- | ριπλουν εφ ημερας τεσσαρας απο επτακαιδεκατηι (l. -ης).
ͺεν ηι ο περιπλους και η του πενθους απολυσις εγενηθη αυτηι
την αρχην· συντελεσαι δ αυτης και | ιερον αγαλμα χρυσουν
διαλιθον εν εκαστωι των πρωτων και δευτερων ιερων, και
καθιδρυσαι εν τωι αγιωι—ο δε προφητης η των εις το αδυτον
ειρημενων (l. εισπορευομενων) | ιερεων προς τον στολισμον των
θεων οισει εν ταις αγκαλαις, οταν αι εξοδειαι και πανηγυρεις
των λοιπων θεων γινωντα(ι), οπως υπο παντων ορωμενον | 60
τιμαται και προσκυνηται, καλουμενον Βερενικης ανασσης
παρθενων—· ειναι δε την επιτιθεμενην βασιλειαν τηι εικονι
αυτης διαφερουσαν της επιτιθεμενης | ταις εικοσιν της μητρος
αυτης βασιλισσης Βερενικης, εκ σταχυων δυων, ων ανα μεσον
εσται η ασπιδοειδης βασιλεια, ταυτης δ οπισω συμμετρον
σκηπτρον | παπυροειδες, ο ειωθασιν αι θεαι εχειν εν ταις χερ-
σιν, περι ου και η ουρα της βασιλειας εσται περιειλημ(μ)ενη,
ωστε και εκ της διαθεσεως της βασιλειας δια- | σαφεισθαι το
Βερενικης ονομα κατα τα επισημα της ιερας γραμματικης· και

l. 59. ἄγαλμα which corresponds to εἰκών in 62, and to the
same word in R 38, Letronne would translate a standing bas-
relief image, as contrasted with ξόανον (R 41), a sitting statue,
and it seems that the HV countenances this. But here the
εἰκών is the same as the ἄγαλμα and can be carried about by
the officiating priest. It is gold and jewelled (διάλιθον). The
words printed ἦ τῶν are blurred on the stone and we should
expect ἤ τις τῶν for which there is no room. The following
words seem to me a jumble of two constructions (1) ἤ τις
τῶν εἰρημένων ἱερέων, and (2) προφ. ὁ τῶν εἰς τὸ ἄδυτον
εἰσπορευομένων ἱερῶν. Probably the cursive Greek from
which the graver copied had here an erasure and correction.

l. 60. The words are repeated in R 42.

l. 61. The omission of ι in subjunctives or in dative forms is
very rare at this early time, as we know from the Petrie Papyri.
In the Revenue Papyrus it only occurs in subjunctives.

ll. 62-4. These details are exactly what we denote as *heraldic*.
βασιλεία is here *crown*, and by its ornaments, as in a mediaeval
coat-of-arms, the mother could be at once distinguished from
her daughter of the same name.

οταν τα Κικηλλια αγηται εν τωι Χοιαχ μηνι προ του περιπλου
του Οσειριος, κατα- | σκευασαι τας παρθενους των ιερεων αλλο.
αγαλμα Βερενικης ανασσης παρθενων, ωι συντελεσουσιν ομοιως
65 θυσιαν και ταλλα τα συντελουμενα νο- | μιμα τηι εορτηι
ταυτηι· εξειναι δε κατα ταυτα και ταις αλλαις παρθενοις ταις
βουλομεναις συντελειν τα νομιμα τηι θεωι. υμνεισθαι δ αυτην
και υ- | πο των επιλεγομενων ιερ(ει)ων παρθενων και τας χρειας
παρεχομενων τοις θεοις, περικειμενων τας ιδιας βασιλειας των
θεων, (ων) ιερειαι νομιζοντα(ι) | εικαι (l. ειναι)· και, οταν ο
προωριμος σπορος παραστηι, αναφερειν τας ιερας παρθενους
σταχυς τους παρα(τε)θησομενους τωι αγαλματι της θεου· αιδειν
δ εις αυτην | καθ ημεραν και εν ταις εορταις και πανηγυρεσιν
των λοιπων θεων τους τε ωιδους ανδρας και τας γυναικας ους
αν υμνους οι ιερογραμματεις γρα- | ψαντες δωσιν τωι ωιδοδιδα-
σκαλωι, ων και ταντιγραφα καταχωρισθησεται εις τας ιερας
βυβλους· και, επειδη τοις ιερευσιν διδονται αι τροφαι εκ

l. 64. About the Kikellia we know nothing, nor does the DV help us.

l. 66. This permission of the laity to join in a feast is paralleled by R 52.

l. 67. We here learn that officiating priestesses wore gold crowns (so DV) of the gods they served, when performing high ceremonies.

l. 68. προώριμος is *the first* in DV. Lepsius translates *Frühsaat*. The ordinary meaning is *premature*. τοὺς παρα-(τε)θησομένους is curiously rendered 'more tall than they are' (*plus haut qu'eux*) by Revillout from the DV. Hence the form, which is right, may mean compared with their own height, if it does not merely mean to be placed beside the image of the goddess.

ll. 69, 70. The custom of the hierogrammateus composing a sacred ode, and then handing it to the teacher of singing for men and women to perform, is interesting, and is a very early form of congregational church music, unless these men and women were a professional choir, which seems very likely from what we see in much earlier Egyptian pictures. Copies of these hymns were *entered* in sacred books.

των | ιερων, επαν επαχθωσιν εις το πληθος, διδοσθαι ταις 70
θυγατρασιν των ιερεων εκ των ιερων προσοδων, αφ ης αν
ημερας γενωνται, την συνκριθησομε-|νην τροφην υπο των
βουλευτων ιερεων των εν εκαστωι των ιερων κατα λογον των
ιερων προσοδων· και τον διδομενον αρτον ταις γυναιξιν | των
ιερεων εχειν ιδιον τυπον και καλεισθαι Βερενικης αρτον.

Ο δ εν εκαστωι των ιερων καθεστηκως επιστατης και
αρχιερευς και οι του ιερου | γραμματεις αναγραψατωσαν τουτο
το ψηφισμα εις στηλην λιθινην η χαλκην Ιεροις γραμμασιν
και Αιγυπτιοις και Ελληνικοις και αναθε-| τωσαν εν τωι
επιφανεστατωι τοπωι των τε ά ιερων και β' και γ', οπως οι
κατα την χωραν ιερεις φαινωνται τιμωντας (l. -τες) τους
Ευεργετας θεους και τα τεκνα αυτων, | καθαπερ δικαιον εστιν. 75

l. 71. When the counsellor priests distribute the dues in kind
to the whole caste, these shall be given to the daughters, wives
of the priests! Wives is here added from the DV. There
seems no reason for the contrast between daughters (71) and
wives (72) of the Greek text.

l. 72. The whole of this last paragraph is missing from the
DV. In the parallel passage of R we have στήλην στερεοῦ
λίθου, and ἐνχωρίοις for Αἰγυπτίοις.

APPENDIX II

Here is an abstract of the text from the outer west wall
of the great temple at Edfu, which gives a full account of
the successive builders of the temple and their work. On the
opposite outer wall, as an ornamental border below the figures,
is inscribed in hieroglyphics a detailed description of the parts
of the building, their various measurements, and the materials
employed. Thus we have an account of the building of this
temple before us without parallel for detail and exactness.

The preamble is written in honour of Ptolemy Alexander, the
eleventh of the series, and is chiefly in exaggerated praise of
the splendours of the building. This part of the inscription
belongs properly to the account of that king's reign. I take
up the text where it begins to instruct us, and translate from

Dümichen's version (*Zeitsch. für Aegypt.* 1870, p. 3). 'The kings of Upper Egypt, engraven are their foundations upon the work, the kings of Lower Egypt, the royal rulers, who have built here, their names are incised upon the walls.

'This fair day of the beginning (of the building in the year 10) of King Ptolemy (III.) Euergetes (I.) a feast of six days it was, during which the ground was opened, and the laying of the foundation-stone celebrated. The temple of Ra-Harmachis was founded, the Edfu of the defender of his father. The king himself in company with the goddess Safech (*i.e.* after careful deliberation, for she is the goddess of wisdom) was occupied in laying the basis of the adytum within and of its side chambers, in the situation determined by the wise, with all that is necessary according to the mind of Thoth. [Here follows a passage not translatable which talks of Ptah as chief architect. Of course there could hardly be an Egyptian text of the kind without a confusion of gods.] So was the temple finished, the inner sanctuary was being completed for the golden Horus up to the year 10, month Epeiph the 7th day, in the time of King Ptolemy (IV.) Philopator. [So far the building had continued for twenty-five years.]

'The wall in it was adorned with fair writing with the great name of his majesty and with pictures of the gods and goddesses of Edfu, and its great gateway completed, and the double doors of its broad chamber up to the year 16 of his majesty [Philopator].

'Then there broke out a revolution, and it happened that bands of the insurgents hid themselves there in the interior of the temple, while the revolution raged both north and south of it. But in year 19 of the reign of the deceased king Ptolemy Epiphanes (V.) the king was victorious, and crushed the revolution in the land ; officially entered is his name, behold it, on the temple.

'In the year 5 Tybi 1 of his beloved son, the deceased king Ptolemy Philometor (VII., if we count the merely nominal Eupator as VI.), there was set up the great wooden gate in the hall of the great victor, and the double doors of the Hai-hall (the second hall with twelve pillars), also the work was taken up again in the inside of the Chamber of Arms in the year 30 of this king.

'The completing of the inscriptions carved upon the stone, with the adorning of the walls with gold and colours, with the carpentry of the doors, with the making of the door lintels of good bronze, with the door-posts and locks, with the laying of gold plates on the doors, with the completing of the inner temple-house, lasted till the 18th of Mesore in the 28th year of the deceased king Ptolemy Euergetes II. (IX.) and his wife, the regent Cleopatra—in all 95 years, from the ceremony of the first hammer-stroke to the feast of the formal entrance-procession, the feast of the dedication by his majesty to his divine lord, Horus of Edfu, etc., etc., the great Techu-feast, the like of which has not been from the creation of the world to this day. [Then follows a description of the festivities—sacrifices, feasting, lavish supply of wine and unguents, brilliant lighting, and reckless enjoyment.] The god of Edfu has taken possession of his adytum [—date, year 30, month Payni 9], the feast of the union of the moon-god Osiris with the sun-god Ra which lasts six days, they began the building of the Chent-hall (the great hall of eighteen pillars), and the roof of the lord of heaven. It was finished in the year 46, 18th of Mesore, 16 years, 2 months, and 10 days after the foundation ; and the fair feast in this house, when the great name of his majesty was inscribed full in the year 48.

'At the close of his life, in the year 54 of this king, on the 11th of Payni, was laid the foundation of the great circuit-wall, and the Pylons of the entrance. As they were busy with this foundation the king died, and his eldest son succeeded to the throne. Engraved with his name is the outer wall of the front hall, as king of Upper and Lower Egypt, Ptolemy (X.) Philometor Soter (II.)

[Here a passage in the text has been broken away]— inscribed is his name upon the circuit-wall as King Ptolemy (XI.) Alexander (I.) 'He fled to Arabia, and his elder brother resumed his sway in Egypt ; for the second time he obtained the diadem as Lord of the Sun.

'These are the monuments of these deceased kings. Your divine souls are in heaven with the sun-god Ra, lasting are your bodies in the grave. Ye walk upon the way in the broad hall of double justice, the judges of the dead justify you with Osiris, lasting are your images upon earth, and your heirs are upon their throne.   Horus of Edfu, the god Api, Lord of heaven, who flames in the horizon, he beholds his house, he knows his beloved son King Ptolemy (X.) Soter Philometor (II.), he establishes him upon his throne for ever.'

The fact that Ptolemy III. was the real founder is also explicitly stated in the sister inscription on the east outer wall describing the building.

CARTOUCHE OF ARSINOE PHILADELPHUS
(Two forms).

CHAPTER VII

PTOLEMY IV. (PHILOPATOR), 222-205 B.C.

§ 150. AT last we emerge from stumbling about amid darkness and uncertainty into the light thrown by Polybius upon the history of Egypt. He tells us that the proper commencement of his work is at the world-moment of the accession of Philip V. of. Macedon, of Antiochus the Great, and of Ptolemy Philopator, and though he gives us many retrospects of previous events, they are only intended to illustrate the rise either of the Roman power, or of the Achaean League, with which Egypt was but little concerned. But now he commences to give us details, of which the following well-known passage (v. 34) is a specimen :—

PTOLEMY IV.

Immediately after his father's death, Ptolemy Philopator put his brother Magas and his partisans to death, and took possession of the throne of Egypt. He thought that he had now freed himself by this act from domestic danger ; and that by the deaths of Antigonus and Seleucus, and their being respectively succeeded by mere children like Antiochus and Philip, fortune had released him from danger abroad. He therefore felt secure of his position and began conducting his reign as though it were a perpetual feast. He would attend to no business, and would hardly grant an interview to the officials about the court, or at the head of the administrative departments in Egypt. Even his agents abroad found him entirely careless and indifferent ; though his predecessors, far from taking less interest in foreign affairs, had generally given them precedence over those of Egypt itself. For being masters of Coele-Syria and Cyprus, they maintained a threatening attitude towards the kings of Syria, both by land and sea ; and were also in a commanding position in regard to the princes of Asia, as well as the islands, through their possession of the most splendid cities, strongholds, and harbours all along the sea-coast from Pamphylia to the Hellespont and the district round Lysimachia. Moreover they were favourably placed for an attack upon Thrace and Macedonia from their possession of Aenus, Maroneia, and more distant cities still. And having thus stretched forth their hands to remote regions, and long ago strengthened their position by a ring of princedoms, these kings had never been anxious about their rule in Egypt ; and had naturally, therefore, given great attention to foreign politics. But when Philopator, absorbed in unworthy intrigues, and senseless and continual drunkenness, treated these several branches of government with equal indifference, it was naturally not long before more than one was found to lay plots against his life as well as his power : of whom the first was Cleomenes, the Spartan.[1]

Concerning the death of Cleomenes we have further the affecting narrative of Plutarch, in one of the most brilliant of his *Lives*.

Cleomenes, therefore, gave up all thought of asking for ships and soldiers from the king. But receiving news that Antigonus was dead, that the Achaeans were engaged in a war with the Aetolians, and that the affairs of Peloponnesus, being now in very great distraction and disorder, required and invited his assistance, he desired leave to depart only with his friends, but

---

[1] The many passages from Polybius which I quote are mainly from the excellent translation of Mr. Shuckburgh (Macmillan 1889).

could not obtain that, the king not so much as hearing his
petition, being shut up amongst his women, and wasting his
hours in bacchanalian rites and drinking parties.   But Sosibius,
the chief minister and counsellor of state, thought that Cleomenes, being detained against his will, would grow ungovern-
able and dangerous, and yet that it was not safe to let him go,
as he was an aspiring, daring man, and well acquainted with
the diseases and weakness of the kingdom.   For neither could
presents and gifts conciliate or content him ; but even as
Apis, while living in all possible plenty and apparent delight,
yet desires to live as nature would provide for him, to range at
liberty, and bound about the fields, and can scarce endure to
be under the priests' keeping, so he could not brook their
courtship and soft entertainment, but sat like Achilles,

> and languished far,
> Desiring battle and the shout of war.

His affairs standing in this condition, Nicagoras, the Mes-
senian, came to Alexandria, a man that deeply hated Cleomenes,
yet pretended to be his friend ; for he had formerly sold Cleomenes a fair estate, but never received the money, because
Cleomenes was either unable, as it may be, or else, by reason
of his engagement in the wars and other distractions, had no
opportunity to pay him.   Cleomenes, seeing him landing, for
he was then walking upon the quay, kindly saluted him,
and asked what business brought him to Egypt.   Nicagoras
returned his compliment, and told him, that he came to bring
some excellent war-horses to the king.   And Cleomenes, with
a smile subjoined, 'I could wish you had rather brought
young boys and music-girls ; for those now are the king's
chief occupation.'   Nicagoras at the moment smiled at the con-
ceit ; but a few days after, he put Cleomenes in mind of the
estate that he had bought of him, and desired his money, protesting that he would not have troubled him, if his merchandise
had turned out as profitable as he had thought it would.   Cleomenes replied, that he had nothing left of all that had been
given him.   At which answer Nicagoras, being nettled, told
Sosibius Cleomenes' scoff upon the king.   He was delighted
to receive the information ; but desiring to have some greater
reason to excite the king against Cleomenes, persuaded

Nicagoras to leave a letter written against Cleomenes, importing that he had a design, if he could have gotten ships and soldiers, to surprise Cyrene. Nicagoras wrote such a letter, and left Egypt. Four days after, Sosibius brought the letter to Ptolemy, pretending it was just then delivered him, and excited the young man's fear and anger ; upon which it was agreed, that Cleomenes should be invited into a large house, and treated as formerly, but not suffered to go out again.

This usage was grievous to Cleomenes, and another incident that occurred, made him feel his hopes to be yet more entirely overcast. Ptolemy, the son of Chrysermas, a favourite of the king, had always shown civility to Cleomenes ; there was a considerable intimacy between them, and they had been used to talk freely together about the state. He, upon Cleomenes' desire, came to him, and spoke to him in fair terms, softening down his suspicions and excusing the king's conduct. But as he went out again, not knowing that Cleomenes followed him to the door, he severely reprimanded the keepers for their carelessness in looking after 'so great and so furious a wild beast.' This Cleomenes himself heard, and retiring before Ptolemy perceived it, told his friends what had been said. Upon this they cast off all former hopes and determined for violent proceedings, resolving to be revenged on Ptolemy for his base and unjust dealing, to have satisfaction for the affronts, to die as it became Spartans, and not stay till, like fatted victims, they were butchered. For it was both grievous and dishonourable for Cleomenes, who had scorned to come to terms with Antigonus, a brave warrior, and a man of action, to wait an effeminate king's leisure, till he should lay aside his timbrel and end his dance, and then kill him.

These courses being resolved on, and Ptolemy happening at the same time to make a progress to Canopus, they first spread abroad a report, that his freedom was ordered by the king, and, it being the custom for the king to send presents and an entertainment to those whom he would free, Cleomenes' friends made that provision, and sent it into the prison, thus imposing upon the keepers, who thought it had been sent by the king. For he sacrificed, and gave them large portions, and with a garland upon his head, feasted and made merry with his friends. It is said that he began the action sooner than he designed, having understood that a servant who was privy to the plot, had gone out to visit a mistress that he loved. This made him afraid of a discovery; and therefore, as soon as it was full noon, and all the keepers sleeping off their wine, he put on his coat, and opening the seam to bare his right shoulder, with his drawn sword in his hand, he issued forth, together with his friends provided in the same manner, making thirteen in all. One of them, by name Hippitas, was lame, and followed the first onset very well, but when he presently perceived that they were more slow in their advances for his sake, he desired them to run him through, and not ruin their enterprise by staying for a useless, unprofitable man. By chance an Alexandrian was then riding by the door; him they threw off, and setting Hippitas on horseback, ran through the streets, and proclaimed liberty to the people. But they, it seems, had courage enough to praise and admire Cleomenes' daring, but not one had the heart to follow and assist him. Three of them fell on Ptolemy, the son of Chrysermas, as he was coming out of the palace, and killed him. Another Ptolemy, the officer in charge of the city, advancing against them in a chariot, they set upon, dispersed his guards and attendants, and pulling him out of the chariot, killed him upon the spot. Then they made towards the castle, designing to break open the prison, release those who were confined, and avail themselves of their numbers; but the keepers were too quick for them, and secured the passages. Being baffled in this attempt, Cleomenes with his company roamed about the city, none joining with him, but all retreating from and flying his approach. Therefore, despairing of success, and saying to his friends, that it was no wonder that women ruled over men that were afraid of liberty, he bade them all die as bravely as became his followers and their own past actions. This said, Hippitas was first, as he desired, run through by one of the younger men, and then each of them readily and resolutely fell upon his own sword, except Panteus, the same who first surprised Megalopolis. This man, being of a very handsome person, and a great lover of the Spartan discipline, the king had made his dearest friend; and he now bade him, when he had seen him and the rest fallen, die by their example.

Panteus walked over them as they lay, and pricked every one with his dagger, to try whether any was alive, when he pricked Cleomenes in the ankle, and saw him turn upon his back, he kissed him, sat down by him, and when he was quite dead, covered up the body, and then killed himself over it.

Concerning Sosibios,[1] we must add for completeness sake a fragment from Polybius' fifteenth book,[2] telling us that Sosibios, the pseudo-steward of Ptolemy, seems to have been 'a wily old baggage (σκεῦος ἀγχίνουν καὶ πολυχρόνιον) and most mischievous to the kingdom, and first he planned the murder of Lysimachus, who was the son of Arsinoe (daughter of Lysimachus) and of Ptolemy,[3] secondly of Magas the son of Ptolemy and Berenike daughter of Magas [hence the king's full-brother], thirdly of Berenike daughter of Ptolemy [rather of Magas] and mother of Philopator,[4] fourthly of Cleomenes the Spartan, fifthly of Arsinoe daughter of Berenike [the king's sister and wife].' It is probably this foul catalogue of crimes which makes Strabo select this reign[5] and the ninth as the worst among the evil series of the later Ptolemies; and so dangers began to thicken about the kingdom of Egypt, which had been kept far off by the energy and wisdom of the first three sovrans.

[1] Of course his influence abroad was great, and hence it has been conjectured that he is the Sosibios son of Dioscurides the Alexandrian who receives city-rights and other honours from Orchomenos, Tanagra, and Knidos in extant inscriptions. Cf. BCH for 1880, pp. 97-98, where Foucart compares these texts.

[2] c. 25, ed. Hultsch.

[3] Philadelphus, hence the present king's uncle. Cf. above § 85, whence it appears he was στρατηγός at Koptos.

[4] A proverb (εὔνους ὁ σφάκτης) is explained by Zenobius (iii. 94) with the remark that the queen was given over to Sosibios, who kept her in such close confinement, that the high-spirited woman committed suicide by poison.

[5] Cp. xvii. 1, § 11. In this opinion Justin's authorities evidently coincided.

Yet Philopator was no child. He must have been over twenty-four years old; he had been associated, though perhaps only nominally, with his father in the government; he had been educated by the best man of his time, Eratosthenes. His very title is said to signify 'the son designated for the throne by his father.'[1]

§ 151. After the abortive attempt of Cleomenes, which can hardly be called a serious danger, came the attack on Coele-Syria by the active and energetic Antiochus, known afterwards as Antiochus the Great.   This prince, succeeding at an early age—he was not twenty-one—whereas the new Ptolemy was twenty-five, found himself beset by many dangers, the revolt of his eastern provinces under Molo, that of Asia Minor under his uncle Achaeus, and yet was already taking measures for the re-conquest of Coele-Syria, when these other dangers stayed his hand. But the wickedness of old Sosibios, who evidently could not tolerate any influence near the throne but his own, had furnished Antiochus with a traitor to help him.   'Theodotus, the Aetolian,[2] governor of Coele-Syria, despising the king for his vices, and mistrusting his court—because recently, after serving the king ably, especially in repulsing the first movements of Antiochus against his province, he not only had received no thanks, but even narrowly escaped with his life, when summoned to Alexandria — for these reasons undertook to confer with Antiochus, and hand him over the cities of Coele-Syria.'

Antiochus, in spite of his activity, his success in crushing the revolt of his eastern provinces, and still more his good fortune in getting rid of his grand vizier Hermeias,[3] was at some loss which enemy to attack next, for on the

---

[1] Cf. Wilamowitz *Weihgeschenk* p. 16, and the quotations there.
[2] Polybius v. 40.   [3] Ibid. 56.

north-west his uncle Achaeus had assumed the diadem and title of king in Asia Minor—perhaps at the instigation of Ptolemy's advisers ; on the south he had pressing invitations from Theodotus to make no delay in occupying the Syrian cities ready to receive him. As, however, it transpired that the troops of Achaeus, when marched as far as Lycaonia, showed plainly that they would proceed no further against their legitimate sovran, Asia Minor evidently afforded no pressing danger, and so Antiochus set himself to attack Ptolemy.

His first great success was the capture of Seleukeia at the mouth of the Orontes, which had been occupied by an Egyptian garrison since the victorious campaign of Euergetes in 246 B.C. Polybius[1] describes at length the capture of this all-important fortress, the possession of which by Egypt was a standing disgrace to Syria ; then he recounts the first victorious campaign of Antiochus against Nicolaus, Ptolemy's new general in Coele-Syria, and the occupation of Tyre and Ptolemais by the treachery of Theodotus. We cannot do better than let Polybius tell the sequel.

§ 152. Being informed that Ptolemy had come out against him, and had reached Memphis, and that all his forces were collected at Pelusium, and were opening the sluices, and filling up the wells of drinking water, he abandoned the idea of attacking Pelusium ; but making a progress through the several cities, endeavoured to win them over by force or persuasion to his authority. Some of the less fortified cities were overawed at his approach and made no difficulty about submitting, but others trusting to their fortifications or the

[1] v. 59 *sq.* I am not aware that any modern researches have been made to verify Polybius' description of the remarkable site of this city. Though many earthquakes may have increased the difficulties of doing so, it ought to be a tempting problem for an explorer.

strength of their situations held out ; and to these he was
forced to lay regular siege and so wasted considerable time.

Though treated with such flagrant perfidy, Ptolemy was so
feeble, and his neglect of all military preparations had been so
great, that the idea of protecting his rights with the sword,
which was his most obvious duty, never occurred to him.

Agathocles and Sosibius, however, the leading ministers
in the kingdom at that time, took counsel together and did
the best they could with the means at their disposal, in view
of the existing crisis.   They resolved to devote themselves to
the preparations for war ; and, meanwhile, to try to retard
the advance of Antiochus by embassies : pretending to confirm
him in the opinion he originally entertained about Ptolemy,
namely, that the latter would not venture to fight, but would
trust to negotiations, and the interposition of common friends,
to induce him to evacuate Coele-Syria.   Having determined
upon this policy, Agathocles and Sosibius, to whom the whole
business was entrusted, lost no time in sending their ambassadors to Antiochus : and at the same time they sent messages
to Rhodes, Byzantium, and Cyzicus, not omitting the Aetolians,
inviting them to send commissioners to discuss the terms of
a treaty.   The commissioners duly arrived, and by occupying
the time with going backwards and forwards between the two
kings, abundantly secured to these statesmen the two things
which they wanted,—delay, and time to make their preparations
for war.   They fixed their residence at Memphis and there
carried on these negotiations continuously.   Nor were they
less attentive to the ambassadors from Antiochus, whom they
received with every mark of courtesy and kindness.   But
meanwhile they were calling up and collecting at Alexandria
the mercenaries whom they had on service in towns outside
Egypt ; were despatching men to recruit foreign soldiers ; and
were collecting provisions both for the troops they already
possessed, and for those that were coming in.   No less active
were they in every other department of the military preparations.   They took turns in going on rapid and frequent visits
to Alexandria, to see that the supplies should in no point be
inadequate to the undertaking before them.   The manufacture
of arms, the selection of men, and their division into companies, they committed to the care of Echecrates of Thessaly

and Phoxidas of Melita. With these they associated Eury-lochus of Magnesia, and Socrates of Boeotia, who were also joined by Cnopias of Allaria. By the greatest good fortune they had got hold of these officers, who, while serving with Demetrius and Antigonus,[1] had acquired some experience of real war and actual service in the field. Accordingly they took command of the assembled troops, and made the best of them by giving them the training of soldiers.

Their first measure was to divide them according to their country and age, and to assign to each division its appropriate arms, taking no account of what they had borne before. Next they broke up their battalions and muster rolls, which had been formed on the basis of their old system of pay, and formed them into companies adapted to the immediate purpose. Having effected this they began to drill the men ; habituating them severally not only to obey the words of command, but also to the proper management of their weapons. They also frequently summoned general meetings at headquarters, and delivered speeches to the men. The most useful in this respect were Andromachus of Aspendus and Polycrates of Argos ; because they had recently crossed from Greece, and were still thoroughly imbued with the Greek spirit, and the military ideas prevalent in the several states. Moreover, they were illustrious on the score of their private wealth, as well as on that of their respective countries ; to which advantages Polycrates added those of an ancient family, and of the reputation obtained by his father Mnasiades as an athlete. By private and public exhortations these officers inspired their men with zeal and enthusiasm for the struggle which awaited them.

All these officers, too, had commands in the army suited to their particular accomplishments. Eurylochus of Magnesia commanded about three thousand men of what were called in the royal armies the Agema, or Guard ; Socrates of Boeotia had two thousand light-armed troops under him ; while the Achaean Phoxidas, and Ptolemy the son of Thraseas, and Andromachus of Aspendus were associated in the duty of drilling the phalanx and the mercenary Greek soldiers on the same ground,—Andromachus and Ptolemy commanding the

---

[1] That is, Demetrius II. and Antigonus Doson.

phalanx, Phoxidas the mercenaries ; of which the numbers were respectively twenty-five thousand and eight thousand. The cavalry, again, attached to the court, amounting to seven hundred, as well as that which was obtained from Libya or enlisted in the country, were being trained by Polycrates, and were under his personal command : amounting in all to about three thousand men. In the actual campaign the most effective service was performed by Echecrates of Thessaly, by whom the Greek cavalry, which, with the whole body of mercenary cavalry, amounted to two thousand men, was splendidly trained. No one took more pains with the men under his command than Cnopias of Allaria. He commanded all the Cretans, who numbered three thousand, and among them a thousand Neo-Cretans, over whom he had set Philo of Gnossus. They also armed three thousand Libyans in the Macedonian fashion, who were commanded by Ammonius of Barce. The Egyptians themselves supplied twenty thousand soldiers to the phalanx, and were under the command of Sosibius. A body of Thracians and Gauls was also enrolled, four thousand being taken from settlers in the country and their descendants, while two thousand had been recently en-listed and brought over : and these were under the command of Dionysius of Thrace.[1] Such in its numbers, and in the variety of the elements of which it was composed, was the force which was being got ready for Ptolemy.

Meanwhile Antiochus had been engaged in the siege of Dura [2] : but the strength of the place and the support given it by Nicolaus prevented him from effecting anything ; and as the winter was closing in, he agreed with the ambassadors of Ptolemy to a suspension of hostilities for four months, and promised that he would discuss the whole question at issue in a friendly spirit. But he was as far as possible from being

---

[1] Thracians we know as settlers long before, but if Gauls were indeed so established, it was a great novelty. I suppose the two thousand imported to have been Gauls, while the four thousand were either κληροῦχοι or τῆς ἐπιγονῆς, viz. the children of privileged foreigners born in the country. Cf. *Addit. Note* p. 491.

[2] Two different towns of this name had already been mentioned (cc. 48, 52). This Dura or Dôra appears to be in Phoenicia ; but nothing is known of it.

sincere in this negotiation : his real object was to avoid being detained any length of time from his own country, and to be able to place his troops in winter quarters in Seleucia ; because Achaeus was now notoriously plotting against him, and without disguise co-operating with Ptolemy. So having come to this agreement, Antiochus dismissed the ambassadors with injunctions to acquaint him as soon as possible with the decision of Ptolemy, and to meet him at Seleucia. He then placed the necessary guards in the various strongholds, committed to Theodotus the command-in-chief over them all, and returned home. On his arrival at Seleucia he distributed his forces into their winter quarters ; and from that time forth took no pains to keep the mass of his army under discipline, being persuaded that the business would not call for any more fighting ; because he was already master of some portions of Coele-Syria and Phoenicia, and expected to secure the rest by voluntary submission or by diplomacy : for Ptolemy, he believed, would not venture upon a general engagement. This opinion was shared also by the ambassadors : because Sosibius fixing his residence at Memphis conducted his negotiations with them in a friendly manner ; while he prevented those who went backwards and forwards to Antiochus from ever becoming eye-witnesses of the preparations that were being carried on at Alexandria. Nay, even by the time that the ambassadors arrived, Sosibius was already prepared for every eventuality.

§ 153. Meanwhile Antiochus was extremely anxious to have as much the advantage over the government of Alexandria in diplomatic argument as he had in arms. Accordingly when the ambassadors arrived at Seleucia, and both parties began, in accordance with the instructions of Sosibius, to discuss the clauses of the proposed arrangement in detail, the king made very light of the loss recently sustained by Ptolemy, and the injury which had been manifestly inflicted upon him by the existing occupation of Coele-Syria ; and in the pleadings on this subject he refused to look upon this transaction in the light of an injury at all, alleging that the places belonged to him by right. He asserted that the original occupation of the country by Antigonus the One-eyed, and the royal authority exercised over it by Seleucus,[1] constituted an absolutely

---

[1] Above, § 43.

decisive and equitable title, in virtue of which Coele-Syria belonged of right to himself and not to Ptolemy ; for Ptolemy I. went to war with Antigonus with the view of annexing this country, not to his own government, but to that of Seleucus. But, above all, he pressed the convention entered into by the three kings, Cassander, Lysimachus, and Seleucus, when, after having conquered Antigonus,[1] they deliberated in common upon the arrangements to be made, and decided that the whole of Syria should belong to Seleucus. The commissioners of Ptolemy endeavoured to establish the opposite case. They magnified the existing injury, and dilated on its hardship ; asserting that the treason of Theodotus and the invasion of Antiochus amounted to a breach of treaty-rights. They alleged the possession of these places in the reign of Ptolemy, son of Lagus ; and tried to show that Ptolemy had joined Seleucus in the war on the understanding that he was to invest Seleucus with the government of the whole of Asia, but was to take Coele-Syria and Phoenicia for himself.

Such were the arguments brought forward by the two contracting parties in the course of the embassies and counter-embassies and conferences. There was no prospect, however, of arriving at any result, because the controversy was conducted, not by the principals, but by the common friends of both ; and there was no one to intervene authoritatively to check and control the caprice of the party which they might decide to be in the wrong. But what caused the most insuperable difficulty was the matter of Achaeus. For Ptolemy was eager that the terms of the treaty should include him : while Antiochus would not allow the subject to be so much as mentioned ; and was indignant that Ptolemy should venture to protect rebels, or bring such a point into the discussion at all.

The approach of spring found both sides weary of negotiations, and with no prospect of coming to a conclusion. Antiochus therefore began collecting his forces, with a view of making an invasion by land and sea, and completing his conquest of Coele-Syria. On his part Ptolemy gave the supreme management of the war to Nicolaus, sent abundant provisions to Gaza, and despatched land and sea forces. The arrival of these reinforcements gave Nicolaus courage to enter

---

[1] Above, § 41.

upon the war, the commander of the navy promptly co-operating with him in carrying out all his orders.   This admiral was Perigenes, whom Ptolemy sent out in command of the fleet, consisting of thirty fully-decked ships and more than four thousand ships of burden.   Nicolaus was by birth an Aetolian, and was the boldest and most experienced officer in the service of Ptolemy.   With one division of his army he hastened to seize the pass at Platanus ; with the rest, which he personally commanded, he occupied the environs of Por-phyrion ; and there prepared to resist the invasion of the king : the fleet being also anchored close to him.

§ 154. Then follows the campaign of Antiochus against the Ptolemaic generals in Syria and Palestine, which ended by his taking the upper country and advancing his next winter quarters to Ptolemais.   The following spring (217 B.C.) brought the decision.

At the beginning of the following spring, having all pre-parations for war completed, Antiochus and Ptolemy determined to bring their claims to Coele-Syria to the decision of a battle. Ptolemy accordingly set out from Alexandria with seventy thousand infantry, five thousand cavalry, and seventy-three elephants.   Being informed of his approach, Antiochus drew his forces together.   These consisted of Daae, Carmani, and Cilicians, equipped as light-armed troops to the number of about five thousand, under the charge and command of Byttacus the Macedonian.   Under Theodotus, the Aetolian, who had de-serted from Ptolemy, were ten thousand picked men from the whole kingdom, armed in the Macedonian fashion, most of whom had silver shields.   The number of the phalanx was twenty thousand, and they were led by Nicarchus and Theo-dotus Hemiolius.   In addition to these there were Agrianes and Persians, who were either bowmen or slingers, to the number of two thousand.   With them were a thousand Thracians, under the command of Menedemus of Alabanda. There was also a mixed force of Medes, Cissians, Cadusians, and Carmanians, amounting to five thousand men, who were assigned to the chief command of Aspasianus the Mede. Certain Arabians also and men of neighbouring tribes, to

the number of ten thousand, were commanded by Zabdibelus.
The mercenaries from Greece amounting to five thousand were
led by Hippolochus of Thessaly.   Antiochus had also fifteen
hundred Cretans who came with Eurylochus, and a thousand
Neo-Cretans commanded by Zelys of Gortyn ; with whom
were five hundred javelin-men of Lydia, and a thousand
Cardaces who came with Lysimachus the Gaul.   The entire
number of his horse was six thousand ; four thousand were
commanded by the king's nephew Antipater, the rest by
Themison : so that the whole number of Antiochus' force
was sixty-two thousand infantry, six thousand cavalry, and one
hundred and two elephants.

Having marched to Pelusium Ptolemy made his first halt
in that town : and having been there joined by the stragglers,
and having given out their rations of corn to his men, he got
the army in motion, and led them by a line of march which
goes through the waterless region skirting Mount Casius and
the Marshes.[1]   On the fifth day's march he reached his
destination, and pitched his camp a distance of fifty stades
from Raphia, which is the first city of Coele-Syria towards
Egypt.

While Ptolemy was effecting this movement Antiochus
arrived with his army at Gaza, where he was joined by some
reinforcements, and once more commenced his advance,
proceeding at a leisurely pace.   He passed Raphia and
encamped about ten stades from the enemy.   For a while the
two armies preserved this distance, and remained encamped
opposite each other.   But after some few days, wishing to remove
to more advantageous ground and to inspire confidence in his
troops, Antiochus pushed forward his camp so much nearer
Ptolemy, that the palisades of the two camps were not more
than five stades from each other ; and while in this position,
there were frequent struggles at the watering-places and on
forays, as well as infantry and cavalry skirmishes in the space
between the camps.

In the course of these proceedings Theodotus conceived
and put into execution an enterprise, very characteristic of an
Aetolian, but undoubtedly requiring great personal courage.
Having formerly lived at Ptolemy's court he knew the king's

---

[1] Called Barathra.   See Strabo xvii. 1, 21.

tastes and habits. Accordingly, accompanied by two others, he entered the enemy's camp just before daybreak; where, owing to the dim light, he could not be recognised by his face, while his dress and other accoutrements did not render him noticeable, owing to the variety of costume prevailing in both armies. He had marked the position of the king's tent during the preceding days, for the skirmishes took place quite close; and he now walked boldly up to it, and passed through all the outer ring of attendants without being observed : but when he came to the tent in which the king was accustomed to transact business and dine, though he searched it in every conceivable way, he failed to find the king ; for Ptolemy slept in another tent, separate from the public and official tent. He however wounded two men who were sleeping there, and killed Andreas, the king's physician ; and then returned safely to his own camp, without meeting with any molestation, except just as he was passing over the vallum of the enemy's camp. As far as daring went, he had fulfilled his purpose : but he had failed in prudence by not taking the precaution to ascertain where Ptolemy was accustomed to sleep.

§ 155. After being encamped opposite each other for five days, the two kings resolved to bring matters to the decision of battle. And upon Ptolemy beginning to move his army outside its camp, Antiochus hastened to do the same. Both formed their centre with their phalanx and men armed in the Macedonian manner. But Ptolemy's two wings were formed as follows :—Polycrates, with the cavalry under his command, occupied the left, and between him and the phalanx were Cretans standing close by the horsemen ; next them came the royal guard ; then the peltasts under Socrates, adjoining the Libyans armed in Macedonian fashion. On the right wing was Echecrates of Thessaly, with his division of cavalry ; on his left were stationed Gauls and Thracians ; next them Phoxidas and the Greek mercenaries, extending to the Egyptian phalanx. Of the elephants forty were on the left wing, where Ptolemy was to be in person during the battle ; the other thirty-three had been stationed in front of the right wing opposite the mercenary cavalry.

Antiochus also placed sixty of his elephants commanded by

his foster-brother Philip in front of his right wing, on which he was to be present personally, to fight opposite Ptolemy. Behind these he stationed the two thousand cavalry commanded by Antipater, and two thousand more at right angles to them. In line with the cavalry he placed the Cretans, and next them the Greek mercenaries; with the latter he mixed two thousand of these armed in the Macedonian fashion under the command of the Macedonian Byttacus. At the extreme point of the left wing he placed two thousand cavalry under the command of Themison; by their side Cardacian and Lydian javelin-men; next them the light-armed division of three thousand, commanded by Menedemus; then the Cissians, Medes, and Carmanians; and by their side the Arabians and neighbouring peoples who continued the line up to the phalanx. The remainder of the elephants he placed in front of his left wing under the command of Myiscus, one of the boys about the court [royal pages].

The two armies having been drawn up in the order I have described; the kings went along their respective lines, and addressed words of encouragement and exhortation to their officers and friends. But as they both rested their strongest hopes on their phalanx, they showed their greatest earnestness and addressed their strongest exhortations to them; which were re-echoed in Ptolemy's case by Andromachus and Sosibius and the king's sister Arsinoe; in the case of Antiochus by Theodotus and Nicarchus: these officers being the commanders of the phalanx in the two armies respectively. The substance of what was said on both sides was the same: for neither monarch had any glorious or famous achievement of his own to quote to those whom he was addressing, seeing that they had but recently succeeded to their crowns; but they endeavoured to inspire the men of the phalanx with spirit and boldness, by reminding them of the glory of their ancestors, and the great deeds performed by them. But they chiefly dwelt upon the hopes of advancement which the men might expect at their hands in the future; and they called upon and exhorted the leaders and the whole body of men, who were about to be engaged, to maintain the fight with a manly and courageous spirit. So with these or similar words, delivered by their own lips or by interpreters, they rode along their lines.

Ptolemy, accompanied by his sister, having arrived at the left wing of his army, and Antiochus with the royal guard at the right: they gave the signal for the battle, and opened the fight by a charge of elephants. Only some few of Ptolemy's elephants came to close quarters with the foe: seated on these the soldiers in the howdahs maintained a brilliant fight, lunging at and striking each other with crossed pikes.[1]   But the elephants themselves fought still more brilliantly, using all their strength in the encounter, and pushing against each other, forehead to forehead.

The way in which elephants fight is this: they get their tusks entangled and jammed, and then push against one another with all their might, trying to make each other yield ground until one of them proving superior in strength has pushed aside the other's trunk; and when once he can get a side blow at his enemy, he pierces him with his tusks as a bull would with his horns.   Now, most of Ptolemy's animals, as is the way with Libyan elephants, were afraid to face the fight: for they cannot stand the smell or the trumpeting of the Indian elephants, but are frightened at their size and strength, I suppose, and run away from them at once without waiting to come near them.   This is exactly what happened on this occasion: and upon their being thrown into confusion and being driven back upon their own lines, Ptolemy's guard gave way before the rush of the animals; while Antiochus, wheeling his men so as to avoid the elephants, charged the division of cavalry under Polycrates.   At the same time the Greek mercenaries stationed near the phalanx, and behind the elephants, charged Ptolemy's peltasts and made them give ground, the elephants having already thrown their ranks into confusion. Thus Ptolemy's whole left wing began to give way before the enemy.

Echecrates the commander of the right wing waited at first to see the result of the struggle between the other wings of the two armies: but when he saw the dust coming his way, and that the elephants opposite his division were afraid even to approach the hostile elephants at all, he ordered Phoxidas to charge the part of the enemy opposite him with his Greek mercenaries; while he made a flank movement with the cavalry

---

[1] Sarissae, the long Macedonian spears.

and the division behind the elephants; and so getting out of the line of the hostile elephants' attack, charged the enemy's cavalry on the rear or the flank and quickly drove them from their ground. Phoxidas and his men were similarly successful: for they charged the Arabians and Medes and forced them into precipitate flight. Thus Antiochus's right wing gained a victory, while his left was defeated. The phalanxes, left without the support of either wing, remained intact in the centre of the plain, in a state of alternate hope and fear for the result. Meanwhile Antiochus was assisting in gaining the victory on his right wing; while Ptolemy, who had retired behind his phalanx, now came forward in the centre, and showing himself in the view of both armies struck terror into the hearts of the enemy, but inspired great spirit and enthusiasm in his own men; and Andromachus and Sosibius at once ordered them to lower their sarissae and charge. The picked Syrian troops stood their ground only for a short time, and the division of Nicarchus quickly broke and fled. Antiochus presuming, in his youthful inexperience, from the success of his own division, that he would be equally victorious all along the line, was pressing on the pursuit; but upon one of the older officers at length giving him warning, and pointing out that the cloud of dust raised by the phalanx was moving towards their own camp, he understood too late what was happening; and endeavoured to gallop back with the squadron of royal cavalry to the field. But finding his whole line in full retreat he was forced to retire to Raphia: comforting himself with the belief that, as far as he was personally concerned, he had won a victory, but had been defeated in the whole battle by the want of spirit and courage shown by the rest.

§ 156. Ptolemy, having secured the final victory by his phalanx, and killed large numbers of the enemy in the pursuit by means of his cavalry and mercenaries on his right wing, retired to his own camp and there spent the night. But next day, after picking up and burying his own dead, and stripping the bodies of the enemy, he advanced towards Raphia. Antiochus had wished, immediately after the retreat of his army, to make a camp outside the city, and there rally such of his men as had fled in compact bodies: but finding that the greater number had retreated into the town, he was compelled to enter it himself also. Next morning, however, before daybreak, he led out the relics of his army and made the best of his way to Gaza. There he pitched a camp: and having sent an embassy to obtain leave to pick up his dead, he obtained a truce for performing their obsequies. His loss amounted to nearly ten thousand infantry and three hundred cavalry killed, and four thousand taken prisoners. Three elephants were killed on the field, and two died afterwards of their wounds. On Ptolemy's side the losses were fifteen hundred infantry and seven hundred cavalry: sixteen of his elephants were killed, and most of the others captured.

Such was the result of the battle of Raphia between kings Ptolemy and Antiochus for the possession of Coele-Syria.

After picking up his dead Antiochus retired with his army to his own country: while Ptolemy took over Raphia and the other towns without difficulty, all the states vying with each other as to which should be first to renew their allegiance and come over to him. And perhaps it is the way of the world everywhere to accommodate one's self to circumstances at such times; but it is eminently true of the race inhabiting that country, that they have a natural turn and inclination to worship success. Moreover it was all the more natural in this case, owing to the existing disposition of the people in favour of the Alexandrian kings; for the inhabitants of Coele-Syria are somehow always more loyally disposed to this family than to any other. Accordingly they now stopped short of no extravagance of adulation, honouring Ptolemy with crowns, sacrifices, and every possible compliment of the kind.

Meanwhile Antiochus, on arriving at the city which bears his own name, immediately despatched an embassy to Ptolemy, consisting of Antipater, his nephew, and Theodotus Hemiolius, to treat of a peace, in great alarm lest the enemy should advance upon him. For his defeat had inspired him with distrust of his own forces, and he was afraid that Achaeus would seize the opportunity to attack him. It did not occur to Ptolemy to take any of these circumstances into account: but being thoroughly satisfied with his unexpected success, and generally at his unlooked for acquisition of Coele-Syria, he was by no means indisposed to peace; but even more inclined to it than he ought to have been: influenced in that direction by the habitual effeminacy and corruption of his manner of life. Accordingly, when Antipater and his colleague arrived, after some little bluster and vituperation of Antiochus for what had taken place, he agreed to a truce for a year. He sent Sosibius back with the ambassadors to ratify the treaty : while he himself, after remaining three months in Syria and Phoenicia, and settling the towns, left Andromachus of Aspendus as governor of this district, and started with his sister and friends for Alexandria : having brought the war to a conclusion in a way that surprised his subjects, when they contrasted it with the 'principles according to which he spent the rest of his life. Antiochus after exchanging ratifications of the treaty with Sosibius, employed himself in making preparations for attacking Achaeus, as he had originally begun doing. Such was the political situation in Asia.

§ 157. We have one accidental reference to the king in the year 216 B.C. from Livy.[1] It is in connexion with Decius Magius, who offered so obstinate an opposition to Hannibal, when the Capuans joined the Punic side, that Hannibal, finding him irreconcilable, put him on board a Carthaginian vessel to be sent to Africa : 'A tempest drove the ships out of their course to Cyrene, which was then in the power of the (Egyptian) kings. There Magius, having taken refuge at the statue of Ptolemy, was brought by the guardians (of the temple) to Alexandria. When he had explained to the king how he was thrown into chains by Hannibal contrary to the terms of the treaty (between Hannibal and Capua) he was set free, and given leave to return either to Rome or Capua, according to his choice. But Magius replied that he was not safe at Capua, and that during the war of Rome and Capua, Rome would be to him rather the abode of a deserter than of a guest. He therefore preferred decidedly to live in the land of that sovran, who was the assertor and procurer of his

[1] xxiii. 10.

liberty.' This is the only glimpse we get of Cyrene for many years, and it also shows to us the king of Egypt as a fair and sensible man, not a compound of all the vices, as the historians tell us.

The sequel of Philopator's history is told briefly by Polybius [1] : 'But it occurred to Ptolemy straightway (εὐθέως) after these conjunctures to be engaged in a war against the Egyptians. For the king by arming the natives for the war against Antiochus pursued a policy successful at the moment, but mischievous in the sequel. The natives being elated by their success at Raphia would no longer submit to his commands, but sought a leader and representative, as being quite able to help themselves. And they ended by doing so, not long after.' Most unfortunately the chapters giving the details of this revolt are lost, nor does any other extant author come to our aid. In the excerpts from the fourteenth book we have but a few words more : 'Ptolemy after the close of the war about Coele-Syria turned from all proper objects to a life of debauchery. But at long last (ὀψὲ δέ ποτε, which hardly agrees with the extract just cited) he was forced by circumstances into the war in question, which, apart from the mutual cruelty and treachery, afforded neither a pitched land nor sea battle, nor a siege, nor anything worthy of narration.' Wherefore, he adds, it was better to treat it once for all, than to mention year by year small and unimportant movements.

§ 158. So much then we can clearly infer. The first [2] of the great native rebellions broke out in this reign, some time after the battle of Raphia, perhaps 213 or 212 B.C. It lasted several years, and was evidently a civil war such

---

[1] v. 107.

[2] This may be qualified by what has been said above, § 131, regarding Euergetes.

as the Germans call *Bauernkrieg*, with many savage cruelties committed by the peasants, and by the troops sent to reduce them to obedience. In a passage,[1] which gives some details of the faithlessness of Epiphanes towards the native chiefs who had headed the revolt of Lycopolis (concerning which more will be said in its place), Polybius adds that the course of this later rebellion was much the same as the former one, in which Polycrates subdued the revolters. This Polycrates is the Argive mercenary leader, the friend of Agathocles, frequently mentioned by Polybius as acting during Philopator's reign, as well as during the first great revolt under Epiphanes.

It is to be noted that if Philopator had been married at or before his accession, the late birth of his son Epiphanes would be remarkable. Arsinoe figures as already possessing great influence in the campaign of Raphia, and yet her son was only four or five years old in 205 B.C. when his father died.[2]

From this and from the fact that in Polybius' narrative of the campaign she is repeatedly spoken of only as the king's *sister*, as well as her *long orphanhood*,[3] I infer that her marriage was subsequent, perhaps as late as 212 B.C.

---

[1] xxii. 7.

[2] He seems to have been associated as an infant with his father in the throne, according to an inscription from Naukratis published in the *Amer. Journal of Arch.* ii. 2 υπερ β]ασιλεως Πτολ. θε[ου | μ]εγαλου Φιλοπατορος σωτηρος | και νικηφορου και του υιου Πτολ. | Ισιδι Σαραπιδι Απολλωνι | κομων Ασκληπιαδου | οικονομος των κατα Ναυκρατιν, and this is supported by the demotic contracts cited by Revillout *RE* iii. 3.

[3] Cf. below, p. 276. According to Jacobs and Susemihl, interpreting an epigram of Damagetos, she dedicated a lock of hair in the same way that her mother did (above, § 126) :—

> Ἄρτεμι, τόξα λαχοῦσα καὶ ἀλκήεντας ὀϊστούς,
> σοὶ πλόκον οἰκείας τόνδε λέλοιπε κόμης

Our Greek authorities tell us little more concerning this king than his debauches, and his literary fancies. They describe him as having totally abandoned all care of foreign affairs, which had been the great glory of his predecessors. His subjection to his mistress Agathocleia, and to her brother Agathocles, became so complete, that when they had put to death his wife Arsinoe, and he shortly after died, they seemed to have the whole kingdom in their hands.

But withal he had literary fancies, and was rather aesthetical than (as his fathers had been) scientific. He composed a play called *Adonis*,[1] to which his flatterer Agathocles wrote a commentary. He built a temple to Homer, which may possibly mark a change in the attitude of Alexandrian critics towards the Father of poetry. For with the sober and prudent Eratosthenes, still more with the brilliant Aristophanes, whose genius was ignored by this king, the free-and-easy way of treating Homer with emendation and alteration adopted by Zenodotus gave way to a reverence for the Father of Greek poetry, and to a strict and scientific handling of the difficulties which his

> Ἀρσινόη, θυόεν παρ' ἀνάκτορον, ἡ Πτολεμαίου
> παρθένος, ἱμερτοῦ κειραμένη πλοκάμου (*Anthol.* vii. 277).

This fully corroborates my theory in the text, that when setting out for the campaign of Raphia, she was still (as Polybius calls her) only the king's sister, and probably very young. Her zeal in encouraging the troops is rhetorically exaggerated in the opening of the 3rd Maccabees, where indeed the victory is attributed to her efforts : ἱκανῶς ἡ 'Α. ἐπιπορευσαμένη τὰς δυνάμεις παρεκάλει, μετὰ οἴκτου καὶ δακρύων τοὺς πλοκάμους λελυμένη, βοηθεῖν ἑαυτοῖς τε καὶ τοῖς τέκνοις καὶ γυναιξὶ θαρραλέως, ἐπαγγελλομένη δώσειν νικήσασιν ἑκάστῳ δύο μνᾶς χρυσίου. This author also calls her the king's sister only, but possibly he is copying from Polybius.

[1] Schol. Aristoph. *Thesmoph.* 1059, who says it was in imitation of Euripides.

language offered to later generations.[1] His queen and
sister Arsinoe was evidently a woman of vigour and of
character, but she seems to have been unable to control
her weak and sensual husband. Her child and heir to
the throne, not born till 210 or 209 B.C., must have been
welcomed with no ordinary rejoicings. But we hear no
details concerning this feast.

§ 159. To the Greek evidence for the dissolute and
worthless character of the king, there may be added
the so-called third book of Maccabees, which gives an
exceedingly turgid account of Philopator's dealings with
the Jews. The author, who evidently has good knowledge
of the king and his history, starts from the circumstances
following the battle of Raphia, when the king visits Jerusalem, and proposes to enter the Holy of Holies, in spite
of the protest of the high-priest and the whole population. The agitation of the city is described with extravagant rhetoric; and then by providential interposition
the king falls in a fit at the very door, and is carried out
by his attendants, which is urged not only as a proof
of divine favour, but as the cause of Philopator's subsequent hostility to the Jews.

Nothing is more probable than that this idle and
sportive king did desire to enter, from mere curiosity, the
holiest shrine of Jewish religion, and that he was with
difficulty dissuaded by the uproar which his proposal
excited. He was not a man of strong resolves, but essentially an easy-going person, as Polybius repeatedly tells us.

When he returned home, we hear from the Jewish
author that he carried with him a rankling spite against
the chosen people, which he first showed by excluding
them from court, unless they sacrificed to the king, or

---

[1] Cf. Susemihl ii. p. 619 on this matter.

perhaps to Dionysus, his patron god, also by ordering that
such as refused should be treated as natives,[1] and the
contumacious even branded with the ivy-leaf of Dionysus,
while those that recanted and were initiated into the
mysteries of this god should have equal privileges with the
Alexandrians.[2]   The great majority of the nation refuses,
and accordingly the king, in an obviously concocted document to the 'generals and soldiers' throughout Egypt,
states that he had indeed wished to treat the Jews with
generosity, and had intended to raise them to the citizenship
of Alexandria and to eligibility for the eponymous priesthood[3] ; but finding that they were irreconcilable, and even
persecuted the few who had accepted loyally his benefits,
he is determined, upon this clear evidence, and 'providing
lest if some sudden insurrection may hereafter occur, he may
not have this impious people traitors behind his back,' to
have them all, men, women and children, catalogued and
sent up to Alexandria, there to be put to death.

§ 160. I will spare the reader the monstrous details that
follow, about the failure of papyrus and pens to register the
vast number of the Jews, about their deportation to the
hippodrome outside the city, where they were to be trampled

---

[1] πάντας τοὺς 'Ιουδ. εἰς λαογραφίαν καὶ οἰκετικὴν διάθεσιν ἀχθῆναι.
This means that there was a census and poll-tax according to residence,
and that this latter could not be changed at will.

[2] ἰσοπολίτας 'Αλεξανδρεῦσιν εἶναι, ii. 28-30.

[3] So I suppose we should translate iii. 21 ἐβουλήθημεν καὶ πολιτείας
αὐτοὺς 'Αλεξανδρέων καταξιῶσαι καὶ μετόχους τῶν ἀεὶ ἱερε(ι)ῶν καταστῆσαι
(though we should have expected ἱερωσυνῶν, the word ἱερεία is used for
priesthood in the Canopus inscription, so I have emended this text
which gives ἱερέων).   The repeated mention of the civic rights *of
the Alexandrians* seems to me to corroborate what I have above
(§ 51) maintained that this franchise was not ordinary Greek liberty
or autonomy, but something peculiar and intermediate between that and
the condition of mere subjects.

to death by intoxicated elephants. The king alternates feasting with fits of fury against his elephantarch, and after sundry providential delays, the elephants turn against their own troops. Then the king is converted, and writes another public letter, much in the style of that of Darius in the sixth chapter of the book of Daniel. In consequence the Jews are all liberated. They hold a great feast at 'Ptolemais called the rose-bearing from the peculiarity of the place,'[1] and appoint a feast lasting from the 25th of Pachon to the 4th of Epeiph—forty days —ending with the three days of the great crisis and liberation.[2]

The *mala fides* of the author, and his deliberate intention to add to the books of Daniel and Esther another instance of divine interposition in favour of the chosen people, are plain enough. But surely the feast kept by the Egyptian Jews at a fixed date cannot be an invention, and must point back to some historical origin. The author not only knows the habits of the king, his perpetual feasting, his devotion to the cult of Dionysus, the strong character of his sister Arsinoe, whose activity at the battle of Raphia is only overcoloured, but he lets us see plainly that the main question with the Jews was that of privileges. Were they to count as mere natives, and be included in the poll-tax ($\lambda\alpha\sigma\gamma\rho\alpha\phi\acute{\iota}\alpha$), or were they to have the privileges of Alexandrian Greeks? That Philopator in some way injured the condition of the Jews, and that they were concerned in the insurrection of the natives, seems very probable; also that the king may have demanded some large contribution from them, and degraded them upon their refusal. They may have regained, or obtained, the privilege of Alexandrian citizen-

[1] vii. 17.   [2] vi. 35-41.

ship by payment of a large sum of money, of which the memory rankled in their hearts, and caused them to regard him as a national enemy.

But to find out the truth from a writer, who deliberately conceals it, is not easy. We can assert with confidence that Philopator earned the hostility of that people, and that they looked back upon his reign as one of oppression and injustice.

§ 161. Yet in spite of these documents, there is no slight evidence that this king's reign was not so worthless and mischievous as it appears. Had Polybius and Plutarch been lost, and inscriptions only been preserved, we should have formed quite another picture of Philopator.

I have already spoken of the earthquake at Rhodes and of the great liberality of Egypt, some of which must be set down to the present king.[1] Had he reversed the policy of his father in this respect, or refused to send the subsidies still due to the Rhodians, we may be sure that we should have heard of it as another instance of his worthlessness.

There is extant an inscription found at Lesbos[2] which shows that his sway still reached to this far island. The date is, however, unknown. There is another found on an altar at Sestos,[3] which shows that at some shrine of the Cabiri at Sestos people thought it worth while to honour the Egyptian king. There were cities on the coast of 'Asia' which recognised his sway to the very end of his life, and which were counted part of the empire of his

---

[1] The long list of the Ptolemaic inscriptions found at the temple of the Paphian Aphrodite commences with this king ; cf. *JHS* ix. p. 253.

[2] Published in the *BCH* iv. 435.

[3] *Mitth.* vi. 208 υπερ βασιλεως Πτολ. και βασιλισσης Αρσινοης θεων φιλοπατορων, και του νου (*sic*) Πτολεμαιου θεοις τοις εν Σαμοθρακηι Αρισταρχη Μικυθου Περγαμηνη.

son.[1]   Then we hear that the Romans sent him an embassy about the tenth year of his reign, when they were in great straits for supplies during the Hannibalic war, to remind him of the old alliance made by Philadelphus, and obtain from him supplies of corn.   Livy does not speak of any want of courtesy or good sense on the part of the king. He also mentions that (in 207 B.C.) he joined the Rhodians, Athenians and Chians in sending an embassy to offer mediation in the war between Philip and the Aetolians, probably from apprehension of the Romans, and tells us the story of Decius Magius.[2]   There is a notable passage of Polybius (v. 106) which though primarily intended to censure the Athenians, nevertheless shows the high esteem in which they held Philopator.[3]   Again, there was recently found in Upper Egypt (Edfu) a votive inscription of Lichas the Acarnanian, the general sent up by this king to capture elephants in far Ethiopia.[4]

As the general Lichas is mentioned (or rather his regiment) in the papyri of the early years of Ptolemy III., it is very likely that this second expedition of his took place during the long preparations for the Syrian War, and

---

[1] Cf. Polybius xviii. c. 1, 14 ; c. 49, 5.   Aenos in Thrace had an Egyptian governor, Livy xxxi. 16.   Livy also mentions the attack (in 197 B.C.) of Antiochus *per omnem oram Ciliciae Lyciaeque et Cariae temptaturus urbes quae in dicione Ptolemaei essent*, xxxiii. 19.   There is an inscription showing that he controlled the taxes of Lycia, *BCH* xiv. 162.   Cf. *Addit. Note* pp. 491-2.

[2] xxxii. 30.   Above, § 157.

[3] They seem to have called a *phyle* Ptolemais and a *deme* Berenikidae after Ptolemy III. and his wife, so that they had constant friendly relations with Egypt.

[4] On this text I have already commented (*BCH* 1894).   It runs as follows, being perfectly preserved and complete : βασιλει Πτολεμαιωι και | βασιλισσηι Αρσινοηι θεοις | φιλοπατορσι και Σαραπιδι και | Ισιδι Λιχας Πυρρου Ακαρναν | στρατηγος αποσταλεις | επι την θηραν των ελεφαν | των (then after a gap) το δευτερον.   It is now in Mr. Wilbour's boat on the Nile.

that some of the beasts which he brought in ships to Alexandria, ran away at the battle of Raphia.

§ 162. These various scraps of evidence do not indeed contradict the estimate in our extant Greek and Jewish writers, but they certainly should have led us to assume that this king was active in foreign affairs, and occupied in pursuing the policy of his predecessors.[1]

When we come to consider the evidences of his buildings in Egypt, this impression is even strengthened. The remains of Philopator's work are more important than any left us by his predecessors, and they extend far beyond them to that region of the Nile which seems hitherto untouched by Ptolemaic influences. Not only did he build at Thebes, not only was he the second founder of Edfu, and busy at Philae, but he began the exquisite little shrine now known as Deyr el Medineh, over against Luxor. In fact we can clearly perceive that his architectural activity extended all over Upper Egypt.

But this is not all. Now for the first time we find Ptolemaic cartouches in buildings as far off as Dakkeh, fully fifty miles above the First Cataract. They are added by Ptolemy Philopator to the inner shrine or adytum built by the Nubian king Ergamenes, who, as Diodorus tells us,[2] broke through the bondage of the priests, and

---

[1] It is not impossible that some of the bad impressions produced upon posterity were due to the anecdotic sketches of the life of Philopator by Ptolemy the Megalopolitan, an able governor of Cyprus under this king, also employed by his successor, who may have permitted himself to use very free language as regards his former master. For the book must certainly have appeared during the reign of Epiphanes. The impression produced by the writer was that he himself had deteriorated with age, as Polybius observes. The evidence is gathered by Susemihl i. 905, but consists only in this remark of Polybius (xviii. 55) and some anecdotes quoted by Athenaeus.

[2] iii. 6.

being educated in Hellenic learning, would not obey their summons to put himself to death.

§ 163. Diodorus says he lived in the time of the second Ptolemy, which seems to me wrong for the following reasons. The naos built by Ergamenes (Arkamen beloved of Isis) tells how the Pharaoh (Per-a-a) gives him the countries of the south. The gods and goddesses of Nubia, and the deified Nile are offering him gifts. Unfortunately he does not specify the Pharaoh in question. But the cartouches assumed by Ergamenes, and indeed by the later Nubian king Azkeramon at Debôt, a few miles north of this, are not only in Egyptian style, but they have the peculiar hieroglyphic signs added to the fourth Ptolemy's name, to distinguish him from his father and grandfather.[1] As it is hardly conceivable that Philopator's cartouche should have copied this detail from Ergamen, it follows that Philopator must have been on the throne when the Nubian made his revolution.

Philopator added a fine porch to this temple, and the row of figures presenting offerings to himself and his wife Arsinoe are, on one side, his father and mother, on the other, his grandfather (Philadelphus) and grandmother. The name is attached to each figure. Later monarchs made additions to the temple in the same way, also giving their names. This architectural combination points to a peaceful settlement between Ptolemy and the Nubian prince; it is probable that the latter purchased his recognition by assisting the king against his revolted subjects in Egypt; but he too must have had learned Egyptians of the higher classes at his

---

[1] This borrowing of types, by a revolting dynast, from his suzerain meets us in the coinage of Arsakes and of Diodotus of Bactria, both of whom copied Seleukid emblems on their coins; cf. the evidence in Holm's *Griech. Gesch.* iv. p. 264.

T

court, and his Greek education was most likely obtained at Alexandria. Probably he was sent as a child, by a very usual arrangement, which both the Romans and we know, to learn letters, and submission, at the court of Ptolemy. He may have grown up and succeeded to his throne during the twenty-five years of Euergetes; his revolution, and assumption of royal state in Nubia, may only date from the middle of Philopator's reign. Thus Diodorus may be defended, while the facts are explained, but it should not be forgotten, that in cursive papyri of the second century B.C. to A.D., B and Δ as figures are hardly distinguishable, being both mere ovals, so that the historian may really have named the fourth king and not the second.

§ 164. The building of so many temples throughout Upper Egypt points to leisure from internal disturbances, a considerable outlay, and a disposition to conciliate the national religion. It may have been the policy of the wily Sosibios, the king's minister, but could hardly have been carried out against the king's consent, so that Philopator, though the Jews believed him to have been very adverse to their religion, was not opposed to that compromise which led ultimately to a re-assertion of the old creed, and of native ideas, against the imported Hellenism.

We now know from the gold plaque found at Alexandria in 1886 that he also built there a temple to Isis and Sarapis.[1]

Athenaeus[2] records another sort of ambitious building on the part of this prince, and gives us extravagant details of the state-ships which he used. First he describes a sea-going ship with 40 banks of oars, 280 cubits long, 38 broad, and 48 high up to the taffrail. The stern indeed was 53 cubits out of the water. It had four rudder-oars 30 cubits

---

[1] Cf. Maspero *Recueil* No. vii., and above, p. 73.
[2] v. 37-9.

long, and 38 oars on the highest bank, loaded at the butt
with lead to keep the blades out.   It was apparently a twin
boat, with two prows and sterns.   It carried 4000 rowers,
and about 4000 of a crew for other purposes.   The other
ship was a state *dahabiyeh*, for going up the river, which was
no less than a floating palace with suites of apartments,
shrines for Dionysus and for Aphrodite, banquetting-rooms,
and lavish ornament in gold, ivory, and precious woods.
The style was evidently a mixture of Greek and Egyptian,
for there were rows of Corinthian columns, and also of the
lotus capital so familiar in the native art.   The luxury of the
arrangements is astonishing.   But is the description trustworthy?   There is printed in the *Journal of Hellenic Studies* [1]
a text which goes to prove that the enormous number of
the banks of oars, at least, was no mere exaggeration.

We have nothing else recorded during the latter years
of Philopator's life, beyond the birth of his heir (presently
associated with the crown), and his continued submission
to his mistress Agathocleia and her brother Agathocles.[2]

§ 165. But when we come to the close of his life,
most fortunately Polybius has given us a very full and
vivid picture of the condition of Alexandria, and of the
tumults that accompanied the accession of the new infant

---

[1] ix. p. 255 β]ασιλευς Πτολεμαιος [ ]οτελην Ζωητος αρχιτεκτονησ-
[αντα] την τριακοντηρη και εικ[οσηρη].   The text is from Cyprus.

[2] It is very remarkable that while the coffins at Gurob were made
chiefly of papyri dating from the second and third Ptolemy, they contain
a few isolated documents of the fifth, but none, actually dated, of the
fourth.   So many are dated, and the dating is so unmistakeable, when
the parents of the king are given, that they could hardly have escaped me
in editing the Petrie Papyri.   Wilcken Göttingen *GA* for 1894 thinks that
one document (II.) xlvii. p. [154] is of this date; if so, it is a solitary
exception to the general result which I have stated.   Epiphanes, born
210-9 B.C., was associated between ∠12 and ∠15 of the reign.   Cf.
Revillout *RE* iii. 5.

king.   Here again we shall do well to let our only good authority speak.   Polybius is often dull and prosaic, but in this and in three or four other famous scenes he is as vivid and interesting as Herodotus.   His picture of Alexandria in tumult is more instructive than all the description of Strabo, or the sermons of Dion Chrysostom.   We cannot but hope that some day the lost portions of his work may be discovered in that very country for whose history they are of such capital importance.   Let us now turn to this passage, so little known and cited among modern scholars.

It was then that all the world at last learnt the truth about the death of queen Arsinoe.   For now that her death was clearly established, the manner of it began to be a matter of speculation.   Though rumours which turned out to be true had found their way among the people, they had up to this time been disputed ; now there was no possibility of hiding the truth, and it became deeply impressed in the minds of all. Indeed there was great excitement among the populace : no one thought about the king ; it was the fate of Arsinoe that moved them.   Some recalled her orphanhood ; others the tyranny and insult she had endured from her earliest days ; [1] and when her miserable death was added to these misfortunes, it excited such a passion of pity and sorrow that the city was filled with sighs, tears, and irrepressible lamentation.   Yet it was clear to the thoughtful observer that these were not so much signs of love for Arsinoe as of hatred towards Agathocles.

[1] As she would not be called an orphan after she married, and was not illtreated by her father and mother, this proves her to have been a late child of Euergetes, and hardly grown up when he died, which agrees with what I said above concerning her marriage to Philopator after the battle of Raphia.   We know that Berenike had a daughter alive in the ninth year of her reign—an infant which died that year.   Arsinoe was probably still younger, and an illtreated orphan till she showed her bravery at Raphia, and perhaps in consequence became queen.   I conjecture that no sooner had she borne an heir than she was set aside, and presently murdered, by Agathocles, whose sister took charge of the infant (below, p. 285).

§ 166. The first measure of this minister, after depositing the urns in the royal mortuary, and giving orders for the laying aside of mourning, was to gratify the army with two months' pay; for he was convinced that the way to deaden the resentment of the common soldiers was to appeal to their interests. He then caused them to take the oath customary at the proclamation of a new king; and next took measures to get all who were likely to be formidable out of the country. Philammon, who had been employed in the murder of Arsinoe, he sent out as governor of Cyrene, while he committed the young king to the charge of Oenanthe and Agathocleia. Next, Pelops thě son of Pelops he despatched to the court of Antiochus in Asia, to urge him to maintain his friendly relations with the court of Alexandria, and not to violate the treaty he had made with the young king's father. Ptolemy, son of Sosibius, he sent to Philip to arrange for a treaty of intermarriage between the two countries, and to ask for assistance in case Antiochus should make a serious attempt to play them false in any matter of importance.

He also selected Ptolemy, son of Agesarchus, as ambassador to Rome : not with a view of his seriously prosecuting the embassy, but because he thought that, if he once entered Greece, he would find himself among friends and kinsfolk, and would stay there ; which would suit his policy of getting rid of eminent men. Scopas the Aetolian he sent to Greece to recruit foreign mercenaries, giving him a large sum in gold for bounties. He had two objects in view in this measure : one was to use the soldiers so recruited in the war with Antiochus ; another was to get rid of the mercenary troops already existing, by sending them on garrison duty in the various forts and settlements about the country ; while he used the new recruits to fill up the numbers of the household regiments with new men, as well as the pickets immediately round the palace, and in other parts of the city. For he believed that men who had been hired by himself, and were taking his pay, would have no feelings in common with the old soldiers, with whom they would be totally unacquainted ; but that, having all their hopes of safety and profit in him, he would find them ready to co-operate with him and carry out his orders.

To return to Agathocles : when he had thus got rid of the most eminent men, and had to a great degree quieted the wrath of the common soldiers by his present of pay, he returned quickly to his old way of life. Drawing round him a body of friends, whom he selected from the most frivolous and shameless of his personal attendants or servants, he devoted the chief part of the day and night to drunkenness and all the excesses which accompany drunkenness, sparing neither matron, nor bride, nor virgin, and doing all this with the most offensive ostentation. The result was a widespread outburst of discontent; and when there appeared no prospect of reforming this state of things, or of obtaining protection against the violence, insolence and debauchery of the court, which on the contrary grew daily more outrageous, the old hatred blazed up once more in the hearts of the common people, and all began again to recall the misfortunes which the kingdom already owed to these very men. But the absence of any one fit to take the lead, and by whose means they could vent their wrath upon Agathocles and Agathocleia, kept them quiet. Their one remaining hope rested upon Tlepolemus, and on this they fixed their confidence.

As long as the late king was alive Tlepolemus remained in retirement ; but upon his death he quickly propitiated the common soldiers, and became once more governor of Pelusium. At first he directed all his actions with a view to the interest of the king, believing that there would be some council of regency to take charge of the boy and administer the government. But when he saw that all those who were fit for this charge were got out of the way, and that Agathocles was boldly monopolising the supreme power, he quickly changed his purpose, because he suspected the danger that threatened him from the hatred which they mutually entertained. He therefore began to draw his troops together, and bestir himself to collect money, that he might not be an easy prey to any one of his enemies. At the same time he was not without hope that the guardianship of the young king, and the chief power in the state might devolve upon him ; both because, in his own private opinion, he was much more fit for it in every respect than Agathocles, and because he was informed that his own troops and those in Alexandria were looking to him to put an end to the minister's outrageous conduct. When such ideas were entertained by Tlepolemus, it did not take long to make the quarrel grow, especially as the partisans of both helped to inflame it. Being eager to secure the adhesion of the generals of divisions and the captains of companies, he frequently invited them to banquets; and at these assemblies, instigated partly by the flattery of his guests and partly by his own impulse (for he was a young man and the conversation was over the wine), he used to throw out sarcastic remarks against the family of Agathocles. At first they were covert and enigmatic, then merely ambiguous, finally undisguised, and containing the bitterest reflections. He proposed the health of the scribbler of pasquinades, the sackbut-girl and waiting-woman; and spoke of his shameful boyhood, when as cupbearer of the king he had submitted to the foulest treatment. His guests were always ready to laugh at his words and add their quota to the sum of vitupera- tion. It was not long before this reached the ears of Agathocles: and the breach between the two thus becoming an open one, Agathocles immediately began bringing charges against Tlepolemus, declaring that he was a traitor to the king, and was inviting Antiochus to come and seize the government. And he brought many plausible proofs of this forward, some of which he got by distorting facts that actually occurred, while others were pure invention. His object in so doing was to excite the wrath of the common people against Tlepolemus. But the result was the reverse; for the populace had long fixed their hopes on Tlepolemus, and were only too delighted to see the quarrel growing hot between them. The actual popular outbreak which did occur began from the following circum- stances. Nicon, a relation of Agathocles, was in the lifetime of the late king commander of the navy.[1] . . .

Another murder committed by Agathocles was that of Deinon, son of Deinon. But this, as the proverb has it, was the fairest of his foul deeds. For the letter ordering the murder of Arsinoe had fallen into this man's hands, and he might have given information about the plot and saved the queen; but at the time he chose rather to help Philammon, and so became the cause of all the misfortunes which followed;

---

[1] I omit the story as not strictly relevant to this history.

while, after the murder was committed, he was always recalling the circumstances, commiserating the unhappy woman, and expressing repentance at having let such an opportunity slip: and this he repeated in the hearing of many, so that Agathocles heard of it, and he met with his just punishment in losing his life. . . .

§ 167. The next step of Agathocles was to summon a meeting of the Macedonian guards. He entered the assembly accompanied by the young king and his own sister Agathocleia. At first he feigned not to be able to say what he wished for tears; but after again and again wiping his eyes with his chlamys he at length mastered his emotion, and, taking the young king in his arms, spoke as follows: 'Take this boy, whom his father on his death-bed placed in this lady's arms' (pointing to his sister) 'and confided to your loyalty, men of Macedonia! Her affection has but little influence in securing the child's safety: it is on you that that safety now depends; his fortunes are in your hands. It has long been evident to those who had eyes to see, that Tlepolemus was aiming at something higher than his natural rank; but now he has named the day and hour on which he intends to assume the crown. Do not let your belief of this depend upon my words; refer to those who know the real truth and have but just come from the very scene of his treason.' With these words he brought forward Critolaus, who deposed that he had seen with his own eyes the altars being decked, and the victims being got ready by the common soldiers for the ceremony of a coronation.

When the Macedonian guards had heard all this, far from being moved by his appeal, they showed their contempt by hooting and loud murmurs, and drove him away under such a fire of derision that he got out of the assembly without being conscious how he did it. And similar scenes occurred among other corps of the army at their meetings. Meanwhile great crowds kept pouring into Alexandria from the up-country stations, calling upon kinsmen or friends to help the movement, and not to submit to the unbridled tyranny of such unworthy men. But what inflamed the populace against the government more than anything else was the knowledge that, as Tlepolemus had the absolute command of all the imports into Alexandria, delay would be a cause of suffering to themselves.

Moreover, an action of Agathocles himself served to heighten the anger of the multitude and of Tlepolemus. For he took Danae, the latter's mother-in-law, from the temple of Demeter, dragged her through the middle of the city unveiled, and cast her into prison. His object in doing this was to manifest his hostility to Tlepolemus ; but its effect was to loosen the tongues of the people. In their anger they no longer confined themselves to secret murmurs : but some of them in the night covered the walls in every part of the city with pasquinades ; while others in the day-time collected in groups and openly expressed their loathing for the government.

Seeing what was taking place, and beginning to fear the worst, Agathocles at one time meditated making his escape by secret flight ; but as he had nothing ready for such a measure, thanks to his own imprudence, he had to give up that idea. At another time he set himself to drawing out lists of men likely to assist him in a bold *coup d'état*, by which he should put to death or arrest his enemies, and then possess himself of absolute power. While still meditating these plans he received information that Moeragenes, one of the body-guard, was betraying all the secrets of the palace to Tlepolemus, and was co-operating with him on account of his relationship with Adaeus, at that time the commander of Bubastus. Agathocles immediately ordered his secretary Nicostratus to arrest Moeragenes, and extract the truth from him by every possible kind of torture. Being promptly arrested by Nicostratus, and taken to a retired part of the palace, he was at first examined directly as to the facts alleged ; but, refusing to confess anything, he was stripped. And now some of the torturers were preparing their instruments, and others with scourges in their hands were taking off their outer garments, when just at that very moment a servant ran in, and, whispering something in the ear of Nicostratus, hurried out again. Nicostratus followed close behind him, without a word, frequently slapping his thigh with his hand.

The predicament of Moeragenes was now indescribably strange. There stood the executioners by his side on the point of raising their scourges, while others close to him were getting ready their instruments of torture : but when Nico-stratus withdrew they all stood silently staring at each other's faces, expecting him every moment to return ; but as time went on they one by one slipped away, until Moeragenes was left alone.   Having made his way through the palace, after this unhoped-for escape, he rushed in his half-clothed state into a tent of the Macedonian guards which was situated close to the palace.   They chanced to be at breakfast, and therefore a good many were collected together ; and to them he narrated the story of his wonderful escape.   At first they would not believe it, but ultimately were convinced by his having appeared without his clothes.   Taking advantage of this extraordinary occurrence, Moeragenes besought the Macedonian guards with tears not only to help him to secure his own safety, but the king's also, and above all their own.   'For certain destruction stared them in the face,' he said, 'unless they seized the moment when the hatred of the populace was at its height, and every one was ready to wreak vengeance on Agathocles.   That moment was *now*, and all that was wanted was some one to begin.'

The passions of the Macedonians were roused by these words, and they finally agreed to do as Moeragenes advised. They at once went round to the tents, first those of their own corps, and then those of the other soldiers ; which were all close together, facing the same quarter of the city.   The wish was one which had for a long time been formed in the minds of the soldiery, wanting nothing but some one to call it forth, and with courage to begin.   No sooner, therefore, had a com-mencement been made than it blazed out like a fire : and before four hours had elapsed every class, whether military or civil, had agreed to make the attempt.

§ 168. At this crisis, too, chance contributed a great deal to the final catastrophe.   For a letter addressed by Tlepolemus to the army, as well as some of his spies, had fallen into the hands of Agathocles.   The letter announced that he would be at Alexandria shortly, and the spies informed Agathocles that he was already there.   This news so distracted Agathocles that he gave up taking any measures at all or even thinking about the dangers which surrounded him, but departed at his usual hour to his wine, and kept up the carouse to the end in his usual licentious fashion.   But his mother Oenanthe went in great distress to the temple of Demeter and Persephone, which was open on account of a certain annual sacrifice ; and there first of all she besought the aid of those goddesses with bendings of the knee and strange incantations, and then sat down close to the altar and remained motionless.   Most of the women present, delighted to witness her dejection and distress, kept silence : but the ladies of the family of Poly-crates, and certain others of the nobility, being as yet unaware of what was going on around them, approached Oenanthe and tried to comfort her.   But she cried out in a loud voice : 'Do not come near me, you monsters ! I know you well ! Your hearts are always against us ; and you pray the goddess for all imaginable evil upon us.   Still I trust and believe that, God willing, you shall one day taste the flesh of your own children.'   With these words she ordered her female attend-ants to drive them away, and strike them with their staves if they refused to go.   The ladies availed themselves of this excuse for quitting the temple in a body, raising their hands and praying that she might herself have experience of those very miseries with which she had threatened her neighbours.

The men having by this time decided upon a revolution, now that in every house the anger of the women was added to the general resentment, the popular hatred blazed out with redoubled violence.   As soon as night fell the whole city was filled with tumult, torches, and hurrying feet.   Some were assembling with shouts in the stadium ; some were calling upon others to join them ; some were running backwards and forwards seeking to conceal themselves in houses and places least likely to be suspected.   And now the open spaces round the palace, the stadium, and the street, as well as the area in front of the Dionysian Theatre, were filled with a motley crowd.   Being informed of this, Agathocles roused himself from a drunken lethargy, — for he had just dismissed his drinking party,—and, accompanied by all his family, with the exception of Philo, went to the king.   After a few words of lamentation over his misfortunes addressed to the child, he took him by the hand, and proceeded to the covered walk which runs between the Maeander garden and the Palaestra, and leads to the entrance of the theatre.   Having securely fastened the two first doors through which he passed, he came to the third with two or three bodyguards, his own family, and the king. The doors, however, which were secured by double bars, were only of lattice work and could therefore be seen through.

By this time the mob had collected from every part of the city in such numbers, that, not only was every foot of ground occupied, but the doorsteps and roofs also were crammed with human beings ; and such a mingled storm of shouts and cries arose, as might be expected from a crowd in which women and children were mixed with men : for in Alexandria, as in Carthage, the children take as conspicuous a part in such commotions as the men.

Day now began to break and the uproar was still a confused babel of voices ; but one cry made itself heard conspicuously above the rest, it was a call for THE KING. The first thing actually done was by the Macedonian guard : they left their quarters and seized the vestibule which served as the audience hall of the palace ; then, after a brief pause, having ascertained whereabouts in the palace the king was, they went round to the covered walk, burst open the first door, and, when they came to the next, demanded with loud shouts that the young king should be surrendered to them. Agathocles, recognising his danger, begged his bodyguards to go in his name to the Macedonians, to inform them that 'he resigned the guardianship of the king, and all offices, honours, or emoluments which he possessed, and only asked that his life should be granted him with a bare maintenance ; that by sinking to his original situation in life he would be rendered incapable, even if he wished it, of being henceforth oppressive to any one.' All the bodyguards refused except Aristomenes, who afterwards obtained the chief power in the state.

This man was an Acarnanian, and, though far advanced in life when he obtained supreme power, he is thought to have made a most excellent and blameless guardian of the king and kingdom. And as he was distinguished in that capacity, so had he been remarkable before for his adulation of Agathocles in the time of his prosperity. He was the first, when entertaining Agathocles at his house, to distinguish him among his guests by the present of a gold diadem, an honour reserved by custom to the kings alone ; he was the first too who ventured to wear his likeness on his ring ; and when a daughter was born to him he named her Agathocleia.

§ 169. But to return to my story. Aristomenes undertook the mission, received his message, and made his way through a wicket-gate to the Macedonians. He stated his business in few words : the first impulse of the Macedonians was to stab him to death on the spot; but some of them held up their hands to protect him, and successfully begged his life. He accordingly returned with orders to bring the king or to come no more himself. Having dismissed Aristomenes with these words, the Macedonians proceeded to burst open the second door also. When convinced by their proceedings, no less than by the answers they had returned, of the fierce purpose of the Macedonians, the first idea of Agathocles was to thrust his hand through the latticed door,—while Agathocleia did the same with her breasts which she said had suckled the king, — and by every kind of entreaty to beg that the Macedonians would grant him bare life.

But finding that his long and piteous appeal produced no effect, at last he sent out the young king with the bodyguards. As soon as they had got the king, the Macedonians placed him on a horse and conducted him to the stadium. His appearance being greeted with loud shouts and clapping of hands, they stopped the horse, and dismounting the child, ushered him to the royal stall and seated him there. But the feelings of the crowd were divided : they were delighted that the young king had been brought, but they were dissatisfied that the guilty persons had not been arrested and met with the punishment they deserved. Accordingly, they continued with loud cries to demand that the authors of all the mischief should be brought out and made an example. The day was wearing away, and yet the crowd had found no one on whom to wreak their vengeance, when Sosibius, who, though a son of the elder Sosibius, was at that time a member of the bodyguard, and as such had a special eye to the safety of the king and the State,—seeing that the furious desire of the multitude was implacable, and that the child was frightened at the unaccustomed faces that surrounded him and the uproar of the crowd, asked the king whether he would ' surrender to the populace those who had injured him or his mother.' The boy having nodded assent, Sosibius bade some of the body-guard announce the king's decision, while he raised the young child from his seat and took him to his own house which was close by to receive proper attention and refreshment. When the message from the king was declared, the whole place broke out into a storm of cheering and clapping of hands.   But meanwhile Agathocles and Agathocleia had separated and gone each to their own lodgings.   Without loss of time soldiers, some voluntary and others under pressure from the crowd, started in search of them.

The beginning of the actual bloodshed, however, was this. One of the servants and flatterers of Agathocles, whose name was Philo, came out to the stadium still flustered with wine. Seeing the fury of the multitude, he said to some bystanders that they would have cause to repent it again, as they had only the other day, if Agathocles were to come there.   Of those who heard him some began to abuse him, while others pushed him about ; and on his attempting to defend himself, some tore his cloak off his back, while others thrust their spears into him and wounded him mortally.   He was dragged into the middle of the crowd breathing his last gasp ; and, having thus tasted blood, the multitude began to look im-patiently for the coming of the other victims.   They had not to wait long.   First appeared Agathocles dragged along bound hand and foot.   No sooner had he entered than some soldiers rushed at him and struck him dead.   And in doing so they were his friends rather than his enemies, for they saved him from the horrible death which he deserved.   Nicon was brought next, and after him Agathocleia stripped naked, with her two sisters ; and following them the whole family.   Last of all some men came bringing Oenanthe, whom they had torn from the temple of Demeter and Persephone, riding stripped naked upon a horse.   They were all given up to the populace, who bit, and stabbed them, and knocked out their eyes, and, as soon as any one of them fell, tore him limb from limb, until they had utterly annihilated them all : for the savagery of the Egyptians when their passions are aroused is indeed terrible. At the same time some young girls who had been brought up with Arsinoe, having learnt that Philammon, the chief agent in the murder of that queen, had arrived three days before

from Cyrene, rushed to his house ; forced their way in ; killed
Philammon with stones and sticks ; strangled his infant son ;
and, not content with this, dragged his wife naked into the
street and put her to death.

Such was the end of Agathocles and Agathocleia and their
kinsfolk.

I am quite aware of the miraculous occurrences and em-
bellishments which the chroniclers of this event have added to
their narrative with a view of producing a striking effect upon
their hearers, making more of their comments on the story
than of the story itself and the main incidents.   Some ascribe
it entirely to Fortune, and take the opportunity of expatiating
on her fickleness and the difficulty of being on one's guard
against her.   Others dwell upon the unexpectedness of the
event, and try to assign its causes and probabilities.   It was
not my purpose, however, to treat this episode in this way,
because Agathocles was not a man of conspicuous courage
or ability as a soldier ; nor particularly successful or worth
imitating as a statesman ; nor, lastly, eminent for his acuteness
as a courtier or cunning as an intriguer, by which latter accomplishments Sosibius and many others have managed to keep
one king after another under their influence to the last day of
their lives.   The very opposite of all this may be said of this
man.   For though he obtained high promotion owing to
Philopator's feebleness as a king ; and though after his death
he had the most favourable opportunity of consolidating his
power, he yet soon fell into contempt, and lost his position and
his life at once, thanks to his own want of courage and vigour.

§ 170. It is necessary to remind the reader, that at this
crisis in the affairs of Egypt, there was no similar change
of sovrans in the sister kingdoms, as had been the case
when Philopator succeeded.   The whole aspect of the
world was changed.   The Romans, after a desperate
struggle of fourteen years, were at last getting the upper
hand in the war with Hannibal, and the unconquerable
general was cooped up in his natural fortress in Calabria.[1]

[1] This is now called the *Grande Sila*, an island of granite which
stands out of the newer formations, and affords on a lofty plateau

King Philip V. of Macedon, by utilising the divisions and jealousies of the Greeks, had maintained himself in power, and during fifteen years of varying success, had felt strong enough, not only to maintain his kingdom, but to enter into a treaty with Hannibal, and provoke the Roman Republic by a wanton interference in the great western quarrel. Antiochus the Great, after sharp struggles to maintain his kingdom in the East and West, had at last become the undisputed and powerful sovran of Syria, though his early campaign against Philopator had been a failure, and he had left Coele-Syria and Phoenicia in the hands of the Egyptians. During the years of the easy-going Philopator the external influence of Egypt had been waning, and her enormous wealth had no doubt often inflamed the cupidity of her ambitious neighbours. But the smaller neutral states, the confederation of the Cyclades, and the commercial queen of the Levant—Rhodes—were old and firm friends of the Ptolemies, and likely to ward off by diplomacy, if not by arms, any wanton attack upon her independence.

both water and arable land, which a small occupying army could hold and cultivate, while the approach of a hostile force could not escape notice, and could be met by an easy concentration at any point. This was the secret of Hannibal's long stay in Italy, after his powers of offence were crippled, nor need he have left, were it not for the imperative call from his native country, invaded by Scipio.

COIN OF PTOLEMY IV.

CHAPTER VIII

§ 171. The circumstances of the stormy accession of the boy-king have been narrated in connexion with the death of his father, and the massacre of the unworthy favourites, who had evidently hoped to succeed to the vacant throne. But when these adventurers were removed by public indignation, and met their cruel though well-deserved fate, what advisers or directors were left to assume the direction of affairs, until the infant came to years of discretion? Upon this interesting question we have but scanty information. Foremost of his mercenary generals was Tlepolemos, who seems to have been about as able and as unscrupulous as the best of his kind.[1]

PTOLEMY V.

Tlepolemus, the chief minister in the kingdom of Egypt, was a young man, but one who had spent all his life in the camp, and with reputation. By nature aspiring and ambitious, he had done much that was glorious in the service of his country, but much that was evil also. As a general in a campaign, and

---

[1] The following passage is from Polybius xvi. 21.

U

as an administrator of military expeditions, he was a man of great ability, high natural courage, and extremely well fitted to deal personally with soldiers. But on the other hand, for the management of complicated affairs, he was deficient in diligence and sobriety, and had the least faculty in the world for the keeping of money or the economical administration of finance. And it was this that before long not only caused his own fall, but seriously damaged the kingdom as well. For though he had complete control of the exchequer, he spent the greater part of the day in playing ball and in matches in martial exercises with the young men; and directly he left these sports he collected drinking parties, and spent the greater part of his life in these amusements and with these associates. But that part of his day which he devoted to business, he employed in distributing, or, I might rather say, in throwing away the royal treasures among the envoys from Greece and the Dionysiac actors, and, more than all, among the officers and soldiers of the palace guard. He was utterly incapable of saying no, and bestowed anything there was at hand on any one who said anything to please him. The evil which he himself thus began continually increased.

In civil affairs we are told that the principal power came into the hands of Aristomenes,[1] who is called the king's tutor, and whose character, so far as we know, was superior to that of the other Greek officials at the Egyptian court. But the task allotted to these ministers was one of no slight difficulty.[2]

Is it not astonishing, says Polybius, that while Ptolemy Philopator was alive and did not need such assistance,

---

[1] Polybius xv. 31, 6.

[2] In the Papyrus I. of the Turin collection, p. 5, 27 (Ed. Peyron) it is stated by the plaintiff in the case that, in consequence of rebellion in the first year of Epiphanes' reign, a large number of soldiers were sent from Thebes to occupy Ombos in the upper country: (ελεγεν) τον εαυτου πατερα μετηλθαι εκ της Διοσπολεως μεθ ετερων στρατιωτων εις τους ανω τοπους εν τηι γενομενηι ταραχηι επι του πατρος των βασιλεων θεου Επιφανους, and he then counts twenty-four years of this reign from the disturbance.

the kings of Macedonia and Syria were ready with offers
of aid, but that as soon as he was dead, leaving his heir
a mere child, whose kingdom they were bound by ties of
nature to have defended, they then egged each other on to
adopt the policy of partitioning the boy's kingdom between
themselves, and getting rid entirely of the heir; and that too
without putting forward any decent pretext to cover their
iniquity, but acting so shamelessly, and so like beasts of prey,
that one can only compare their habits to those ascribed to
fishes, among which, though they may be of the same species,
the destruction of the smaller is the food and sustenance of
the larger? This treaty of theirs shows, as though in a mirror,
the impiety to heaven and cruelty to man of these two kings,
as well as their unbounded ambition. However, if a man were
disposed to find fault with Fortune for her administration of
human affairs, he might fairly become reconciled to her in this
case; for she brought upon those monarchs the punishment
they so well deserved, and by the signal example she made of
them taught posterity a lesson in righteousness. For while
they were engaged in acts of treachery against each other, and
in dismembering the child's kingdom in their own interests,
she brought the Romans upon them, and the very measures
which they had lawlessly designed against another, she justly
and properly carried out against them. For both of them,
being promptly beaten in the field, were not only prevented
from gratifying their desire for the dominions of another, but
were themselves made tributary and forced to obey orders from
Rome. Finally, within a very short time Fortune restored the
kingdom of Ptolemy to prosperity; while as to the dynasties
and successors of these two monarchs, she either utterly
abolished and destroyed them, or involved them in misfortunes
which were little short of that.

§ 172. Tlepolemos being therefore rather a war
minister or prime minister, who would not leave the
centre of affairs, the charge of the frontier province of
Palestine and Phoenicia was entrusted to Skopas. For
the kings of Macedon and Syria having combined to
divide the kingdom of the infant Ptolemy, Antiochus had

apparently seized Palestine upon the first news of the death of Philopator.

Philip was thwarted by his own lawlessness and cruelty. The progress of his fleet through the Aegean was marked by such atrocities, that Attalus and the Rhodians joined their forces to crush him as the enemy of civilisation. In the pitched battle off Chios, the Rhodian admiral, like the allied admirals at Navarino, forced a conflict with a power against whom the Rhodians had not declared war, and on the grounds of humanity towards the islanders of the Aegean. Though the result was indecisive, the heavy losses on each side disabled the allies, and also so shook the confidence of Philip in his fleet that though, according to Polybius, he might have, and ought to have, sailed directly to Alexandria, he shirked this bold step, and so left his Syrian ally without proper support during his campaign against Skopas.

Unfortunately this campaign is only touched here and there in our fragments of Polybius. At first Skopas, a notorious Aetolian, who had formerly been president of his League, but who now preferred the enormous pay of the Egyptian service—£40 a day—seems to have re-occupied the whole disputed province.[1] But in the following campaign he was defeated at the great battle of Panion, on the upper Jordan. Polybius, however, refers to the battle only to expose the ignorance of the historian Zeno, whose account of the tactics was absurd and self-contradictory.[2]

§ 173. In the end Antiochus was victorious, and all lower Syria and Palestine, which had for a century been almost a settled possession of Egypt, passed into his hands. This practically permanent transference of Palestine from the control of Egypt to that of Syria is specially

---

[1] Josephus *Antt.* xii. 3.   [2] xvi. 18.

noted by Josephus,[1] and is remarkable because we know
that for a century or more the Ptolemies had been most
popular in Judaea. Even now, though the transference
of allegiance was sudden, it was not completed without all manner of concessions and favours on the part of
Antiochus,[2] and not without a strong protest on the part
of the Jewish aristocracy, many of whom migrated per-

[1] He speaks of the sturdy loyalty of Gaza, which stood a siege from
Antiochus rather than join the cities of Palestine in going over to the
Syrian side (xvi. 22).

[2] Cf. his letter to his general Ptolemy quoted by Josephus *Antiqq.*
xii. 3, 3 :—' Since the Jews, upon our first entrance on their country,
demonstrated their friendship towards us ; and when we came to their
city [Jerusalem], received us in a splendid manner, and came to meet
us with their senate, and gave abundance of provisions to our soldiers,
and to the elephants, and joined with us in ejecting the garrison of the
Egyptians that were in the citadel, we have thought fit to reward them,
and to retrieve the condition of their city, which hath been greatly
depopulated by such accidents as have befallen its inhabitants, and to
bring those that have been scattered abroad back to the city ; and, in
the first place, we have determined, on account of their piety towards
God, to bestow on them, as a pension, for their sacrifices of animals
that are fit for sacrifice, for wine and oil, and frankincense, the value of
twenty thousand pieces of silver, and [six] sacred artabae of fine flour,
with one thousand four hundred and sixty medimni of wheat, and three
hundred and seventy-five medimni of salt ; and these payments I would
have fully paid them, as I have sent orders to you. I would also have
the work about the temple finished, and the cloisters, and if there be
anything else that ought to be rebuilt ; and for the materials of wood,
let it be brought them out of Judaea itself, and out of the other countries,
and out of Libanus, tax-free ; and the same I would have observed as
to those other materials which will be necessary, in order to render the
temple more glorious ; and let all that nation live according to the
laws of their own country ; and let the senate and the priests, and the
scribes of the temple, and the sacred singers, be discharged from poll-
money and the crown-tax, and other taxes also ; and that the city may
the sooner recover its inhabitants, I grant a discharge from taxes for
three years to its present inhabitants, and to such as shall come to it,
until the month Hyperberetaeus. We also discharge them for the future

manently to Egypt, where they soon obtained great influence in the counsels of the court.

Still there must have been special circumstances in the condition of Judaea during the closing years of Philopator's reign to account for the apparently sudden change of public feeling. The third book of Maccabees, whether true or false in its details, at all events proves to us that Philopator was regarded with hatred by the Jews, unless indeed we adopt the unlikely hypothesis that it was fabricated to justify their defection from Egypt soon after his death. The letter of Antiochus just referred to speaks of decay and poverty in the city of Jerusalem, so that the province seems not to have been flourishing under Egypt. Nothing is more likely to make a government unpopular than this want of prosperity. Perhaps extortions on the part of Skopas may have intensified the evil. We know, too, that Judaea was upon the eve of a great national restoration, and very probably such aspirations would hope to find freer scope under a new protectorate, which was bound to make itself popular with the Jews. Such diverse causes, co-operating with the natural ungratefulness of subjects to their rulers, were sufficient to produce this great and permanent, though apparently sudden change.

§ 174. Meanwhile Philip with his fleet took and plundered various cities in the Hellespont and the Aegean, and that some of these were still regarded as Egyptian, appears from the demand of Titus Flamininus, his Roman conqueror, 'that he should restore

from a third part of their taxes, that the losses they have sustained may be repaired; and all those citizens that have been carried away, and are become slaves, we grant them and their children their freedom; and give order that their substance be restored to them.'

to Ptolemy all the cities which he had seized after the death of Philopator.'[1] But the remaining extracts do not tell the number of these cities. They were of course 'the cities of Asia, which were ranged under Ptolemy,'[2] which shows that the power of Philopator over the Aegean was kept up all through that king's reign. The various details of the naval war between Philip and the allies cannot be easily unravelled; most authors assume two naval battles, one at Lade, the other off Chios. As far as the fragments of Polybius inform us, there seems to have been only the one great action, in which Philip lost so heavily, that though he maintained himself for some time on the coast of Caria, the Rhodian fleet soon became his superior, and he was obliged to evade it, in order to return to Europe, where war from the Romans was threatening him.[3]

Moreover the Romans soon found another opportunity to check the second enemy of Egypt. It appears from Livy[4] that at the end of the second Punic war they sent a polite embassy to announce officially their success, and to thank the Egyptian king for his friendly neutrality, which must chiefly have consisted in supplying them with Egyptian wheat at a reasonable price during their greatest difficulties. Here again the policy of Philopator appears to have been anything but silly or immoral.

But we next hear that the young king's guardians were so alarmed at the progress of Antiochus and Philip that they volunteered to offer the protection of his interests to the Roman Republic. Such is the story of Justin.[5] We may well suspect him of having given us only a superficial

---

[1] Polybius xviii. 1, 14 ; Livy xxxii. 33.

[2] Polybius xviii. 49, 5.

[3] Cf. the details and citations concerning this war in Hertzberg *Gesch. Gr.* i. 55 and notes.

[4] xxxi. 2.   [5] xxx. 3.

account of the transaction.   Let us consider what he says
by the light of other evidence.

§ 175. Livy tells us that three ambassadors, C. Claudius
Nero, M. Aemilius Lepidus, and P. Semp. Tuditanus
were sent on the courteous embassy just named, but is
silent concerning the action of the Alexandrian court,
or concerning any extraordinary honour conferred upon
the Romans.   Justin ignores this embassy, and says
that the Alexandrians sent to Rome a message, begging
the Republic to undertake the guardianship of the young
king, now threatened by his neighbours of Macedon and
Syria, and that Lepidus alone was then sent to Egypt,
while other ambassadors were despatched to check Antiochus and Philip.   The next book [1] is not consistent with
this, but says that the boy had been entrusted to the
Romans by the last request of his dying father.   There is
nothing in the narrative of Philopator's death to countenance this.   I do not think any critic, considering the persistent silence of Livy, who had all Polybius before him,
would have accepted Justin's story, were it not that there
is actually extant a coin of M. Lepidus, supposed to have
been struck when he was consul, in the eighteenth year
of this reign, on which he represents himself crowning
a youth, with the motto *Tutor regis*.   On the reverse is
the personified Alexandria.   But according to Mommsen,[2]

---

[1] xxxi. 1.

[2] Cf. the evidence cited in Pauly-Wissowa's *Encyclopaedia* Art.
AEMILIUS, No. 68. Val. Maximus says he was Pontifex Max. when he
undertook the charge of the prince, which is certainly false.   His high
offices came later than his embassy.   I am glad to see that Bandelin
(*Inaug. Diss.* p. 14) agrees with my view.   The misleading coin was
probably issued in regard of the controversies about the restoration of
Auletes to his kingdom, but in whose interest I cannot tell.   Bandelin
thinks the story was one of the inventions of Valerius Antias, which was
copied by later historians. Cf. *Addit. Note* p. 492.

this coin was really issued by one of his descendants
in 54 B.C., so that what any careful survey of the facts
would suggest, is not contradicted by contemporary evidence. We may therefore safely set aside both Justin
and Val. Maximus, for if the patriotic Livy had known
the fact, he could not have failed to mention it.
Polybius, as now extant, is so fragmentary, that we can
argue nothing from his silence. We know, however,
with certainty from Livy,[1] that this Lepidus, who was
the *youngest* of the three ambassadors, did not remain in
Egypt, but was present (on his way home) when Philip was
besieging Abydos, and was shortly after appointed Pontifex
at Rome, where he filled many other offices of dignity in
the succeeding years. As therefore Ptolemy Epiphanes
remained at Alexandria, the notion of any personal control
over the king cannot be entertained. The very submissive embassy from Ptolemy in 200 B.C.,[2] asking whether
the Romans would be pleased to accept his help for Athens
against Philip, or would prefer to do without him, may

[1] xxxi. 18.
[2] Ibid. 9. The meaning of Livy's statement has given rise to some
difference of opinion : *Athenienses adversus Philippum petisse ab rege
auxilium. ceterum etsi communes socii sint, tamen nisi ex auctori-
tate populi Romani neque classem neque exercitum defendendi aut
oppugnandi cuiusquam causa regem in Graeciam missurum esse. vel
quieturum eum in regno, si populo Romano socios defendere libeat ;
vel Romanos quiescere, si malint, passurum, atque ipsum auxilia, quae
facile adversus Philippum tueri Athenas possent, missurum.* Mommsen
thinks that the diplomatic object was to keep any Roman fleet from
appearing in the Aegean—a source of danger to all Hellenism. It
seems to me that it was an indirect and obsequious bidding for Roman
support against Antiochus, who was seriously threatening Egypt. For
Ptolemy was bound by no formal treaty to consult Rome. The Romans
merely replied that they would take care of their own allies, which
promised nothing, and they delayed at least three years before they
interfered diplomatically with Antiochus' attack on Egypt.

have been dictated by a Roman at Alexandria, but not by Lepidus. In 199 B.C. it is Lucius Cornelius who is sent with other ambassadors (who join him on the way) to command Antiochus to desist from attacking any of Ptolemy's possessions, and then it is that Antiochus, while questioning diplomatically the title of Egypt to any part of the old kingdom of Lysimachus, once conquered by the Syrian Seleukos, adds that he is about to make such family alliance with the young Egyptian king as will settle the strife about the occupied provinces of Palestine and Philistia. This betrothal took place in the year 198 B.C., the seventh of the young king's reign. I cannot therefore but think that the Lepidi in after years exaggerated their influence over the king, and that the title of Protector was not a public or recognised dignity.[1]

§ 176. It is more easy to see the reasons which actuated the wise Aristomenes to bid high for Roman support, and enlist, so far as he could, the interest and influence of great Roman nobles. The dangers which beset this able minister were not so much from the ambitious monarchs, whose joint attack upon Egypt was sure to be foiled by the energy of the Rhodians, the king of Pergamum, and the Greek island-cities, as from the Scylla and Charybdis of Aetolian condottieri and native insurgents.

We have already quoted the sketch of Tlepolemos drawn by Polybius. A little further on he gives a very similar sketch of Skopas, the general who had defended Coele-Syria with some ability against Antiochus, and who after his defeat came back to Alexandria to enjoy his

---

[1] Possibly the Egyptian court wanted a formal protector of Egyptian interests at Rome, and M. Lepidus may have undertaken this duty as a guest-friend. He could not, of course, be called the king's *Patronus*, so the title *Tutor* may have been used in familiar conversation at Rome.

extravagant rewards with the usual insolence of a successful Greek.

Many people have a yearning for bold and glorious under-takings, but few dare actually attempt them. Yet Scopas had much fairer opportunities for a hazardous and bold career than Cleomenes. For the latter, though circumvented by his enemies, and reduced to depend upon such forces as his servants and friends could supply, yet left no chance untried, and tested every one to the best of his ability, valuing an honourable death more highly than a life of disgrace. But Scopas, with all the advantages of a formidable body of soldiers and of the excellent opportunity afforded by the youth of the king, by his own delays and halting counsels allowed himself to be circumvented. For having ascertained that he was holding a meeting of his partisans at his own house, and was consulting with them, Aristomenes sent some of the royal bodyguards and summoned him to the king's council. Whereupon Scopas was so infatuated that he was neither bold enough to carry out his designs, nor able to make up his mind to obey the king's summons,—which is in itself the most extreme step,—until Aristomenes, understanding the blunder he had made, caused soldiers and elephants to surround his house, and sent Ptolemy son of Eumenes in with some young men, with orders to bring him quietly if he would come, but, if not, by force. When Ptolemy entered the house and informed Scopas that the king summoned him, he refused at first to obey, but remained looking fixedly at Ptolemy, and for a long while preserved a threatening attitude as though he wondered at his audacity ; and when Ptolemy came boldly up to him and took hold of his chlamys, he called on the bystanders to help him. But seeing that the number of young men who had accompanied Ptolemy into the house was large, and being informed by some one of the military array surrounding it outside, he yielded to circum-stances, and went, accompanied by his friends, in obedience to the summons.

On his entering the council-chamber the king was the first to state the accusation against him, which he did briefly. He was followed by Polycrates lately arrived from Cyprus ; and he again by Aristomenes. The charges made by them all were much to the same effect as what I have just stated ; but there was now added to them the seditious meeting with his friends, and his refusal to obey the summons of the king. On these charges he was unanimously condemned, not only by the members of the council, but also by the envoys of foreign nations who were present. For when Aristomenes was about to commence his accusation he brought in a large number of other Greeks of rank to support him, as well as the Aetolian ambassadors who had come to negotiate a peace, among whom was Dorimachus son of Nicostratus. When these speeches had been delivered, Scopas endeavoured to put forward certain pleas in his defence : but gaining no attention from any one, owing to the senseless nature of his proceedings, he was taken along with his friends to prison. There after nightfall Aristomenes caused Scopas and his family to be put to death by poison ; but did not allow Dicaearchus to die until he had had him racked and scourged, thus inflicting on him a punishment which he thoroughly deserved in the name of all Greece. For this was the Dicaearchus whom Philip, when he resolved upon his treacherous attack on the Cyclades and the cities of the Hellespont, appointed leader of the whole fleet and the entire enterprise : who being thus sent out to perform an act of flagrant wickedness, not only thought that he was doing nothing wrong, but in the extravagance of his infatuation imagined that he would strike terror into the gods as well as man. For wherever he anchored he used to build two altars, to Impiety and Lawlessness, and, offering sacrifice upon these altars, worshipped them as his gods.[1]

These were the men who seemed necessary to Egypt, as military leaders, and yet were likely at any moment to throw off their allegiance and turn kings for themselves. The old Egyptian monarchy had been more than once upset by such men, notably by the Libyan Shishak, well known in Jewish history.

On the other hand, the native princes that remained, favoured and perhaps incited by the priests, were ever

[1] Polybius xviii. 54.   Cf. *Addit. Note* p. 492.

dreaming of recovering the land from Macedonian and Greek invaders. During the brilliant reigns of the first three Ptolemies, we do not hear of them. No sooner does the fourth king arm the natives again, than the first of those bloody insurrections breaks out, which were renewed during the reigns of many of his successors. It must have been such an insurrection, only to be subdued by insubordinate mercenary leaders in the pay of the government, which terrified Aristomenes, and the prudent part of the Synedrion, or Council, into behaving with great deference and even submission to the Romans.

§ 177. We may regard it, however, rather as a piece of internal, than of external, policy, to hurry on the announcement of the young king's personal accession to the throne, the so-called ἀνακλητήρια (196-5 B.C.), in which the established religion of the country and its priests had so powerful a voice. Polybius [1] merely mentions the fact, and that it was promoted by Polycrates, the former governor of Cyprus, who had not only been a faithful servant of the previous king, but had preserved the island during the great initial dangers of the new reign, and had brought considerable savings in treasure to assist the anxious Court of Alexandria. Fortunately the famous Rosetta stone contains the formal document drawn up by the priests on this occasion, and from this we can learn, as from the earlier Canopus inscription,[2] much of the methods of the Ptolemaic administration. The fate of this famous text in the world of Greek letters has been very curious. When first discovered, nearly 100 years ago, its capital importance as affording the key to the hieroglyphic script was recognised, and no stone was more quoted and studied. But when Champollion had attained to the solution, so far as the

---

[1] xviii. 55.   [2] Above, § 149.

mutilated hieroglyphic text was concerned, no one in earlier days took any further trouble to translate the two Egyptian texts independently until the demotic studies of H. Brugsch, and then of Revillout,[1] of which even the latter, dating from 1880, are probably in many points now antiquated. It is said by competent Egyptologists that even yet an honest translation of Ptolemaic hieroglyphics — a very late and highly complicated development of this writing—is not easily to be had. Thus we cannot yet freely use the two Egyptian versions to elucidate the difficulties of the Greek. Of this latter, the text and commentary of Letronne, published half a century ago, seems to be still the standard work, though the discovery of many other inscriptions and MSS. on papyrus has added much to our knowledge of the titles, and of the technical words employed. We must therefore endeavour, with the help of some valuable hints derived from later essays on kindred subjects, but mainly from the information of new texts, to understand this all-important document.

§ 178. There has been some controversy as to the priority of the various parts of the inscription. Though the hieroglyphic version stands first, and that is the order which is mentioned in this and other bi-lingual texts, both Letronne, in the commentary to his text,[2] and Franz[3] maintain that the Greek is the original, and the Egyptian a translation. There are some suggestions from Champollion that the hieroglyphics do not accurately represent the sense of the Greek, and that they show ignorance on the part of the scribe. Until the Egyptian part in its two

---

[1] In his *Chrestomathie démotique.*

[2] Müller's *FHG* i., Appendix. There is also a monograph of Drumann on the inscription.   [3] In the *CIG.*

forms is thoroughly understood, much weight cannot be attached to this criticism. On the other hand, the very preamble of the document, containing the king's titles, is such as can hardly have been composed by a Greek. The titles at least, with their mythological intricacies, must have been copied from the dictation of an Egyptian priest. So must the details of the escutcheon, at the close of the text, which in Egypt was a peculiar head-dress, distinguishing each king from the rest. I am not aware that in the whole mass of Greek inscriptions—some of them quite as formal —there is anything of the kind. Take for example the inscription of Adule.[1] All the king's titles, composed by Greeks, are in accordance with Greek notions. This is here far from being the case. As the whole decree was passed by the priests, and affected their interests, and those of the other natives, it is obvious enough that the resolution must have been originally passed in their synod, and first taken down in demotic, from which one scribe constructed the hieroglyphic part, while another, who knew some Greek, dictated the same to a Greek secretary, who copied it in cursive, and then gave it to a Greek workman to enter upon the stone.[2]

I am glad to say this conclusion, based upon general considerations, agrees with the opinion of Wescher on the Canopus inscription, and is strongly corroborated by the judgment of Revillout, who, in publishing the Greek and demotic versions with a *verbum verbo* translation, in

---

[1] Above, § 128, note.

[2] It is remarkable that the workman entrusted with punching the inscription on the gold plaque of Ptolemy IV. (above, p. 73) was ignorant of Greek letters, and made such mistakes as an ignorant decipherer of Greek now makes, *e.g.* Ƹ for E. It seems likely, therefore, that a native workman was employed, and that the work was not even revised by a Greek superior.

parallel columns, and asserting as past controversy that the Canopus inscription shows evidence of a priority in the Greek, of which he says the demotic is but a slavish and ignorant copy, declares the very reverse to be the case with that of Rosetta. Here the priests are speaking in Egyptian style, using Egyptian titles, which would have been quite strange to Euergetes. Hence the demotic version is in this case fuller and more explicit than the Greek.

The perusal of his version does not leave any strong impression of the kind, though the general probability of the case confirms him. He rightly sees in the document an accommodation of Greek to Egyptian, whereas the earlier text he calls a mere accommodation of Egyptian to Greek. It is also to be noticed that the hieroglyphic and demotic versions, without the Greek, are found repeated on a stele at Philae. Throughout the whole document it is Ptah of Memphis and his worship which are exalted apparently in opposition to Amon Ra of Thebes, which city, as we shall see anon, was the centre of the national rebellion. Alexandria is for the time laid aside, and the interests of Memphis espoused against Thebes.[1]

The composition is in the usual official style, using quite correctly the terms which we find in earlier and later papyri, but is clumsy and not faultless, though fairly grammatical. The text is so seldom to be found in ordinary private libraries, that I think it well to give a complete trans-literation with a commentary in an appendix to this chapter.

Hence I need here only give a brief summary. After a pompous and purely Egyptian enumeration of the king's titles, and the elaborate dating, the decree says that the Egyptian priesthood, assembled in solemn conclave at

---

[1] While I accept all that Revillout says about the later text, I have given my reasons for differing from him concerning the earlier.

Memphis, when the king celebrated his formal accession
in the temple of Ptah—in consideration of his benefits to
the temples, both by donations and remission of taxes, his
benefits to the population in the same respects, his victorious
subjugation of a dangerous rebellion, his further benevolences to priests and temples—decrees to set up statues of
him in all the shrines of the greatest deities, with a special
head-dress marking his name and titles, and to establish
special feast-days in his honour.

§ 179. Thus the young king seemed to have overcome
his greatest difficulties, and to be at last entering upon a
prosperous reign. The wise administration of Aristomenes
had warded off, with the aid of Roman diplomacy, the
most pressing dangers. Antiochus the Great had been
obliged to turn his conquest of Syria into a doubtful gain,
only to be retained by betrothing his daughter, with a
great dowry, to the boy king.[1] Philip had been humbled
at Cynoscephalae, and the Romans were so busy with the
affairs of Greece and Asia Minor, that they had no leisure
for closer interference in Egypt. The outbreak of the
natives was overcome with the aid of Polycrates, and
apparently without any extravagant cruelty. The young
king himself was being trained in manly exercises by
Aristonikos, an eunuch who was brought up with him,
and who was remarkable for his sporting talents. It was
reported to Polybius by an Egyptian ambassador that the
young king had even killed a wild bull from his horse.[2]

---

[1] S. Jerome *ad Dan.* xi. 17.

[2] xxii. 22 : 'Just at that time Demetrius of Athens came on a mission
from Ptolemy, to renew the existing alliance between the king and the
Achaean League. This was eagerly accepted, and my father, Lycortas,
and Theodoridas, and Rositeles of Sicyon were appointed ambassadors
to take the oaths on behalf of the Achaeans, and receive those of the
king. And on that occasion a circumstance occurred, which, though

When he was not seventeen years old, the Syrian princess Cleopatra, betrothed to him five or six years before, was brought by her father with great pomp to Raphia on the common frontier, where she was married (193 B.C.), with the taxes of Coele-Syria and Palestine as her dowry. It has been well pointed out that this by no means implies the cession of the disputed provinces to the king of Egypt.[1] It only meant that the taxes, or probably the items of the taxes considered as the royal fiscus, were paid over yearly to the princess. The events at the opening of the next reign show clearly that Syrian governors and Syrian troops held Palestine. It was permanently lost to Egypt. So also the Greek island-cities·which had been wrested from Egyptian influence by Philip's fleet at the opening of Epiphanes' reign, though released from Philip's barbarous ravages, seem never to have come again under Egyptian rule, though the first demand of the Romans had been, that they should be restored to Ptolemy by Antiochus.[2] Either they were made 'free' at the demand of the Romans,[3] or they entered the Confederacy of Rhodes. It was therefore during the infancy of Epiphanes, not during the slothful reign of Philopator, that the external provinces and influence of Egypt were curtailed, so

not important perhaps, is still worth recording.   After the completion of this renewal of alliance on behalf of the Achaeans, Philopoemen entertained the ambassador ; and in the course of the banquet the ambassador introduced the king's name, and said a great deal in his praise, quoting anecdotes of his skill and boldness in hunting, as well as his excellence in riding and the use of arms ; and ended by quoting, as a proof of what he said, that the king on horseback once transfixed a bull with a javelin.'   But as courtiers of all epochs show an irresistible propensity to lie about their princes, the whole story may be an invention.

[1] Stark *Gaza* p. 426.   [2] Polybius xviii. 1 *fin.*
[3] Ibid. 47, and 49-51.   Cf. *Addit. Note* pp. 492-3.

that of its foreign possessions only Cyprus [1] and Cyrene remained.

§ 180. We hear of no effort on the part of Epiphanes to regain his provinces ; though during the war of Antiochus with Rome, or even after the battle of Magnesia, he might easily have seized Syria and Palestine. And yet his queen is said to have sided loyally with her husband, where his interests clashed with those of her native country. She was a vigorous and prudent woman, and she certainly introduced new blood into a stock likely to degenerate from the constant unions of close blood-relations. But unfortunately she brought by her name another confusion into the annals of the Lagidae. Old historians, and we too, are puzzled enough with the recurring Arsinoes and Berenikes. Now come the Cleopatras, who add to the older names a new confusion of their own.

If Epiphanes waged no foreign wars, he kept up friendly diplomatic relations with the Achaean League, even sending an embassy (about 188 B.C.) to offer large gifts, and seek the renewal of his former treaty.[2] The famous Lycortas and others were sent for this purpose to Alexandria, but upon their reappearance before the League a scene of confusion arose, which is one of the most curious passages in Polybius' history.

The next subject introduced for debate was that of king Ptolemy. The ambassadors who had been on the mission to Ptolemy were called forward, and Lycortas, acting as spokesman, began by stating how they had interchanged oaths

[1] Cyprus, which had been held for his father by Polycrates, was now held for him safely by the able and economical Ptolemy the Megalopolitan (Polybius xxvii. 13).

[2] Cf. above, p. 305, note 2. Modern historians assign no importance to these missions of politeness, which were then much in fashion. Cf. Hertzberg *Gesch. Griech.* i. p. 152. Polybius evidently thought

of alliance with the king; and next announced that they brought a present from the king to the Achaean League of six thousand stands of arms for peltasts, and two thousand talents in copper money.   He added a panegyric on the king, and finished his speech by a brief reference to his goodwill and active benevolence towards the Achaeans.   Upon this the Strategus of the Achaeans, Aristaenus, stood up and asked Lycortas and his colleagues in the embassy to Ptolemy 'which alliance it was that he had thus renewed?'

No one answering the question, but all the assembly beginning to converse with each other, the Council chamber was filled with confusion.   The cause of this absurd state of things was this.   There had been several treaties of alliance formed between the Achaeans and Ptolemy's kingdom, as widely different in their provisions as in the circumstances which gave rise to them : but neither had Ptolemy's envoy made any distinction when arranging for the renewal, merely speaking in general terms on the matter, nor had the ambassadors sent from Achaia; but they had interchanged the oaths on the assumption of there being but one treaty. The result was, that, on the Strategus quoting all the treaties, and pointing out in detail the differences between them, which turned out to be important, the assembly demanded to know which it was that they were renewing.   And when no one was able to explain, not even Philopoemen himself, who had been in office when the renewal was made, nor Lycortas and his colleagues who had been on the mission to Alexandria, these men all began to be regarded as careless in conducting the business of the League; while Aristaenus acquired great reputation as being the only man who knew what he was talking about; and finally, the assembly refused to allow the ratification, voting on account of this blunder that the business should be postponed.

A subsequent embassy of the Achaeans to this king was interrupted by his death.[1]

differently, as will appear from the debate which he describes.   It follows from the language of Lycortas that to strangers at least Epiphanes appeared a courteous and reasonable sovran.

[1] Polybius xxiv. 6.

In both cases Polybius speaks of Ptolemy as the moving cause, and the Achaeans as acquiescing in his initiative. But the reasons of this policy are not stated.

§ 181. In the year 191 B.C., when the Romans declared war against the Aetolians, Epiphanes sent an embassy to Rome, with a gift of 1000 lbs. of gold and 20,000 lbs. of silver, which, however, as well as his proffered troops, were politely declined by the Romans. At this time the struggle with Antiochus was imminent, and it was the obvious policy of all the other eastern powers to side with the great western republic. It was in accordance with this that presently 'ambassadors were sent from Ptolemy and Cleopatra, sovrans of Egypt, with congratulations that Manius Acilius the consul had driven King Antiochus from Greece, and advising the Romans to send their army over to Asia; that all Syria as well as Asia was in a panic; that the sovrans of Egypt were prepared to do whatever the Senate resolved. A vote of thanks was passed to the sovrans, and a donation given to the ambassadors.'[1] It is noteworthy that Livy speaks of *reges Aegypti*, the king and queen, as of equal importance, just as the second Ptolemy and Arsinoe, the Brother Gods, had been associated.[2] We know of no special act associating the queen in the case of Epiphanes, but with a strange persistence the queens of this royal house seem superior in character and vigour to their husbands.

The meaning, however, of Ptolemy's persistent offers of help to the Romans, is not more clear than the meaning of

[1] Livy xxxvii. 3.

[2] It is, however, not impossible that Livy is thinking of Cleopatra and her young son Ptolemy Philometor, with whom she reigned formally for some years during his minority.

their equally persistent, though polite refusals. The object of the Egyptian was to recover from Antiochus his lost provinces.[1] The Greek island-cities had been declared free, and the Roman phil-Hellenism was so sentimentally violent on that point, that Epiphanes never hoped for a favourable reply. But he must have expected to recover Palestine and Coele-Syria, especially after the Roman victory of Magnesia, and the complete submission of Antiochus. Still though the Greek cities profited something, though the kingdom of Pergamum and the republic of Rhodes gained yet more by the settlement, Egypt got nothing. The fact was that Antiochus was fined an enormous war indemnity; it was not the policy of Rome to deprive him of any rich Oriental province, while he was raising this sum from his subjects. After the death of Antiochus III. in 187 B.C., his successor Seleukos IV. maintained the same military control over these provinces, though their heavy taxes, and the threatened plunder of the temples by Heliodorus, the στρατηγός of the Syrian king, made men again think of returning to Ptolemy as a Protector, whose queen was now a Syrian princess, always striving to spread her influence towards the north.

§ 182. But for the present there was no open threat of war. We may be sure that the second great home rebellion, which Epiphanes was obliged to face, occupied him and his ministers to the full extent of their powers. We hear that Epiphanes had grown worse with age. He had put to death by poison his wise minister Aristomenes, who had allowed himself too much freedom in dealing

---

[1] A Lycian inscription in favour of Epiphanes appears to commemorate the fact that though he had lost Lycia in the settlement of 189 B.C., he sent help subsequently to the Lycians in their war against the Rhodians (Letronne *Recherches* i. p. 52).

with his royal pupil.[1]   The favourite general Polycrates,
who took all trouble off his hands, is also said by Polybius
to have degenerated with age, and it is evident that the
compromises which led to the decree of the priests at
Memphis in the ninth year of his reign, must have been
violated by the crown.   A document among the Petrie
Papyri, dating in the eighteenth year of his reign, shows
that the tax of one-sixth on wine, called ἀπόμοιρα, which
had been monopolised by the deified queen of the second
Ptolemy, and had been ceded to the priests for their
temples in the Rosetta decree, was again absorbed by
the deified queens.[2]   In other words the great revenue
of the temples had been again absorbed by the crown.
This and other injustices led to a dangerous revolution in
Upper Egypt.   It was led by at least four native princes
or *dynasts*, whom Polybius names.   The events of this
revolution were so similar to those of the former, which
is noticed in the Rosetta stone, that there was long felt
some difficulty in distinguishing to which of them the four
fragments of Polybius and Diodorus refer.

After mentioning the death of Aristomenes, the latter
proceeds[3] 'Becoming gradually more brutal and aiming
at a tyrant's lawlessness rather than a monarch's sway,
he became odious to the Egyptians, and ran the risk of

[1] From Agatharchides we have a curious fragment, containing an
exhortation to a young Ptolemy to undertake a war against Aethiopia.
It is agreed among critics that the king in question was Epiphanes, and
they put the speech into the mouth of this Aristomenes, cf. Krall *Studien*
ii. 45.

[2] II. xlvi.   It also appears that the cleruchs, a class not mentioned in any later papyri, but frequent in the Arsinoite documents
of the second and third Ptolemies, still existed, at least in that province,
for they appear as witnesses etc. in the group of documents which I have
printed in the same vol. (xlvi).

[3] Vol. iv. p. 106 of Dindorf's text.

losing his throne.' In Polybius we have a mutilated passage [1] discussing the alleged divine right of kings, and their consequent right to break their obligations, evidently in connexion with the treachery of Epiphanes and the rebels. The historian proceeds:

> When this same Ptolemy was besieging Lycopolis, the Egyptian nobles surrendered to the king at discretion : and his cruel treatment of them involved him in manifold dangers. The same was the result at the time Polycrates suppressed the revolt. For Athinis, Pausiras, Chesuphus, and Irobastus, who still survived of the rebellious nobles, yielding to necessity, appeared at the city of Sais and surrendered at discretion to the king. But Ptolemy, regardless of all pledges, had them tied naked to the carts and dragged off, and then put to death with torture. He then went to Naucratis with his army, where he received the mercenaries enlisted for him by Aristonicus from Greece, and thence sailed to Alexandria, without having taken any part whatever in the actual operations of the war, thanks to the dishonest advice of Polycrates, though he was now twenty-five years old. . . .

§ 183. Revillout has found [2] two demotic Theban contracts, the one dated in the fourth year of Horhetep, the second in the fourteenth year of Anchtu, the latter of which is countersigned by the *fifth* section of priests of Amon Ra, whose establishment is ordained by Euergetes in the Canopus decree. Hence he infers that both these dynasts must have held titular power after that reign at Thebes, and at least for eighteen years. This hardly agrees with the statement of the hieroglyphic inscription concerning the building of the Edfu temple, [3] which describes this place as a centre of the rebellion which broke out in the sixteenth year, and even as occupied by a rebel dynast from the sixteenth till the nineteenth year of Epiphanes,

---

[1] xxii. 6-7.   [2] *Chrest. dém.* p. xcii.   [3] Above, p. 240.

when this king began to add to the buildings of his predecessors. On the other hand dated documents among the Petrie Papyri (II. xlvi-viii) show that in the fourth and the eighteenth years of Epiphanes, the Ptolemaic law-courts and the farming of taxes, etc., were undisturbed in the secluded Arsinoite nome.[1] We have also the departure, apparently permanent, of Greek troops from Thebes for the south mentioned in the Turin Papyrus.[2] These dynasts then were probably local kings like Inaros or Amyrtaeos, during part of Epiphanes' reign.

Diodorus' words also imply that what Polybius relates was not the end of the insurrection, though Epiphanes was now twenty-five years old (184 B.C.) and though we know that at the time of his death, four years later, he was preparing for an invasion of Syria. S. Jerome,[3] in his Commentary on Daniel xi., tells us (from Porphyry) that when Epiphanes' generals asked him how he would provide for his increased forces, he replied that his treasure was in the number of his *friends*, probably, in the official sense, of his nobility, for friend of the king was now a title like the *cousins* of modern monarchs. The friends in question thereupon disposed of him by poison in the twenty-ninth year of his age, and twenty-fourth of his reign (182-1 B.C.) As I

---

[1] Krall thinks (*Studien* ii. 43, note), in my opinion rightly, that these insurgent kings counted their years as kings of Aethiopia, not of Upper Egypt, hence the long period of eighteen years of successful rebellion is not necessary.

[2] Above, p. 290, note 2. On Inaros, etc. cf. Thucyd. i. 104.

[3] *Porro Porphyrius non vult hunc esse Seleucum, sed Ptolemaeum Epiphanem, qui Seleuco sit molitus insidias, et adversum eum exercitum prepararit, et idcirco veneno sit interfectus a ducibus suis. quod cum unus ab illo quaereret, tantas res moliens ubi haberet pecuniam: respondit sibi amicos esse divitias. quod quum divulgatum esset in populis, timuerunt duces ne auferret eorum substantiam, et idcirco eum maleficis artibus occiderunt.*

have said above,[1] this probably means that he intended to
sell the title of *Friend*, and so impair the privileges of the
existing official nobility.   Revillout[2] refers to the stele of
Philae (a hieroglyphic and demotic text much damaged,
published by Brugsch) dated in this king's nineteenth year,
wherein he renews the φιλάνθρωπα of the Rosetta inscription,[3] but Revillout adds that in his twentieth year there
was imposed a new and vexatious tax of 5 per cent, to be
paid by the buyer upon all sales, the ἐγκύκλιος εἰκοστή
which appears so often in the papyri, and the receipt of
which in the royal bank is taken as evidence of such sale
in the courts.   Euergetes II. in the late years of his reign
even raised it to 10 per cent.   The imposing of this tax
may have been one of the causes of Epiphanes' murder:
it is at all events a symptom of his financial difficulties,
and an evidence of his oppressive attempts to mend them.

§ 184. As might be expected, we have but few evidences from inscriptions of internal benefits conferred by
this king.   There is a votive offering of one Acoris at
a grotto near the site of the ancient Tehneh,[4] in Greek.
The cartouche of the king is among the rarest found
upon Ptolemaic buildings.   He continued the building
of the great temple at Edfu.   At Philae, the so-called
chapel of Aesculapius is declared by its inscription to be
founded by Ptolemy Epiphanes and Cleopatra, and their
son, to Imhotep, the son of Ptah.   The mention of their
son seems to place this inscription in a late portion of
the reign.[5]

---

[1] p. 214, note 2.   [2] *Chrest. dém.* p. xiii.

[3] A remission of the taxes paid by the natives to the local dynasts
during their sway must have been the main indulgence of this decree.

[4] Murray ii. p. 404.   Cf. also *Rev. arch.* xiv. 89 υπερ βασ. Πτολ. θεου
Επιφανους μεγαλου ευχαριστου Ακωρις Ερωεως Ισιδι Μωχιαδι σωτειρα(ι).

[5] We have another record of this king in a small stele with a very

The copy of the decree on the Rosetta stone, at the same temple, has already been mentioned. A temple at Antaeopolis, built by this king and queen, was undermined by the Nile, and so destroyed, in the present century.

effaced inscription, in the museum of Gizeh (room 39), which runs thus: υπερ βασιλεως Πτολ. του Πτολ. θεου Επιφανους και ευχαριστου Ισιδι θεαι μεγαληι τον ναον και το ιερον και τα προσοντα αυτωι ταμιεια και τα συνκυροντα παντα Θεων Ηρακλειδου Μαρωνευς. Unfortunately, after deciphering the inscription, I could get no information of its *provenance*, and as it has no date, and we know nothing of Theon of Maroneia from other sources, we can as yet draw no further conclusions from the text. Strack (*Mitth.* for 1894, p. 224) and Wilcken think that *Maroneus* is formed from Maron, one of the mythical ancestors of Ptolemy, who gave their names to Alexandrian demes, so that Theon would be an Alexandrian of the deme of Maron.

CLEOPATRA I.

APPENDIX

The Decree of Memphis (Rosetta Stone) 196 b.c.

§ 185. βασιλευοντος του νεου, και παραλαβοντος την βασιλειαν παρα του πατρος, κυριου βασιλειων, μεγαλοδοξου, του την
Αιγυπτον καταστησαμενου, και τα προς τους | θεους ευσεβους,
αντιπαλων υπερτερου, του τον βιον των ανθρωπων επανορ-
θωσαντος, κυριου τριακονταετηριδων, καθαπερ ο Ηφαιστος ο
μεγας· βασιλεως καθαπερ ο ηλιος, | μεγας βασιλευς των τε
ανω και των κατω χωρων, εκγονου θεων Φιλοπατορων· ον ο
Ηφαιστος εδοκιμασεν, ωι ο ηλιος εδωκεν την νικην· εικονος
ζωσης του Διος, υιου του ηλιου, Πτολεμαιου | αιωνοβιου,
ηγαπημενου υπο του Φθα· ετους ενατου, εφ ιερεως Αετου του
Αετου Αλεξανδρου και θεων Σωτηρων και θεων Αδελφων και
θεων Ευεργετων και θεων Φιλοπατορων και | θεου Επιφανους
Ευχαριστου· αθλοφορου Βερενικης Ευεργετιδος Πυρρας της

The observations already made on the decree of Canopus
will enable us to treat the present text far more briefly. The
circumstances of the issuing of the decree will be found at
§ 177. Square brackets indicate a loss, or supply of lost
letters, or a superfluous word ; round brackets a few obvious
corrections.

ll. 1-3. Here at the very opening we come upon one of the
greatest contrasts between the sister decrees, and probably that
which persuaded Revillout that while the original of the former
was Greek, this must have been demotic. On Greek principles,
the opening should run : βασιλευοντος Πτολ. του Πτολ. και
Αρσινοης θεων Φιλοπατορων, ετους ενατου, εφ ιερεως Αετου
κτλ., instead of which we have long-winded formulae quite
foreign to any known or possible Greek dating.

l. 5. ἐπιφανής means a god manifesting his presence ;
εὐχάριστος, *displaying his beneficence* ; not full of grace, in the

Φιλινου, κανηφορου Αρσινοης Φιλαδελφου Αρειας της Διογενους,
ιερειας Αρσινοης Φιλοπατορος Ειρηνης | της Πτολεμαιου· μηνος 5
Ξανδικου τετραδι, Αιγυπτιων δε Μεχειρ οκτω και δεκατηι·
ΨΗΦΙΣΜΑ. οι αρχιερεις και προφηται και οι εις το αδυτον
εισπορευομενοι προς τον στολισμον των | θεων και πτεροφοραι
και ιερογραμματεις και οι αλλοι ιερεις παντες, οι απαντησαντες
εκ των κατα την χωραν ιερων εις Μεμφιν τωι βασιλει προς την
πανηγυριν της παραληψεως της | βασιλειας της Πτολεμαιου,
αιωνοβιου ηγαπημενου υπο του Φθα θεου Επιφανους Ευχαριστου,
ην παρελαβεν παρα του πατρος αυτου, συναχθεντες εν τωι εν
Μεμφει ιερωι, τηι ημεραι ταυτηι ειπαν | ΕΠΕΙΔΗ βασιλευς
Πτολεμαιος αιωνοβιος ηγαπημενος υπο του Φθα, θεος Επιφανης
Ευχαριστος, ο εγ βασιλεως Πτολεμαιου και βασιλισσης
Αρσινοης θεων Φιλοπατορων, κατα πολλα ευεργετηκεν τα θ
ιερα, και | τους εν αυτοις οντας και τους υπο την εαυτου
βασιλειαν τασσομενους απαντας· υπαρχων θεος εκ θεου και θεας

sense of attractive or delightful. Ηφαιστος and Φθα are
used in the Greek indifferently for the same demotic sign, or
rather where Ptah appears in the king's cartouche, the word is
preserved in the Greek. The somewhat senseless repetition
of the same god three times is relieved by considering that
Ptolemy, living for ever, beloved of Ptah, is the transcription
of the king's oval, or ordinary Egyptian name, given at the
head of Chapter VIII. του Διος (l. 3) is in the DV Amon.

ll. 7, 8. This occasion is then the formal coronation of the
young king upon his coming of age (14), and at Memphis, in
the temple of Ptah. We may well doubt whether the earlier
kings condescended to this ceremony. They were probably
crowned at Alexandria. M. Revillout (*RE* iii. 4 *sq.*) thinks
this was the third formal ceremony connected with Epiphanes'
succession, viz. (1) an association with his father, about 208-7
B.C., when the prince, born 210-9, was a mere infant; (2) his
actual accession described by Polybius; (3) the present coronation.

l. 9. The king's Egyptian name and description is again
given, before coming to his ordinary Greek description.

l. 10. Benefits to priests are by them always stated as

καθαπερ Ωρος ο της Ισιος και Οσιριος υιος, ο επαμυνας τωι
10 πατρι αυτου Οσιρει, τα προς θεους | ευεργετικως διακειμενος,
ανατεθεικεν εις τα ιερα αργυρικας τε και σιτιχας προσοδους·
και δαπανας πολλας υπομεμ[ε]νηκεν, ενεκα του την Αιγυπτον
εις ευδιαν αγαγειν, και τα ιερα καταστησασθαι· | ταις τε εαυτου
δυναμεσιν πεφιλανθρωπηκε πασαις και απο των υπαρχουσων
εν Αιγυπτωι προσοδων, και φορολογιων τινας μεν εις τελος
αφηκεν, αλλους δε κεκουφικεν, οπως ο τε λαος και οι αλλοι
παντες εν | ευθηνιαι ωσιν επι της εαυτου βασιλειας. τα τε
βασιλικα οφειληματα α προσωφειλον οι εν Αιγυπτωι και οι εν
τηι λοιπηι βασιλειαι αυτου, οντα πολλα τωι πληθει, αφηκεν·
και τους εν ταις φυλακαις | απηγμενους και τους εν αιτιαις
οντας εκ πολλου χρονου απελυσε των ενκεκλημενων.   προσεταξε

distinct from, and more important than, benefits to the rest of
the population. The use of ἑαυτοῦ here and ll. 12, 13 for
αὐτοῦ is a fault not uncommon at this period.

l. 11. We know now that σιτιχας (-κας) τε και αργυρικας
corresponds to a distinction in the fiscal management of the
exchequer, there being separate offices for each. Cf. the texts
quoted by me in *Hermathena* for 1895. εὐδία, *peace*, is
usually coupled with εὐθηνία, *plenty*, in C and in this text.

l. 12. Letronne thought that πεφιλανθρώπηκε should be
rendered as a neuter verb. It is more likely that it means
φιλάνθρωπα ποιεῖν with an object understood, and the demotic
seems to mean 'he gave presents to all the soldiers under
his authority.' This also agrees better with the demotic.
φορολογία also appears as a technical word in the Revenue
Papyrus. φιλάνθρωπα was the usual word for royal concessions or benevolences, as we know from other inscriptions.
κεκούφικεν is in the DV *gave them* (the Egyptians) *the
control of*, *i.e.* gave them back to the priests, to collect and to
use. λαός means the native population, as elsewhere.

l. 13. I think it better to construe πολλὰ τῷ πλήθει
together, not τῷ πλήθει ἀπέδωκε, which would mean that he
gave the remissions to the corporation of the priestly caste
only.

l. 14. The words point to the great hardships of long
imprisonments without trial. This is evidently the fear in the

δε και τας προσοδους των ιερων και τας διδομενας εις αυτα κατ
ενιαυτον συνταξεις σιτι | κας τε και αργυρικας ομοιως δε και
τας καθηκουσας απομοιρας τοις θεοις, απο τε της αμπελιτιδος
γης και των παραδεισων και των αλλων των υπαρξαντων τοις
θεοις επι του πατρος αυτου | μενειν επι χωρας· προσεταξεν δε 15
και περι των ιερεων οπως μηθεν πλειον διδωσιν εις το τελεστικον
ου ετασσοντο εως · του πρωτου ετους επι του πατρος αυτου·
απελυσεν δε και τους εκ των | ιερων εθνων του κατ ενιαυτον εις

minds of various petitioners in the Petrie Papyri, who beg that
they may not be allowed to 'rot in prison.'· ἀπηγμένους
seems to be the technical word for being *arrested*.

l. 14. The σύνταξις, for which the demotic gives a mere
transcript of the word, was the yearly grant which the
Ptolemies made to the priests instead of former properties or
rights on land, which had been taken into the treasury.

l. 15. In particular the ἀπόμοιρα to the gods, consisting of
a ἕκτη, $\frac{1}{6}$, which was levied from the vines of the country,
whether in vineyards or gardens, had been turned into a tax
for Arsinoe Philadelphus in the twenty-third year of the second
Ptolemy's reign. This appears from the Revenue papyrus.
If the statement of the text be true, the priests had recovered
this large source of income during the reign of Philopator.
The very expression μένειν ἐπὶ χώρας, 'to remain on its old
footing,' seems to point back to the former disturbance of it.

l. 16. The DV seems to make it certain that the τελεστικόν
was a tax paid on becoming a priest, and this had now been
fixed, curiously enough, at the sum payable under the late
king's first year. Letronne, greatly puzzled by the otiose ἐπί,
if we translate thus, proposed to render: 'the tax which the
priests paid up to (the end of) their first year, in his father's
time,' which is even more awkward. Perhaps a mere inversion
of the clauses would be simpler, viz. 'they should not pay
more than they had paid under his father, up to the first year
of the present reign,' which would imply that Epiphanes'
ministers, probably in distress for money at his accession, had
imposed an increase of this tax, which was now remitted.
The DV here gives us no help.

l. 17. The ἔθνη seem to be the various classes included in

Ἀλεξανδρειαν καταπλου· προσεταξεν δε και την συλληψιν των
εις την ναυτειαν μη ποιεισθαι· των τ εις το βασιλικον συντε-
λουμενων εν τοις ιεροις βυσσινων | οθονιων απελυσεν τα δυο
μερη· τα τε εγλελειμμενα παντα εν τοις προτερον χρονοις
αποκατεστησεν εις την καθηκουσαν ταξιν, φροντιζων οπως τα
ειθισμενα συντεληται τοιξ θεοις κατα το | προσηκον· ομοιως
δε και το δικαιον πασιν απενειμεν καθαπερ Ερμης ο μεγας και
μεγας· πρ(ο)σεταξεν δε και τους καταπορευομενους εκ τε των
μαχιμων και των αλλων των αλλοτρια | φρονησαντων εν τοις

the πλῆθος of· the priests. In the DV it is the men 'among
the authorities of the temple.' This remission that they
should no longer pay their formal respects yearly at Alexandria was a great concession to national feeling. The DV
indicates that σύλληψις εἰς ναυτείαν means compulsory (naval)
service, like our old press-gang, though there seems to be no
equivalent for the words εἰς τὴν ναυτείαν.

l. 18. The sail-cloth seems to have been manufactured at
the temples, and by the priestly caste. In a new papyrus
(Grenfell Papyri I) brought home (1895) by Mr. Grenfell,
ὀθόνιον is distinctly used for outer garment or cloak. ἐγλε-
λειμμένα is in the DV *out of order*, and seems to refer not
to omissions, but to irregular exactions. τοιξ is of course a
mistake for τοῖς.

l. 19. The expression Hermes (Thoth) μέγας καὶ μέγας,
which even appears as μέγας μέγας when applied to Souchos
in inscriptions of the Fayyum, is not Greek but Egyptian, and
one more proof that the original was in demotic. The allusion
to the warrior caste, as still existing, is remarkable. But for
this we should have imagined it long since extinct (though
the word occurs in Plutarch's *Moralia* iii. 7 and 9), and
replaced by foreign mercenaries; and so it may have been,
till the natives, probably of this caste, were armed again and
trained before the battle of Raphia, and hence assumed the
courage to revolt. The text implies that the insurrection was
mainly military, but of course the priests would conceal their
share in it, in this document. This is the ταραχή here
mentioned. καταπορευομένους is in the DV future, *who will
come* (back).

κατα την ταραχην καιροις κατελθοντας μενειν επι των ιδιων
κτησεων· προενοηθη δε και οπως εξαποσταλωσιν δυναμεις
ιππικαι τε και πεζικαι και νηες επι τους επελθοντας | επι την 20
Αιγυπτον κατα τε την θαλασσαν και την ηπειρον, υπομεινας
δαπανας αργυρικας τε και σιτικας μεγαλας οπως τα θ ιερα και
οι εν αυτηι παντες εν ασφαλειαι ωσιν· παραγινομε- | νος δε
και εις Λυκων πολιν την εν τωι Βουσιριτηι η ην κατειλημμενη
και ωχυρωμενη προς πολιορκιαν οπλων τε παραθεσει δαψιλε-
στεραι και τηι αλληι χορηγιαι πασηι, ως αν εκ πολλου | χ(ρ)ο-
νου συνεστηκυιας της αλλοτριοτητος τοις επισυναχθεισιν εις
αυτην ασεβεσιν, οι ησαν εις τε τα ιερα και τους εν Αιγυπτωι
κατοικουντας πολλα κακα συντετελεσμενοι, και αν- | τικαθισας
χωμασιν τε και ταφροις και τειχεσιν αυτην αξιολογοις περι-
ελαβεν· του τε Νειλου την αναβασιν μεγαλην ποιησαμενου εν
τωι ογδοωι ετει και ειθισμενου κατακλυζειν τα | πεδια κατεσχεν

l. 20. This sending out an army and fleet is generally
supposed to allude to the campaigns of Scopas against
Antiochus the Great in Palestine (203-2 B.C. ?)   But I think
it rather applies to forces sent to the frontiers, south or
south-east, to repel raids of Nubians and others, who sought
to profit by the troubles of the country.   For the foreign
campaigns are quite out of chronological order in this place.
Here, as in the Canopus decree, such expeditions are regarded
as undertaken by the king at his own expense.   Hence there
seems to have been no war-tax among the many imposts with
which the people were burdened.

l. 22. This campaign of Lycopolis has been discussed § 182.
The DV adds : 'which had passed into the hands of the
impious.'   From τάφροις to ὀχυρώσας, the Greek is only a
very free rendering of the DV.   We know that in some cases
the insurgents seized the temples, and used them for forts, as
in the case of Edfu.

l. 23. D adds : 'having abandoned the path of obedience
to the king and the gods.'

ll. 24-26. The operation described is the damming aside of
the overflowing Nile, so that it might not flood the king's camp,
and stop the siege.   By this means the insurgents, who hoped

εκ πολλων τοπων οχυρωσας τα στοματα των ποταμων χορηγησας
εις αυτα χρηματων πληθος ουκ ολιγον· και καταστησας ιππεις
25 τε και πεζους προς τηι φυλακηι | αυτων εν ολιγωι χρονωι την
τε πολιν κατα κρατος ειλεν και τους εν αυτηι ασεβεις παντας
διεφθειρεν, καθαπε[ρ Ερμ]ης και Ωρος ο της Ισιος και Οσιριος
υιος εχειρωσαντο τους εν τοις αυτοις | τοποις αποσταντας
προτερον· τους [τ] αφηγησαμενους των αποσταντων επι του
εαυτου πατρος και την χωραν ε[κταραξ?]αντας και τα ιερα
αδικησαντας, παραγενομενος εις Μεμφιν, επαμυνων | τωι πατρι

for relief from the inundation, were driven to despair.   I am
in doubt about the usual translation of πρὸς τῇ φυλακῇ
αὐτῶν (25-6) which both Letronne and Revillout interpret of
the watching of the new dykes with horse and foot.   I rather
incline to translate : ‘when the Nile made a very high inundation in the eighth year, and would naturally have covered all
the flat land (Lycopolis being on a mound), he stayed the
river (which no antecedent king had ever attempted to do,
DV) by stopping at many points, and at great expense, the
mouths of the canals which brought the rising Nile into the
lands about Lycopolis, and so, having set horse and foot to
invest them (αυτων the insurgents), presently stormed the
city.’ His dykes enabled him to keep his troops investing
the city.   The DV throws no light on αὐτῶν.

l. 26.   It was a usual formula of flattery to say whatever
a Ptolemy had done, had been done of old in the same way,
and in the same place, by some Egyptian god.   To διέφθειρεν
the DV adds : *and annihilated them*, as etc.

l. 27.   ἀφηγησάμενοι is a curious word for the leaders of a
revolt, whom Polybius calls δυνάσται or local chiefs.   Xenophon
uses it for the *van* of an army under march.   DV says :
‘the impious who had collected troops.’   Some of these men
had been for years maintaining a civil war.

I think the suggestion ε[νοχλησ]αντας of Letronne too
weak, as he thinks ε[ρημωσ]αντας (Porson) too strong (though
Letronne might have quoted in his own support Appian’s use of
the word (*Bell. Civ.* iv. 61), who describes Cleopatra pleading to
Cassius that Egypt was *bothered* (ἐνοχλουμένην) with pestilence
and·famine).   Perhaps ἐκταράξαντας, a word found in Plutarch

και τηι εαυτου βασιλειαι, παντας εκολασεν καθηκοντως καθ
ον καιρον παρεγενηθη προς το συντελεσθη[ναι αυτωι τα] προσ-
ηκοντα νομιμα τηι παραληψει της βασιλειας· ΑΦΗΚΕΝ
δε και τα ε[ν] | τοις ιεροις οφειλομενα εις το βασιλικον εως του
ογδοου ετους οντα εις σιτου τε και αργυρ(ι)ου πληθος ουκ ολιγον,
ωσαυ[τως δε κ]αι τας τιμας των μη συντετελεσμενων εις το
βασιλικον βυσσινων οθ[ονι-] | ων και των συντετελεσμενων τα
προς τον δειγματισμον διαφορα εως των αυτων χρονων· απελυσεν
δε τα ιερα και της α[ποδιδο?]μενης αρταβης τηι αρουραι της ιερας
γης και της αμπελιτιδος ομοι[ως | το κεραμιον τηι αρουραι· τωι 30
τε Απει και Μνευει πολλα εδωρησατο και τοις αλλοις ιεροις ζωιοις
τοις εν Αιγυπτωι, πολυ κρεισσον των προ αυτου βασιλε(ι)ων

and in Athenaeus, in sense of *greatly troubling*, may be
accepted. After τὰ ἱερά the DV adds : 'being out of the way
(obedience) of the king and his father, the gods granted him
to strike.'

1. 28. The execution of the rebel leaders formed part of
the coronation ceremonies, for which the king came specially
to Memphis. The priests now revert again to their favourite
topic, the remissions of taxes—here of the arrears of taxes due
up to the eighth year. These were, I suppose, the special
φιλάνθρωπα at Epiphanes' coronation, as distinguished from
those granted at his accession.

1. 30. 'And of those sail-cloths which had been actually
contributed, the cost (διάφορα) of having them verified (πρὸς
τὸν δειγμ.)' is Letronne's version. But the meaning of the
latter word is quite uncertain. The DV says : the complement
for pieces of cloth which had been kept back (*écartées*).
I have not printed the usual α[ποτεταγ]μενης here, because there is not room for it in the gap, according to the
ordinary spacing of the letters, though there are places to be
found in the inscription, where letters are crowded considerably,
viz. ll. 48-9. Another possible word is ἀ[φφορισ]μένης.

1. 31. The κεράμιον is stated to be = ἀμφορεύς, and this =
½ μετρητής. Apis and Mnevis appear as in C 9. τοῖς ἄλλοις
ζώοις is in the DV aux autres *bœufs*, in C 9 it is *animaux*.
τὰ τελισκόμενα, DV, 'the expenses that arise.'

φροντιζων υπερ των ανηκον[των εις] | αυτα δια παντος· τα τ εις
τας ταφας αυτων καθηκοντα διδους δαψιλως και ενδοξως και τα
τελισκομενα εις τα ιδια ιερα μετα θυσιων και πανηγυρεων και
των αλλων των νομι[ζομενων] | τα τε τιμια των ιερων και της
Αιγυπτου διατετηρηκεν επι χωρας ακολουθως τοις νομοις, και
το Απιειον εργοις πολυτελεσιν κατεσκευασεν, χορηγησας εις αυτο
χρυσιου τε κ[αι αργυρι | ου και λιθων πολυτελων πληθος ουκ
ολιγον· και ιερα και ναους και βωμους ιδρυσατο· τα τε προσ-
δεομενα επισκευης προσδιωρθωσατο εχων θεου ευεργετικου εν
τοις ανηκου[σιν εις το] | θειον διανοιαν· προσπυνθανομενος τε
τα των ιερων τιμιωτατα ανενεουτο επι της εαυτου βασιλειας ως
καθηκει· ανθ ων δεδωκασιν αυτωι οι θεοι υγιειαν νικην κρατος
35 και ταλλ αγαθ[α παντα] | της βασιλειας διαμενουσης αυτωι και
τοις τεκνοις τον απαντα χρονον· ΑΓΑΘΗΙ ΤΥΧΗΙ ΕΔΟΞΕΝ
τοις ιερευσι των κατα την χωραν ιερων παντων τα υπαρχοντα
τ[ιμια παντα] | τωι αιωνοβιωι βασιλει Πτολεμαιωι ηγαπημενωι
υπο του Φθα θεωι Επιφανει Ευχαριστωι ομοιως δε τα των
γονεων αυτου θεων Φιλοπατορων και τα των προγονων θεων
Ευεργ[ετων και τα] | των θεων Αδελφων και τα των θεων
Σωτηρων επαυξειν μεγαλως· στησαι δε του αιωνοβιου βασιλεως
Πτο(λε)μαιου θεου Επιφανους Ευχαριστου εικονα εν εκαστωι

l. 33. He adorned the temple of Apis (near Memphis)
with gold, and silver, and *precious stones*, in great quantity.
For this both the DV and the HV give gold, silver, and *corn*,
a curious variant. The DV further amplifies the sentence.
The phrase λιθεία πολυτελής occurs in an inscription of the
gathering of precious stones in the Arabian desert, p. 394, note.

ll. 34, 35. As might be expected, the king's architectural
activity is a feature specially praised, though but little of it
now remains. His share in the Edfu temple is noticed p. 240.
ἱδρύσατο, which properly means *founded*, translates a word
meaning *amplified* in D.

· ll. 35, 36. For a shorter formula, cf. C 20. The DV is
even longer—*victory, triumph, safety, health.*

ll. 38 *sq.* These honours are far more extravagant than
those given to Euergetes, and are to be compared to the

ιερωι εν τωι επιφα[νεστατωι τοπωι] | η προσονομασθησεται
Πτολεμαιου του επαμυναντος τηι Αιγυπτωι, ηι παρεστηξεται
ο κυριωτατος θεος του ιερου διδους αυτωι οπλον νικητικον α
εσται κατεσκευασμεν[α τον επιχωριον?] | τροπον· και τους
ιερεις θεραπευειν τας εικονας τρις της ημερας· και παρατιθεναι
αυταις ιερον κοσμον και ταλλα τα νομιζομενα συντελειν καθα
και τοις αλλοις θεοις, εν [ταις εν τηι Αιγυπτωι? πα] | νηγυρεσιν· 40
ιδρυσασθαι δε βασιλει Πτολεμαιωι θεωι Επιφανει Ευχαριστωι
τωι εγ βασιλεως Πτολεμαιου και βασιλισσης Αρσινοης θεων
Φιλοπατορων ξοανον τε και ναον χρ[υσα εν εκαστωι των | ιερων·
και καθιδρυσαι εν τοις αδυτοις μετα των αλλων ναων και εν ταις
μεγαλαις πανηγυρεσιν εν αις εξοδειαι των ναων γινονται και τον
του θεου Επιφανους Ευ[χαριστου ναον συνε] | ξοδευειν· οπως δ
ευσημος ηι νυν τε και εις τον επειτα χρονον, επικεισθαι τωι
ναωι τας του βασιλεως χρυσας βασιλειας δεκα αις προσ-
κεισεται ασπις [καθαπερ και επι πασων] | των ασπιδοειδων
βασιλειων, των επι των αλλων ναων· εσται δ αυτων εν τωι
μεσωι η καλουμενη βασιλεια ψχεντ ην περιθεμενος εισηλθεν
εις το εν Μεμφ[ει ιερον οπως εν αυτωι συν] | -τελεσθηι τα
νομιζομενα τηι παραληψει της βασιλειας· επιθειναι δε και
επι του περι τας βασιλειας τετραγωνου κατα το προειρημενον βασιλειον φυλακτηρια χρυ[σα δεκα οις εγγραφθησεται
ο-] | τι εστιν του βασιλεως, του επιφανη ποιησαντος την τε 45
ανω χωραν και την κατω. και επει την τριακαδα του(του)
Μεσορη εν ηι τα γενεθλια του βασιλεως αγεται, ομοιως δε και
[την του μεχειρ επτα και δεκα την] | εν ηι παρελαβεν την βασι-

honours assigned to the dead child Berenike, at the moment
of her parent's grief, C 47 *sq.* Letronne thinks the εἰκών was
a relief on the wall, such as there are many extant of Ptolemies,
in contrast to the ξόανον, a sitting figure in a shrine.
Revillout renders εἰκών, *statue* ; ξόανον, *statue divine.*

l. 43. Letronne has given a full commentary on the
heraldic designs of this summit of the Ναός with illustrations.
The DV is somewhat more explicit than the Greek, especially
in explanation of the *phylacteries.*

λειαν παρ(α)του πατρος επωνυμους νενομικασιν εν τοις ιεροις,
αι δη πολλων αγαθων αρχηγοι πασιν εισιν, αγειν τας ημερας
ταυτας εορτ[ην και πανηγυριν εν τοις κατα την Αι-] | γυπτον
ιεροις κατα μηνα· και συντελειν εν αυτοις θυσιας και σπονδας
και ταλλα τα νομιζομενα καθα και εν ταις αλλαις πανηγυρεσιν,
τας τε γινομενας προθε[σμιας? . . . . . πα] | ρεχομενους εν
τοις ιεροις· αγειν δε εορτην και πανηγυριν τωι αιωνοβιωι και
ηγαπημενωι υπο του Φθα βασιλει Πτολεμαιωι θεωι Επιφανει
Ευχαριστωι κατ ενι[αυτον εν τοις ιεροις τοις κατα την] | χωραν
απο της νουμηνιας του θωυθ εφ ημερας πεντε εν αις και
στεφανηφορησουσιν, συντελουντες θυσιας και σπονδας και
ταλλα τα καθηκοντα· προσαγορε[υεσθαι δε τους ιερεις των
50 αλλων θεων] | και του θεου Επιφανους Ευχαριστου ιερεις
προς τοις αλλοις ονομασιν των θεων, ων ιερατευουσι, και κατα-
χωρισαι εις παντας τους χρηματισμους και εις τους δ[ακτυ-
λιους ους φορουσι προσεγκολαπτεσθαι την] | ιερατειαν αυτου·
εξειναι δε και τοις αλλοις ιδιωταις αγειν την εορτην και τον
προειρημενον ναον ιδρυεσθαι και εχειν παρ αυτοις συντελου[σι
. . . . . . ταις τα κατα μηνα? και | τα]ις κατ ενιαυτον οπως
γνωριμον ηι διοτι οι εν Αιγυπτωι αυξουσι και τιμωσι τον θεον
Επιφανη Ευχαριστον βασιλεα καθαπερ νομιμον εστ[ιν· το δε
ψηφισμα τουτο αναγραψαι εις στηλην | σ]τερεον λιθου τοις τε
ιεροις και ενχωριοις και Ελληνικοις γραμμασιν και στησαι εν

l. 48. προθεσμίας or προθέσεις is very doubtful, nor is the
general sense certain. The DV has *les offrandes saintes* qu'on
les assigne.

l. 51. The parallel phrase in C enables us to restore the
gap here. It is there εις τους δακτυλιους ους φορουσι προσεγκολαπτεσθαι και την ιερωσυνην των Ευ. θεων. The phrase
may have been shorter here, probably εις τους δ[ακτυλιους
προσεγκολαπτεσθαι την] ιερατειαν etc., which gives the likely
number (29) of missing letters. That the Greek version was
not copying a fixed Greek formula is obvious from the variation ἱερατεία (used both by Aristotle (*Pol.*), and in the N. T.),
for ἱερωσύνη. καταχωρίσαι is to *enter* in writing.

l. 54. The concluding phrase in C 75 is missing here,

εκαστωι των τε πρωτων και δευτερω[ν και τριτων ιερων προς τηι
του βασιλεως εικονι ?]

apparently because the graver did not choose to begin a new
line. The supplement is taken from the HV as given by
Champollion. The DV agrees with the HV, but does not add
anything beyond it.

COIN OF ARSINOE PHILOPATOR.

CHAPTER IX

§ 186. WE have now reached the moment when the history of Egypt under the Macedonian dynasty declines

PTOLEMY VII.

in dignity and increases in complication. Hitherto, though it was usual to associate the queen, or the prince royal, in the government, there is no doubt about the reigning king. From henceforth, we have almost constantly rival brothers asserting themselves in turn, queen mothers controlling their king sons—intestine feuds and bloodshed in the royal house, till the stormy end of the dynasty with the daring Cleopatra VI. The historian is bound to chronicle these wretched complications, to unravel these problems of chronology, and yet they only affect the reigning house, and tell us nothing of interest to posterity. We must have recourse to private papers, journals, extracts of obscure persons, bills of stewards and lists of tax-gatherers, to learn something of the gradual relapse of the country from Hellenism into the ineradicable Egypt of the native race.

Even the accession of Philometor, though attested unanimously by all remaining historians as following at once upon the death of Epiphanes, is not without serious difficulties. For we have several papyri[1] which give the list of the Ptolemies down to Lathyrus, in which there is a Eupator inserted between them—a king who seems to occupy no time, and for whom there is no place. Yet we can hardly ascribe to business texts a wanton invention, and must seek for some solution. What has been suggested is this : we know that Philometor was not born till 188 B.C., five years after the marriage of his father, and that other children followed quickly. It is therefore more probable than not that there was an elder son, who may have lived long enough to survive his father a week or two, and so attain the titles and the recognition of royalty. We shall find another such case later on, namely in the son of Philometor, and this too without distinct knowledge of the historians.[2]

This is the argument of Lepsius, in his well-known article on Ptolemaic chronology.[3] He says that nine hieroglyphic inscriptions and several demotic texts support his view. His decision has been accepted, and it is for that reason that Philometor is now known as the seventh—

---

[1] Viz. the *Casati* papyrus (cf. the discussion of the question in *CIG* no. 2618) and the texts (C, D, F) obtained by Mr. Grenfell in 1895.

[2] There can hardly be a doubt concerning the dedication found at Apello in Cyprus (Le Bas iii. 2809) to βασ. Πτολ. θεον Ευπατορα τον εγ βασ. Πτολ. και βασ. Κλεοπ. θεων Φιλομητορων. It refers to a nephew of the Eupator in question, elsewhere called Philopator Neos.

[3] *Transactions of the Berlin Academy* for 1852, pp. 456 *sqq.*

and not the sixth—reigning sovran.   It was not till 1895
that Mr. Grenfell found a *Greek* papyrus, containing the
full list as determined from Egyptian documents forty
years ago.[1]

§ 187. Our difficulties have been increased by the
absurd habit of repeating the same names.   Cleopatra, the
wife of Epiphanes, in other respects a sane, and perhaps
able woman, thought fit to call her two sons Ptolemy and
her daughter Cleopatra, so that we have to distinguish
Ptolemies and Cleopatras, without the obvious mark of a
distinct name.   It is no wonder that we hear of the habit
of giving nicknames as very prevalent in Alexandria.   The
smart wits of the people are not so obvious a cause as the
necessities of life.

This Cleopatra (I.), who bears an excellent character in
Egyptian history, was made regent, while her elder son,
now a child of seven years old, formally ascended the
throne, and it is a strong corroboration of the opinion
expressed concerning her good sense, that during the
seven remaining years of her life, the history of the
country is perfectly uneventful.   The rest of the Hellenistic
world was either occupied with home politics, such as the
continuous quarrels in the Peloponnesus, or was in the
hands of unambitious sovrans, such as Perseus of Macedonia,
who was perhaps already gathering treasure for his war
with Rome, or Seleukos IV. (Philopator) of Syria, whose
twelve years of power (187-75 B.C.) are among the quietest
in the agitated history of that kingdom.   The payment
of the heavy tribute to the Romans may have crippled the
resources of Syria.   The Romans, secure from any danger

---

[1] The Aswân stele now in the British Museum contains important
genealogical corroborations of these papyri. Cf. for details below, p.
374, note.

arising out of Egypt, were keeping their armies in practice by obstinate wars with the Ligures and Istrians, who made both northern exits from Italy, either to Spain or northern Dalmatia, perilous even to troops. At the same time their moneyed men were watching with jealous greed the rising wealth of Carthage, their politicians the strengthening of Macedonia under Perseus, and were preparing for the coming troubles. Hence we hear not a word about Egypt till we come to the *Anacleteria* of the young Philometor, to which all the world sends embassies.[1]

§ 188. We may now infer from the inscription found near the head of the Delta, beside the Rosetta branch, in 1891, that the marriage of the young king to his sister Cleopatra took place soon after the death of his mother, and as early as 173 B.C. For though the earliest text which mentions her as queen does not specify its own precise date, certain officers, who have served in the king's eighth and ninth year, offer a dedication to him *and his wife*, presumably in his tenth year.[2]

But a combination of adverse circumstances made a great change in the quiet East about this time. In the first place the prudent Cleopatra, who, while she was keeping peace, was extending Egyptian influences through Palestine and Lower Syria, from whence she still drew her

---

[1] Polybius xxviii. 12 ; Livy xlii. 6 ; 2 Macc. iv. 21, where the feast is called πρωτοκλισία. It appears that Antiochus' ambassador took the opportunity to discover the policy of the Egyptian court towards Syria.

[2] The text is given by Krebs in the December number of the Göttingen *Nachrichten* for 1892, viz. βασιλει Πτολ. και βασιλισσηι Κλεοπατραι θεοις Φιλομητορσι τοις εγ βασιλεως Πτολ. και βασ. Κλεοπ. θεων Επιφανων και Ευχαριστων χρηματισται οι το η̄ και δ̄ ∠ κεχρηματικοτες εν τωι Προσωπιτηι και τοις αλλοις τοις μεμερισμενοις νομοις. Six names follow. The abbreviations are of course mine. Krebs says the text is dated year 10. That does not appear from his transcript.

dowry, died (174-3 B.C.), leaving her son in the hands of an eunuch Eulaeus and a Syrian Lenaeus,[1] evidently members of her personal household; and these men at once suggested ambitious schemes for the recovery of the Syrian provinces. The uneasiness felt at Rome is shown by the sending of an embassy in 173 B.C. to have a look at Egypt.[2]

Meanwhile Heliodorus, the powerful minister of the Syrian Seleukos IV., thought to attain a practical sovranty by removing his master, and acting as tutor to his young son Demetrius. He had apparently succeeded in his purpose, when the king's brother, the active and ambitious Antiochus IV., who had been for fourteen years a hostage at Rome, and had just returned as far as Athens, promptly got the assistance of the king of Pergamum and asserted himself as king of Syria. This new king, having learned the plans of the minister, Heliodorus, and perceived that the Egyptians were preparing to seize Judaea and Coele-Syria, determined to take the first step. He occupied Judaea, making himself popular with the inhabitants, while the Egyptian ministers, dilatory in their preparations, and incapable in the field, thought it sufficient to send large offers of help to the Romans for their approaching war with Macedonia.[3]

---

[1] Eulaeus was important enough to mark the young king's coinage with the first syllable of his name. Cf. Poole *Coins* &c. p. 80. Both men are called *regents* by S. Jerome *ad Dan.* xi.

[2] Livy xlii. 6; *renovandae amicitiae causa* is the excuse.

[3] The newest and clearest treatment of the complicated wars of Antiochus IV. with Egypt will be found in the art. ANTIOCHUS of U. Wilcken in Pauly-Wissowa's *Encyclopaedia* (1894). Bandelin (*Inaug. Diss.* p. 20) does not date the young king's formal accession, with the embassy of the Achaeans, till 169 B.C., observing that Livy speaks of him as still under tutors in 171 B.C. (xlii. 29). But this disturbs so many other dates, that I cannot accept it, nor is Livy's authority of sufficient weight to make us reform our chronology.

§ 189. Early in the year 171 B.C. the contending powers of Syria and Egypt came into decisive conflict on the borders of Egypt between Mt. Casius and Pelusium. The Egyptians were completely defeated. Antiochus advanced with but a small[1] army to Memphis—the ordinary route from Pelusium to Alexandria—and there, it seems, got possession of young Ptolemy Philometor, and was himself crowned king *ex more Aegyptio*. His complete conquest of the land must now have appeared easy. But the people of Alexandria, who spoke more completely the voice of Egypt than Paris does of France, determined to resist, and forthwith raised to the throne his younger brother, who took the title Euergetes, and is consequently known as Euergetes II. in history. This boy was not more than fifteen or sixteen, but his subsequent career shows him to have been a strong and ambitious person. He accordingly counted the twelfth year of his brother's reign as his own year of accession. This usurpation gave Antiochus the excuse of advancing on Alexandria under the pretence of restoring Philometor.

Meanwhile both sides had been working hard to obtain the favour of the Roman Senate. Antiochus, who had been very well treated as a royal hostage at Rome, and had of course many friends among the Roman aristocracy, not only sent an embassy immediately upon his usurpation, but again when beginning his campaign, this latter to explain that he was only forestalling an attack upon his southern provinces which he held by right of his father's conquest. The Egyptian royalties could only plead the ancient friendship of their house with Rome, and the

---

[1] 1 Maccabees describes Antiochus' army as a great host; I prefer to follow the *cum modico populo* of S. Jerome *ad Dan.* xi.

injustice of having their kingdom dismembered by a wanton invasion.[1]

§ 190. When Antiochus advanced from Memphis down the river to attack the new boy-king at Alexandria, he met on the way two several embassies from Greek allies of Egypt, concerning which Polybius tells us :—

When Antiochus was actually in occupation of Egypt, Comanus and Cineas, after consultation with king Ptolemy Physcon [Euergetes II.], determined upon summoning a conference of the most distinguished Egyptian nobles to consult about the danger which threatened them. The first resolution the conference adopted was to send the Greek envoys who were then at

[1] Cf. the arguments in Polybius xxviii. 1 : 'When the war between the kings Antiochus and Ptolemy for the possession of Coele-Syria had just begun, Meleager, Sosiphanes, and Heracleides came as ambassadors from Antiochus, and Timotheos and Damon from Ptolemy. The one actually in possession of Coele-Syria and Phoenicia was Antiochus ; for ever since his father's victory over the generals of Ptolemy at Panium all those districts had been subject to the Syrian kings. Antiochus, accordingly, regarding the right of conquest as the strongest and most honourable of all claims, was now eager to defend these places as unquestionably belonging to himself : while Ptolemy, conceiving that the late king Antiochus had unjustly taken advantage of his father's orphan condition to wrest the cities in Coele-Syria from him, was resolved not to acquiesce in his possession of them. Therefore Meleager and his colleagues came to Rome with instructions to protest before the Senate that Ptolemy had, in breach of all equity, attacked him first ; while Timotheos and Damon came to renew their master's friendship with the Romans, and to offer their mediation for putting an end to the war with Perseus ; but, above all, to watch the communications made by Meleager's embassy. As to putting an end to the war, by the advice of Marcus Aemilius they did not venture to speak of it ; but after formally renewing the friendly relations between Ptolemy and Rome, and receiving a favourable answer, they returned to Alexandria. To Meleager and his colleagues the Senate answered that Quintus Marcius should be commissioned to write to Ptolemy on the subject, as he should think it most to the interest of Rome and his own honour. Thus was the business settled for the time.' . . . Hence it appears that our best authority justifies Antiochus. Livy takes the opposite view.

Alexandria as envoys to Antiochus to conclude a pacification. There were at that time in the country two embassies from the Achaean League, one which had been sent to renew the alliance between the League and Egypt, and which was composed of Alcithus of Aegium, son of Xenophon, and Pasiodes, and another sent to give notice of the festival of the Antigoneia.[1] There was also an embassy from Athens led by Demaratus on the subject of some present, and two sacred embassies, one in connexion with the Panathenaea under the presidency of Callias the pancratiast, and the other on the subject of the mysteries, of which Cleostratus was the active member and spokesman. There were also there Eudemus and Hicesius from Miletus, and Apollonides and Apollonius from Clazomenae. The king also sent with them Tlepolemus and Ptolemy the rhetor as envoys. These men accordingly sailed up the river to meet Antiochus.[2] . . .

In the course of these same days envoys sailed in from Rhodes to Alexandria, headed by Pration, to negotiate a pacification ; and a few days afterwards presented themselves at the camp of Antiochus. Admitted to an interview, they argued at considerable length, mentioning their own country's friendly feelings to both kingdoms, and the ties of blood existing between the two kings themselves, and the advantage which a peace would be to both. But the king interrupted the envoy in the middle of his speech by saying that there was no need of much talking, for the kingdom belonged to the elder Ptolemy, and with him he had long ago made terms, and they were friends, and if the people wished nòw to recall him Antiochus would not prevent them. . . .

He besieged Alexandria for some time, and even caused a famine in the city, but either from the insufficiency of troops, the want of supplies, or some home disturbances, possibly even at the advice of the Romans, he raised the

---

[1] The Antigoneia was a festival established in honour of Antigonus Doson, who had been a benefactor of the Achaeans. In Polybius xxx. 23 it is mentioned as being celebrated in Sikyon. The benefactions of this Macedonian king to the Achaeans are noticed by Pausanias (viii. 8, 12).

[2] Cf. *Addit. Note* p. 493.

siege, and retired by the highway of Memphis.[1]   If he was indeed crowned king of Egypt at Memphis,[2] the timid assertion of it in his coins,[3] and the silence of our remaining historians, cause us some surprise.

§ 191. What became of Philometor after his defeat, and capture by his uncle, is unknown.   Polybius[4] (and Diodorus after him) comments strongly on the resolve of the young prince to abandon his kingdom and retire to Samothrace, as a mean and cowardly act in a youth who afterwards showed not only ability but valour.   And they attribute this early mistake to the influence of the eunuch Eulaeos, evidently on mere grounds of general probability.   But at what moment this resolve was made known, and whether it was really carried out, and how long, are points upon which we as yet have no evidence.   On the other hand, Justin's account of him[5] shows that he confused him with some other Ptolemy: *segni admodum et cotidiana luxuria ita marcenti, ut non solum regiae maiestatis officia intermitteret, verum*

[1] Bandelin *op. cit.* p. 23.   Cf. the narrative in Livy xliv. 19, xlv. 11.

[2] Jerome *in loc.* and implied in 1 Maccabees i. 16.

[3] 'The usurpation of Antiochus IV. was marked not only by the countermarking [with the Seleukid anchor] of the current copper, but by the issue of a new copper currency for Egypt with his own name, two of the obverse types of which, the heads of Sarapis and Isis, were borrowed from his sister's, the [Egyptian] regent Cleopatra's, money,' Poole *Coins of the Ptolemies* p. lxiii.   It appears from Babelon (*Monnaies de Syrie* pp. c-ci.) that though this Antiochus certainly issued coins in Egypt, probably during his siege of Alexandria, the larger of which have on the reverse the eagle of the Ptolemies with Epiphanes' name, and on the obverse a head of Zeus or Sarapis, only a couple of the very smallest copper coins have his head radiated, in place of the god.   In a proud and boastful king like Epiphanes, this would seem too cautious an attempt to feel public opinion, and see how the natives would accept him as king.   Yet I am at a loss to understand the facts otherwise.

[4] xxviii. 21.   [5] Justin xxxiv. 2.

etiam sensu hominis nimia sagina careret. This remark does
not fit even the fattest Ptolemy (IX.) whose mind was most
active. At all events, Antiochus left Philometor either as
his associate or deputy at Memphis, and returned home,[1]
leaving a strong garrison in the fort of Pelusium. This
latter precaution opened the eyes of Philometor to the
dangers of the situation, and he began to make overtures
to his brother and sister, with the result that they came to
terms, and began to reign conjointly (170 B.C.)[2]

§ 192. The combination of the Egyptian princes
brought back Antiochus with a new invasion, much more
systematic and dangerous than the others. He occupied
most of Cyprus with a fleet; he advanced leisurely to his
fort of Pelusium, and then through lower Egypt,[2] courting
the favour of the population. The two young kings sent,
among other embassies for help, a mission to the Achaean
League, of which the account is preserved by Polybius.

They entreated the Achaeans, in view of the greatness of
the danger surrounding the king of Egypt, not to neglect the
right moment for acting; but keeping in mind their mutual
agreement and good services, and above all their oaths, to fulfil
the terms of that agreement.

The people were once more inclined to grant the aid when
they heard this: but Callicrates and his party managed to
prevent the decree being passed, by staggering the magistrates
with the assertion that it was unconstitutional to discuss the
question of sending help abroad in public assembly. But a

---

[1] Wilcken (*op. cit.*) prefers to assume *three* expeditions of Antiochus
to Egypt, owing to Livy xlv. 11 *si reducendi eius* [*Philometoris*] *causa
exercitum Aegyptum induxisset,* which means, he thinks, a second invasion.
I interpret it merely of his prosecuting his victory beyond the limits he
had professed. It seems to me that all the facts can be explained by
two invasions, as is implied 2 Macc. v. 1. Wilcken thinks the first
siege of Alexandria must have lasted a long time to produce a famine.
Such a city, fed from without, would feel famine in a week's siege.

[2] Cf. *Addit. Notes* pp. 494-5.

short time afterwards a meeting was summoned at Sicyon, which was attended not only by the members of the council, but by all citizens over thirty years of age; and after a lengthened debate, Polybius especially dwelling on the fact that the Romans did not require assistance,—in which he was believed not to be speaking without good reason, as he had spent the previous summer in Macedonia at the headquarters of Marcius Philippus,—and also alleging that, even supposing the Romans did turn out to require their active support, the Achaeans would not be rendered incapable of furnishing it by the two hundred horse and one thousand foot which were to be despatched to Alexandria,—for they could, without any inconvenience, put thirty or forty thousand men into the field,—the majority of the meeting were convinced, and were inclined to the idea of sending this aid. Accordingly, on the second of the two days on which, according to the laws, those who wished to do so were bound to bring forward their motions, Lycortas and Polybius proposed that aid should be sent. Callicrates, on the other hand, proposed to send ambassadors to reconcile the two Egyptian kings with Antiochus. So once more, on these two motions being put, there was an animated contest; in which, however, Lycortas and Polybius got a considerable majority on their side. For there was a very wide distinction between the claims of the two kingdoms. There were very few instances to be found in past times of any act of friendship on the part of Syria to the Greeks,—though the liberality of the present king was well known in Greece,—but from Egypt the acts of kindness in past times to the Achaeans had been as numerous and important as any one could possibly expect. By dwelling on this point Lycortas made a great impression, because the distinction between the two kingdoms in this respect was shown to be immense. For it was as difficult to count up all the benefactions of the Alexandrine kings, as it was impossible to find a single act of friendship done by the dynasty of Antiochus to the Achaeans. . . .

For a time Andronidas and Callicrates kept on arguing in support of their plan of putting an end to the war : but as no one was persuaded by them, they employed a stratagem. A letter-carrier came into the theatre (where the meeting was being held), who had just arrived with a despatch from Quintus

Marcius, urging those Achaeans who were of the Roman party to reconcile the kings; for it was a fact that the Senate had sent a mission under T. Numisius to do so. But this really made against their argument: for Titus Numisius and his colleagues had been unable to effect the pacification, and had returned to Rome completely unsuccessful in the object of their mission. However, as Polybius and his party did not wish to speak against the despatch, from consideration for Marcius, they retired from the discussion: and it was thus that the proposal to send an aid to the kings fell through. The Achaeans voted to send ambassadors to effect the pacification: and Archon of Aegeira, and Arcesilaus and Ariston of Megalopolis were appointed to the duty. Whereupon the envoys of Ptolemy, being disappointed of obtaining help, handed over to the magistrate the despatch from the kings, in which they asked that he would send Lycortas and Polybius to take part in the war.

It was not till Antiochus had reached Eleusis, within four miles of Alexandria, that the despairing embassies of the Ptolemies to Rome, coupled with the decisive victory at Pydna, produced their effect. The mission of the Senate is fortunately described to us in an extant fragment of Polybius from which Livy has given us a very clear narrative.[1]

When Antiochus had advanced to attack Ptolemy, he was met by the Roman commander Gaius Popilius Laenas. Upon the king greeting him from some distance, and holding out his right hand to him, Popilius answered by holding out the tablets which contained the decree of the Senate, and bade Antiochus read that first: not thinking it right, I suppose, to give the usual sign of friendship until he knew the mind of the recipient, whether he were to be regarded as a friend or foe. When the king, after reading the despatch, said that he desired to consult with his 'friends' on the situation, Popilius did a thing which was looked upon as exceedingly overbearing and insolent. Having a vine stick in his hand, he drew a circle round Antiochus with it, and

---

[1] Polybius xxix. 27 (11); Livy xlv. 12.

ordered him to give his answer to the letter before he stepped out of it. The king was taken aback by this haughty proceeding. After a brief interval of embarrassed silence, he replied that he would do whatever the Romans demanded. Then Popilius and his colleagues shook him by the hand, and one and all greeted him with warmth. The tenor of the despatch was an order to put an end to the war with Ptolemy at once. Accordingly a stated number of days was allowed him, within which he withdrew his army into Syria, in high dudgeon indeed, and groaning in spirit, but yielding to the necessities of the time.

Popilius and his colleagues then restored order in Alexandria; and after exhorting the two kings to maintain peaceful relations with each other, they took ship and sailed for Cyprus, with the intention of promptly ejecting from the island the forces that were also gathered there. When they arrived, they found that Ptolemy's generals had already sustained a defeat, and that the whole island was in a state of excitement. They promptly caused the invading army to evacuate the country, and remained there to keep watch until the forces had sailed away for Syria. Thus did the Romans save the kingdom of Ptolemy, when it was all but sinking under its disasters. Fortune indeed so disposed of the fate of Perseus and the Macedonians, that the restoration of Alexandria and the whole of Egypt was decided by it; that is to say, by the fate of Perseus being decided previously [at Pydna]: for if that had not taken place, and been well ascertained, I do not think that Antiochus would have obeyed these orders.

§ 193. It was on his final return to Syria after stepping out of Popilius' circle, that Antiochus committed those shocking violences to the religion of the Jews which have earned him their undying hate. In the books of the Maccabees and in Daniel he is represented as the very personification of the most impious wickedness. He had already, upon his previous return (170 B.C.), plundered the temple and put to death some of the nationalist opponents of his Hellenism. As a promoter of this kind of culture he would be hated by all pious Jews, and presently his persecutions produced the great patriotic revolt of the Maccabees, which he was unable to quell.

Yet I think his savage outbreak at Jerusalem, where he sacrificed swine upon the altar, defiled the Holy of Holies, and forced all the priests to pollute themselves, must have been caused by some more special personal injuries on their part than the mere resistance to his innovations. Our information is so scanty, that we can only guess. In some way the nationalist party in Judaea, and their relations in Egypt, must have thwarted his advance and marred his campaign. We hear that his third advance was slow; had he reached Alexandria but a few days sooner, he might have seized the capital, murdered the royal princes, and then made his peace with the Romans when the game was won. It seems likely that the opposition of the patriotic party in Judaea hindered his march, and so caused his signal failure at the moment of victory.

Under such circumstances we can quite understand his fury. It is some corroboration of this conjecture to note that in the reign of Philometor we first find Jews in high favour, and rising to great state offices in Egypt, also that the reception of Antiochus by the natives seems not to have been unfriendly. At least we hear of no great national uprising on behalf of the established dynasty. Probably the cruelties and treacheries of the late king, and the long insurrections in the Delta and in Upper Egypt, had shaken men's loyalty, and Egypt was no longer the firm and united kingdom which it seemed to be under the first three Ptolemies. Moreover, from the battle of Pydna onward, all the remaining kings of the Hellenistic East were under Roman protectorate, all bidding for Roman favour, all dreading Roman wrath. It seems hardly possible that such sovrans should inspire loyalty or devotion in their subjects.

§ 194. Nevertheless, the present royalties, Ptolemy Philometor, his brother Euergetes II., and his sister Cleopatra were not wanting in high qualities, though their position as regards the Romans was one of dependence. They were obliged to surrender the Rhodian Polyaratos, charged with intrigues in favour of Perseus, though the disgrace was softened by sending him back to Rhodes and not straight to Rome.[1] They were obliged to set free the Lacedaemonian Menalkidas, who had profited by their recent troubles to make himself important, we know not how. And both these acts were at the request of the all-powerful man of the circle, Popilius Laenas.

It is certain that at this time Philometor had already married his energetic sister Cleopatra, as it was in her name, as well as his, that an embassy was received at Rome, offering congratulations for the victory over Perseus, and thanks, apparently couched in abject language, for the interference of Popilius Laenas.[2]

§ 195. We get a few valuable lights on the history of Philometor, and his brother, in the years immediately succeeding the withdrawal of Antiochus Epiphanes from Egypt, in the excerpts from Diodorus found by C. Müller in the Escurial.[3] It seems that Dionysius surnamed Petosiris one of the 'king's friends' undertook to wrest the power into his own hands and so brought the crown into great dangers. 'For being the most influential man at court, and a long way the first of all the natives (καὶ πάντων Αἰγυπτίων προέχων) he despised both kings for

---

[1] Polybius xxx. 9.　　[2] Livy xlv. 13.　　[3] *FHG* ii. pp. viii *sq.*

their youth and inexperience.   Alleging therefore that
he had been approached by the elder to commit a family
murder (φόνον ἐμφύλιον), he spread reports that the younger
Ptolemy was in danger from his brother.   But when the
mob gathered into the stadium, and all were so infuriated
that they were about to slay the elder, and put the sovranty
into the hands of the younger, and the news of the riot
reached the court, then the king sending for his brother
justified himself with tears, imploring him not to trust the
man who was seeking to appropriate the kingdom, and
had insulted their youth ; but if any doubts yet made him
afraid, the king bid him assume the crown and the government.   So when the youth readily absolved his brother of
all suspicion, they went out together in their royal apparel to
the populace, showing publicly that they were in perfect
harmony.   Thereupon Dionysius, when his scheme broke
down, disappeared from Alexandria, and first of all he
sent round to tamper with the soldiers whom he thought
likely to join him in the prospects of a revolt, and at
Eleusis received those who were ready for a revolution,
and collected of the disorderly soldiery about 4000.   But
the king attacked and defeated them, slaying some and
pursuing the rest, so that he forced Dionysius to swim
naked across an arm of the river, and taking refuge with the
Egyptians to excite that populace to revolt.   And being
an active man and highly popular among the natives, he
quickly found large support.'   We hear nothing elsewhere
of this mischievous Dionysius, but may conclude that the
affair just narrated must have taken place in 167 or
166 B.C., when the two brothers had reigned conjointly
but a short time.

§ 196. The next fragment to be cited (x.) tells us,
probably in connexion with the machinations of Dionysius,

that another disturbance arose in the Thebaid, a taste for revolution having invaded the natives. 'But King Ptolemy having gone up against them with a large force easily subdued the other parts of the province; only into Panopolis [now Akhmîn] a city built upon an ancient mound, which seemed strong and difficult of approach, the most active of the rebels threw themselves. But Ptolemy, despising both the despair of the defenders and the strength of the place, at once besieged it, after great hardships carried it by assault, and having punished the delinquents returned to Alexandria.'[1]

But it is more than likely that his absence on the campaign gave his thankless and unscrupulous brother the opportunity for treasonable plots at Alexandria, in consequence of which Philometor, in spite of his private virtues and military deserts, was driven from Alexandria. Yet this event is placed by Livy apparently in the seventh year of their joint reign, so that Philometor may have had time to do many things before his expulsion. Our authorities leave us in the dark on these matters.

§ 197. Several of them are, however, quite explicit as to the miserable plight in which Philometor made his appearance (163 B.C.) on the coasts of Italy.[2] He came as a private person of no means attended only by an eunuch and three slaves, and made the journey on foot! We are told that the Syrian prince Demetrius son of Seleukos,

[1] This must have happened about 165 B.C., and I gravely doubt whether it was on this occasion (that the king carried his campaign as far as Debot in Nubia, where he appears to have dedicated a temple, as Letronne says, *Journal des Savants* for 1840).

[2] It is likely that a Roman embassy had already been sent (164 B.C.) to the East, with directions, amid other business, to settle the rising quarrel between the brothers. This, Bandelin thinks, is the embassy mentioned by Polybius xxxi. 1.

who was still kept a hostage at Rome (though he was the rightful heir to the Syrian throne), having learned these facts, sent out a long distance to meet him with servants, purple robes, diadem etc., in order that one of his own class, a royal personage from the East, should not make so sorry a figure at the world's capital. But Philometor, evidently from policy, rejected all these attentions, and having found out the lodging of one Demetrius, an Alexandrian painter (Diodorus says τοπογράφου), went to stay there. When the Senate learned this, Philometor was invited to come to the Senate, where he was tendered elaborate apologies that they had not, according to ancient precedent, sent out a quaestor to meet him, or received him as a guest of the state.[1]

The result of his application to be restored was, however, not so satisfactory. The arguments used in the Roman Senate are not preserved, but we can supply them with tolerable completeness from analogous discussions then constantly taking place. The Senate decided according to two equally dishonest and weak arguments. The first was the advice of the timid, that no allied kingdoms in the East should be allowed to regain strength, for that their difficulties were Rome's opportunity. The second was the advice of the ignorant, who probably could not follow arguments urged in Greek, and who professed that they were not worth following. Must there not be claims and faults on both sides? Let us divide the kingdom and this will rid us both of a possible danger and an actual perplexity.[2] It also appears from two inscriptions found at Delos, that Euergetes had enlisted on his side another

---

[1] Valerius Max. v. 1.

[2] Cf. the curious parallel of the division of Cappadocia between Ariarathes V. and Orophernes in 157 B.C. P.-W. *Encycl.* ii. 818.

powerful Roman interest, that of the merchants who lived
at Alexandria, as they did at Delos, and required the
protection of the king. It was probably through them
that he was enabled, time after time, to work a bad case,
and make the worse reason appear the better. The chief
inscription referred to [1] is a dedication to Apollo at Delos
thanking Lochus, the 'cousin' of King Euergetes and
Queen Cleopatra, for his kindness to the Roman merchants
and shippers on the occasion of the taking of Alexandria.
Though we cannot tell whether it was his first expulsion
of his brother, or his final conquest of the city that is here
intended, the inference remains valid.

It seems then that Philometor acquiesced, or was
obliged to acquiesce, in handing over to his brother the
rich province of Cyrene, with (as we hear presently) a
large allowance of corn yearly from Alexandria.

§ 198. But Euergetes was not satisfied with this decision.
Though he was obliged to surrender the capital to his elder
brother, and probably at once took possession of Cyrene,
he had learned by this time that he had made a great mistake in not going personally to the capital to promote his
interests. It was plain enough that people at Rome, especially the old gentlemen in the Senate, were very imperfectly
informed regarding Eastern affairs. Indeed it is astonishing
that at this time the Romans never thought of keeping
accredited political agents at Corinth, Pergamum, Antioch,
or Alexandria, where they could learn things on the spot, and
could send authorised reports to the Senate and receive

---

[1] Cf. *BCH* viii. 107 Ρωμαιοι οι ευεργετηθεντες ναυκληροι και εμποροι
εν τηι γενομενηι καταληψει Αλεξανδρειας υπο βασιλεως Πτολεμαιου θεου
Ευεργετου, Λοχον Καλλιμηδου τον συγγενη βασ. Πτολ. και βασ. Κλεοπ.
αρετης ενεκεν και ευεργεσιας της εις εαυτους Απολλωνι. The second
text is a similar dedication of gratitude by Lucius and Gaius Pedius,
misinterpreted by Letronne, as Boeckh has shown, *CIG* 2285.

directions from it.[1]   All this foreign political work was done without any permanent Foreign Office at Rome, without any responsible ambassadors or ministers abroad.   The Senate trusted altogether to successful generals, aided by special Commissioners, or to the wisdom of envoys sent out from Rome to examine and settle each problem as it arose. Hence the Hellenistic powers had no other effectual means of having their case heard, than to crowd to Rome in embassies, pay private visits to influential Senators, bribe those who would take money, and then argue their case in the Senate before judges for the most part prejudiced, in no small degree ignorant.

§ 199. Polybius tells us of the progress of the second discussion of the Senate concerning the kingdom of Egypt:

(xxxi. 18) After the Ptolemies had made their partition of the kingdom the younger brother arrived in Rome desiring to set aside the division made between himself and his brother, on the ground that he had not acceded to the arrangement voluntarily, but under compulsion, and yielding to the force of circum-

---

[1] This appears plainly from Polybius xxxii. 21, where Charops conceals the decision of the Senate, and sends home an account of his own, and again c. 28, in which the words used are most significant. 'After his defeat by Prusias Attalus appointed his brother Athenaeus to accompany Publius Lentulus to Rome to inform the Senate of what had happened.   At Rome they had not paid much attention when a previous messenger named Andronicus had come from Attalus, with news of the original invasion ; because they suspected that Attalus wished to attack Prusias himself, and was therefore getting up a case against him beforehand, and trying to prejudice him in their eyes by these accusations ; and when Nicomedes and some ambassadors from Prusias, headed by Antiphilus, arrived and protested that there was not a word of truth in the statement, the Senate was still more incredulous of what had been said about Prusias.   But when after a time the real truth was made known, the Senate still felt uncertain, and sent Lucius Apuleius and Gaius Petronius to investigate what was the state of the case in regard to these two kings.'

stances. He therefore begged the Senate to assign Cyprus to his portion ; for, even if that were done, he should still have a much poorer share than his brother. Canuleius and Quintus supported Menyllus, the ambassador of the elder Ptolemy, by protesting that 'the younger Ptolemy owed his possession of Cyrene and his very life to them, so deep was the anger and hatred of the common people towards him[1]; and that, accordingly, he had been only too glad to receive the government of Cyrene, which he had not hoped for or expected ; and had exchanged oaths with his brother with the customary sacrifices.' To this Ptolemy gave a positive denial : and the Senate, seeing that the division was clearly an unequal one, and at the same time wishing that, as the brothers themselves were the authors of the division being made at all, it should be effected in a manner advantageous to Rome, granted the petition of the younger Ptolemy with a view to their own interest. Measures of this class are very frequent among the Romans, by which they avail themselves with profound policy of the mistakes of others to augment and strengthen their own empire, under the guise of granting favours and benefiting those who commit the errors. On this principle they acted now. They saw how great the power of the Egyptian kingdom was ; and fearing lest, if it ever chanced to obtain a competent head, he would grow too proud, they appointed Titus Torquatus and Gnaeus Merula to establish Ptolemy Physcon in Cyprus, and thus to carry out their own policy while satisfying his. These commissioners were accordingly at once despatched with instructions to reconcile the brothers to each other, and to secure Cyprus to the younger. . . .

It is a great pity we have not more of Polybius' narrative extant, for he tells us farther on[2] that the Menyllos of Alabanda here mentioned, who argued the case of the elder Ptolemy, was a particular friend of his own at Rome. We might so have heard, from the Roman gossip of the day, when it was that Euergetes made the acquaintance of

---

[1] The anger of the Alexandrians had been excited against Ptolemy Physkon by his having, for some unknown reason, caused the death of Timotheus, who had been Ptolemy Philometor's legate at Rome. See Polybius xxviii. 1. Diodor. Sic. fr. xi.   [2] xxxi. 20, 28.

Cornelia, mother of the Gracchi (then little children) and offered her what is called his hand and heart, but really her chances of becoming Queen of Egypt. Plutarch, who mentions the fact, tells us she refused him. A Cornelia on the throne at Alexandria would have been a real novelty among the Cleopatras. But the great Roman lady probably held him in such esteem as an English noblewoman now would hold an Indian Rajah proposing marriage.

We have, however, another important fragment from Polybius.

After this the younger Ptolemy arrived in Greece with the Roman commissioners, and began collecting a formidable army of mercenaries, among whom he enlisted Damasippus the Macedonian, who, after murdering the members of the council at Phacus, fled with his wife and children from Macedonia, and after reaching Peraea, opposite Rhodes, and being entertained by the people there, determined to sail to Cyprus. But when Torquatus and his colleagues saw that Ptolemy had collected a formidable corps of mercenaries, they reminded him of their commission, which was to restore him ' without a war,' and at last persuaded him to go as far as Side (in Pamphylia), and there disband his mercenaries, give up his idea of invading Cyprus, and meet them on the frontiers of Cyrene. Meanwhile, they said that they would sail to Alexandria, and induce the king to consent to their demands, and would meet Euergetes on the frontiers, bringing the other king with them. The younger Ptolemy was persuaded by these arguments, gave up the attack upon Cyprus, dismissed the mercenaries, and first sailed to Crete, accompanied by Damasippus and Gnaeus Merula, one of the commissioners ; and, after enlisting about a thousand soldiers in Crete, put to sea and crossed to Libya, landing at Apis.

Meanwhile Torquatus had gone to Alexandria and was trying to induce the elder Ptolemy to be reconciled to his brother, and yield Cyprus to him. But Ptolemy, by alternate promises and refusals and the like, managed to waste the time, while the younger king lay encamped with his thousand

Cretans at Apis in Libya, according to his agreement. Becoming thoroughly irritated at receiving no intelligence, he first sent Gnaeus Merula to Alexandria, hoping by this means to bring Torquatus and those with him to the place of meeting. But Merula was like the others in protracting the business: forty days passed without a word of intelligence, and Euergetes was in despair. The fact was that the elder king, by using every kind of flattery, had won the commissioners over, and was keeping them by him, rather with their will than against it. Moreover, at this time the younger Ptolemy was informed that the people of Cyrene had revolted, that the cities were conspiring with them, and that Ptolemy Sympetesis had also taken their side. This man was an Egyptian by birth, and had been left by the king in charge of his whole kingdom when he was going on his journey to Rome. When the king was informed of this, and learned presently that the Cyreneans were encamped in the open country, afraid lest, in his desire to add Cyprus to his dominions, he might lose Cyrene also, he threw everything else aside and marched towards Cyrene. When he came to what is called the Great Slope, he found the Libyans and Cyreneans occupying the pass. Ptolemy was alarmed at this: but, putting half his forces on board boats, he ordered them to sail beyond the difficult ground, and show themselves on the rear of the enemy; while with the other half he marched up to their front and tried to carry the pass. The Libyans being panic-stricken at this double attack on front and rear, and abandoning their position, Ptolemy not only got possession of the pass, but also of Tetrapyrgia, which lay immediately below it, in which there was an abundant supply of water. Thence he crossed the desert in seven days, the forces under Mochyrinus coasting along parallel to his line of march. The Cyreneans were encamped eight thousand five hundred strong: for having satisfied themselves as to the character of Ptolemy from his conduct at Alexandria, and seeing that his government and policy generally were those of a tyrant rather than a king, they could not endure the idea of becoming his subjects, but were determined to venture everything in their desire for freedom. . . .

At this time Gnaeus Merula also came from Alexandria, informing the king (Physcon) that his brother would consent to none of the proposals, but maintained that they ought to abide by the original agreements. On hearing this, Physcon selected the brothers Comanus and Ptolemy to go as ambassadors to Rome with Gnaeus, and inform the Senate of his brother's selfish and haughty behaviour. At the same time the elder Ptolemy sent away Titus Torquatus also without having attained the object of his mission. Such was the state of things in Alexandria and Cyrene. . . .

At the same time as the Senate despatched Opimius to the war with the Oxybii, Ptolemy the younger arrived at Rome; and being admitted to the Senate brought an accusation against his brother, laying on him the blame of the attack against his life. He showed the scars of his wounds, and speaking with all the bitterness which they seemed to suggest, moved his hearers to pity; and when Neolaidas and Andromachus also came on behalf of the elder Ptolemy, to answer the charges brought by his brother, the Senate refused even to listen to their pleas, having been entirely prepossessed by the accusations of the younger. They commanded them to leave Rome at once; while they assigned five commissioners to the younger, headed by Gnaeus Merula and Lucius Thermus, with a quinquereme for each commissioner, and ordered them to restore Ptolemy (Physcon) to Cyprus; and at the same time sent a circular to their allies in Greece and Asia, granting permission to them to assist in the restoration of Ptolemy. . . .

§ 200. All these machinations, however, failed not only against the diplomacy, but against the warlike energy of Philometor. When Euergetes attacked Cyprus, he was there encountered by the lawful king with his army, and after being for some time besieged was forced to surrender.[1] According to all the notions of the day, he should have at

---

[1] We now know from the excavations at Cyprus (*JHS* ix. p. 233) that statues to Philometor, and to his wife, and other votive offerings, were set up at the temple of the Paphian Aphrodite. This was also done for his successors. The usual body dedicating is *the Assembly of Cilicians* or *of Lycians, serving in the island.* Or else it is a dignitary who is not only cousin of the king, and general, but high-priest of the island, and even τροφεύς of the king.

once been put to death, and there is little doubt what would have happened had the fortunes of war gone against Philometor. But this king, who showed considerable skill in his diplomacy, and treated Roman interference as ably as his position permitted, was afraid to break utterly with the party at Rome that supported his brother. His own gentle nature prompted him in the same direction, and so the infamous Euergetes was pardoned and restored to Cyrene, even with his yearly allowance of corn from Alexandria. This is what we gather from the excerpt of Diodorus.[1] If we take these various discussions and conflicts to have lasted their natural time, and consider the place which the last journey of Euergetes takes in Polybius' thirty-third book, the final settlement of this long dispute cannot have taken place till about 154 B.C.[2] But for the last eight or nine years of his reign, at all events, Philometor had rest from his brother, whose position indeed was most insecure at Cyrene, owing to the insurrections caused (we are told) by his cruelty and tyranny.

[1] *Excerpt. de virt.* p. 588, ed. Dindorf.

[2] I propose this date with some confidence, as we learn from the great Turin Papyrus (No. 1) that Philometor issued an indulgence, confirming all actual holders of property in their possessions, in his twenty-sixth year. No historian or commentator has assigned a special reason for these φιλάνθρωπα, of which we shall meet another instance in the next reign. But it was surely to allay the apprehension that he would annul the acts and decisions of his brother, who held the throne for a short time alone (when he had expelled Philometor) until he was removed to Cyrene by the interference of the Roman Senate. During the struggle which ensued Philometor was occupied either in persuading the Senate, or coercing his brother, so that he was not sure of his throne. This edict confirming the acts of the interregnum was therefore a mark that the struggle was over, and that any illegalities committed under the usurper's sway (*e.g.* paying him tax) would not now be punished. It is possible, however, that it was a mere bid, during the crisis, for the support of all vested interests.

§ 201. It is well too for the historian to be able to turn from these miserable personal quarrels, which need never be told, if they were not the quarrels of kings, and endeavour to glean what we can of the internal condition of Egypt, concerning which historians are almost silent.

The cruelties of Antiochus Epiphanes must have produced a great revulsion of Jewish feeling from Syria to Egypt, nor would there be wanting proofs of this change on the face of history, but that the tyranny over Judaea had been overthrown, not by foreign help, but by the native valour of Judas Maccabaeus, and the national party. Although therefore friendly relations with the Egyptian king rapidly increased; though many of the rich, and with them the cowards, fled to Egypt, and courted the protection of Philometor, the policy of the Maccabees was rather to play one powerful neighbour against the other, and to maintain the religion and liberties of the Jews by force of native arms, not by depending upon foreign support.

Yet there are not wanting in Josephus ample indications that the policy of this king was distinctly philo-Judaic. We feel great hesitation in believing that Onias (known as Onias IV. in Jewish history), the exiled son of a high-priest, became Philometor's principal general, and his right-hand man, so that he was able to direct the policy of Egypt. That is one of the usual exaggerations made by any semi-subject race endeavouring to substantiate lofty historical claims. But the fact of Onias' exile, and the importance of his being a Jew of royal descent living in Egypt, come out in the foundation of the opposition Temple, if we may so call it, in the nome of Arabia, near Heliopolis (about 154 B.C.),[1] where a disused and ruined

---

[1] Cf. the arguments in Grätz iii. 34, and Isaiah xix. 18.

shrine of Bubastis Agria 'was set up with priests and ritual according to those of Jerusalem—a day of feasting and rejoicing for the Jews of Egypt, a day of mourning for those of Palestine, who were seriously religious and saw clearly the danger of disunion and of apostacy if any separate centre were tolerated for the religion of Jehovah.'

§ 202. The narrative of Josephus has absurdities mixed up with real history.

But then the son of Onias the high-priest, who was of the same name with his father, and who fled to king Ptolemy, called Philometor, lived now at Alexandria, as we have said already. When this Onias saw that Judaea was oppressed by the Macedonians and their kings, out of a desire to purchase to himself a memorial and eternal fame, he resolved to send to king Ptolemy and queen Cleopatra, to ask leave of them that he might build a temple in Egypt like to that at Jerusalem, and might ordain Levites and priests out of their own stock. The chief reason why he was desirous so to do, was, that he relied upon the prophet Isaiah, who lived above six hundred years before, and foretold that there certainly was to be a temple built to Almighty God in Egypt by a man that was a Jew. Onias was elevated with this prediction, and wrote the following epistle to Ptolemy and Cleopatra :—' Having done many and great things for you in the affairs of the war, by the assistance of God, and that in Coele-Syria and Phoenicia, I came at length with the Jews to Leontopolis, and to other settlements of their nation, where I found that the greatest part of our people worshipped in an improper manner, and that on this account they bare ill will one against another, which has happened to the Egyptians also by reason of the multitude of their temples, and the difference of opinion about divine worship. Now I found a very fit place in a fort that hath its name from Agria Bubastis ; this place is full of materials of several sorts, and replenished with sacred animals : I desire, therefore, that you will grant me leave to purge this shrine, which belongs to no master, and is fallen down, and to build there a temple to Almighty God, after the pattern of that in Jerusalem, and of the same dimensions, in honour of ($\dot{\upsilon}\pi\acute{\epsilon}\rho$) thyself, and thy wife and children ; that those Jews who dwell in Egypt may have a place whither they may come and meet together in mutual harmony, and be subservient to thy advantages ; for the prophet Isaiah foretold, that "there should be an altar in Egypt to the Lord God " : and many other such things did he prophesy relating to that place.'

And this was what Onias wrote to king Ptolemy.[1] Now any one may observe the king's piety, and that of his sister and wife Cleopatra, by the epistle which they wrote in answer to it ; for they laid the blame and the transgression of the law upon the head of Onias. And this was their reply :—'King Ptolemy and Queen Cleopatra to Onias, send greeting. We have read thy petition, wherein thou desirest leave to be given to thee to purge that temple which is fallen down at Leontopolis, in the Nome of Heliopolis, and which is named from Agria Bubastis ; on which account we cannot but wonder that it should be pleasing to the God to have a temple erected in a place so unclean, and so full of sacred animals. But since thou sayest that Isaiah the prophet foretold this long ago, we give thee leave to do it, if it may be done according to your law, so that we may not appear to have at all offended the God herein.'

So Onias took the place, and built a temple, and an altar to God, like indeed to that at Jerusalem, but smaller and poorer. I do not think it proper for me now to describe its dimensions, or its vessels, which have been already described in my seventh book of the Wars of the Jews. However, Onias found certain other Jews like himself, both priests and Levites, that there performed divine service. But we have said enough about this temple.

Now it came to pass that the Alexandrian Jews, and those Samaritans who paid their worship to the temple that was built in the days of Alexander at mount Gerizzim, did now make a sedition one against another, and disputed about their temples before Ptolemy himself, the Jews saying that, according to the law of Moses, the temple was built at Jerusalem ; and the Samaritans saying that therefore it was built at Gerizzim. They desired therefore the king to sit with his friends and hear the debates about these matters, and punish those with

---

[1] This letter and the next are manifest and stupid forgeries.

death who were defeated. Now Sabbaeus and Theodosius managed the argument for the Samaritans, and Andronicus, the son of Messalamus, for the people of Jerusalem ; and they took an oath by God and the king, to make their demonstrations according to the Law ; and they desired of Ptolemy, that whomsoever he should find that transgressed what they had sworn to, he would put him to death. Accordingly, the king took many of his friends into the council, and sat down, in order to hear what the pleaders said. Now the Jews that were at Alexandria were in great concern for those men, whose lot it was to contend for the temple at Jerusalem ; for they took it very ill that any should take away the reputation of that temple, which was so ancient and so celebrated all over the habitable earth. Now when Sabbaeus and Theodosius had given leave to Andronicus to speak first, he began to demonstrate out of the Law, and out of the successions of the high-priests, how they every one in succession from his father had received that dignity, and ruled over the temple ; and how all the kings of Asia had honoured that temple with their donations, and with the most splendid gifts dedicated thereto : but as for that at Gerizzim, as being a thing of nought, none made account of it, or ever regarded it. By this speech, and other arguments, Andronicus persuaded the king to determine that the temple at Jerusalem was built according to the laws of Moses, and to put Sabbaeus and Theodosius to death. And these were the events that befell the Jews at Alexandria in the days of Ptolemy Philometor.

The story of the religious controversy between Jews and Samaritans carried on publicly before the king and his peers, and resulting in the execution of the unsuccessful Samaritans, is another fable, but probably resting on some historic basis. And from all such stories the policy at least of the good and gentle king may be fairly concluded. But whether the concession was a matter of influence exerted by Onias, or a matter of deliberate statecraft, we can now hardly tell. So strong did the philo-Jewish complexion of this king appear to Grätz, when he wrote his well-known *History of*

the Jews, that he attributed the whole scheme of the translation of the LXX to this king, and not to Philadelphus.[1]
He suggested that the writer of the 'letter of Aristeas'
threw back the date in order to make the support of the
Jews by the Egyptian Court as ancient and important as
the first attack upon them ascribed to Manetho, who lived
under the second king. This argument, which appeared
very strong when first advanced, has, however, been
shaken by the researches of Freudenthal and others,
who show that the Jewish chronicler Demetrius, some of
whose fragments are preserved by Alexander Polyhistor,
counts his dates down to the reign of the fourth Ptolemy,
thus showing that he did not live later, and yet that his
book seems to show distinct knowledge of the LXX. Thus
the date alleged in the Epistle of Aristeas seems after
all correct.

§ 203. Nevertheless the establishment of the Oneion
near Heliopolis, and the title of Arabarches,[2] or governor
of the nome of Arabia, given to Onias, mark an
epoch in the history not only of the Jews, but of
the Egyptians. For now was developed that curious
polemical literature of Greeks and Egyptians against
Jews, of Jews against Greeks and Egyptians, which
has coloured Hellenistic history with its mendacity, and
lowered the sense of truth in the whole literary world

[1] Cf. his *History of the Jews* vol. iii. Appendix 2.

[2] It was afterwards repeated in Roman times as Alabarches, in the
sense of taxing officer, and it is probably this transference which makes
Josephus assert that Philometor made Onias chief of the taxes derived
from the river-transport and the harbours of Egypt. We have in the
Revenue Papyrus (col. 37) Λιβυαρχαι, but not Αραβαρχαι, though both
these outlying nomes are mentioned. In Pauly-Wissowa's *Encyclopaedia*, Alabarches is treated as a perfectly distinct word, and derived
from *alaba*, which was (Hesychius) a word for ink.

of the second century B.C. The blame for this crime, generally thrown altogether on the Jews, has been apportioned to both sides with firmness and judgment by Freudenthal, whose concluding pages are to be commended as a model not only of style, but of historical insight.[1]

§ 204. There is a remarkable group of papyri, found years ago in an earthen pot at the site of Memphis, and now scattered through the principal museums of Europe, which have been frequently discussed, from the famous edition of the Turin part by A. Peyron in 1826, to the princely publication of the British Museum in 1893. They tell us of the private affairs of sundry persons (especially a recluse named Ptolemy and Twin priestesses or acolytes) attached to the Serapeum at Memphis, as well as of sundry quarrels regarding property, and petitions for state allowances. We need not here enter into details beyond those which tell us of the condition of the various layers of population settled in Upper Egypt. In the first place it is remarkable that there is no mention of Jews. It has been noted above (§ 114) that there is evidence both of Jews and Samaritans in the Fayyum about seventy years earlier. For the present group of papers date from about 170 B.C., in the reign of Philometor, down to the divided reigns in the next century.[2]

---

[1] *Hellenistische Studien* i., *Alexander Polyhistor*, with fragments of various writers appended, Breslau, 1875.

[2] One of the group (29 of the Paris papyri), a petition from the Twins, speaks of εν τοις περι στασιν αμεικτοις καιροις—a moment when Greeks and natives could not live together. They go on to specify the king's visit to Memphis (probably 160 B.C.) thus : και καθ ον μεν καιρον, μεγιστε βασιλευ, διασωθεις κατα το δικαιον εκ των εξωθεν τοπων ανεβης εις το ιερον θυσιασαι (*Notices* p. 280). The king and queen are addressed as τους ευχαριστους θεους. In Pap. 39 of the same collection they are called θεοι σωτηρες ευεργεται, so that we see that such titles were used somewhat at random by the local scribes, in their fulsome compliments. The concluding formulae are of this kind : υμιν γενοιτο κρατειν πασης ης

§ 205. In the petitions and complaints which occupy most of the British division we can easily perceive a considerable approach towards fusion between the foreign and native elements. The very temple, or collection of temples, called the Great Serapeum, contains shrines not only of Egyptian, but of Greek, and even of Syrian deities—Astarte and Aesculapius are settled in the same enclosure as Ptah and Sarapis. We find that men of foreign origin were allowed to come and settle there as anchorites, making a vow to refrain from leaving the precincts for a series of years. The Serapeum seems indeed to have been a sort of *Liberty*, in which there was not only an asylum, where both people like Ptolemy, the son of Glaucias, and even people accused of crimes lived, but also various inns, one apparently that of Protarchus (unless he was an official), another that for Arsinoite visitors. It seems that the police had their eye upon the refugees, and that the sons of Glaucias were acting for the police, in reporting whether the suspected criminals (they are called ἀλάστορες) slipped out of the asylum by night. Hence (Revillout thinks) the various persecutions of these Greeks, such as beating them, seizing their goods, and refusing to sell them what they wanted, arose. We find Ptolemy, son of a Glaucias, a Macedonian formerly resident at the little village of Psychin in the Heracleopolitan nome, such a family friend of his Egyptian neighbour that he spends all his energies fighting the case of twin girls, the daughters of his neighbour, whose names, Thaues and Taous, show them to have been natives, and whose Egyptian mother, Nephoretis, had turned against them on account of a liaison with a Greek soldier called Philip. We find through these papers a mixture

αν αιρησθε χωρας και . . . . . . συν τοις υμετεροις τεκνοις, την τε χωραν υμων ειναι εν ηι προνοεισθε δ[ια]θεσε[ι.

of Greek and Egyptian names even in the same family, which either proves mixed marriages, or that Egyptians were assuming Greek names, or Greeks adopting Egyptian translations of their names.   No doubt all these cases were common enough.   Dionysius surnamed Petosiris, and Ptolemy Sympetesis, a leading officer under Euergetes II. (pp. 342, 350) at Cyrene, are cases in point.

§ 206. It is quite in accordance with this growing fusion that the documents now before us should be degenerate in their Greek when compared with the earlier (Arsinoite) papyri.   There is not one among the scores of writers in the Petrie collection who spells so badly as Ptolemy son of Glaucias ; and yet he is above the average of the synchronous writers.   If we take at random one page (26) of the British Museum publication, we find ἐπιδή, νεότερον, βοίηθον, ἰλήφασιν, πολοῦσιν, ὡμοίως, and many more such blunders, which the two volumes of the *Petrie Papyri* could not exhibit.   The decadence in this respect in sixty years is very rapid, unless we assume that there was better Greek talked in the Fayyum than at Memphis, for which I see no reason.[1]

Nor are the Greeks (Macedonians) any longer a dominant race.   We may infer that both in Ptolemy's, and in other cases, the men who went into retreat in the Serapeum did so from personal danger, ἐν τοῖς τῆς ταραχῆς χρόνοις, when disputes among kings or rebellions of the natives impaired the security of life.   Pap. xxiv. of the collection, written in

---

[1] On a papyrus (II. of the Louvre) of which the verso has been used by a recluse of the Serapeum to record silly dreams (about 160 B.C.), we find sentences from many of the great Greek poets—Ibykos, Thespis?, Sophocles, Anacreon, Pindar, Euripides, Timotheos—but unfortunately only as specimens of the various forms of affirmative and negative propositions.   This at least shows that the settlers were still familiar with the names, and with some fragments, of their old national poets.

161 B.C. when the king was busily engaged in his quarrel with
his brother, tells us, in the complaint of the same Ptolemy
the Macedonian, secluded in the shrine of Astarte, that a
party of Egyptians broke into the temple, and ill-treated
him *because he was a Greek*, a reason we should in vain
seek under the second or third Ptolemy.[1] A formal visit
of the king and queen to Memphis in the year 160 B.C.
is also mentioned, as an occasion for laying petitions
before them, so that the need was evidently felt at court
to win popularity throughout the country.   In these papers
we hear no longer of *cleruchs*, even when cavalry soldiers,
but of κάτοικοι and of regiments stationed at Memphis, at
Hermonthis, or at Thebes, into which men seek enrolment
as a means of getting small pay and allowances of food.
There is no hint that these troops had done duty in foreign
campaigns, though there is mention of camp-duty and of
hardships, apparently during local disturbances, in the Grenfell papyri. They seem a poor, resident soldiery, still consisting not of natives, but of the imported Greeks, for even
the Macedonians had now learned to call themselves Greeks,
as the broad term including all the Hellenistic population.

§ 207. We have already seen that Philometor was
obliged to put down serious internal revolt, not like
Epiphanes in the Delta, but in Upper Egypt. It is
probably on account of this anti-Macedonian feeling
among the natives of the south country, that his few
Egyptian temples are in Upper Egypt, at Antaeopolis,
Kom-Ombos, Philae, even at Debôt in Nubia, some
fifteen miles south of Philae.[2] In general we find his

---

[1] Louvre Pap. 36, 11 ενεβιαζοντο βουλομενοι εκσπασαι με και αγαγησαι,
καθαπερ και εν τοις προτεροις χρονοις επεχειρησαν, ουσης αποστασεως, παρα
το Ελληνα ειναι. Cf. for similar complaints, B. M. Pap. 44 (p. 34).

[2] *CIG* 4712 ; 4859 is a dedication from the horse and foot stationed
at Ombos ; 4979 at Debôt *circa* 164 B.C. ; 5185 (Cyrene) is very curious,

work taken up and completed by his brother and successor, whose building is much more extensive and prominent. Indeed, if we consider the length of Philometor's reign, we may say that he was not remarkable in this respect; I am not aware that we have a single monument of his left in Lower Egypt.

This comparative neglect of the national party may have been owing to a strong turn for foreign politics, as is manifest not only in the closing scenes of his life, to which we shall come presently, but in a curious Cretan inscription, where in an arbitration case between the Itanians and Hierapytnians, the former rehearse that (l. 38) being pressed in war by their neighbours the Praesians, they invited King Ptolemy to take charge of their city, and adjoining islands which belonged to them, also that upon his death the people he had set in charge went away, leaving the Itanians to take care of themselves.[1] There is an inscription in his honour at Methana in Argolis,[2] one at Thera,[3] as well as one at Cyprus, as we should naturally expect. These evidences are sufficient to show that in spite of the growing Roman jealousy, which sought to isolate all the remaining Hellenistic powers, Philometor

---

for it is dedicated to him as the brother of the reigning sovran and his wife, hence possibly set up in his memory after his death, viz. βασ. Πτολ. τον βασιλεως Πτολ. και βασιλισσης Κλεοπ. αδελφον, θεον φιλομητορα, η πολις (viz. Ptolemais in the Cyrenaica).

[1] *CIG* vol. ii. Addenda 2561 b θλιβόμενοι κατά τινας καιρούς ὑπὸ τῶν παρορούντων Πραισίων, ἐπεσπάσαντο χάριν βοηθείας καὶ φυλακῆς τῆς τε πόλεως καὶ τῆς χώρας, ἔτι δὲ καὶ τῶν νήσων, τὸν Αἰγύπτου βασιλεύσαντα Πτ., ὡς τὰ παρατεθέντα [   ] περὶ τούτων γράμματα περιεῖχεν, καὶ τούτῳ τῷ τρόπῳ κατεῖχον τοὺς προειρημένους τόπους· τελευτήσαντος δὲ τοῦ Φιλομήτορος βασιλέως Πτ. καὶ τῶν ἀποσταλέντων ὑπ' αὐτοῦ χάριν τοῦ συντηρεῖν τοῖς 'Ιτανίοις τήν τε χώραν καὶ τὰς νήσους ἀπαλλαγέντων κτλ.

[2] *CIG* 1191.   [3] Ibid. 2451.

carried out the old policy of his house towards the islands and coasts of the Aegean.

§ 208. The last act in the life of Philometor is recorded by several independent historians, and the facts are not in dispute, though any fair critic cannot but express his doubts concerning the motives suggested for Philometor's action. We find him taking an active part in the affairs of Syria. Here the Demetrius known as Soter,—who had befriended Philometor when he went to Rome[1] and whose own escape from his ill-disguised bondage as a royal hostage Polybius has so graphically described[2] — seems to have turned all his subjects, especially those of Antioch, against him by his cruelties. Probably it was the Jews who urged Philometor to interfere, and to support a new claimant Alexander Bala, who went to Rome, and obtained the authority of the Senate to recover the kingdom of Syria. Polybius[3] evidently considers that the Senate was hood-winked, but then the actual king, though he had been practically recognised, had really escaped from Rome without leave, and had established a very dangerous precedent. However, the decree cited by Polybius quite justifies Philometor in helping Alexander. There seems also to have been some treachery employed by Demetrius in the matter of Cyprus, which he attempted to gain for a bribe of 500 talents from the Egyptian governor Archias. This plot Philometor discovered and stopped in time.[4] He promised Bala his daughter Cleopatra in marriage, and came in person to escort the bride as far as Ptolemais in Palestine, where the marriage took place; apparently in 150 B.C. At this time Alexander had already defeated and slain in battle Demetrius, and was king of Syria. Josephus tells

[1] Above, § 197. [2] xxxi. 19 *sqq.* [3] xxxiii. 16.
[4] Ibid. xxxiii. 3.

us that both Philometor and Bala did great honour to Jonathan, the high-priest of the Jews, whom they invited to the marriage, and whom Alexander even insisted on dressing in purple, instead of his national dress, seating him beside himself as a royal personage,[1] and declaring him the 'first among his friends' or peers.

Nevertheless Alexander Bala was not honestly disposed to the Jews, but allowed his local governors to carry on war with them.   This and other weaknesses in the management of Syria emboldened Demetrius Nicator, son of the Soter just named, to land with a force of Cretan mercenaries on the coast of Cilicia (147 B.C.)

§ 209. We may tell the sequel in the words of Josephus (*Antt.* xiii. 4):

About this time it was that king Ptolemy, who was called Philometor, led an army, part by sea and part by land, and came to Syria, to the assistance of Alexander [Bala], who was his son-in-law ; and accordingly all the cities received him willingly, as Alexander had commanded them to do, and conducted him as far as Ashdod ; where they all made loud complaints about the temple of Dagon, which was burnt, and accused Jonathan of having laid it waste, and destroyed the country adjoining with fire, and slain a great number of them.   Ptolemy heard these accusations, but said nothing.   Jonathan also went to meet Ptolemy as far as Joppa, and obtained from him hospitable presents, and those glorious in their kinds, with all the marks of honour ; and when he had conducted him as far as the river called Eleutherus, he returned again to Jerusalem.

But as Ptolemy was at Ptolemais, he was very near to a most unexpected destruction ; for a treacherous design was laid for his life by Alexander, by the means of Ammonius, who was his friend : and when the plot was discovered, Ptolemy wrote to Alexander, and required of him that he should bring Ammonius to condign punishment, informing him what snares had been laid by Ammonius, and desired that he might be

[1] *Antiqq.* xiii. 4, 2.

accordingly punished for it ; but when Alexander did not comply
with his demands, Ptolemy perceived that it was he himself
who laid the design, and was very angry with him. . . .

Hereupon Ptolemy blamed himself for having given his
daughter in marriage to Alexander, and for the league he had
made with him to assist him against Demetrius [Soter] ; so he
dissolved his relation to him, and took his daughter away from
him, and immediately sent to Demetrius [Nicator], and offered
to make a league of mutual assistance and friendship with him,
and agreed with him to give him his daughter in marriage, and
to restore him to the principality of his fathers.   Demetrius was
well pleased with this embassage, and accepted his assistance,
and his daughter ; but Ptolemy had still one more hard
task to do, and that was to persuade the people of Antioch to
receive Demetrius, because they were greatly displeased at
him, on account of the injuries his father Demetrius had done
them ; yet did he bring this about ; for as the people of
Antioch hated Alexander on Ammonius's account, as we have
shown already, they were easily prevailed with to cast him
out of Antioch ; who, thus expelled out of Antioch, came
into Cilicia.   Ptolemy came then to Antioch, and was made
king by its inhabitants, and by the army ; so that he was
forced to assume two diadems, the one of Asia, the other of
Egypt ; but being naturally a good and righteous man, and
not desirous of what belonged to others, and besides these
dispositions, being also a wise man in reasoning about
futurities, he determined to avoid the envy of the Romans ; so
he called the people of Antioch together to an assembly, and
persuaded them to receive Demetrius ; and assured them that
the latter would not be mindful of what they did to his father
in case he should be now obliged by them ; and he undertook
that he would himself be a good monitor and governor to the
new king ; and promised that he would not permit him to attempt
any bad actions ; but that, for his own part, he was contented
with the kingdom of Egypt.   By which discourse he persuaded
the people of Antioch to receive Demetrius.

But now Alexander made haste, with a numerous and great
army, and came out of Cilicia into Syria, and burnt the country
belonging to Antioch, and pillaged it ; whereupon Ptolemy,
and his son-in-law Demetrius, brought their army against him

(for he had already given him his daughter in marriage), and beat Alexander, and put him to flight; and accordingly he fled into Arabia. Now, it happened in the time of the battle, that Ptolemy's horse, upon hearing the noise of an elephant, cast him off his back, and threw him on the ground; upon the sight of which accident his enemies fell upon him, and gave him many wounds upon his head, and brought him into danger of death, for when his guards caught him up he was so very ill, that for four days' time he was not able either to understand or to speak. However, Zabdiel, a prince among the Arabians, cut off Alexander's head and sent it to Ptolemy, who so far recovering of his wounds, as to recover his understanding, on the fifth day, heard at once a most agreeable hearing, and saw a most agreeable sight, which were the death and the head of Alexander; yet a little after this his joy for the death of Alexander, with which he was so greatly satisfied, he also departed this life.

It was by a strange retribution of fortune, that the very king whom Antiochus Epiphanes had defeated, and whose crown in Egypt he had assumed, should be the very king who came to occupy by conquest his victor's throne, and be proclaimed Lord of Syria. His actual, though brief, reign in Syria is still attested by coins both silver and copper, which represent him with his diadem as king, not of Egypt, but of Syria.[1] This account seems plain enough, but the account of the author of the first Maccabees differs in one important point. I will quote the whole passage, omitting the detail it gives us concerning the taxing of provinces by the Seleukids, which I have already used for the analogous case of the Ptolemies.

§ 210. In the hundred and sixtieth year Alexander, the son of Antiochus surnamed Epiphanes, went up and took Ptolemais: for the people had received him, by means whereof he reigned there.

---

[1] Cf. *Coins of the Ptolemies* p. lxv., and Babelon *Rois de Syrie* No. 1057.

Now when king Demetrius [Soter] heard thereof, he gathered together an exceeding great host, and went forth against him to fight. Moreover Demetrius sent letters unto Jonathan with loving words, so as he magnified him. For said he, Let us first make peace with him, before he join with Alexander [Bala] against us : else he will remember all the evils that we have done against him, and against his brethren and his people. Wherefore he gave him authority to gather together an host, and to provide weapons, that he might aid him in battle : he commanded also that the hostages that were in the tower should be delivered him. . . .

This done, Jonathan settled himself in Jerusalem, and began to build and repair the city.

Now when king Alexander had heard what promises Demetrius had sent unto Jonathan : when also it was told him of the battles and noble acts which he and his brethren had done, and of the pains that they had endured, he said, Shall we find such another man ? now therefore we will make him our friend and confederate. Upon this he wrote a letter, and sent it unto him, according to these words, saying, King Alexander to his brother Jonathan sendeth greeting : we have heard of thee, that thou art a man of great power, and meet to be our friend. Wherefore now this day we ordain thee to be the high priest of thy nation, and to be called the king's friend (and therewithal he sent him a purple robe and a crown of gold) : and require thee to take our part, and to keep friendship with us.

So in the seventh month of the hundred and sixtieth year, at the feast of the tabernacles, Jonathan put on the holy robe, and gathered together forces, and provided much armour. Whereof when Demetrius heard, he was very sorry, and said, What have we done, that Alexander hath prevented us in making amity with the Jews to strengthen himself ? I also will write unto them words of encouragement, and promise them dignities and gifts, that I may have their aid.

He sent unto them therefore to this effect . . . [1] :

Now when Jonathan and the people heard these words, they gave no credit unto them, nor received them, because they remembered the great evil that he had done in Israel ;

---

[1] Cf. above, § 117.

for he had afflicted them very sore. But with Alexander they were well pleased, because he was the first that entreated of true peace with them, and they were confederate with him always.   Then gathered king Alexander great forces, and camped over against Demetrius [Soter]. And after the two kings had joined battle, Demetrius' host fled : but Alexander followed after him, and prevailed against them.   And he continued the battle very sore until the sun went down : and that day was Demetrius slain.

Afterward Alexander sent ambassadors to Ptolemy king of Egypt with a message to this effect : Forasmuch as I am come again to my realm, and am set in the throne of my progenitors, and have gotten the dominion, and overthrown Demetrius, and recovered our country ; for after I had joined battle with him, both he and his host was discomfited by us, so that we sit in the throne of his kingdom : now therefore let us make a league of amity together, and give me now thy daughter to wife : and I will be thy son-in-law, and will give both thee and her gifts according to thy dignity.

Then Ptolemy the king gave answer, saying, Happy be the day wherein thou didst return into the land of thy fathers, and satest in the throne of their kingdom.   And now will I do to thee, as thou hast written : meet me therefore at Ptolemais, that we may see one another ; for I will marry my daughter to thee according to thy desire.   So Ptolemy went out of Egypt with his daughter Cleopatra, and they came unto Ptolemais in the hundred threescore and second year [1] : where king Alexander meeting him, he gave unto him his daughter Cleopatra, and celebrated her marriage at Ptolemais with great glory, as the manner of kings is.

§ 211. Now king Alexander had written unto Jonathan, that he should come and meet him.   Who thereupon went honourably to Ptolemais, where he met the two kings, and gave them and their friends silver and gold, and many presents, and found favour in their sight. . . . So the king honoured him, and wrote him among his chief friends, and made him a duke, and partaker of his dominion.   Afterward Jonathan returned to Jerusalem with peace and gladness.   Furthermore in the

---

[1] Viz. from 312 B.C., the year from which Seleukos counted his accession, and therefore 150 B.C.

hundred threescore and fifth year came Demetrius [Nicator] son of Demetrius out of Crete into the land of his fathers : whereof when king Alexander heard tell, he was right sorry, and returned into Antioch.

Then Demetrius made Apollonius the governor of Coelesyria his general, who gathered together a great host, and camped in Jamnia, and sent unto Jonathan the high priest, saying, Thou alone liftest up thyself against us, and I am laughed to scorn for thy sake, and reproached : and why dost thou vaunt thy power against us in the mountains ? Now therefore, if thou trustest in thine own strength, come down to us into the plain field, and there let us try the matter together : for with me is the power of the cities. . . .

Then brought Simon forth his host, and set them against the footmen (for the horsemen were spent), who were discomfited by him, and fled. The horsemen also, being scattered in the field, fled to Azotus, and went into Beth-dagon, their idol's temple, for safety. But Jonathan set fire on Azotus, and the cities round about it, and took their spoils ; and the temple of Dagon, with them that were fled into it, he burned with fire. Thus there were burned and slain with the sword well nigh eight thousand men. And from thence Jonathan removed his host, and camped against Ascalon, where the men of the city came forth, and met him with great pomp. After this returned Jonathan and his host unto Jerusalem, having many spoils. Now when king Alexander heard these things, he honoured Jonathan yet more. And sent him a buckle of gold, as the use is to be given to such as are of the king's blood : he gave him also Accaron with the borders thereof in possession.

And the king of Egypt gathered together a great host, like the sand that lieth upon the sea shore, and many ships, and *went about through deceit to get Alexander's kingdom, and join it to his own.* Whereupon he took his journey into Syria in peaceable manner, so as they of the cities opened unto him, and met him : for king Alexander had commanded them so to do, because he was his father in law. Now as Ptolemy entered into the cities, he set in every one of them a garrison of soldiers to keep it. And when he came near to Azotus, they showed him the temple of Dagon that was burnt, and

Azotus and the suburbs thereof that were destroyed, and the
bodies that were cast abroad, and them that Jonathan had
burnt in the battle ; for they had made heaps of them by the
way where he should pass.   Also they told the king whatso-
ever Jonathan had done, to the intent he might blame them :
but the king held his peace.   Then Jonathan met the king
with great pomp at Joppe, where they saluted one another, and
lodged.   Afterward Jonathan, when he had gone with the
king to the river called Eleutherus, returned again to Jerusalem.   King Ptolemy, therefore, having gotten the dominion
of the cities by the sea unto Seleucia upon the sea coast,
imagined wicked counsels against Alexander.   Whereupon he
sent ambassadors unto king Demetrius, saying, Come, let us
make a league betwixt us, and I will give thee my daughter
whom Alexander hath, and thou shalt reign in thy father's
kingdom : for I repent that I gave my daughter unto him, for
he sought to slay me.   Thus did he slander him, because he
was desirous of his kingdom.   Wherefore he took his daughter
from him, and gave her to Demetrius, and forsook Alexander,
so that their hatred was openly known.   Then Ptolemy
entered into Antioch, where he set two crowns upon his head,
the crown of Asia and of Egypt.

In the mean season was king Alexander in Cilicia, because
those that dwelt in those parts had revolted from him.   But
when Alexander heard of this, he came to war against him :
whereupon king Ptolemy brought forth his host, and met him
with a mighty power, and put him to flight.   So Alexander
fled into Arabia, to find refuge there ; but king Ptolemy was
exalted : for Zabdiel the Arabian took off Alexander's head,
and sent it unto Ptolemy.   King Ptolemy also died the third
day after, and his men that were in the strongholds were
slain by the inhabitants of them.[1]

The author of this narrative is in general a sober and a
good authority, but his interpretation of the motives of
Philometor differs so completely from that of Josephus,
who frequently follows him, that we perceive unmistakeably
a philo-Syrian conflicting with a philo-Egyptian tradition.

---

[1] 1 Macc. x.-xi. 18 (with a few omissions).

The other acts of Philometor compel us in the present case to take the side of Josephus, and reject the latter narrative, so far as it alleges treachery on the Egyptian side, as a calumny against the gentle and able Philometor.

§ 212. This was the end of one of the best kings of Egypt, in the forty-first year of his age (?) and the thirty-fourth of his reign. We are not told whether his body was embalmed and brought to Egypt for burial, as we now know to have been the case with the Egyptian king, whose actual mummy, with a deadly axe-wound in the skull, was found and unrolled a few years ago at the museum of Gizeh. Polybius, who was in Egypt very shortly after Philometor's death, and who must have known him personally at Rome during his adversities, has left us a short character-sketch of him, of great interest owing to Polybius' authority and intimate knowledge of the men and the politics of the day.

Ptolemy, king of Syria, died from a wound received in the war : a man who, according to some, deserved great praise and abiding remembrance, and according to others the reverse. If any king before him ever was, he was mild and benevolent; a very strong proof of which is that he never put any of his own 'friends' to death on any charge whatever ; and I believe that not a single man at Alexandria either owed his death to him. Again, though he was notoriously ejected from his throne by his brother, in the first place, when he got a clear opportunity against him in Alexandria, he granted him a complete amnesty ; and afterwards, when his brother once more made a plot against him to seize Cyprus, though he got him body and soul into his hands at Lapethus, he was so far from punishing him as an enemy, that he even made him grants in addition to those which formerly belonged to him in virtue of the treaty made between them, and moreover promised him his daughter. However, in the course of a series of successes and prosperity, his mind became corrupted ; and he fell a prey to the dissoluteness and effeminacy characteristic of the Egyptians : and these vices brought him into serious disasters. . . .

Polybius is therefore not the least disposed to overestimate him, and indeed seems to depreciate him more than the facts would have seemed to warrant. The last joy of his life, that of gazing on the head of a defeated enemy, is the very last joy we should have supposed him to seek.[1] But the express statement of the historian must have been based upon some well-known detail concerning the king's dying moments, and can hardly, I think, have been put in by way of general scenery for the picture. The operation upon his skull was probably trepanning, one known not only to the civilised Egyptians, but to many savage races all over the globe. It would seem to us more probable that the operation took place while he was unconscious, and that by it he recovered his senses, but died shortly after. Livy's epitome states that he died under the operation.[2]

Fortunately, we can supplement the descriptions of historians by some trustworthy evidence regarding the king's appearance.   There has been found[3] in the sea at Aegina and brought to Athens the colossal head of the king, indicated by the tall royal head-dress of the Ptolemies, and by a fragmentary hieroglyph text on the back, which shows it to have been some gift or dedication of Philometor and his wife. Though the quality of the stone and the dress point to Egypt, the head and hair are distinctly Greek in fashion, and so far as the mutilated nose allows us, we must consider him a very handsome youth with a countenance full of sweet expression.   It is conjectured that this fragment

---

[1] Cf. *Addit. Notes* pp. 495-6.

[2] Epit. lii. *inter curationem, dum medici ossa terebrare contendunt, expiravit.*

[3] Cf. Six on this portrait in *Mitth.* (Athens), xii. 212.

comes from the neighbouring Methana, where Pausanias saw a temple of Isis. The splendid coin commemorating his coronation as king of Syria,[1] though representing him a much older man, corroborates fairly the marble head, and persuades us that he was the handsomest and most refined-looking of the whole dynasty.[2]

§ 213. We must add a word concerning the princess who was so prominent a figure in this Syrian war. She had been handed on from one Syrian prince to another as if she had no more will in the matter than her precious trousseau. When her second husband Demetrius was taken prisoner in the East (140 B.C.), she forthwith sent for his brother, then a wandering adventurer, and set him on the throne as Antiochus Sidetes. But when Demetrius returned, after nine years of captivity, she murdered Sidetes, it is said from jealousy, and her son Seleukos, who attempted to assume the crown, in 125 B.C. At last she met her match in her second son Antiochus Grypus, who made her swallow the loving cup of poison, which she had prepared for him on his return from hunting. These adventures belong to the history not of Egypt, but of Syria, yet they may fairly find brief mention here, as they show in another instance the daring and the recklessness with which the princesses of that day played their part in the wars and the intrigues of Hellenistic courts. They seem quite as free of their persons as are the princes. Their marriages and murders are alike without compunction.

---

[1] Poole xxxii. 9, reproduced at the close of this chapter.

[2] Gutschmid (Sharpe p. 267) judges him very harshly, and says that in spite of some personal good qualities, it was he who allowed the whole kingdom to go to pieces, so that it required all the energy and ability of Euergetes II. to repress insurrections and hold the reins of government. On the other hand, Revillout, judging from financial measures, thinks Philometor just and wise, and Euergetes the reverse.

We shall have more to say of the younger Cleopatra, this queen's sister, who spent her life in Egypt. When modern people wonder at the daring of the last of the series, who has been embalmed in the prose of Plutarch, and the verse of Shakespeare, they seldom know or reflect that she was but the last of a long series of princesses, probably beautiful and accomplished, certainly daring and unscrupulous, living every day of their lives in the passions of love, hate, jealousy, ambition, wielding the dominion over men or dying in the attempt. But alas! except in the dull and lifeless effigies on coins, we have no portraits of these terrible persons, no anecdotes of their tamer moments, no means of distinguishing one Cleopatra from the rest, amid the catalogue of parricides, incests, exiles, bereavements!

§ 214. Upon hearing the news of her husband's death, the widowed queen Cleopatra (II.), supported, we may infer, by the Jewish party in Alexandria, sought to set upon the throne his son, and had him proclaimed king as Ptolemy Neos Philopator (II.)[1] An inscription found in

---

[1] Lepsius (Berlin *Abh.* for 1852, p. 468) argued that although all our Greek authors ignore it, this youthful son of Ptolemy Philometor is known in hieroglyphic lists of ancestors worshipped by the later Ptolemies as Philopator or Young Philopator, according to the translation of the Egyptian texts. He therefore designated the eighth king as Philopator II. Until now we should have preferred to call him Eupator II., on the evidence of a Cyprian coin, which Lepsius did not know (cf. Poole's *Coins* etc., p. lxvii.), combined with the inscription of Apello, which says expressly βασιλεα Πτολεμαιον, θεον Ευπατορα, τον εγ βασιλεως Πτ. και βασιλισσης Κλεοπατρας, θεων Φιλομητορων. I suppose then that the hieroglyphics for Eupator have been confused with those for Philopator by the gravers. This identity of name in the titular kings before and after Philometor also accounts for the fact that Eupator appears sometimes before, sometimes after, in those inscriptions that show only one Eupator: cf. above, § 186. But the question has at last been settled in Lepsius' favour by two documents: (1) on a mutilated granite stele, brought from Aswân to the British Museum in 1887 (cf. my

Cyprus shows that he was actually acknowledged there. But his reign was only nominal. Euergetes, who had no doubt been long planning another invasion from Cyrene, started at once at the head of his army, and with the help of a large faction at Alexandria, asserted himself as king upon the understanding that he should marry the widowed queen his sister. If she hoped to save her son, as the narrative in Justin seems to imply, of course she failed. The young prince is said to have been murdered on the very day, and amid the pomp, of the nuptial feast. Thus did this pardoned brother requite his brother's magnanimous forbearance! History is silent concerning the character of the ill-fated youth. We only know that his education had been entrusted to Aristarchus, the famous critical editor of Homer, and the prince of grammarians.[1] It seems to me possible, that the inscription cited above (§ 197) refers to this capture of Alexandria, which was probably not accomplished without disturbance and blood-

publication of it in *Hermathena* xxii.), which commemorates privileges granted to the local priests of the kings from Philadelphus to Soter II., we have l. 16, θεων Ε]πιφανων και θεου Ευπατορος και θεω[ν Φιλομητορων : and again l. 33 θεων Φιλο]μητορων και θεου νεου Φιλοπατορος και θεου [Ευεργετου (not θεων Ευεργετων, probably because Cleopatra III. was still alive); (2) a contract of the eighth year of Soter II., bought in Egypt by Mr. Grenfell in 1895, which for the first time gives us *in Greek*, the complete list of the first ten Ptolemies, *e.g.* βασιλευοντων Κλεοπατρας και βασιλεως Πτολεμαιου θεων Φιλομητορων Σωτηρων ετους η εφ ιερεως του οντος εν Αλεξανδρειαι Αλεξανδρου και θεων Σωτηρων και θεων Αδελφων και θεων Ευεργετων και θεων Φιλοπατορων και θεων Επιφανων και θεου Ευπατορος και θεου Φιλομητορος και θεου Φιλοπατορος νεου και θεου Ευεργετου και θεων Φιλομητορων Σωτηρων ιερου πωλου Ισιδος μεγαλης αθλοφορου Βερενικης Ευεργετιδος κανηφορου Αρσινοης Φιλαδελφου ιερειας Αρσινοης Φιλοπατορος των ουσων εν Αλεξανδρειαι εν δε Πτολεμαιδι της Θηβαιδος εφ ιερεων και ιερειων και κανηφορου των οντων και ουσων μηνος μεχειρ ια εν Κροκοδιλων πολει του Παθυριτου επι Σωσου αγορανομου ομολογει κτλ.

[1] Cf. Susemihl i. 451 for the evidence.

shed. But to keep the young Philopator, the just heir, alive, must have seemed quixotic to a man of Euergetes temper. He had been recognised as the crown prince over the whole empire, not only at Cyprus, but at Philae, for Mr. Sayce[1] found on the island of Huseh a granite slab, which had supported figures of the king and queen with this youth standing between them.[2] These evidences show that his claims to the throne were not to be set aside so long as he was alive.[3]

[1] *Academy* for March 23, 1895.

[2] The text runs: βασ. Πτολ. και βασ. Κλεοπ. | θεους Φιλομητορας και Πτολεμαιον τον υιον αυτων. Under it Ισις και Ωρος, over an erasure, and a demotic translation of the text. Unfortunately the prince's titles seem to have been erased.

[3] But cf. my conjecture below, p. 380 note 2.

SYRIAN COIN OF PHILOMETOR.

CHAPTER X

§ 215. WE come now to a reign of exceptional duration, and of varied interests, during which not a little that is characteristic in the Ptolemaic remains of Egypt found its origin. And yet no figure in the series would seem less likely to last long; no man less likely to do anything for the good of his country. The verdict of the remaining historians is unanimous that he was a monster of cruelty and vice; that he spent his early life in persistent intrigues and rebellions against his elder brother; that he never showed respect or gratitude for any favour. He conciliated no party of his motley population

CLEOPATRA III.   PTOLEMY IX.[1]

which might leave us any records of his merits; he is set down by Strabo along with the fourth and the last, as by far the worst in a series which was rich in vices. The crimes of the present king moreover occurred quite

---

[1] His second, or throne-name, is seldom distinguishable from that of his brother (p. 328).

publicly, were not disputed, and were the talk of all the Hellenistic world, yet there was still in Rome, now giving the tone to the Eastern world, a Scipionic circle which not only knew what occurred in the East, but which visited Egypt; there was the elder Cato, ready to 'attack all abuses in the provinces, whose indignation should have been enough to remove a monster steeped in murder and. incest. Nevertheless Euergetes II. lived on and prospered, and died in peace at a ripe old age.

Surely these extraordinary anomalies require some explanation which has not been vouchsafed us by the writers of the day.[1]

§ 216. Let us first, however, rehearse the facts of his life, restating briefly the part he had taken in public affairs during his brother's reign. Compared with Philometor, he seems consistently to have shown a more vigorous disposition. The people of Alexandria set him up as king, as soon as his elder brother had fallen under the power of Antiochus Epiphanes. He cannot then have been so much as sixteen years old, and yet no sooner does his able sister make a reconciliation or junction between the brothers to resist the Syrian invader, than we perceive in him the ambition to oust that gentle and forgiving youth, and make himself sole king. In all the various disputes which ensued, ending in the actual

---

[1] I cannot but think that the opinion of Polybius influenced all succeeding writers, and though much of what he said about this Euergetes is lost, his strong censure of him is clearly expressed. But may not Polybius have been unduly prejudiced? He tells us that Menyllos, the confidential agent and ambassador of Philometor, was an intimate of his own at Rome, and from this man he must have heard all Euergetes' vices dwelt upon, and perhaps considerably blackened. May it not be the gossip of this bitter opponent of Physkon which has crept into history as the verdict of Polybius?

expulsion of Philometor, who was restored by Rome with
a division of the kingdom, none of our authorities ever
hints that Euergetes had a good cause. He is hated at
Alexandria; he is hated at Cyrene; and yet he manages
to persuade a party at Rome to support his claims, and
award him the province of Cyrene, to which he had no
right whatever. He must have been intimate with high
Roman society, if it be true that he proposed for the
celebrated Cornelia, mother of the Gracchi.[1] Not content with the Senate's award, he bids for Cyprus; he
persuades the Senate to give him the province without
armed intervention, then with armed intervention; even
to break off diplomatic relations with Philometor. But
all his schemes fail against the polite passive resistance
of the king to the Roman behests, coupled with his
superiority in arms when the two brothers meet in actual
conflict. Defeated, pardoned, silenced, but not reconciled,
Euergetes was sent home by his merciful brother to the
province of Cyrene, where the inhabitants had rebelled
against him, and hated him for his cruelties. Though
history is silent concerning him during the last eight or
nine years of Philometor's reign, we can see from his
promptness to seize the vacant throne[2] that he must have
been watching for any reverse which might happen to his
brother in Syria; it is even quite possible that the attempt
at murder, which Philometor set down to the agency of
Alexander Bala, was really suborned by Euergetes.

§ 217. At all events he invaded Egypt apparently
before the Egyptian army had returned from Syria, and

---

[1] Above, § 199.
[2] Justin says he was offered the crown (*per legatos*) by the Alexandrians, and that Cleopatra's attempt was only that of a faction.
Bandelin errs in assuming that the *legati* were from Rome.

compelled the population of Alexandria, which had sided with the widowed queen Cleopatra in setting up her son Philopator Neos as king, to accept him according to the usual fashion of the Ptolemies, as the second husband of his sister, probably with some vague pretence that this Philopator (II.), his stepson, should succeed.[1] Of course he had not the smallest intention of keeping this contract; he only desired to seize the power, that he might secure himself against all claimants. But it appears to us not only cynical and senseless, but most impolitic, cruelty, that he should murder the young prince publicly, during the very marriage feast, and even before the eyes of his queen and sister.[2] And yet the outraged mother, the distracted bride, continued to live with him, and brought him within a year a son, while he was residing in state at Memphis, whom he called, out of compliment to the circumstance, Memphites! If the queen was of nearly the same age as her brother, which seems to have been the case, she must have been now at least thirty-five years of age, when (in that climate) the usual age of childbearing would have passed. Hence the extraordinary exultation of Euergetes at this late heir,

---

[1] Josephus (*contra Apion.* ii. § 5) and Justin (xxxviii. 8) ascribe the whole management of the defence to Onias, and seem to imply that a Roman envoy named Thermus was responsible for the terms of the surrender, which were unjust, owing to Thermus being bribed by Euergetes.

I distrust Josephus' polemical tract altogether, but in this case we know that there was an oration of Cato against Q. Minucius Thermus, from which A. Gellius (xviii. 9) quotes a sentence accusing him of venality.

[2] Justin is so liberal in his accusations of murder (cf. § 147, note), that it is quite probable the sudden and opportune death of Philopator II. from natural causes may have been set down to his uncle's crime. It is more reasonable to assume this and so avoid the monstrous sequel which historians would have us believe.

'born out of due season.' This event was said to have taken
place during his 'coronation' at Memphis [1]—at which time,
I think, he first assumed the title θεὸς Εὐεργέτης. Diodorus
is express that he was crowned according to the Egyptian
custom,[2] and this gives us a key to much of his after life.

The Jews also believed that he had set his mercenaries
upon them at Alexandria, owing to their support of
Philopator II., and that he was prevented from execut-
ing a wholesale massacre by the intercession of his concubine Irene. The details seem to be borrowed from, or
identical with, those which form the substance of the third
book of Maccabees, and which are there attached to Philopator (cf. above, §§ 159, 160). Diodorus adds that he
murdered a number of his old subjects the Cyreneans,
who had accompanied him, because they used too free
language about the same concubine.

§ 218. But there was a larger policy in this severity.
Polybius, who visited Alexandria, probably within a very

---

[1] Cf. Wilcken in Droysen's *Kl. Sch.* ii. 442. See what was said
above, p. 317, on the ceremony commemorated by the Rosetta stone.
We cannot tell with certainty whether the present was the actual
coronation or the solemn entry into the temple of Ptah.

[2] κατὰ τὴν Μέμφιν ἐνθρονιζόμενος τοῖς βασιλείοις κατὰ τοὺς Αἰγυπτίων
νόμους, *de Virt.* p. 594. We know from Pap. 15 of the Louvre (col.
3, ll. 58 *sq.*) that he issued a decree of benevolences in his twenty-sixth
year at Memphis, probably upon his coronation, and the birth of
Memphites, *e.g.* παραθεμένου δε και προσταγματα και μερος εκ του
εκτεθεντος εν τωι κσ L προσταγματος, etc. His first sole year of royalty
at Alexandria he called his twenty-sixth, *i.e.* from 171 B.C. This decree
gave a legitimate title to those who had property without any such
title, on the ground of possession, as is amply confirmed by the last
column of the Turin Pap. i. 9, 20 παραθεμενων δε και προσταγματος
μερος του εκτεθεντος εν τωι κσ L περι των φιλανθρωπων περι των
κεκρατηκοτων (*sc.* ουσιας). There must have been some sort of Act
of Settlement required, but it did not last till the end of the reign,
when another such Benevolence was proclaimed. Cf. below, § 224.

few years of Euergetes' accession, speaks of repeated massacres of the Alexandrian population by the mercenaries let loose upon them, and he describes the Alexandrians, whom he considers substantially Greeks, as quite distinct from the natives.

A personal visit to Alexandria filled me with disgust at the state of the city. It is inhabited by three distinct races,— native Egyptians, an acute and civilised race; secondly, mercenary soldiers (for the custom of hiring and supporting men-at-arms is an ancient one), who have learnt to rule rather than obey owing to the feeble character of the kings; and a third class, consisting of native Alexandrians, who have never from the same cause become properly accustomed to civil life, but who are yet better than the second class; for though they are now a mongrel race, they were originally Greek, and have retained some recollection of Greek principles. But this last class has become almost extinct, thanks to Euergetes Physcon, in whose reign I visited Alexandria; for that king being troubled with seditions, frequently exposed the common people to the fury of the soldiery and caused their destruction. So that in this state of the city the poet's words only expressed the truth—

'To Egypt 'tis a long and toilsome road.'[1]

Athenaeus[2] also, quoting from an Alexandrian historian called Menekles, says that there was a great revival of learning throughout Greek lands in the days of this king, usually called Kakergetes at Alexandria: 'For he having massacred many Alexandrians, and exiled many more who had grown up in his brother's time, filled all the islands and cities with grammarians, philosophers, geometers, musicians, painters, trainers, physicians, and other artists,[3]

---

[1] Homer *Odyss.* iv. 483.   [2] iv. c. 83.

[3] The absence of rhetors in this enumeration has been noticed by Brzoska (cf. Susemihl ii. 463), and accounted for by the fact known since the researches of Blass, that rhetoric, or even commenting upon the orators, was not developed at Alexandria till the days of Didymus.

who giving lessons, owing to their poverty, produced many distinguished pupils.' With this my predecessor, Sharpe, aptly compares the results of the capture of Constantinople by the Turks upon the learning of Europe.

Yet no intelligent reader will have accompanied me thus far without seeing that one consistent policy underlies all these acts—the rehabilitation of the native population, at the expense of the Hellenistic settlers and Jews. It was from this time on that Alexandria began to revert to the Egyptian type, and to lose its distinctive Hellenism. There were, of course, many Greeks, and learned Greeks, left; this king was himself an author, a critic, and a patron of Greek learning. But the mass of the population changed its character.

§ 219. We are left without dates, and must guess the sequence of events, but it is probable that the famous visit of Scipio, with Panaetius, and a modest retinue of five slaves, took place in consequence of complaints from the exiled Greeks.[1] He was sent ostensibly on a friendly mission, and was shown all the kingdom, and the glories of it, by Euergetes, who was already so fat and unwieldy that he came with great difficulty, on foot, to receive and escort the Romans. We do not hear of any charges being made against the king by his people, or any censure on the part of the Romans, though we cannot but suspect that Scipio must have warned him not to try the long-suffering or in-

Justin (xxxviii. 8) goes on to say that Alexandria was so much deserted that the king invited foreign (*peregrinos*) settlers by proclamation. I suspect that the foreigners invited were native Egyptians.

[1] Clinton quotes Cic. *Acad. priora* ii. 6 *in legatione illa nobili, quam ante censuram obiit* ; and adds that his censorship, according to the Fasti Capitolini, was in 142 B.C. But the *Somnium Scip.* § 11 seems to contradict this, and as he was elected consul, *in his absence*, in 134 B.C. Bandelin (p. 33) adopts this date ; I prefer the former.

difference of the Romans too severely. Cato's attack on Thermus must have been fresh, and any bribing of the present embassy impossible. The king was probably put on his good behaviour, and treated with good-natured contempt for his luxury by the frugal Roman hero : 'The embassy headed by Scipio Africanus came to survey the whole kingdom. But Ptolemy having received them with great pomp and circumstance prepared extravagant feasts and brought them round to show them the palaces, and the rest of the royal treasures. The eminent Roman ambassadors, however, insisted upon eating only slight and wholesome food and despised the king's luxuries, as being injurious to both mind and body. They also paid no attention to the things which the king thought splendid, but were most diligent in studying what was really worth seeing, the situation and the size of the city, and the peculiar arrangements of the Pharos ; and then, sailing up to Memphis, the excellence of the soil, and its irrigation by the Nile, also the great number of the towns, the countless myriads of inhabitants, and the security of the whole country, admirably suited for a great and safe empire if ruled by a worthy sovran.' [1]

Still Euergetes II. knew how to deceive or persuade his masters. We do not hear of any movement at Rome to deprive him of his blood-stained crown.

Diodorus [2] tells us that his power was sustained by his minister or general Hierax, who even paid from his own purse the mercenaries who were about to revolt to one Galaestos, because their allowances were in arrear. Yet

---

[1] Diod. Sic. *Legat.* 32. It was believed that he actually appointed a Roman, named Marcus, not only a peer, but an *epi-strategus*, one of the highest (nominal) dignities in Egypt. Marcus' friends set up a statue of him at Delos. But the text only gives us]μαρ(χ?)ον. Cf. *CIG* 2285.

[2] *Excerpt. Virt.* p. 598.

for fifteen years this king occupied the throne without
serious danger. Early in that period, but probably after
the visit of Scipio, may be placed the family tragedy
mentioned by Justin[1] that he violated, then married
the youthful daughter of his wife, his own niece and
step - daughter, called Cleopatra, divorcing the elder
wife. But the divorce was long delayed. For we know
that his first queen and sister was for years after
(certainly in the years 141 and 136 B.C.) named in
public acts, along with the younger Cleopatra (III.)
What should we not give for a closer insight into the
character and sentiments of these extraordinary women!
There is to be found in Mr. Paton's collection of inscriptions from Kos one of peculiar interest, in which the king
and his two queens honour with a golden crown and
a gilded image the tùtor of their children, who seem therefore to have been educated at Kos. This was quite what
we should expect from a prudent king, but hardly from
Euergetes II., yet I gladly record the fact as giving us one
more item of evidence whereby to judge him less harshly.[2]

§ 220. But while the verdict of the Greek historians is
so decided against him, if we had no other evidence than
the Egyptian monuments, we should call him the greatest
of the Ptolemies. Not only does his sway extend into
Nubia, far beyond that of his predecessors, but all over

---

[1] xxxviii. 8.

[2] Mr. Paton dates this text (No. 73) from the second period (after
127 B.C.) that gives us the three royal names in official documents. I
prefer to put it earlier, before the divorce, while the children of Cleopatra III. were still young, perhaps 140 to 135 B.C. Here is the text:
βασιλευς Πτολεμαιος και βασιλισσα | Κλεοπατρα η αδελφη και βασιλισσα |
Κλεοπατρα η γυνη θεοι Ευεργεται | Ιερωνα Σιμου των πρωτων φιλων | επι-
τροπευσαντα των τεκνων ημων | ετειμησαν στεφανωι χρυσεωι και ικο|νι
χρυσεηι αρετης ενεκα και | ευνοιας της εις αυτους και τεκνα.

Upper Egypt, we find his name upon temple after temple as the builder, restorer, adorner of the national monuments. Even from these material proofs we might know that this sovran led a reaction against the foreigner in the land, and professed to spend his wealth not in salaries to strangers, but in promoting the creed and the traditions of the natives. The private papyri of this period also contain what I think unheard of in the earlier collection, which we owe to Mr. Petrie. There are alleged encroachments, and even violences, on the part of natives against Greeks, which the latter ascribe to the fact that they are Greeks. In earlier days we find natives subject to violence from Greeks. To this fact I have already called attention.[1]

The natives have left us no literature wherein to criticise or defend the character of their king. Their constant appeals in legal actions to his justice are mere official formulae addressed to the crown. But it is not impossible that as the rancour of the Roman nobles has blackened the character of more than one emperor in the gloomy pages of Tacitus, so the persecuted Greeks and Jews have taken revenge upon this Ptolemy, whom they called Physkon, or Kakergetes, and have exaggerated the horror of his crimes.[2] Some such hypothesis seems almost demanded to explain away the otherwise inconceivable callousness of the men and women who seem to be satisfied with a day's lamentation for a deliberate murder, and live on together with the murderer as if nothing had happened.

§ 221. The catalogue of temples built or restored by this king is probably not at all complete, for he was active everywhere, but the following details will give some support to the general statement which I have made.[3]

---

[1] Cf. above, § 205. [2] Cf. Josephus c. Ap. ii. 5 for a clear instance.
[3] Here is a list of the principal papyri which we can ascribe with

So far as excavations and chance discoveries have as yet informed us, there is hardly a trace of the activity of either Philometor or Euergetes II. in Lower Egypt or even at Memphis, though we may be taught any day that our ignorance of these things is for want of proper search. But as soon as we reach Thebes, we find no reign so marked as that of Physkon. In many cases the work is dedicated to the gods by Philometor, and his intentions carried out by Euergetes II., in others it is the work of the younger brother alone. On the other hand I am not aware of any temple founded by Philometor, which was not enlarged or completed by his successor. At the temple of Karnak both kings appear on a doorway in the second Pylon. In the neighbourhood Euergetes II. has left his name on the temple of Medamut, where he used the older materials of Pharaonic buildings. He restored what is known as the small temple of Dayr-el-Medîneh on the western side of the Nile, and built the small temple at Medinet-Abu. Excavated in the rock behind the famous terraces of Hatasu, the inmost chamber again shows his name, where a high official had appropriated for his tomb an older resting-place. The rock temple of El-Kab was his work, though improved by Ptolemy X. He built at the great temple of Edfu all his life. He added to the temple

certainty to his reign, for they differ widely from those of the early Ptolemies, and, if dated higher than the year 36, cannot belong to Philometor. At Turin (I quote from A. Peyron's edition) Pap. I. II. (a rough copy of the Paris Pap. 15²) III. IV. VIII. XI. XII. XIII., all dated either ∠ 44, or ∠ 51·3. At Leyden Pap. L. (Catal. Leemans); at Paris (ed. Brunet de Presle) 6, 8, 14, 15, 16, 61·3. In the British Museum Pap. XV. and perhaps III. The papyri of Zois (Peyron part iii.) and Pap. XIII. of Turin being dated ∠ 31 and ∠ 34 may be of Philometor's time. It is from these legal documents—trials, petitions, contracts, depositions—that we can gather impressions of the state of things at Thebes, and some other spots in Upper Egypt.

of Ombos founded by Philometor.[1] He has left his mark upon Syene Elephantine, Philae, in many places.

He built part at least of the temple of Debot in Nubia. So also at Dakkeh, we have his inscription over the portal of the temple, which is the highest point on the Nile that any Ptolemaic cartouche has been found.

This interest in the national religion, coupled with the large outlay from the royal purse which such buildings implied, go some way to corroborate Gutschmid's opinion that though he may have been worthless as a man, he was a model regent of Egypt.[2]

§ 222. Such are the evidences, to me conclusive, that his so-called massacres of his Hellenic subjects were not random violences, but caused by a despot's will to protect and promote the native population against the imported Graeco-Macedonians. These doubtless gave him an excuse for his severities by some outbreak, some insubordination, perhaps some persecution of the natives. There is not one word said of his having shown any harshness to the latter.

This explanation seems all the more probable as his persecution of the Alexandrians, though it could not but affect all classes, cannot have been directed primarily against literary men; it was surely, in the first instance, political, for the king showed unmistakeable taste for Greek learning, and is even the only one of the series whose authorship is to us more than a name. Though he may not have been, as some of the ancients asserted, a pupil of Aristarchus, he was no doubt well acquainted with that eminent man, and his critical methods.[3] The

---

[1] Above, § 207.   [2] Sharpe i. p. 267.

[3] Susemihl i. 451. If Aristarchus was the tutor of Euergetes II., he must also have been the tutor of Philometor, and yet he is called

courtiers found it pleased him to discuss problems
of the Homeric text far into the night, and one of his
emendations has actually survived.[1]

It seems likely enough that the anecdote told by Galen
of the conflict for preeminence in libraries between Pergamum and Alexandria, and the means taken to secure books
from ships, may refer to this Euergetes, and not to his
older namesake, and the citations by Athenaeus from his
Memoirs, though they are trivial enough, show a keen
interest in geography and in natural history, as his emendation also suggests.[2] If indeed mathematical studies,
then chiefly prosecuted by oral teaching (in the absence of
convenient notation), seem to have received a mortal
blow by the exile of the learned from his capital, geographical discovery, such as we hear of it in the case of
Eudoxus and Agatharchides, was in high fashion. It is
even conjectured that the complaint of Agatharchides at
the end of his book, that he could not finish it owing to
his want of access to the State archives on the subject,
points to the disturbances which exiled the king after
his fifteen years of undisputed reign.[3] We have then
before us no mere wild beast, no *Missgeburt von Blut und
Dreck*, but at all events a man who understood the

the tutor of Philometor's son Eupator. He may possibly have taught
all three, and probably fled from Egypt on the murder or death of
Eupator. Cf. Suidas *sub voc.*

[1] Πτολεμαῖος ὁ δεύτερος Εὐεργέτης παρ' Ὁμήρῳ (ε 72) ἀξιοῖ γράφειν
"ἀμφὶ δὲ λειμῶνες μαλακοὶ σίου ἠδὲ σελίνου." σία γὰρ μετὰ σελίνου
φύεσθαι ἀλλὰ μὴ ἴα, Athen. ii. 61 C, and also οὕτως δὲ καὶ Πτ.
φιλομαθεῖν δοκοῦντι περὶ γλώττης καὶ στιχιδίου καὶ ἱστορίας μαχόμενοι
μέχρι μέσων νυκτῶν ἀπέτειναν, cf. Susemihl i. 9.

[2] The only passage which indicates his style is the remarkable sketch
of the strange character of Antiochus Epiphanes, which has passed
through Polybius into Athenaeus x. 52.

[3] Susemihl i. 688, 735, 757 ; ii. 413, 667 for the texts utilised above.

pleasures of literature, and was from some points of view a patron of learning.

The studies of recent years upon the apocryphal writings of the Hellenistic Jews have shown that this was the moment when polemical tracts for and against the Jews were much in vogue. The preface to the book of Ecclesiasticus shows us that the translator had all the canonical books of the LXX ready before him.[1] Physkon's enmity against the Jews, as supporters of his brother and his brother's son Eupator, must have excited in his courtiers a desire to damage that nation in dignity as well as importance, and hence arose scurrilous and mendacious attacks upon the Jews, met by that clever people with the same weapons. But whatever the value of these pamphlets, they add to the evidence given us in geographical studies, that the Alexandria of Ptolemy Physkon, from which all the learned were supposed to have fled, was still the home of scientific inquiry and of literary activity. The Sibylline oracles, of which the oldest in our collection are also ascribed to this reign,[2] are perhaps too special a subject to admit of discussion in the pages of this book.

§ 223. The next passage in this history is even more enigmatical. Physkon, after having reigned fifteen years at Alexandria, finds himself (in 130 B.C.) so hated for his cruelties, and in such danger of assassination, that he flies secretly to Cyprus, taking with him his son Memphites (now about fourteen years old), and *uxore*

---

[1] οὐ γὰρ ἰσοδυναμεῖ αὐτὰ ἐν ἑαυτοῖς Ἑβραϊστὶ λεγόμενα καὶ ὅταν μεταχθῇ εἰς ἑτέραν γλῶσσαν· οὐ μόνον δὲ ταῦτα, ἀλλὰ καὶ αὐτὸς ὁ νόμος καὶ αἱ προφητεῖαι καὶ τὰ λοιπὰ τῶν βιβλίων οὐ μικρὰν ἔχει τὴν διαφορὰν ἐν ἑαυτοῖς λεγόμενα. ἐν γὰρ τῳ ή καὶ λ' ἔτει [viz. of his age] ἐπὶ τοῦ Εὐεργέτου βασιλέως παραγενηθεὶς εἰς Αἴγυπτον καὶ συγχρονίσας, κτλ.

[2] Susemihl ii. 637-8.

matris pellice, whereupon the Alexandrians confer the royalty again upon his sister and discarded queen, Cleopatra II.[1] By way of vengeance he murders his son, and having cut the body into pieces, sends it in a box to the boy's mother, who receives this horrid present on her birthday.[2] But we only hear of the grief of the mother, and the complete alienation of the population, except from Justin,[3] who tells us that Cleopatra prepared to resist with an army Euergetes, who came to invade Egypt by the Syrian frontier! In the battle which ensued he conquered, and though Cleopatra solicited the help of Demetrius Nicator, who had just returned from his captivity in the East, she was unable to maintain herself in Egypt, and joined Demetrius in Syria.

The war with which Physkon was now threatened he evaded by setting up Alexander Zabinas, as a son of Alexander Bala, to claim the Syrian throne, in which the adventurer was actually successful (128 B.C.) But presently his creature revolted from obeying him, and thereupon the king of Egypt marries his second daughter Tryphaena to Antiochus Grypus, and sends him to play the same tragi-comedy with the same success in Syria. The climax of absurdity remains to be told. Letronne is persuaded by the evidence of monuments that the exiled Cleopatra II., condoning the murder and mutilation of her son Memphites, returned to Egypt, and is again recognised with her brother and her daughter (Cleopatra III.) as a reigning queen.

[1] To this period Revillout (*RE* vii. 40) refers a document dated in the second year of Cleopatra's reign. Cf. *Addit. Notes* pp. 496-7.

[2] Diodorus *Excerpt.* p. 602 is fullest, and with rhetorical touches; cf. also Livy *Epit.* lix.; Justin xxxviii. 8.

[3] *iam etiam populo peregrino invisus,* says Justin. What does this mean? Is it 'even the Egyptians'? I think so.

§ 224. It is with great impatience that a historian feels himself compelled to set down such a jumble of facts, without reasonable motives, as the chronicle of a civilised kingdom in civilised days. The Romans were now so busy with the Gracchan revolution that they had no time or inclination to attend to foreign affairs. They had indeed acquired Pergamum by the bequest of the last king, and were obliged to put down Aristonikos, the natural heir, by arms. But as regards the rest of the Hellenistic world, they were content that it should be torn by discords, wracked by rival claimants for the thrones, and so prepared to fall easily into the tentacles of the all-devouring Republic.

There must indeed have been some internal disturbances. For the pleader in a legal papyrus [1] argues the case of his client on the ground ετι δε των μεγιστων βασιλεων απολελυκοτων τους υπο την βασιλειαν παντας αιτιων πασων των εως Θωυθ ιβ του νγ∠, and this quasi-Papal indulgence is spoken of as one of a series of φιλάνθρωπα — Benevolences or Indulgences—ordained by this king and his ancestors. In the particular case argued, this decree in the 53rd year of the king made actual possession equivalent to possession with title—an expedient which points to an Act of Settlement after great disorders, and depreciation of property from the uncertainty of its tenure. I take it to signify that the elder Cleopatra was just dead. She had ruled at Alexandria for some time during Physkon's last exile, and it was in order to legalise her acts and protect them from being annulled that upon his return he was compelled to associate her with his throne. When she died this danger recurred, and it was probably to allay public uneasiness that he enacted his φιλάνθρωπα, which

_____
[1] Turin i. col. 7, ll. 13-15 (ed. Peyron).

legalised all the transfers of property done under her authority.[1]

§ 225. Even after all his adventures, the king lived some years, for he did not die till 117 B.C. But of his last years we only know from inscriptions and papyri that the affairs of Upper Egypt were actively and carefully administered. His 53rd and 54th (really 28th and 29th) years appear frequently among the dates remaining: the many absurdities with which his life teems are probably to be attributed, as I have already said, to the inventions and distortions of partisan historians, Jews and Greeks, who took literary revenge upon the monarch who destroyed their influence in the land of Egypt.

§ 226. Let us now turn to a far more interesting subject—the indications of the internal state of the country during this reign from the stray information conveyed by the private documents in the publications of the respective papyri of the museums of Leyden, Paris, London, also Vienna and Rome. Those of the British Museum are indeed the only collection recently and scientifically edited, but the studies of Peyron, Lumbroso, Letronne, Revillout,[2] have told us most of what we could learn,

---

[1] This conclusion is directly opposed to the argument of Lepsius (Berlin *Abh.* 1852, p. 470) who reports that in demotic contracts he has found both queens mentioned in the headings of the years 141 and 136 B.C., and again in 124 and 118 B.C., while the younger Cleopatra alone appears in some of 126-4 B.C. Hence he desires to read in the dedication of the temple of Pselchis με (45), as only one Cleopatra is mentioned. I do not believe in the accuracy of these demotic documents, and think they may have omitted or added a name at random. Cf. *Addit. Notes* pp. 496-7. Had she been alive in 117 B.C. we should probably have heard of her, in the doubtful condition of the succession.

[2] This is only the case with the particular texts which he has re-handled, but there remains much to be done for the Paris papyri. The whole collection as it stood in 1862 was edited in vol. viii. of the *Notices et Extraits* of the MSS. of the Louvre, from the papers of Letronne, by Brunet de Presle. A folio volume of facsimiles was also

even by a photographic reproduction such as the English
authorities have supplied. Unfortunately there is no
comprehensive study of the social aspects of these papers.
The economic side has been probably exhausted by the
admirable essays of G. Lumbroso and U. Wilcken. As
was said long ago, the information to be obtained from
the many hieroglyphic inscriptions of this king is almost
nothing; the demotic documents are not deciphered with
any certainty. A few valuable Greek inscriptions, and
a good many documents of a legal character, coming from
the Serapeum at Memphis—these are the materials at our
disposal.

§ 227. We may first dispose of the few inscriptions on
stone, which show, at least in the king's later years, a careful attention to the southern frontiers of his kingdom, and
in accordance with his life-policy, an attention to the
claims of his native subjects. I have above mentioned
the votive offering of Soterichos of Gortyn.[1] It teaches us

then produced. But these, done by pre-photographic processes, are not
to be safely trusted, and Brunet's reading constantly deviates even from
what they present. Every page of the work will show discrepancies
of this kind. He was evidently one of those clever decipherers
who are not content to confess their failure, but set down their conjectures as readings of the text. The important text numbered 62 was
re-copied by Mr. Grenfell in 1895, and republished in the appendix to
the Revenue Papyrus of Philadelphus. But this instance will not show
how much the rest of the collection demands adequate reproduction, for
it is far less faulty than the other transcriptions. Wilcken's forthcoming
Corpus Papyrorum will comprise revised copies of all these treasures.

[1] § 118. Here is the text : υπερ βασιλεως Πτολεμαιου και | βασιλισσης
Κλεοπατρας της γυναικ[ος | θεων Ευεργετων και των τεκνων αυ[των |
Σωτηριχος Ικαδιωνος Γορτυνιος τω[ν | αρχισωματοφυλακων απεστα[λ | μενος
υπο Παωτος του συγγενους και | στρατηγου της Θηβαιδος επι την
συναγ[ω | γην της πολυτελους λιθειας και επι των | πλων και παρεξομενος
την ασφαλειαν τ[οις | κατακομιζουσι απο του κατα Κοπτον ορου[ς | τα
λιβανωτικα φορτια και τα αλλα ξενια | Πανι ευοδωι και τοις αλλοις θεοις
| πασι και πασαις ∠μα θυθι. Cf. also *CIG* 4838.

many curious facts. The date is ∟ 41, viz. 129 B.C., and
then Cleopatra II. his sister, whom he had so maltreated,
must have been either in exile or dead, for if not, she
would have been mentioned along with her daughter, his
second wife.[1] But we should have expected even the
latter to be called his sister, according to the usual formula.
The officer in question was sent out to collect precious
stone, and we hesitate between the *mafkat*, or turquoise,
which the old Egyptian kings had sought in the peninsula
of Sinai, and the porphyry, which is found in that very
region, and which was far the most precious architectural
stone found in Egypt. But Letronne[2] asserts that there
is not a single instance of the use of porphyry in any
of our Egyptian antiquities, and indeed the expression of
the text does not seem to suit quarrying so well, as the
gathering of some precious stone (emeralds) found in the
desert. This too couples better with the cargoes of
spices which must have come by sea either to Berenike
or to Myos Hormos, and thence by caravan to Koptos.

Very striking is the fact that Soterichos, a high official,
and a Greek, is under the control of one Paos, evidently

---

[1] Strack (*Mitth.* for 1894, p. 230) notes that while the historians
have fixed 127 B.C. as the date of the king's return from his exile, this
inscription proves that he was reigning in Egypt in 129 B.C. We have
another proof of the king's activity in protecting the southern trade-
route in an inscription found at Berenike, and now at Alexandria,
which runs

υπερ βασιλε]ως Πτολ[εμαιου
και βασιλισσ]ης Κλεο[πατρας
της αδελφ]ης και βασ[ιλισσης
Κλεοπατρα]ς της γυναικος
θεων Ευεργ]ετων και των
τεκν]ων Εχεφυδος
son of X. Π]ολυρρηνιος
των σωμ]ατοφυλακων.

[2] *Inscriptions* i. pp. 137 *sq.*

an Egyptian, who has the higher titles of cousin to the
king, and military governor of the whole Thebaid, that
is of all the south country from Kynopolis to Syene.[1]   Nor
is this a solitary case.   The group v. vi. vii. of the Turin
Papyri is addressed to a Phommous (or -outes), who held
the same dignities in the early years of the succeeding
reign, as appears from the text of the Aswân stele to be
noticed presently.   The votive offering of the βασιλισται
on the little island of Sehele just above the Cataract
is still more curious.   The dedication is made to a
number of local Egyptian deities, whose Greek names
are in each case added.   The greatest of Greek gods
were here identified with local deities.   The daemons
of the Cataract are also added.   But the list of names,
containing fifteen Greeks, the sons of Greeks, also contains five Egyptians, the sons of Egyptians, who are thus
enrolled with the rest in a religious confraternity of the
Greek kind, and offer worship, and keep feast days to
Egyptian deities, whose Greek names must have been a
mere recent accommodation.[2]

§ 228.   But if these Egyptian deities have Greek names
appended to them, so there are Greek private individuals
who appear in the legal documents of the day with
Egyptian names added—Apollonios, also called Psemmonthes, son of Hermias, also called Petenephotus,[3] and

---

[1] I notice that in two of the Paphian inscriptions (Nos. 43, 89) of
this date, the soldiers quartered in Cyprus set up statues to a general
called the στρατηγὸς αὐτοκράτωρ of the Thebaid.   This title is new to
me.   Is it the same as στρατηγου και επιστρατηγου of other inscriptions ?
In any case it shows the importance of the military forces in Upper
Egypt, which kept in check the Nubian and Arabian neighbours.

[2] Cf. the text and comm. in *CIG* 4893.

[3] Leiden Pap. F.   Thus we have in Pap. 7 of the Louvre (99 B.C.)
Asclepias also called Senamouthin, daughter of Panas, a Persian woman.

though earlier critics have assumed that these persons were natives who had adopted Hellenistic names, I think the evidence in this case leans the other way. On the analogy of the inscription just cited the order, in such case, should be different, it should be Psemmonthes, also called Apollonios, and it is idle to argue that the natives were required or thought it advisable to appear in Ptolemaic courts with Greek names, for in the same Turin collection, and of the same epoch, are suits brought by natives against one another concerning affairs of purely Egyptian interest before the Ptolemaic magistrates. A clear example is the Turin Papyrus viii., in which one corporation of Paraschists, who performed the most offensive part of the embalming of mummies in the necropolis of Thebes, prosecute another corporation or joint-stock company for having violated the conditions of a transaction whereby a large number of villages were reserved for the practice of the buyers—not only were they alone to have the right of opening dead bodies in that district, but that of collecting contributions in wine, oil, etc., from the people of the prescribed district. And this case is brought before Heracleides, the royal A.D.C., and Epistates, and over the revenues of the Theban district! Nor were the native courts abolished. We know from the same collection that there were native judges (λαοκριται) and native courts; that legal contracts were often made in demotic, we know from extant specimens. Here are evidences of fusion such as we should have looked for in vain before the national rising against Epiphanes.

§ 229. But there is further evidence. On a small obelisk or stele found at Philae, the priests of the temples commemorate a relief granted them by this king from the heavy burden of entertaining all the government officials who had been in the habit of exacting hospitality at this famous station. The text,[1] which I cite in a note, is interesting in this, that it shows how firm a hold Physkon had obtained of lower Nubia, at least as far as Pselchis.

[1] This important text is now in the possession of Mr. Bankes of Kingston Hall. The first two parts of it, viz. (A) the answer from the crown to the priests of the temple, enclosing (B) an order to the strategos of the district to see that their petition is granted and the evil of which they complained abated, are so effaced (being only painted in red upon the stone) that their reconstruction is not easy. What is possible to be done will be seen in Wilcken's Essay in *Hermes* for 1887, pp. 1 *sqq.* He there establishes that the hieroglyphic text on the sides of the stone is not a version of the Greek, but an account of some earlier φιλάνθρωπα granted by the king. These were commemorated upon two obelisks which have not yet been discovered. Wilcken in the same essay corrects the reconstruction of Letronne, and the conclusions he drew which identified the priest of Alexander, etc., with the metropolitan ecclesiastic of all Egypt. The last part (C) is fortunately complete, and tells us what the complaint was, viz. (with some abbreviations of the obvious formulae) : βασιλει Πτ. και βασ. Κλεοπ. τηι αδελφηι, και βασ. Κλεοπ. τηι γυν. θεοις Ευεργ. χαιρειν οι ιερεις της εν τωι Αβατωι και εν Φιλαις Ισιδος, θεας μεγιστης. Επει οι παρεπιδημουντες εις τας Φιλας στρατηγοι, και επισταται, και θηβαρχαι, και βασ. γραμμ. και επισταται φυλακιτων, και οι αλλοι πραγματικοι παντες, και αι ακολουθουσαι δυναμεις, και η λοιπη υπηρεσια, αναγκαζουσι ημας παρουσιας (entertainment) αυτοις ποιεισθαι ουχ εκοντας, και εκ του τοιουτου συμβαινει ελαττουσθαι το ιερον και κινδυνευειν ημας του μη εχειν τα νομιζομενα προς τας γενομενας υπερ τε υμων και των τεκνων θυσιας και σπονδας · δεομεθ' υμων, θεων μεγιστων, εαν φαινη- ται, συνταξαι Νουμηνιωι, τωι συγγενει κα[ι επιστο]λογραφωι γραψαι Λοχωι, τωι συγγενει και στρατηγωι της Θηβαιδος, μη παρενοχλειν ημας προς ταυτα, μητ' αλλωι μηδεν επιτρεπειν το αυτο ποιειν, και ημιν διδοναι τους καθη- κοντας περι τουτων χρηματισμους, εν οις επιχωρησαι ημιν αναθειναι στηλην, εν ηι αναγραψομεν την γεγονυιαν ημιν υφ' υμων περι τουτων φιλανθρωπιαν, ινα η υμετερα χαρις αειμνηστος υπαρχηι παρ' αυτης εις τον απαντα χρονον. τουτου δε γενομενου εσομεθα και εν τουτοις, και το ιερον της Ισιδος, ευεργετημενοι. ευτυχειτε. The Aswân stele, set up under the next king (below, § 235) cites Benevolences granted by letter to officials at Syene in the 53rd year of his reign, showing that his active interest in the southern country lasted up to the end of his life.

This petition has to me the air of a new grievance, which had not existed of old, just like the petition of the crown gooseherds,[1] who complain a century earlier that the king's fiscal officer, Ischurias, demands from them twelve geese for his hospitalities. In both cases the complainants do not venture to allege any personal claims for justice, but lay stress only on the fact that their service to the king is being impaired. Also, though a few of the troublesome officials were Egyptians, the great majority was Greek, as distinguished from the purely Egyptian priests. When endowed with official importance, they were able to assert themselves over the pliant natives, but we may be sure that in any time of disturbance isolated foreigners would have fared at Philae as the recluse Ptolemy did at the Serapeum of Memphis in the preceding reign. The reaction had set in, and was tending to restore Egypt to its original inhabitants.

§ 230. Meanwhile let us remember that the king at Alexandria did not carry this policy so far as to despise Greek letters. His reign marks the acme of the Museum, and also the beginning of its decay. Aristarchus was the greatest, but also the last, of the great Alexandrian critics. But the king was even an author, and as the first Ptolemy had put on record the chronicle of his expeditions and victories in the far East, so the ninth wrote memoirs of his expeditions and diplomacies in the West —but naturally on the trivial side of these humiliating transactions, on the curiosities of Greece or the islands, especially in delicacies for the table, on the mistresses of his ancestor Philadelphus, and such things, which the reader will find in the couple of pages devoted to his fragments by the laborious Carl Müller.[2]

[1] In the *Petrie Papyri* II. p. [25].   [2] *FHG* iii. p. 186.

If many of the learned had been expelled from his capital in former years, there remained an ample supply of salaried scholars in the Museum, to give a literary flavour to his entertainments. But whatever may have been the condition of Alexandria, there is good evidence from the law reports still extant that the upper country was prudently and justly governed. No case in antiquity is more completely and fairly reported than that of Hermias *v.* the Choachytae, which was tried and decided at Thebes in the fifty-third year of Physkon. There is (at Turin) a papyrus of nine columns long, admirably preserved, giving the cases of both plaintiff and defendants, and the decision, as drawn up by the deciding court, upon hearing the arguments of counsel on either side. Nothing can be more sensible or business-like than the whole document. Though there was an Act of Settlement of the previous year, whereby all actual holders of property were confirmed in their holdings, the defendants, while citing it, do not rely upon it.

§ 231. The plaintiff Hermias, son of Ptolemaeus, claimed a house and premises in Diospolis (Thebes) as his hereditary possession, which during his absence on permanent military service at Ombos had been occupied by a corporation of Choachytae, who resisted eviction, and when ordered to retire to their own side of the river (to the Memnonia) came back again ; when summoned before the courts, declined to appear. The plaintiff could only stay a short time at Thebes, and was obliged to return to duty at Ombos. He further pleads that these attendants upon the dead had polluted the temples adjoining his house by storing dead bodies there—an impiety deserving a separate punishment. As regards the plea of defendants that they had purchased the premises from a certain woman named Lobais, he produces an affidavit from her, that she never had any rights over the property.

Hermias' case, as the judge sums it up from the arguments of counsel and the enclosed documents, seems very strong indeed.

But when we come to the defence, the whole aspect of the facts changes. The defendants produce evidence of a series of purchases by which they acquired this property from the twenty-eighth to the thirty-fifth years of the previous king, not from Lobais alone, but from a number of joint-owners; they not only produce the Egyptian contracts, translated into Greek, but the entries of the tax paid to the State on these sales.[1] These transactions were not questioned for thirty-seven years, not to speak of the *indulgences* which gave a secure title to actual possessors, even if their titles were not clear. They then show that it was now eighty-eight years since the first year of Epiphanes, when the plaintiff's father had left Thebes to settle at Ombos, and that during all that time the plaintiff, who was now very old, had produced no evidence of title. The affidavit of Lobais was irrelevant, for it did not establish his title, nor touch the ownership of the other partners of the property, who had sold to defendants.

---

[1] E. Revillout (*Chrestomathie démotique* pp. xxxvii. *sq.*) has added much information from demotic papyri, which I note here on his authority. He shows that there were two distinct actions against these Choachytae, the first concluded in ∠44, wherein Apollonios called Psemmonthes, after several proceedings, is finally 'squared' by the Choachytae for a sum of money, as appears from Turin Pap. iv. Then begins the action for a younger son of Ptolemy, who did not live at Thebes. We still have the demotic contracts whereby the Choachytae acquired bit by bit the property on which they built. He adds (p. lvi.) that the Choachytae were regular usurers in wheat, as appears from many demotic contracts, some of them made by women on their own account without a κύριος.

They further charge her with being in collusion with the plaintiff.

I need not pursue the details further. The judge decides : that as the defendants have produced (1) clear evidence of title, (2) clear evidence of undisturbed possession, and (3) the indulgence of the twenty-sixth year of Philometor to prove the title of the vendors, whereas the plaintiff shows (1) no evidence of title, (2) lachesse in asserting his claims, (3) no previous decision in his favour, though he has been for nine years prosecuting the defendants—the case is dismissed, and the plaintiff warned to cease from disturbing defendants in their possession.

§ 232. Nothing can be more convincing that the country, in spite of the quarrels of its kings, was upon the whole in a settled and safe condition. In this property case, the evidence goes back for eighty-eight years ; the public records of the previous generation are at hand. The arguments are all such as would be used before a judge in an English court. The only point in which the Greek tries to raise odium against the Egyptian is that by keeping mummies near the temples of Greek gods, they are committing impiety. The defendants show that he has confused their office, one thoroughly pure, and consistent with entry into temples, with that of the actual embalmers (παρασχισταί).

It is, however, interesting that a very aged Greek soldier should have sought to oust an Egyptian corporation from their property. Probably he remembered former days, when such things had taken place. His father had once lived at Thebes, and possibly had left this very site without thinking of preserving his rights. At all events, he had never asserted any claim. When his son, in extreme old age, began the prosecution, the Choachytae probably made delays and postponement in the hope that he would die, and with him his troublesome .claims. When the case is actually heard, the decision is given within a month of the hearing, and upon strictly objective grounds.

Although therefore M. Revillout contrasts the government of Physkon, as unjust and oppressive, with that of his brother, so far as I know the Papyri of the period, there is more evidence of disturbance in the internal management of Egyptian affairs under the worthy Philometor, than there is under the unworthy Physkon.

The same may be said of his arrangements concerning Cyrene. The whole history of that very turbulent province lapses into a silence which implies pacification if not contentment. The old king had appointed to govern it, probably during his life, an illegitimate son, known as Ptolemy Apion, concerning whom we hear nothing save that he continued to rule at Cyrene in perfect independence and quite aloof from the sanguinary quarrels of the royal house, till his death in 97 B.C.

§ 233. The last years of Physkon were no doubt saved from the greatest of all dangers, that of Roman interference, by the fierce internal struggles caused by the Gracchi, which occupied the Senate so completely as to produce a cessation of all foreign policy. But the dangerous, indeed the fatal, precedent of the Pergamene kingdom passing by the bequest, real or suborned, of the last Attalus to the Roman people, must have shown Physkon very clearly what was likely to arise as soon as the Romans had their hands free to plunder their Oriental allies.

All the remaining pretences of virtue and honour had disappeared from among the Roman nobles during the last fifty years. There was nothing to be had at Rome, or from Rome, but by shameless bribery. This is the moral which Sallust's *Jugurthine War* conveys; and Jugurtha's case was only one of many.. Both in Syria and in Egypt there were rival claimants, illegitimate branches, quarrels luxuriating round every throne; and every throne was ready to be sold to the highest bidder.

Such was the aspect of the Hellenistic world when Euergetes II., after his long and eventful reign over an Egypt extended far south of the limits which his predecessors had accepted, died at the age of about sixty-five. His vices, which are so much noted by the historians, had not been able to cut him off prematurely. Let us believe that as in the case of the emperor Tiberius, these things have been exaggerated by the anecdote-mongers, and that Physkon, as he had intellect enough, so he showed discretion enough, to avoid the physical ruin of his health. At all events the history of Ptolemaic Egypt might fairly close with his death. There is nothing of public interest to follow till we come to the last scene, and the notorious Cleopatra VI. Not that her ancestor Cleopatra III., the reigning queen of Euergetes' later life, was not a very strong and remarkable woman. Being niece of the king, she must have been considerably younger, and some of her children, especially her younger son Alexander, are spoken of as still under age when Physkon died. At all events, we hear from Pausanias,[1] in a passage very important, amid our want of information from other sources, that she had persuaded her failing husband to send away her elder son, the natural successor, to Cyprus, under the title of governor, but really to have the field clear for her own intrigues.

[1] i. 9.

COIN OF CLEOPATRA II.

CHAPTER XI

CLEOPATRA III. AND HER SONS PHILOMETOR, SOTER II. (OR
LATHYRUS) AND PTOLEMY ALEXANDER (117-81 B.C.)

§ 234. OUR authorities do not, so far as I know, explain
how it was that the people of Alexandria so frequently
acquiesced in a reigning queen, in
the presence of legitimate male heirs.
That a royal princess, the sister of
the king, should be associated with
him as his queen in public acts, seems
natural enough. But in the present,
as in other cases, when the old king
dies, no one seems to dispute the
right of the queen-mother to retain her
position and control the state. And
yet the association with one of her
sons as king seems also to be pre-
supposed as unavoidable. We must
conclude from these facts that when

PTOLEMY X.

once a queen, who was also the eldest female heir of the
royal family by birth, was officially raised to the rank
of partner with the king in public acts, with the usual
deification, her right to the throne was permanent, and was

not affected by her husband's death. Hence it is that the elder Cleopatra (II.), Physkon's former wife and sister, is named in public acts to the end of her life along with the reigning king and queen. Hence it is that when Physkon died, his queen remains in possession of the throne, though her son also has recognised rights of succession. We are told by Justin [1] and Pausanias that her first object was to persuade the Alexandrians to associate her younger son Alexander in the sovranty. But when the people would not hear of it, she sent Alexander for safety to Cyprus, and accepted her elder son, known as Soter II. or nicknamed Lathyrus, with the compromise that he should divorce his elder sister and wife Cleopatra (IV.), and marry his younger sister Selene.[2] We can hardly doubt that by this arrangement she meant to avoid the association of the young queen with her son's and her own name in public acts, as had been the case when she was herself the younger Cleopatra. For there was probably some strong Egyptian sentiment against giving these peculiar royal, and divine, honours, to the younger members of the family.

§ 235. So the new joint reign began amid such mutual suspicion and fear, that Pausanias even reports a [false] tradition that the title Philometor (II.), also given to this king in public acts, was given to him ἐπὶ χλευασμῷ, in

---

[1] xxxix. 3.

[2] Porphyry (*FHG* iii. 721) tells us quite another story ; βασιλεύει δὲ πρότερος ὁ πρεσβύτερος ὑπὸ τῆς μητρὸς ἀναδειχθείς. δοκῶν δὲ αὐτῇ εἶναι πειθήνιος, ἄχρι μέν τινος ἠγαπᾶτο. ἐπεὶ δὲ κατὰ τὸ δέκατον ἔτος τῆς ἀρχῆς τοὺς φίλους τῶν γονέων ἀπέσφαξεν, ὑπὸ τῆς μητρὸς διὰ τὴν ὠμότητα τῆς ἀρχῆς καθῃρέθη, καὶ εἰς Κύπρον ἐφυγαδεύθη, etc. What are we to make of such wholly contradictory materials? This seems to represent the story told by Cleopatra's adherents, and is inconsistent with the subsequent acts of Lathyrus ; but who can tell?

derision of the notorious enmity which existed between mother and son. Externally, however, the situation was not critical. We see from the account just given that the old traditional habit of having the king declared by the 'Macedonians,' *i.e.* the free citizens of that country assembled under arms, was still maintained though Macedon had been wiped out of the list of nations, and the armed assembly at Alexandria retained but very little of the blood of Alexander's companions in their veins. But Syria was sunk into hopeless civil war among the rivals for its throne. Rome was busy with dangers nearer home.

For some months indeed, while the queen was striving to carry out her designs, she was the sole regent, and Agatharchides tells us she was the sovran who sent out Eudoxus on the second of his adventurous voyages, whereas when he returned the young king was ruling, and she was no longer in power. This is hardly consistent with the public documents which mention her and him together as joint queen and king. The inscription on the temple of Kous (Apollonopolis Parva) runs in the name of 'Queen Cleopatra and King Ptolemy gods Philometores, Soteres, and his children.' The young queen is not mentioned, as was natural according to what has just been said. We now know from an inscription on a granite stele found at Aswân in 1885, and brought to the British Museum, the fact that in the second year of his reign (115 B.C.), the young king visited Elephantine, and was waited upon by the priests of the gods of the Cataract, who were also the priests of the series of the Ptolemies, as gods associated with the old national deities, and that they asked for certain privileges, which the king granted. The whole transaction, with his orders to Phommous, the local governor, whom he entitles his brother, and the documents appended, were engraved and set up

on this stele.[1]   Probably it was found politic to remit to the
priests some of the burdens imposed by Physkon.   It is
remarkable that in this document, so far as we possess it,
there is no evidence that the queen-mother was with her
son or included in the government.[2]

For the purpose of securing her favourite son Alexander,
she had him appointed in the third year of her reign
independent king of Cyprus, and from this year (114 B.C.)
he counted all the years of his reign not only here, but
subsequently in Egypt.[3]

§ 236. It is not our task to follow in detail the fortunes
of the Egyptian princesses who were settled in foreign
countries.   The subsequent career of the divorced Cleopatra (IV.) was, however, so characteristic, that even the
hasty compendium of Justin delays over the exhibition of
such violent sisterly hate.   She offered herself, with her
riches, and a mercenary army raised in Cyprus, to Antiochus
Cyzicenus, who was struggling for the throne of Syria

[1] Unfortunately only the central portion of the stone, which was cut
vertically into three shafts, for lintel stones, or the like, is extant, and
so the beginnings and ends of all the lines are lost ; the lower portion
being moreover almost effaced.   For the fullest decipherment, cf. my
text in *Hermathena* xxii. with a commentary for the details, and for the
inferences which seem reasonable.

[2] E. Miller reports in the *BCH* for 1885, p. 145, the heading of a
similar granite stele, but only επι βασιλεως Πτ[and then θεου Φιλομητορος
επ[, so that it may belong to the first Philometor, and not to Philometor
Soter, as Lathyrus is usually called in inscriptions.   The Epistrategos
Phommous, whom the king calls his brother, was appealed to for justice
against the exactions of the fiscal steward Isidoros, by the pastophori
of the Amenophium over against Thebes four years later.   Cf. *Turin
Papyri* V-VII.

[3] Inscriptions in his honour, and part of a curious open letter to him
from an Antiochus (Grypus?) concerning the privileges of the 'sacred
asylum of the Seleucians in Pieria,' were found in Cyprus by the ex-
cavators of the temple of the Paphian Aphrodite, and published in the
Journ. Hell. Studies for 1888, p. 231.

with Antiochus Grypus, his brother, married to her sister Tryphaena. But falling into the hands of the latter, she was put to death promptly, and her new husband was only able to avenge her death by putting Tryphaena to death, when the reversed fortunes of war put her in his power. It must have been the personal wealth of these Egyptian princesses, Cleopatra, Tryphaena, and by and by Selene, which gave them the power of assembling armies, waging wars, and marrying royal claimants in the distracted Syria.

This was the period when the Maccabean dynasty, adopting the military organisation of the Hellenistic powers, and adding even some Hellenistic culture to their strong nationalistic policy, were extending the sway of the Jews over all the country which had been gradually filched from them by Syrian and Egyptian city-foundations. At this moment Hyrcanus was besieging Samaria, and Soter II., or Lathyrus, as Josephus consistently calls him, sent a force of 6000 men to help Antiochus Cyzicenus in relieving that hardly pressed city.[1] But this was opposed to the policy of the queen-mother who had two distinguished Jews, Chelkias and Ananias, the sons of Onias of Heliopolis, for her generals in Palestine, and these were doubtless acting in the interest of the Jews against the Samaritans.[2] So the succours of Lathyrus failed, and Samaria was taken and razed to the ground.

§ 237. It is quite possible that this interference of the king against the Jewish interests in Palestine threw the balance of power even at Alexandria into his mother's hands. It is moreover certain from the evidence of

[1] *Antiqq.* xiii. 10, § 2.

[2] Josephus, knowing well that he has been exaggerating the influence of the Jews in Hellenistic history, cites Strabo to establish the importance of Chelkias and Ananias at the Egyptian court.

coins, that during the period from his eighth to his eleventh year (110-7 B.C.), Lathyrus must have assumed the sole authority, for we have a change in the coinage of Egypt at that moment, the double cornucopiae and headdress of Isis disappearing, and the date being simply the year of Lathyrus.[1] Then, however, partly by intrigues, and partly by actual force, she set the populace against · him, and he was obliged to depart to Cyprus, from which his younger brother Ptolemy, also called Alexander, returned to Egypt and took the throne.[2]

It is remarkable that the building of temples to the national gods was not stayed by these dynastic quarrels. The great temple at Esneh shows the cartouches of these joint sovrans, and there are besides at Latopolis, over against it, remains of their work. They were busy at Edfu and at Philae.

§ 238. The further fortunes of the exiled Lathyrus are narrated to us by Josephus.[3] No sooner was he secure from his mother, than he turned his attention to Palestine and the coast of Philistia, where the Seleukids, owing to their protracted family quarrels, had lost all power, and the question remained whether the Hellenistic (mostly Ptolemaic) foundations in the country, and especially along the coast, could maintain themselves against the rising military power of the Maccabee despot Alexander Jannaeus. The

---

[1] This fact is clearly brought out in Mr. Poole's *Coins of the Ptolemies* pp. 107-8.

[2] *Antt.* xiii. 10, § 4. It is best to refer to this moment the statement of Justin (xxxix. 4), *nec filium regno expulisse contenta* [Cleopatra] *bello Cypri exulantem persequitur ; unde pulso interficit ducem exercitus sui, quod vivum eum e manibus dimisisset, quanquam Ptolemaeus verecundia materni belli non viribus minor ab insula recessisset.* Yet it was from Cyprus as a basis of operations that Lathyrus made his great expedition to the coast of Palestine, so that the narrative is hopelessly inconsistent.

[3] *op. cit.* xiii. 12.

course of the campaign is quite clear from Josephus, though the alleged numbers of the armies engaged are of course absurd. Ancient historians almost always deal with such numbers in a very liberal way. Lathyrus was the last Ptolemy who made the attempt to bring Palestine again under permanent Egyptian rule, and he would easily have succeeded in making for himself a strong position on the coast, but for the decision of the people of Ptolemais not to receive him as a friend, though they had but a choice between Egyptian and Jewish domination. They held out against him, and disappointed his first great hope. But it led to their own destruction. Ptolemy was indeed received at Gaza, and Jannaeus retired from his campaign with expressions of friendship towards Lathyrus. But the Maccabee was only gaining time while he sent to Cleopatra and the new king of Egypt to warn them that Lathyrus was about to make a kingdom in Palestine. So nearly was this true that Lathyrus, with the help of the tactician Philostephanos, inflicted a crushing defeat near the Jordan on Jannaeus, whose double dealing he had discovered. But then came Cleopatra with an army, her son Alexander with a fleet, and though Lathyrus tried a bold diversion upon Egypt, which he sought to invade from his stronghold Gaza, the war ended by his plans being completely foiled. The account of his cruelties to the inhabitants of the surrounding villages, after his great victory at the Jordan, is probably the exaggeration of some violences committed by his mercenaries.

§ 239. Alexander, counting his years of reign from his appointment at Cyprus, assumed the Egyptian throne in the eleventh year of Cleopatra, and his own nominal eighth (106 B.C.) Cleopatra,[1] who, upon the opening of her

---

[1] *op. cit.* xiii. 13, § 1.

campaign in Palestine, had felt the situation so grave that she sent her grandchildren with treasure and her will to safe keeping at Kos,[1] was now so powerful that she seemed able to subdue Jannaeus, and do what Lathyrus had failed to do,—to add Palestine to her dominions.   But the protests of the Egyptian Jews, possibly the fear of Roman interference, and insecurity at home, deterred her from this step.   She contented herself with marrying Selene, her younger daughter, and second wife of Lathyrus, whom she had taken from him, we know not how, to Antiochus Grypus, in order to keep open the quarrel between the Syrian claimants to the throne of Antioch. During the next seven years, Greek and Egyptian texts quote 'Queen Cleopatra and King Ptolemy, also called Alexander, gods Philometores, Soteres,' so that the titles already adopted by the queen and her elder son were not changed.

§ 240.   The best historians assign to 97-6 B.C. the death of Ptolemy Apion, the illegitimate son of Physkon, who left the kingdom of Cyrene by his will to the Roman people.   Nothing is more obscure than the life of this person.   We know not by what right he obtained the province, still less why the ambitious Cleopatra and her sons should never have made the least attempt to recover it.   For some twenty years he may have exemplified the adage, *bene qui latuit vixit.*   He seems to have left no mark, even upon the coinage of Cyrene.

When he bequeathed his kingdom to the Roman people, the hideous consequences of such a bequest to the

---

[1] Among these Egyptian regalia was an heirloom alleged to be the actual *chlamys* of Alexander the Great, which Pompey wore at his triumph over Mithradates, who had carried it off from Kos.   This is told by Appian as a story which he does not believe, *Mith.* 117.

province of Asia must already have been plain enough, for the intense hatred of Roman oppression, which found its expression in the great Mithradatic massacres, must have already been loud in the world. But for the moment, the Romans were so busy with their own quarrels that they actually left this rich source of plunder untouched, and the Cyrenean cities were allowed to enjoy the disorders of Greek liberty for a season.

§ 241. From the year 100 to 98 B.C., we find a young queen, known to modern historians as Berenike III., quoted sometimes with, sometimes without, the queen-mother. This princess was a daughter of Soter II. (Lathyrus) but is commonly held not to have been the first of the sisters [1] whom Alexander I. married. For his son Alexander II., who succeeded him, was ordered by the Romans, or rather by Sylla, to marry this very lady, who was his step-mother, the union of actual son and mother being intolerable even in those days, and in that society. The appearance of this young queen—she is called the 'only legitimate' daughter of Lathyrus, whatever that may mean—can with certainty be associated with the stories of the quarrels which broke out between mother and son so violently, that the latter, preferring a quiet life to perpetual danger, retired from the throne. As is conjectured by Letronne, the recognition of his wife Berenike in public acts may have been part of the compromise by which his mother induced him to return. But why Cleopatra could not rule without him, is what none of our authorities think fit to tell us. If the Jew Ananias (Chelkias had been killed in the war against Lathyrus) was indeed popular and powerful, it should have been his interest to

---

[1] Letronne thinks (*op. cit.* i. p. 70) she was a daughter not of Lathyrus, but of his father Physkon.

act for the queen his patroness alone. At all events, while documents of B.C. 99 and earlier cite the three royal names, those of 90 - 88 B.C. only mention Alexander and Berenike.[1] The evidence of the extant coins supplements this fact, for while down to 101 B.C. we have them with double dates thus $\angle\frac{IC}{I\Gamma}$, from the king's fourteenth year onward to his twenty-third they appear with his year of reign only. Thus it will be seen that the double dating on the papyri overlaps the single dating on the coins— quite a natural fact, for the scribes would go on copying a formula stupidly, even though part of it had become obsolete. Not so the coinage, which marks 101 B.C. as the date when Alexander's sole sovranty officially began.[2]

§ 242. But there are now texts known, not indeed contracts, where the king's name only appears. There is in Room 39 of the Gizeh museum a well-cut inscription on a slab of black granite dated in the twentieth year (94 B.C.) of 'Ptolemy also called Alexander the god Philometor' Lysanias being Strategus and over the revenue of the Arsinoite nome, in which the Oeconomus Aniketos is stated to have given a tax from his own salary and those of his subordinates of half an artaba of wheat daily to the temple of the mighty god Soknopaios, with the further

---

[1] Cf. Lepsius, in Berlin *Abh.* p. 483 and Letronne *Recueil* i. pp. 52 *sq.*, who here agree in their chronology. I am not disposed to lay as much stress as Lepsius does upon the appearance or non-appearance of a third name in the dating of legal documents. It is quite likely that people at Memphis or Thebes may either have copied a heading which had recently become technically obsolete, or may have forgotten to put in a third name, where it ought to have appeared. Thus the occurrence of Berenike proves something, the occasional omission of Cleopatra very little indeed.

[2] Cf. *Coins of the Ptolemies* p. 113.

direction that all his successors in office shall do the same.[1]

This local god Soknopaios is identical with Souchos, who is the Sobk, or crocodile god of the district, and to him are most, if not all, the dedications which have been brought from the Fayyum.

There is one dated in the year 19 of the same king, similarly described, at Gizeh ; another now in the library of Trinity College, Dublin, dated year 16, almost identical in expression—both white limestone cippi with the god Souchos depicted as a crocodile adorned with the *pshent*,—marking the boundaries of the τόπος or locale of a company of ephebi. This Attic custom of *epheby*, which became so prominent in the third century B.C. at Athens, and elsewhere in Greek lands, seems therefore to have made its way now into Egypt, as far as the Arsinoite nome. In the Petrie Papyri of 150 years earlier there is no trace of it, nor indeed of the local gods, save once of Souchos and Arsinoe.[2] These clubs are described

---

[1] υπερ βασ. Πτολ. | του και Αλεξ. θεου Φιλο|μητ. και Λυσανιου του | συγγενους και στρατηγου | και επι των προσοδων του Αρ|σινοιτου Λκ αθυρ ȝ | επ᾽ Ανικητου οικονομου σιτικων | της Ηρακλ. μεριδος κατηρ|τισθη διδοσθαι παρα τε εαυτου | και των υπασχολουμενων εν | τηι οικονομιαι δια της μεριδος | κατ ενιαυτον απαρχην εις το | ιερον του μεγιστου θεου Σοκνο|παιου πυρου

Αρτ ρπβ∠ κτλ. Very similar is the stele now in Berlin, which comes from Dimeh, and which has been published and discussed by Krebs in the Göttingen *Nachrichten* for December 1892, and also in the *Z. für Aeg.* vol. xxxi. pp. 31 *sq.*, cf. my comments on the two texts in *Hermathena* No. xxi. In this case the temple of Dimeh, hitherto unidentified, was dedicated to Soknopaios and Isis under a new and strange name. Krebs quotes from Brugsch the identification of the two names of Sobk, the longer being in Egyptian *Souk, the Lord of the island*. And accordingly the present Dimeh, when the lake was far higher, was an island, and so known in the district as Σοκνοπαιου νῆσος.

[2] Cf. *Pet. Pap.* I. p. 70, according to Wilcken's correction.

as of those who have been ephebi their second year, and belong to the *heresy* of Asklepiades, or of Ammonios, whatever that special term afterwards so notorious in philosophy and theology (as a *sect*) may here signify. The size of the plot is then given in measures from east to west and from north to south, 'up to the road,' or the drying place.[1] Thus we find, both in a binding ordinance of the state, and in texts of private character, the same omission of the queen Berenike, whose name in papyri of the very same year 16, and in one of the year 26,[2] is carefully given. In the reply annexed to the former, she is even called the goddess Philadelphus.

§ 243. These texts are worth quoting not only for the sake of their dates, but because they show a distinctly Greek fashion maintained in the very Hellenistic settlement of the Fayyum province, which seems like a reaction against the Egyptianising of the Greeks during the last reign.

As regards papyri on the law business of the natives, we are exceptionally rich at this moment. In addition to the papyri Mr. Grenfell has obtained in the spring of 1895, which are contracts with dates (not yet published), a whole series of the Leiden Papyri G–O are of this reign (*circa* 100-90 B.C.), and so is the great Casati papyrus[3] in the Paris collection. But none of them gives us any information regarding public affairs, though these contracts point to the fact that law and order prevailed in the upper country, and that the rights of property were not disturbed.

---

[1] υπερ | βασ. Πτολ. του | επικαλουμενου Αλεξ. | Σουχωι θεωι μεγαλωι | μεγαλωι τοπο[s] των | το βL εφηβευκοτων | της Αμμωνιου αιρεσεως | ου
μετρα νοτου επι βορραν | ιγ λιβος επ απηλιωτην | εως ψυγμου[$\overset{\mu}{}$] Lıs φα ια. This is the Dublin stele. For explanations cf. *Hermathena* xxi.

[2] Pap. G and H of the Leiden collection.

[3] So also the papyrus of Nechutes (105 B.C.) at Berlin.

Pausanias, in his brief sketch of Cleopatra III. and her two sons, says that the Athenians, on account of various kindnesses not worth specifying, had set up at Athens bronze statues of Soter II. and his daughter Berenike, who was 'his only legitimate child.' Apart from the odd expression, why should they choose the king and his daughter, who was married to Alexander? Seeing that both kings were known by the same titles, and the latter only distinguished by the τοῦ καὶ Ἀλεξάνδρου, which may possibly have been omitted, I take this dedication to have been in this case to Alexander and his queen, and to be another hint of the Hellenic tendency, just noted as existing in the Fayyum.

Do we want a third? Cleopatra sends her grandchildren and treasure to Kos, so that the children of this very Alexander are put into Hellenic keeping, and if they were still young enough (which is doubtful), committed to Hellenic instructors in a purely Greek city. But if Pausanias be correct it only shows that Soter II. was of the same way of thinking.

And yet the hieroglyphic account of the building of the great Edfu temple begins with praise of this very king Alexander I., who built the magnificent circuit-wall, planned, but not carried out, in the end of Physkon's reign. It was at this period, and by both the kings, that the structure was completed (Auletes only added doors), and the circuit-wall in particular, with its elaborate historical and geographical texts, is still one of the finest and most perfect things in Egypt. It is also certain that the crypts of the temple of Denderah, finished by Cleopatra VI., were commenced, according to an ancient plan, by the tenth and eleventh Ptolemies. Their Hellenic tendencies, therefore, did not induce them to reverse the consistent policy of the whole dynasty to spend a vast amount of treasure in building and endowing temples to the national gods.

§ 244. We left Alexander in voluntary exile, and his mother seeking to recall him. But he evidently thought it was only a plot to secure his death. He made a successful counterplot, and got rid of this desperate queen, whose long career is one hardly to be paralleled in any other civilised society. Perhaps among the despots of the Italian Renaissance we might find a princess as daring and as unscrupulous, but not successful for forty-five years ! [1]

It would appear from the form of Pausanias' statement, that Alexander's crime was only discovered after a time,[2] while the fragments of Porphyry indicate that this author did not believe Cleopatra to have been murdered, for he speaks simply of her death as the time from which onward Alexander's name appeared alone in official documents. This agrees with the texts cited above, and would place her death perhaps as far back as his sixteenth year. Porphyry also attributes his exile to a quarrel he had with his army. Possibly the charge of murdering his mother was only trumped up against him then ; at all events he was obliged to fly from Alexandria (88 B.C.) and make way for his long-exiled brother Lathyrus, who returned with many expressions of good-will from the fickle populace, now called by them ποθεινός—the Desired.[3] His gentleness in not

---

[1] There is no good reason to call her Cleopatra Cocce, as Sharpe does, though the *Chron. Pasch.* p. 347, 13 says it was her nickname. The passage in Strabo, ὁ Κόκκης καὶ Παρείσακτος ἐπικληθεὶς Πτολ., rather points to the king being called *Cocces.*

[2] i. 9, 3 τοῦ δὲ ἔργου φωραθέντος κτλ.

[3] The *Chron. Pasch.* p. 347, 15 says he was called ὁ ἐξωσθείς, which I do not believe any more than that Alexander I. was called παρείσακτος. This latter term could only refer to a spurious claimant.

warring directly against his unnatural mother is noted as exceptional in that age when filial piety was an obsolete virtue.   This gentleness did not cause him to prevent the close pursuit of Alexander by the Egyptian forces under Pyrrhus, a Peer of the Realm (συγγένους τοῦ βασιλέως), who first defeated Alexander on sea, and drove him with his wife and daughter to Thyra in Lycia, from whence he crossed to Cyprus, only to be killed in battle by Chaereas, the naval commander of that station.   The only personal notice of him from Posidonius [1] is perhaps borrowed from Physkon.   It is said he was so fat that he walked with men supporting him on either side.   Almost every Ptolemy was fat, but almost every Ptolemy was also very active.

§ 245. The close of Ptolemy Alexander's life, his relations to his mother and to the Alexandrians, are so confused in our only authorities, Justin, Porphyry, Pausanias, that it is worth while to attempt a theoretical reconstruction of the whole story.   The army, the Jews, now very powerful, and probably the populace of Alexandria were strongly in favour of the queen-mother, whose overbearing and tyrannical conduct to her once favourite son did not, we may be sure, soften with age.   Hence Alexander began to find life there so intolerable that he ' left Egypt,' or retired, no one tells us whither,[2] for the sake of peace, but still to some place from which the queen-mother is most anxious to call him back.   This must

[1] *FHG* iii. 265.

[2] That it was to Syria is only an inference from Strabo xvii. 1, § 8, which passage probably refers to a different person. ' Leaving Egypt' might well be a loose phrase for leaving Alexandria and lower Egypt for Nubia and the upper country.   It is also highly improbable that a king who had already reigned at Alexandria for many years should choose this moment for plundering the golden coffin of Alexander the Great.   To this last fact I shall revert, § 256.

have been Upper Egypt, probably Thebes, where he began, or was suspected of beginning, another national revolution. Hence he only returns upon special terms, and why? Not to murder his mother, who probably died from natural causes, but because he wished to organise a naval attack upon Alexandria with an army of mercenaries, while the natives rose in the south. This was the policy which so enraged the Alexandrians, that they not only rose against him, but promptly pursued him by sea, and conquered him in a naval battle (Porphyry), which implies that he had already collected some power. They even pursued him to the death, and hastened to summon back Lathyrus, for the insurrection in the upper country was not allayed, but was bursting into flame. Had Ptolemy Alexander been given time to gather an army in the north to bring against Egypt (which Porphyry says he intended to do) he would have subdued Alexandria, and possibly treated it as Physkon had done, if not as his brother presently treated Thebes.

This combination of the main facts would at least give us a logical narrative, instead of the random statements which previous historians have essayed to use, and which I felt obliged to repeat. If what I have here suggested be sound, new arguments will no doubt, in due time, confirm it. Meanwhile I commend it to those who make this period their special study.

§ 246. Porphyry adds that as soon as Alexander had fled, Soter was formally invited by the Alexandrians to resume the throne, which he held for seven and a half years longer (up to 81 B.C.) We are also told by Porphyry that he returned 'from Cyprus.' The last fact we heard about him was that he was driven from that island, barely escaping with his life, by his mother in 107 B.C. Where had he been living, and what had he been doing in this long interval? If we assume his pursuit by his mother Cleopatra, and his expulsion from Cyprus to have taken place after his campaign in Palestine, we should be obliged to consider him a wandering exile for nineteen years. But the deliberate closing of that war without any decisive success on either side, points to a compromise, according to which Lathyrus returned to Cyprus. Coins of his found there, and dated from his eighteenth to his twenty-first years (99-6 B.C.), make this inference quite certain, though our remaining historical notices do not confirm it. Possibly he visited Athens during this period, and became a favourite in that city. Rome was all the while torn with such dissensions, that it was hardly a place of agreeable resort for an Eastern king.

At all events, his return to the sovranty of Egypt was almost synchronous with the invasion of Asia Minor by Mithradates, and the great massacre of the Italians in Asia (88 B.C.) which reminds us of the *Sicilian Vespers*. When the Pontic king controlled the Aegean he found at Kos the Egyptian princes and the treasure which Cleopatra III. had deposited there, and is said to have seized[1] some or all of the treasure, while he kept with him in royal state the prince Alexander, now the next male heir to the throne of Egypt.[2]

§ 247. The reappearance of Roman armies going with Sylla to the East lifts the veil which has so long lain over our Egyptian history. Sylla, though having success in Greece, found himself unable to cope with the Pontic king without a fleet, and accordingly (87 B.C.) sent his able and active lieutenant, Lucullus, to raise one in all haste. But

---

[1] Appian *Mith.* 115 says the Koans gave him what had been entrusted to them. [2] Appian *Mith.* 23.

so distracted was Rome, and so doubtful her future, that naval assistance could not be exacted by her, nor was it offered by her Eastern allies, who were watching in suspense the issue of her trials in foreign war coupled with home dis-sension. So[1] when Lucullus made his way with great risk of capture from pirates to the coast of Africa, his mission was to *persuade* the allies of Rome to send him help of their own accord. Coercion he was unable to apply. Passing from Crete to Cyrene, he found this group of cities, which had been allowed to drift their own way since the death of Ptolemy Apion, in confusion from constant tyrannies and dissensions. They desired him to act as umpire, a pro-posal which he must have received with no little impatience; for he had come to find ships for Sylla, not to spend his time in mongering constitutions for idle Greeks. Instead of drawing them up laws, he told them that they were too rich to expect to live in peace, and hurried on to Egypt. He lost most of his boats on the way through pirates, but arrived safely at Alexandria, where his advent was expected. For a whole fleet went out to meet him, in the state array then customary for receiving a royal visit, and Lathyrus even showed the young Roman the unheard-of attention of establishing him as a guest in one of the royal palaces. We hear from *Aristeas' letter* that in older days there was a special officer of state to receive distinguished strangers, and attend to their comforts in some public house of reception. In this case the king added an allowance for his maintenance four times greater than what was tradi-tional, and sent him presents worth 800 talents, which Lucullus refused. They must have been gifts which could not or dare not be turned into money, for Sylla's war-chest was too low to despise such help.

[1] The narrative which follows is from Plutarch's *Lucullus*.

It is also plain from Plutarch's narrative that Lucullus was pressed to go up the country and see Memphis and its splendours, but he said that he was no idle tourist, but a lieutenant who had left his chief encamped in the open air before a hostile city. Beyond profuse civilities, however, Lathyrus would not go. He declined to help Rome, and merely pressed upon his guest a precious seal-ring (which Lucullus was loth to refuse), and sent ships to escort him to Cyprus.

§ 248. With the adventures of Lucullus we have no more concern, and Lathyrus took no further part in the Mithradatic war, his attention being absorbed by a great revolt in Upper Egypt, which cost him three years to subdue. No details are preserved beyond the signal fact, that Thebes, as a city, and a centre of national life, was destroyed, its fortifications were razed, and the population henceforth obliged to live κωμηδόν, or in distinct villages.[1] The conflict must therefore have been severe and critical, and the policy of preferring Memphis to Thebes, which we noticed in the reign of Epiphanes, here found its last expression. Whether the priests of Ptah were jealous enough of those of Amon to set the king against them, we do not know. If theological spites were as they now are, we may suspect that these rivals hated one another more than they did the foreigners who had usurped the power and privileges of both. Thebes henceforth disappears from the list of Egyptian cities, though its gigantic temples survived, and have lasted to our own days, as a monument of its whilome splendour. A very

---

[1] This is the more remarkable as extant inscriptions on the so-called small temple of Tothmes III., at Thebes, and at Medamut in the vicinity, show that this king had built a pylon and added other ornaments to this temple, thus keeping up the tradition of the old Egyptian dynasties.

curious inscription of this time has turned up among the
Paphian inscriptions published by three English scholars.[1]

In 81 B.C. Ptolemy Soter II. (Lathyrus) died, we know
not from what cause.   He was an elderly man, probably
sixty years old, or even more.   He leaves upon us an

impression more agreeable than the
other later kings, and seems in many
points like his uncle Philometor
(Ptolemy VII.)   There is the same
gentleness and absence of cruelty, the
same tendency to avoid diplomatic
difficulties by social amenities, yet
when occasion served him he fought
his enemies with the sword, and not
with procrastination.   We know too
little of him to draw a more definite
picture, but he is one of the series
whom we should willingly know better,
and whose virtues should be insisted

PTOLEMY XI.

upon in the face of those who brand the whole dynasty
as steeped in vice and crime.[2]

[1] In the *JHS* ix. p. 240

Αφροδιτηι Παφιαι | η πο]λις η Παφιων Ονησανδρον Ναυσικρατους | τον
σ]υνγενη και ιερεα δια βιου βασιλεως Πτολεμαι|ου θεου σω|τηρος και του
ιδρυμενου υπ αυτου ιερου Πτολε|μαιειου τον] γραμματεα της Παφιων πολεως
τεταγμενον δε | επι της εν Α]λεξανδρειαι μεγαλης βυβλιοθηκης ευνοιας |
ενεκεν.

Here is a Chief Librarian never yet heard of !

[2] This judgment differs widely from that of Gutschmid (Sharpe ii. 5),
who thinks that he was praised by partial historians to the detriment of
his mother and brother, and that the adverse judgment of Porphyry is
based on more trustworthy sources.

COIN OF CLEOPATRA III.

CHAPTER XII

BERENIKE III. AND PTOLEMY XII. (ALEXANDER II.) 81 B.C.,
PTOLEMY XIII. (AULETES) 81-52 B.C.

§ 249. UPON the death of Soter II., his eldest daughter
Berenike (III.), widow of his brother Alexander, who
was the legitimate heir, ascended the throne with the
consent of the Alexandrians, as is the usual phrase in
these days. The rest of the country seems to count for
nothing in the eyes of Hellenistic historians. For six
months, according to Porphyry, she reigned alone, but at
the end of that period, the son of her former husband by
another wife, Ptolemy Alexander II., the prince whom
Mithradates had found at Kos, and treated royally, but who
had escaped to Rome, was sent back from there by Sylla,[1]
or was called by the Alexandrians, to a share in the throne.
Porphyry states it in the latter way—μετάκλητος ἦλθεν
εἰς 'A.—but there is indirect evidence of the former in the
second speech of Cicero against Rullus (c. 16), who says
that the king had made a will leaving his kingdom to the
Roman people. When he arrived in Egypt, he succeeded
in marrying the queen his stepmother, owing no doubt to

[1] Appian *Bell. Civ.* i. 102.

strong pressure upon her either in Alexandria or from
Rome ; but he is said to have murdered her nineteen days
after, and he himself fell a victim at once to the vengeance
of her household troops.[1]   The will therefore, if genuine,
must have been made or promised as a bribe by the new
king to his Roman supporters, and yet at this moment Sylla
was dictator, and not at all the man to enter upon or permit
so disgraceful a bargain.   But the fact that there was such
a will was doubted, says Cicero, though the king's private
money, deposited at Tyre, was actually taken possession
of, according to the alleged testament.   'We sent ambassadors,' says Cicero, 'to recover the money he had deposited
for our people.'   But Cicero avoids giving us his opinion
on the transaction ; his only point is that under the law
proposed by Rullus, this and other very doubtful questions
will be settled off-hand, and without discussion, by the new
court of decemvirs for realising the property of the Roman
people.   I think the evidence is against any such will in
this case.   It was doubted even in the case of the last
Attalus.   Here it seems like a bold attempt to claim the
rich Egypt for another prize such as the province of Asia.
At all events, there followed no practical assertion of the
Roman claims beyond the seizing of the money at Tyre.[2]

---

[1] It is remarkable that Appian (*Bell. Civ.* i. 102), in telling the facts,
seems ignorant of Berenike's murder, viz. ἀλλὰ τὸν μὲν οἱ Ἀλεξανδρεῖς,
ιθ ἡμέραν ἔχοντα τῆς ἀρχῆς, καὶ ἀποπώτερον σφῶν, οἷα Σύλλᾳ πεποιθότα,
ἐξηγούμενον, ἐς τὸ γυμνάσιον ἐκ τοῦ βασιλείου προαγαγόντες ἔκτειναν—
probably a military revolt, caused by a refusal to grant a large present
of money to the household troops.

[2] It is argued by Cless (Pauly *Real-Encyc.* art. PTOLEMAEUS, p.
226) and more fully by Clinton (*Fasti* iii. p. 392) that the Ptolemy who
left his kingdom by will to Rome was not Alexander II., but another
claimant, whom he calls Alexas, or Alexander III., who was not set
up till 66 B.C., and died in exile at Tyre in 65 B.C.   But I cannot find
that the passages which Cless cites can be all verified, or that they carry

§ 250. With this double assassination, the legitimate succession of the Lagidae became extinct. Yet there were both princes and princesses alive who could have claimed the throne under any modern laws of succession. I cannot but think that the constant assertion of the illegitimacy of Egyptian princes and princesses was an invention of Hellenistic historians in the interest of the Romans. So now it seems that what is called a natural son of Lathyrus, Ptolemy Auletes in our histories, who had been also living in Syria, and knew the conditions of the game he had to play, assumed the derelict sovranty, without any active intervention of the Romans, and with the approval of the native population. This latter may be safely inferred from the absence of any internal revolution, and from the character of the inscriptions at Philae, which date from the early years (second to eighth) of his reign.

They are all dedications to Isis, the special goddess of Philae, by visitors to her shrine, quite similar to those of Roman officers in subsequent times at Dakkeh and Kalabsheh in Nubia. In these the king appears as the young Dionysus, φιλοπάτωρ and φιλάδελφος: and in his twelfth year, a dedication by the πάρεδρος Lysimachus includes his queen and his children. But this is not all. One of these texts is dedicated by an officer who is still entrusted with the Red Sea coast down to Ethiopia.[1]

out his view, which has not been accepted by later critics. Mommsen *Röm. Gesch.* iii. 51, note, even discusses the opinions of those (Niebuhr, etc.) who hold that the will was made by Alexander I. in his exile. But as he rightly says, it was only the last legitimate heir who had even an ostensible right to bequeath his kingdom. There is an excellent note on the various possibilities of the question by Gutschmid in Sharpe ii. 17 (Germ. ed.) Cicero says plainly that the will was made after the Consuls of 88 B.C., in which year, if not sooner, Alexander I. was dead.

[1] Letronne II. lxxii. Καλλιμαχος | ο συγγενης και επι|στρατηγος και στρα|τηγος της Ινδικης | και ερυθρας θαλασσης | ηκω προς την κυριαν Ισιν

From this we may assume that his power really extended to the southern limits of Ptolemaic Egypt. But except that from his title have been inferred his devotion to the cult of Dionysus and his consequent excesses, nothing is known of his early years. Syria was helpless; the Romans too busy with home troubles, with the approaching Spanish and pirate wars, and the threatening conflict with Mithradates, to interfere with him, or oust him from his kingdom. On the other hand he obtained from the Senate no formal recognition, though he sought it with many intrigues, and of course with bribes.

§ 251. The year 75 B.C. brought on the impending crisis in the East. For there Nikomedes III., the last king of Bithynia, bequeathed his kingdom to the Romans, who now made no delay, and not only took possession of the bequest at once, but made good their negligence concerning Cyrene, which had remained *in statu quo* since 96 B.C., by sending thither a Roman governor. These steps drove Mithradates to declare his second war against .Rome (74 B.C.) Even then, with the will of Ptolemy Alexander for their title, the Romans did not seize the richer prize, which would have been so valuable in supplying food and pay to their Eastern armies, apparently, as Mommsen says,[1] because it was the interest of powerful individuals to keep up the weak rulers in Egypt who supplied them with a veritable income in bribes; still more because it was the interest of the tottering oligarchy not to let so powerful and isolated a kingdom pass into the hands of any ambitious leader, who would use it against the rest, and so overthrow the senatorial régime.

| και πεποηκα το προσκυνημα | του κυριου βασιλεως θεου | νεου Διονυσου φιλοπατορος | [και φιλ]αδελφου | ∠θ παχων ε̄. The same officer is called θηβαρχης της Θηβαιδος in addition, ibid. lxxiii.   [1] *RG* iii. 51.

§ 252. Meanwhile Auletes continued to reign without recognition, but without interference from Rome. He married a Cleopatra (V.), surnamed Tryphaena, by whom he had children, but possibly she was not his first wife,[1] though it is more likely that this princess was the mother of his heiress-daughter Berenike, and not of Cleopatra (VI.)   Probably in 77 B.C. this eldest daughter Berenike (IV.) was born, another of the typical Egyptian princesses, as we shall presently see.   It appears from Cicero[2] that in the year 72, two Syrian princes, the sons of the Egyptian princess Selene and of Antiochus Grypus,[3] came to Rome, not to make any claim upon Syria, but upon Egypt, to which they asserted a better right than Auletes.   But they failed to move the Senate, *temporibus reipublicae exclusi*, and one of them, Antiochus, returning by way of Sicily, was robbed of a magnificent present, which he had intended for the Senate, by Verres.   Within a few years of this date, but not (I think) before 68 B.C.,[4] was born Auletes' second and most famous daughter, the Cleopatra who well nigh changed the course of the world. There were three other younger children, an Arsinoe, and two sons, who both came to the throne with their sister, and who must have been born before 64 B.C., in which year at latest they were betrothed to two daughters, Mithradatis and Nyssa, of Mithradates.[5]   It is the gap in age between Berenike and the rest which makes us suspect that Auletes may have married a second wife, who was the mother of the latter children, and there are not wanting statements that the great Cleopatra was

---

[1] It has been shown by Lepsius that he was already married to the princess Cleopatra Tryphaena in his third year, from an Egyptian text.

[2] *in Verrem* ii. 4, 27.   [3] Above, § 239.

[4] Clinton iii. 394 says the close of 69.   [5] Appian *Mith.* iii.

'illegitimate.' But we have no positive evidence of any second marriage.

§ 253. The course of the third Mithradatic war probably opened the eyes of the leading men at Rome to the necessity of absorbing the rich land of Egypt to meet their financial difficulties. In 65 B.C. Crassus, as censor, relying on the alleged will, proposed the reducing of Egypt to a Roman province, and was only baulked by the determined resistance of his colleague Catulus, who felt outraged at this wanton and barefaced proposal to plunder an old ally of Rome.[1] In the following year Julius Caesar, then aedile, asked the people to put it under his charge,[2] and if this had indeed been done, he would have conquered the republic in a far different way than from the snows of Gaul. Hardly a year after came the bolder proposal of the tribune Rullus, to appoint decemvirs, who should discover and valuate the property of the Roman people, without limit of authority, for the purposes of an agrarian law. Cicero, in discussing the project, assumes that the plunder of Egypt will be one of their first objects. The claim would be based on the will of the prince Ptolemy Alexander, which was a doubtful one, and the whole future of Egypt would depend upon the good pleasure (*i.e.* the corruptibility) of Rullus.[3]

---

[1] Plutarch *Crassus* 13. The king was not yet expelled by his people. It is to this discussion that Mommsen rightly refers the speech of Cicero *de rege Alex.*, which would have been idle after the decree in Caesar's consulship, and yet Mommsen is misled by Suetonius (*RG* iii. 177, which does not agree with p. 163).

[2] Cf. Suetonius *Caesar* c. 11, who adds that he made the proposal on the ground that the people of Alexandria had expelled their king, formally named ally and friend by the Roman Senate. But both this recognition, and the expulsion of Auletes, took place several years later.

[3] Quid Alexandria cunctaque Aegyptus ? ut occulte latet ! ut recondita est ! ut furtim tota decemviris traditur ! Quis enim vestrum hoc

But even in this bold bill the seizure of Egypt by the Roman tax-farmers was not openly asserted; it was tacitly implied, with the hope that the measure might pass without criticism of so grave a consequence.

In the face of these dangers, Auletes had merely made the foolish countermove of accepting Mithradates' offer of a double alliance, which was set aside by that king's defeat and death in 63 B.C.[1]

ignorat, dici illud regnum testamento regis Alexandri populi Romani esse factum? Hic ego consul populi Romani non modo nihil iudico, sed ne quid sentiam quidem profero. Magna enim mihi res non modo ad statuendum, sed etiam ad dicendum videtur esse. Video, qui testamentum factum esse confirmet : auctoritatem senatus exstare hereditatis aditae sentio, tum quando, Alexandro mortuo, legatos Tyrum misimus, qui ab illo pecuniam depositam nostris recuperarent. Haec L. Philippum saepe in senatu confirmasse memoria teneo ; eum, qui regnum illud teneat hoc tempore, neque genere, neque animo regio esse, inter omnes fere video convenire. Dicitur contra, nullum esse testamentum : non oportere populum Romanum omnium regnorum appetentem videri : demigraturos in illa loca nostros homines, propter agrorum bonitatem et omnium rerum copiam. Hac tanta de re P. Rullus cum ceteris decemviris, collegis suis, iudicabit? et verum iudicabit ? Nam utrumque ita magnum est, ut nullo modo neque concedendum neque ferendum sit. Volet esse popularis : populo Romano adiudicabit. Ergo idem ex sua lege vendet Alexandriam, vendet Aegyptum : urbis copiosissimae pulcherrimorumque agrorum iudex, arbiter, dominus, rex denique opulentissimi regni reperietur. Non sumet sibi tantum, non appetet ? iudicabit, Alexandriam regis esse, a populo Romano abiudicabit. Primum populi Romani hereditatem decemviri iudicent, quum vos volueritis de privatis hereditatibus centumviros iudicare? Deinde quis aget caussam populi Romani? Ubi res ista agetur? Qui sunt isti decemviri, quos perspiciamus regnum Alexandriae Ptolemaeo gratis adiudicaturos? Quod si Alexandria petebatur, cur non eosdem cursus hoc tempore, quos L. Cotta, L. Torquato consulibus, cucurrerunt? cur non aperte, ut antea? cur non item, ut quum directo et palam regionem illam petierunt? an Quirites ii, qui per cursum rectum regnum tenere non potuerunt, nunc taetris tenebris et caligine se Alexandriam perventuros arbitrati sunt?

[1] There were not indeed wanting Eastern politicians, who thought Rome bankrupt, and Mithradates the winning horse, and in the case

When Pompey was settling the affairs of all the East, he had many invitations to include Egypt. But he did not enter this country, says Appian,—though the people were in insurrection against the king, and though the king also asked him to come, and sent gifts of money and clothes to all the army—whether from fear of the envy of the gods, or of his enemies, or for other reasons which Appian promises to tell in his (lost) Egyptian history.

§ 254. But continued bribing had its effect, and though Auletes could not obtain his public recognition from Pompey in 63-2 B.C., he obtained it from Julius Caesar as consul in 59. But it was only in return for huge promises of money! His brother, Ptolemy of Cyprus, though he had the money in his coffers, would not part with it; and so in the following year a decree of the democratic party, moved by the villain Clodius, seized the rich island under pretence of its participation in piracy, and sent the rigid Cato to perform a duty which filled him with rage and humiliation. But resistance to a Roman commissioner, even so gentle and considerate as Cato,[1] and without an army, was impossible; the king took poison, and his treasure of 7000 talents passed into the Roman treasury— a strong incitement to repeat such measures elsewhere. But the people of Alexandria rose in indignation. The king had not helped his brother; he had allowed the Romans to make another experiment, which must lead to the absorption of Egypt; his nominal recognition had not been obtained, or rather bought, without oppressive taxation. The series of his coins leads us to believe that among the causes of Alexandrian indignation was the

of Egypt he had apparently taken up the young prince Alexander II. as a threat to Lathyrus, twenty years sooner. Cf. the note of Gutschmid in Sharpe ii. 14.   [1] Plutarch *Cato* 34-37.

debasement of his silver coinage, which sank to a condition quite disgraceful among the issues of the Lagidae.   In his second reign, after his return, there is a considerable improvement, in spite of the extortions of Rabirius.   This must have been caused by the fear of a new revolt.[1]   So it came that in 58 B.C. he was driven from his kingdom, and took refuge, like every such exile, in the centre of all the political intrigues of the world, in Rome.   On his way he called at Cyprus to see Cato, and Plutarch gives us a graphic account of the conference between the Stoic magnate and the dissolute king.

In the meantime, Ptolemy, king of Egypt, who had left Alexandria, upon some quarrel between him and his subjects, and was sailing for Rome, in hopes that Pompey and Caesar would send troops to restore him, on his way thither desired to see Cato, to whom he sent, supposing he would come to him.   Cato had taken purging medicine at the time when the messenger came, and make answer, that Ptolemy had better come to him, if he thought fit.   And when he came, he neither went forward to meet him, nor so much as rose up to him, but saluting him as an ordinary person, bade him sit down. This at once threw Ptolemy into some confusion, who was surprised to see such stern and haughty manners in one who made so plain and unpretending an appearance ; but afterwards, when the king began to talk about his affairs, he was no less astonished at the wisdom and freedom of his discourse.   For Cato blamed his conduct, and pointed out to him what honour and happiness he was abandoning, and what humiliations and troubles he would run himself into ; what bribery he must resort to and what cupidity he would have to satisfy when he came to the leading men at Rome, whom all Egypt turned into silver would scarcely content.   He therefore advised him to return home, and be reconciled to his subjects, offering to go along with him, and assist him in composing the differences. And by this language Ptolemy being brought to himself, as it

[1] I draw this inference from the facts stated in *Coins of the Ptolemies* p. lxxx.

2 F

might be out of a fit of madness or delirium, and discerning
the truth and wisdom of what Cato said, resolved to follow his
advice; but he was again over-persuaded by his friends to the
contrary, and so, according to his first design, went to Rome.
When he came there, and was forced to wait at the gate of
one of the magistrates, he began to lament his folly, in having
rejected, rather, as it seemed to him, the oracle of a god, than
the advice merely of a good and wise man.

Being separated from his treasury and his fellahs, whom
he could no longer tax, Auletes had recourse to borrowing
large sums of money at Rome from one Rabirius Postumus,
a knight and tax-farmer, who no doubt lent at exorbitant
interest upon so doubtful a security.

§ 255. The formal demand of Auletes was that he,
though declared to be a friend and ally of the Roman
people, had been driven out by his subjects, and that
he should be restored again by the proconsul Lentulus
Spinther, who had obtained Cilicia as his province. The
Alexandrians, says Appian, were for a time ignorant of his
movements, and even thought that he was dead, which was
their excuse for setting up his daughter Berenike as queen.[1]
But when they learned where he was, and what he was
doing, they sent an embassy of 100 men to Rome, to
defend themselves, and make countercharges against the
king. This embassy he met by various counterplots.
Some, before they reached Rome, he sent to diverse
destinations. (We cannot understand why they obeyed
him.) Many of them he had assassinated on their journey,
or upon their arrival, and the rest he either cowed or
bribed into silence. The matter became so notorious that
there was a motion before the Senate to inquire into both
the alleged assassination and the bribery, and the head of

---

[1] But this implies a year's delay, as his wife Tryphaena ruled till her
death. Appian is therefore probably wrong here.

the embassy, the philosopher Dio, who had so far escaped, was summoned before the Senate. But the money of Auletes still prevailed, and his henchmen in the Senate baulked the inquiry. Presently even Dio was murdered, a fact attested by Cicero,[1] and yet though the fact was notorious, the influence of Pompey prevented any inquiry. The king seems to have openly asserted his right to slay a revolting subject, and kept bribing the Senators as before.

The accident of lightning striking the statue of Jupiter in the Alban Mount, however, upset his calculations and adjourned the fulfilment of his hopes. For superstition came to the aid of honesty, and from the Sibylline books a prophecy was produced saying: 'if a king of Egypt comes asking for aid, deny him not friendship, but do not assist him with numbers; if ye do, ye will have trouble and danger.' The surprising aptness of this prophecy led the people, not to suspect its genuineness, but to follow Cato as tribune, and rescind all their votes (what were they?) in favour of the king. But then there arose a further controversy about publishing the oracle in Latin, and more discussions about the king.

It appears from Cicero,[2] that while there was a general opinion in favour of restoring the king, there was great disagreement how it should be effected, lest the fortunate restorer might make it an occasion of seizing the country. Hence a committee of three was proposed; some excluding Pompey as already too powerful, etc. etc. After long discussions no decision was made, and the king retired in disgust to live in the temple at Ephesus, till he could persuade some party leader to do what the Senate would not determine.[3]

---

[1] *pro Coelio* § 23.　　　　　[2] *Epp. ad Fam.* i. 1-8.
[3] Dio xxxix. 16, and Plutarch *Pompey* 49.

§ 256. Meanwhile Cleopatra (V.) Tryphaena, whom some authorities call his eldest daughter, but who was certainly his wife, assumed the sole throne during one year, at the end of which she died, and her eldest daughter Berenike (IV.) became queen—the other children being apparently as yet infants, or under age. She ruled for two years (57-6 B.C.) and during that time showed that she possessed all the talents and daring of her race. She observed no restraint, even though she was in imminent danger from Rome, but sent for a Seleukos of the royal house of Syria to be her husband,[1] and share her throne and the conflict with her father. But no sooner did she find that he was an insignificant person, and moreover a man of vulgar manners[2] —the Alexandrians called him *Kybiosaktes*, the pickled-fish monger—than she at once got rid of him, and chose an Archelaos, then high-priest at Komana, upon the same terms. This arrangement Gabinius, the Governor of Syria under Pompey, and the recipient of bribes from Auletes,

---

[1] Strabo (xvii. 1, § 11) in telling the story calls him merely κυβιο-σάκτην τινα, who pretended to be of the Syrian royal house, and says the queen strangled him (ἀπεστραγγάλισεν), a very unusual term in his history, and not an Egyptian method of execution. The nickname was in use till the days of Vespasian, and applied to him by the impudent Alexandrians, so that it was evidently the ordinary name of a low trade, and so used (not as a proper name) by Strabo. It means the packer of salt fish (the πηλαμύs) which was cut into junks (κύβοι) for the purpose, hence possibly the packing of Alexander's pickled body into a cheaper case. τάριχοs is used both for salt fish, and for a mummy.

[2] I agree with Sharpe that this was the person who stole the golden coffin of Alexander the Great, and replaced it with one of glass. The words of Strabo (xvii. p. 794) are : the body of Alexander still lies in Alexandria, but not in the original coffin, which was gold, whereas now it is of glass ; the other was plundered by ὁ Κόκκηs καὶ Παρείσακτοs ἐπικληθεὶs Πτολ., ἐκ τῆs Συρίαs ἐπελθὼν καὶ ἐκπεσὼν εὐθύs, ὥστ' ἀνόνητα αὐτῷ τὰ σῦλα γενέσθαι. I think he means Seleukos Kybiosaktes.

was glad to permit, thinking it would raise the terms for
Auletes' restoration.   For the latter had come with letters
from Pompey, recommending this restoration.   The Senate
indeed had decided nothing, after much debate, as we hear
from Cicero, who had once made a speech in favour of the
king ; but the new plan was to have it carried out with an
armed force by Gabinius before he could be prevented by
the powers at home.   Gabinius demanded and received
6000 talents for the job.[1]   All this we hear from Dio
Cassius[2] who had not only Cicero's earlier speech *de rege
Alexandrino* before him, but other materials now completely
lost.   He proceeds : 'so Gabinius marched to Pelusium
without opposition, and, starting thence with his army in
two divisions, met and defeated the Egyptians the same
day.[3]   After this he again defeated them on the river and
on land.   For the Alexandrians are extremely ready at
making a bold show, and reckless in speaking out their
opinions, but when they meet the real dangers of war
are quite useless, although they are well versed in a long
series of home revolutions, with frequent murders, and
think nothing of human life in comparison to the gaining
of their point at the moment, nay even pursuing any
destruction of life which it entails as the most desirable of
objects.   Gabinius then having conquered them, and slain
Archelaos and many others, and forthwith becoming lord
of all Egypt, handed over the land to Ptolemy, who then
put to death his daughter (Berenike) and many other rich
and distinguished men, being in sore want of money.'

---

[1] Plutarch *Antony* 3 says 10,000.   [2] xxxix. 57 *sq.*

[3] His master of the horse was Antony, who then for the first time
met Cleopatra, a girl of 15, and was struck, says Appian, with her
beauty (*Bell. Civ.* v. 8).   Plutarch (*Antony* 3) says Antony was the main
instigator of the expedition, was the main cause of Gabinius' victories,
and stayed so far as he could Auletes' bloodthirsty vengeance.

§ 257. We are not concerned with the storm which this high-handed and illegal proceeding excited at Rome, except that a great deal of Gabinius' bribe was borrowed from Rabirius Postumus, his former creditor, and when this speculator could not recover his money, Auletes consented to make him his Chancellor of the Exchequer (διοικητής), so that the taxes of the country might pass through his hands. I do not think the real significance of this curious concession has been appreciated by historians. It was then without precedent,[1] but has in recent times its parallel in the cession of Turkish taxes made by the Sultan to secure the interest of their loans to his foreign creditors. The real creditor was not the obscure Rabirius, but the powerful Julius Caesar. For when he came to occupy Egypt after Pompey's death, he claimed that the supplies for his small army were only the repayment of a fraction of the 17,000,000 sesterces due to him from the late king.[2] And hence, perhaps, the zeal of a political party to prosecute the obscure Roman knight. According to Cicero, who defended him when Gabinius was convicted of peculation, and Rabirius was implicated in the case, he was first obliged to take his dangerous post at Alexandria, because it was otherwise impossible to recover his foolish loan; he was obliged to abandon all appearance of being a Roman, and dress as a Greek; he was obliged to submit to the humours of a despotic king, and see his friends imprisoned, and his own life in danger. But the fact that he at last had to escape naked for his life points to the other side of the story. With the aid of the Roman garrison left him by

---

[1] Though Physkon had done something of the kind (above, § 219) it was only an honorary office which he conferred upon a Roman.

[2] Plutarch *Caesar* 48.

Gabinius, he was guilty of such ferocious oppression and extortion, that the people of Alexandria rose against him, and would have murdered him, no doubt justly, if they had caught him. It is to be hoped that he did not recover his money, and it is certain that in spite of Cicero's speech (54 B.C.) he was condemned to pay some of the bribe which could not be recovered from Gabinius.

Auletes, restored in 55 B.C., only reigned till 51 B.C., when death removed the most idle and worthless of the Ptolemies. There is nothing more left to record about him. We need only sum up in a word what impression he has left upon the world. Idle, worthless, devoted to the orgies of Dionysus (whence his title) and disgracing himself by public competitions on the flute (whence his nick-name), he has not a good word recorded of him. If we believe Cicero, he was pliant and persuasive when in need, making boundless promises to men of influence and of money at Rome, but tyrannical and ruthless when in power, taking little account of human life when it thwarted his interests or even baulked his pleasure. He poses at Rome as king of Alexandria. Probably the ruin of Thebes by his father had crushed the national aspirations, for we hear of no revolt of the natives during his oppressive reign. With the priesthood and their religion he seems to have stood on friendly terms.

§ 258. But we are indeed fortunate in having, from Auletes' later years, not only the impressions of Cicero concerning the country, but the personal record of Diodorus Siculus, who visited Alexandria, and some of the upper country about 60 B.C., and reports with faithfulness what he saw and what he heard from the Greek expounders of the old Egyptian civilisation in the great religious centres of the country. There was no longer the same difficulty which had debarred Herodotus four centuries earlier from informing himself. There were now plenty of bilingual people, possibly priests, certainly scribes and other men learned in Egyptian lore; there were Greeks who lived all their life in great establishments like the Serapeum, and could not avoid learning from the priests most of what they knew or pretended to know. Diodorus' impressions, or rather the impressions we receive from his account, correspond very well with what we learn from the monuments, and our other authorities.

First as to Alexandria. He unfortunately gives us only one personal anecdote of what he saw in that city.[1] He is telling us that if any one kill an ibis or a cat, whether deliberately or by accident, he must inevitably die, for the crowd comes together and hounds him to death, without legal inquiry. This in itself proves that the mob of Alexandria was no longer Greek, as it professed to be, but deeply saturated with native blood, for no Hellenistic mob ever showed such deep intolerance on a matter of local superstition. This feeling in the crowd of Alexandria is so strong, he adds, 'that at the time when king Ptolemy was not yet acknowledged as a friend by the Roman people, and the populace was most anxious to show every respect to people from Italy who were sojourning there, and to give no pretext or excuse for a quarrel through their fear of Rome, a Roman happened to kill a cat, and when the mob attacked the house where he lived, neither the officers sent by the king nor the public fear of Rome sufficed to save his life, though he had done it unintentionally. This fact we report not from hearsay, but having ourselves witnessed it during our stay in Egypt.' Can anything correspond

[1] i. 84.

better with what has been quoted just now from Appian, that this populace acted with violence and cruelty on the spur of the moment, without regarding the consequences? In the present case, I cannot but think that, in spite of Diodorus, the fact of the felicide being a Roman gave him a smaller chance, for the Romans, always unpopular abroad for their rude and overbearing manners, were now well known throughout the East as the most cruel and heartless extortioners, so that the mob may have naturally seized a religious pretext for its vengeance. Diodorus also tells us [1] that at the time of his visit, the population of Alexandria (free citizens) was according to the official census more than 300,000, and the king's revenue from the rest of Egypt more than 6000 talents. Strabo,[2] however, quotes Cicero to the effect that Auletes' revenue was 12,500 talents.[3]

§ 259. Beside the great city mob was the mob of the soldiery, an accurate prototype of the Praetorian guard in the days of the Roman Empire, the descendants in tradition, though now very slightly in blood, of those free Macedonians, who had once made and unmade real sovrans. They still asserted their ancient privileges, and what the best observer of the day—Julius Caesar—found them, he tells with his usual clearness in his third book on the Civil War.[4]

Concerning the Jews, as a separate item in the population, we hear nothing but that they sided with the Romans, and that they surrendered the frontier forts near Pelusium to Gabinius.[5]

[1] xvii. 52.   [2] xxvi. 1, 13.
[3] Neither of them specifies the particular talent he means to employ, but the metrologists have made out that they agree, and that the amount is about three millions sterling.
[4] Below, § 267.   [5] Josephus *Antt.* xiv. 6, § 2.

When we come to consider the inner country, how great is the contrast ! *Ut occulte latet! ut tota recondita est!* exclaims Cicero, feeling that his words were true even apart from their connexion with his argument. Diodorus translates us into the far past, when he repeats from the priests their traditions of the old royalty and the old religion of Egypt. Hellenism seems powerless among such people. Diodorus feels that in the priests and their ritual, in the manners and customs of the people, in the legislation which surrounded the old monarchy, in the strange beast-worship, he describes a country and a race still foreign to the new civilisation of the world, but possessed of an equally advanced though a primaeval culture. Even in his own day, the keepers of sacred animals had been known to spend 100 talents upon their obsequies.[1] Throughout the reign of Auletes, we find the usual votive inscriptions, and devotions to the national gods on the part of the king[2] who was probably the least atten-tive of all the series to the sentiments of his people. He completed the great temple of Edfu, at which every Ptolemy since the Founder Euergetes I. had laboured, in 58 B.C. and put his dedication upon it, along with that of his queen, Cleopatra (V.) Tryphaena. On the great pylon we see colossal reliefs of the king smiting his enemies. He enlarged the temple of Kom Ombos, building the still extant *hypostyle pronaos*. One of the pylons at Philae was decorated by him, and he even built a small temple on the island of Biggeh, close to Philae. The crypts at Dendera, an altar of black granite at Koptos, and several temples at Karnak show his cartouche and consequently his dedica-tion of labour and money to the national gods ; in the last case the destruction of the city by Lathyrus had not

[1] i. 85.   [2] Murray's *Egypt* ii. pp. 427, 429, 431.

abolished the sanctity of the temples which it contained. Under his children's reign we shall find the building of great Egyptian temples more active than it had been under many a native dynasty.

§ 260. But there is one source, which by some accident dries up at this time, though it is abundant enough in the next century.   We have hardly any papyri of the reigns of Auletes or of Cleopatra to give us an insight into the internal state of the country.   Diodorus could learn from the priests their traditions and could wonder at their hereditary corporate dignities; he can describe, but from the much older Greek source Agatharchides, the horrors of the Nubian gold mines; he can copy from Hecataeus (of Abdera) the account of the conquests of Osymandyas (Ramses II.) as they appeared in relief or in text on the great temples at and over against Thebes.   But most of his account is at second hand.   Like Strabo after him, indeed like most Greek authors, he preferred copying from books, to setting down personal observations, and so his painstaking and trustworthy account is very deficient in such personal anecdotes as that I have above cited.   Here and there we surprise him in something modern, as when he speaks of catching quails by raising nets along the coast,[1] into which they fly by night in their passage, as any one may now see on the southern coasts of Italy any May-time. We feel that he has been on the Nile, when he notes that it is a most tortuous river, departing from its general course northward in bends to the east and west, or even to the south, and that in high summer the inundations make the country look like the Aegean with its Cyclades.[2]   He also knows the *sakya*, which he tells us was the invention of Archimedes, and this is probably

---

[1] i. 60.   [2] i. 32, 36.

true, for the old Egyptians only used the shadoof.[1] We
know further that he produces a true general impression,
when he says that the queens received greater honours
than the kings, and that even in ordinary marriage settlements the husband was bound by contract to respect his
wife.[2] He knows too about the use of kiki oil for lamps,

and about sundry industries like the
feeding of geese,[3] which are amply
corroborated by the papyri. His
account of the ordinary legal process[4] by written documents, and
not by oral pleading, is also correct,
as well as the curious statement that
the educators of the people objected
on theory both to music and gym-
nastic in education, as injurious to
mind and body. But even in these
matters it is most difficult to say
how far he has himself seen, and
how far he has copied from books.

PTOLEMY XIII.

Thus his account of Thebes and of the tombs of the kings
seems to me all borrowed from Hecataeus, and even as
regards the pyramids, his statements are open to the same
suspicion. He speaks of inscriptions on them, and of
other details which cannot be verified, and so he gives us
but one more example of the very reprehensible habit of
Greek historians, who ordinarily passed off second-hand
information as if it were observation of their own.

[1] i. 34.
[2] His language however is probably too strong (27) ἐν τῇ τῆς προικὸς
συγγραφῇ προσομολογούντων τῶν γαμούντων ἅπαντα πειθαρχήσειν τῇ
γαμουμένῃ.   [3] Ibid. 74.   [4] Ibid. 75.

CHAPTER XIII

§ 261. Now at last, at the close of our long search for materials among fragments, allusions, and conjectures, evidence is suddenly multiplied, and Egypt, coming into close connexion with the world's masters, becomes the stage for some of the most striking scenes in ancient history. They seem to most readers something new and strange—the pageants and passions of the fratricide Cleopatra as something unparalleled—and yet she was one of a race in which almost every reigning princess for the last 200 years had been swayed by like storms of passion, or had been guilty of like

PTOLEMY CAESAR(ION).

daring violations of common humanity. What Arsinoe, what Cleopatra, from the first to the last, had hesitated to murder a brother or a husband, to assume the throne, to raise and command armies, to discard or adopt a partner of her throne from caprice in policy, or policy in caprice? But hitherto this desperate gambling with life had been carried on in Egypt and Syria; the play had been with Hellenistic pawns — Egyptian or Syrian princes; the last Cleopatra came to play with Roman pieces, easier apparently to move than the others, but implying higher stakes, greater glory in the victory, greater disaster in the defeat. Therefore is it that this last Cleopatra, probably no more than an average specimen of the beauty, talent, daring, and cruelty of her ancestors, has taken an unique place among them in the imagination of the world, and holds her own even now and for ever as a familiar name throughout the world.

§ 262. Ptolemy Auletes, when dying, had taken great care not to bequeath his mortgaged kingdom to his Roman creditors. In his will he had named as his heirs the elder of his two sons, and his daughter who was the eldest of the family. He had called all the gods, and all his treaties with the Roman people to witness, adjuring it to carry out his intentions.[1] He had taken care to forward one copy by his ambassadors to Rome, to be deposited in the treasury—it had actually come into Pompey's possession, but (perhaps for fear of falsification) a duplicate with his seal was preserved at Alexandria.[2] But the public preoccu-

[1] The form of this will must therefore have differed *toto coelo* from those of his Greek subjects, who abstained from all such imprecations, cf. *Pet. Pap.* I. pp. 35 *sq.*

[2] This is Caesar's express statement, *de Bello Civ.* iii. § 108 : *In testamento Ptolemaei patris heredes erant scripti ex duobus filiis maior, et ex duabus ea quae aetate antecedebat. Haec uti fierent, per omnes deos, perque foedera, quae Romae fecisset, eodem testamento Ptolemaeus populum Romanum obtestabatur. Tabulae testamenti, unae per legatos eius Romam erant allatae, ut in aerario ponerentur (hae, quum propter publicas occupationes poni non potuissent, apud Pompeium sunt depositae), alterae, eodem exemplo, relictae atque obsignatae Alexandriae proferebantur.* It is delightful to find so clear and express a

pation, which did not even allow enough attention to the Egyptian will to have it formally deposited in the treasury, saved it from any discussion or dispute. Nobody thought of claiming Egypt for a heritage of the Roman Republic, when the whole world was the prize proposed in the civil conflict. For though the war of Caesar and Pompey had not actually broken out, the political sky was lowering with blackness, and the coming tempest was muttering its thunder through the sultry air. So Cleopatra, now about sixteen or seventeen years of age, and her much younger brother (about ten) assumed the throne as was traditional, without any tumult or controversy, either on the part of the Alexandrian mob, or of the soldatesca, called Macedonian, but really made up of all manner of Greeks, and the most disreputable and turbulent of Roman refugees.[1]

§ 263. The opening discords came from within the royal family. The tutors and advisers of the young king, among whom Pothinos, an eunuch brought up with him as his playmate, according to the custom of the court, was the ablest and most influential, persuaded him to assume sole direction of affairs, and to depose his elder sister. Cleopatra was not able to maintain herself in Alexandria, but went to Syria as an exile, where she promptly collected an army, as was the wont of these Egyptian princesses, who seem to have resources always under their control, and returned (within a few months, says Caesar) by way of Pelusium, to reconquer her lawful share in the throne. This happened in the fourth year

statement anywhere in this history. It seems to me that the *tabulae* were not a papyrus roll, but some more solid material, and that the precautions taken were owing to the doubts and disputes about the genuineness of previous royal testaments.

[1] Cf. *Addit. Note* p. 497.

of their so-called joint reign (48 B.C.) at the very time that Pompey and Caesar were engaged in their conflict for a far greater kingdom. The details of the flight of Pompey are preserved to us in several accounts of surprising agreement, especially the *Life of Pompey* by Plutarch, and the close of Caesar's *Civil War.* We shall do best to follow in the main the latter, a first-rate authority, which omits indeed many affecting details supplied by Plutarch, but for that very reason spares the reader all digressions from the facts which concern Egyptian history.

§ 264. Pompey, passing in his flight to the coast of Asia, soon found that he and his party were unwelcome guests to the Greek cities, which were expecting the advent of the victorious Caesar. Being therefore compelled, if he chose to continue the war, to seek allies farther off, he himself proposed, as Plutarch tells us, to go to Parthia,[1] but was dissuaded by his faithful follower Theophanes of Mytilene from attempting such a journey, risking his own life and that of his devoted wife among such little known barbarians, when Egypt was but three days' sail distant, ruled by a boy king, whose father had been under great obligations to Pompey.[2] So Pompey set sail with the funds he had collected, and about 2000 armed followers from Cyprus, not to Alexandria, but to Pelusium, where he found Ptolemy with a large army encamped over against his sister's forces. He sent a message on shore to ask for hospitality in Alexandria and protection in his calamity. The bearers did not fail to talk with the Romans in the Egyptian camp, and urge the claims of the illustrious exile. For there were

---

[1] Caesar says *deposito adeundae Syriae consilio,* as if this had been Pompey's alternative—the Syrian states and cities which he had reduced to order and peace in 62 B.C.   [2] *Pompey* 76.

here not a few soldiers, left by Gabinius with Ptolemy
Auletes, and now of influence in Egypt. Whereupon the
king's friends, more especially the eunuch Pothinos, who
was practically the prime minister, debated what should
be done, whether they should harbour Pompey, or
decline that dangerous honour. Plutarch tells us they
were persuaded by the sophist Theodotos to do neither,
but to receive him with pretended civility, and murder
him, in order to gain Caesar's gratitude.[1] The Alexandrian Achillas and L. Septimius, who had served under
Pompey, were sent out in a boat to bring him to land
with fair promises. As he was stepping on shore these
men murdered him.

§ 265. Caesar, pursuing with his wonted celerity,
arrived very soon after at Alexandria, with nominally two
legions, 800 horse, and some fifteen Rhodian and Asiatic
ships of war. But the legions had melted down to a force
of 3200 men, the rest being left behind wounded or sick.
Yet the conqueror thought his reputation would make him
safe anywhere with this small force. Upon entering the
port of Alexandria, the head and signet ring of Pompey
were presented to him by Theodotos, from which he turned
in horror, and took every means to save the remaining
followers of his foe, who were dispersed through Egypt.
Had he felt secure enough he would certainly have
punished the murderers, but this must have led at once to a
rupture with the king's advisers. However he disembarked,
and was surprised by the hostile attitude of the soldiers
who had been left by Ptolemy to protect the capital. He
even found himself riotously assaulted, because his lictors
with their fasces went before him, which assertion of his

---

[1] This reason is not given by Caesar, but comes to us from Livy,
and from those who followed him. Cf. Bandelin p. 45.

imperium the mob interpreted as an insult to their sovran.[1]
Even after this tumult was allayed, there were daily disturbances, and Caesar lost many soldiers by assassination in the streets.   He therefore sent in haste for the
legions he had formed in Asia, and would (he says) have
left Alexandria, but that he was held *necessario* by the
prevalent north winds, which then characterised that coast
in summer.[2]   Meanwhile he expressed his opinion that
the quarrel of the sovrans in Egypt concerned the Roman
people, and himself as consul, the more so as it was in
his previous consulate that the recognition of, and alliance
with, their father had taken place.   So he signified his
decision that Ptolemy and Cleopatra should dismiss their
armies, and should discuss their claims before him by
argument and not by arms.   All our authorities, except Dio
Cassius, state that he sent for Cleopatra that she might
personally urge her claims, but Dio[3] tells us, with far
more detail, and I think greater probability, 'that at first
the quarrel with her brother was argued for her by friends,
till she, learning the amorous character of Caesar, sent
him word that her case was being mismanaged by her
advocates, and she desired to plead it herself.   She was
then in the flower of her age (about twenty) and celebrated for her beauty.   Moreover she had the sweetest of

[1] Bandelin (p. 47) prefers to follow the account of Appian and
Plutarch, who say or imply that Caesar was at first well received.   But I
think he suspects Caesar's narrative too much.   So great a person is
generally superior to petty falsifications.   To mention his own relations
with Cleopatra would have been foreign to the dignity of his narrative.
This omission therefore stands upon different grounds.

[2] They now blow in late winter and spring, but not I think so constantly in summer as to deserve the name of *etesiae*; and in any
case, as he himself adds, he thought it his duty to settle the royal
quarrel in Egypt.   Cf. Bandelin p. 48, and *Bell. Civ.* iii. 107.

[3] xlii. 34.

voices, and every charm of conversation, so that she was
likely to ensnare even the most obdurate and elderly man.
These gifts she regarded as her claims upon Caesar. She
prayed therefore for an interview, and adorned herself in
a garb most becoming, but likely to arouse his pity, and so
came secretly by night to visit him.' If she indeed arrived
secretly, and was carried into the palace by one faithful
follower as a bale of carpet, it was from fear of assassination by the party of Pothinos. She knew that as soon
as she had reached Caesar's sentries she was safe; as
the event proved, she was more than safe. For in the
brief interval of peace, and perhaps even of apparent
jollity, while the royal dispute was under discussion, she
gained an influence over Caesar which she retained till
his death. Caesar adjudicated the throne according to
the will of Auletes; he even restored Cyprus to Egypt,
and proposed to send the younger brother and his sister
Arsinoe to govern it; but he also insisted on a repayment
in part at least of the enormous outstanding debt of
Auletes to him and his party. To meet this the young
king's plate was ostentatiously pawned, and Caesar treated
with insolence by Pothinos as an usurer pursuing trivial gains.
In these complaints the eunuch found support among the
king's friends, and silently brought the Egyptian troops
back to Alexandria, appointing Achillas their commander.
Caesar, who was anxiously awaiting reinforcements under
a cloak of court festivities, was surprised by their arrival,
and found himself unable with his small force to fight them
outside the city. He could only put his soldiers under
arms, occupy the palace and its approaches, and send
ambassadors to treat with and delay Achillas. As he does
not tell us one word concerning the army of Cleopatra,
which had recently been encamped against Ptolemy at

Pelusium, we must infer that a battle had there been fought, that her forces had been defeated, and, as was usual with such mercenary troops, had passed over to the winning side, leaving her a mere claimant to the throne without an army. This assumption explains both the boldness of Pothinos, his prompt return to Alexandria from Pelusium, and the subsequent arrival of Cleopatra. But though the ambassadors (Dioscorides and Serapion) sent by Caesar were men who had been ambassadors at Rome for Auletes, Pothinos set his soldiers upon them as soon as they appeared, so that one was killed, the other carried off for dead by his retinue. This being an extreme declaration of war, Caesar at once secured the person of the young king who had been pleading before him, so that he might act with the nominal authority of the native sovran.

§ 266. Dio gives a different account of the matter in detail, though not modifying the general course of events. He says[1] that when the boy king suddenly saw his sister with Caesar in the palace, he was indignant, and rushed out to the people shouting that he was betrayed, tearing the diadem from his head and dashing it on the ground. When a great tumult arose, Caesar's guards at once seized the king, but the population set upon the palace, and would then and there have become masters of it, as Caesar was taken by surprise, and had no force under arms to meet this sudden outbreak, had he not come forward, and, standing in a safe place, declared to them that he would grant all that they desired. Then going to a formal assembly, he set Cleopatra and Ptolemy before them and read the will of their father, directing them to marry and reign according to hereditary custom, but that

[1] xlii. 35.

the Roman people should be their guardian. He said that
he as dictator represented the Roman people, and would
carry out the terms of the will. It was moreover through
fear that he actually increased the kingdom by the proposed restitution of Cyprus to the younger princes of the
royal family.

§ 267. The forces under Achillas' command, says Caesar,
'were not to be despised either as to numbers or fighting
quality. He had under arms some 20,000 men consisting
(1) of Gabinian soldiers, who had adopted the habits and
license of Alexandrian life and forgotten Roman discipline.
Most of them had married there and had families; (2) of
a mixed multitude of pirates and brigands from Syria,
Cilicia, and the regions round about.' There is no mention
made of native Egyptians. But there were also (3) 'many
criminals and exiles from Italy, and fugitive slaves, to
whom Alexandria had been for years a safe refuge, on the
understanding that they should be enrolled as soldiers. If
any were claimed by his master he was rescued by his
comrades. This was the body that would demand the
death of an unpopular minister; that would pillage
private property; that would besiege the palace to extort
higher pay; that exiled or recalled whom they would
according to the old traditions of the Macedonian garrison
at Alexandria. They had 2000 horse. They had seen
many wars; had restored Auletes to his kingdom; had
murdered the two sons of Bibulus [we know not for what
cause]; had warred against the natives. This was their
history.'

With these forces Achillas occupied all the city round
Caesar's quarters, and even strove to storm them, but in
vain. At the same time he tried to seize a large fleet of
ships, seventy-two in number, lying ready and equipped in

the harbour.[1]   Had these passed into Alexandrian hands, Caesar was blockaded by sea and land, and probably lost. In this extremity Caesar was obliged to set fire to the ships, and with it the naval arsenal was burnt.   A far greater disaster is said to have ensued.   The famous Library, situated close to the dockyards, took fire and was burnt. As Caesar only urges the necessity of his action, and its success as regards the ships, we cannot tell the amount of the collateral loss.   But possibly his silence implies that the worst had happened.   If he had set his soldiers to save what they could from the flames, it is more than likely that he would have said a word on the subject.   On the other hand, his silence is no satisfactory denial of what is recorded by several other credible authorities.   Still I am disposed to consider the whole story a fabrication.   So far as I know, the contemporary Cicero, in all his literary talk, never alludes to a catastrophe which ought to have affected him most deeply as a man of letters.   Strabo, who visited Egypt about twenty-five years after these events, is absolutely silent regarding the Library.   Although therefore he certainly did not come to study in it, as some have thought, he could hardly have failed to notice its loss in connexion with the Museum, which he briefly describes, and of which it was really a part, though of course in a separate building.   The earliest mention of the disaster is in a rhetorical passage of Seneca, already quoted.[2]

[1] As Caesar only speaks of one harbour, and that defended by the lighthouse fort, he must mean the eastern or royal harbour.   He makes no mention of the so-called Eunostos.   *Bell. Civ.* iii. 111.

[2] Above, § 64.   Bandelin, in his careful discussion of the events, is absolutely silent concerning the Library, and so is Mommsen in his narrative (*RG* iii. 439), so that they evidently discredit the story, though they were certainly bound to discuss the evidence.   The language of Dio xlii. 38 is not what we should expect : πολλὰ δὲ καὶ κατεπίμπραντο·

Not content with destroying this fleet, Caesar advanced to the capture of Pharos, the old island, and now lighthouse fort, which commanded the entrance to the N.E. or royal harbour, which was the only one he had attempted to hold. He mentions a curious survival of ancient barbarism in the inhabitants of this island. Whatever ships, whether by bad weather or by bad steering, missed the entrance to either port and were stranded on its rocks, were, as a matter of course, looted by the people, who were no doubt by ancient descent a population of wreckers. This is perhaps the most extreme instance known of Egyptian license. Whether it had been permitted under the early and orderly Ptolemies we cannot tell. The possession of Pharos made it possible for him to receive by sea the succour of troops and provisions of which he was urgently in need. For he was losing men daily in the fighting around the fortified palace, which the Alexandrians, army and populace combined, kept attacking with great vigour till he had constructed defences sufficient to check them.

§ 268. Meanwhile the younger princess Arsinoe, who saw that Caesar was devoted to Cleopatra, and who knew the fierce hatred which this beautiful fiend with her bewitching smiles bore to all her possible rivals in ambition or in love, though she had received from Caesar the title of sovran of Cyprus, fled secretly, with the assistance of her eunuch Ganymedes, from the palace and joined the insurgents, causing at once discord in the camp, for she and Achillas sought to bid for the exclusive favour of the

ὥστε ἄλλα τε καὶ τὸ νεώριον, τάς τε ἀποθήκας καὶ τοῦ σίτου καὶ τῶν βίβλων (πλείστων δὴ καὶ ἀρίστων, ὥς φασι, γενομένων) καυθῆναι. Surely he must mean some store of books intended for sale, or for sorting, and not the great Library, of whose excellence ὥς φασι is not the expression we should expect. The proximity of *corn-stores* supports my view.

soldiers.[1]   Arsinoe must have been barely grown up, and
we may best explain the persistent hatred Cleopatra showed
to her by assuming that she too was beautiful and attractive.   Her present daring act showed that she had the
spirit of the Ptolemies.   Pothinos was detected in the
meaner game of corresponding secretly from the palace with
the insurgents, and was then put to death, no doubt with
real satisfaction, by Caesar.[2]

Caesar had still with him in his fortress Cleopatra, now
his acknowledged mistress, with the two young Ptolemies,
now practically his prisoners, and hardly 2000 veterans,
to oppose the army of Achillas or Ganymedes, and the
furious armed mob of Alexandria, who were bent upon
destroying him.   They endeavoured to ruin his water
supply by letting sea water into the conduits that supplied
the palace, but his legionaries found what had never before
been suspected; without digging to any great depth they
came upon ample wells of fresh water.[3]   The Alexandrians
then seem to have retaken Pharos, and to have compelled
his ships to lie outside, in danger from the weather, and
from any attack they chose to make from the western
harbour, but though they boldly sailed out with their fleet,
they were unable to prevent Domitius, arriving with the
xxxviith legion and sundry supplies in a large convoy of
ships, from entering the royal harbour.   The brunt of this
naval action was borne by Caesar's Rhodian ships, whose

---

[1] Dio says, if his text be slightly corrected (προδόντα for προδοῦσαν
xlii. 40), that Ganymedes persuaded her to slay Achillas as a traitor,
and was practically general till king Ptolemy was sent out by Caesar;
so also *Bell. Alex.* 4.

[2] At this point Caesar's *Civil War* breaks off, and the sequel is to
be obtained from Dio, or from the appendix by Hirtius, called the
Alexandrian War (Ed. R. Schneider, Berlin, 1888).

[3] There are no such wells now known at Alexandria.

admiral, Euphranor, greatly distinguished himself,[1] not only in this, but in the succeeding battle, which Caesar provoked, by sailing round to the mouth of Eunostos and challenging the fleet which the Egyptians had been repairing and building with great zeal and energy. Caesar defeated them, but had no power to follow up his attack, when they retired to the protection of the shore. It was to obtain this support for his fleet in future engagements that he managed to retake the lighthouse fort and island of Pharos, but when advancing to attack the enemy along the causeway which led to the city, which had two bridges to allow a water-passage between the harbours, he was surprised in the rear by a sudden charge of boats, and had more than 100 men driven into the water along with himself, so that he was only saved by swimming,[2] while the Alexandrians set up his scarlet cloak in triumph on the trophy with which they adorned the spot.

§ 269. Meanwhile his succours were approaching, though most of the isolated ships which came to the coast were decoyed by false signals and captured. It was in an action against the Alexandrian vessels, for the purpose of raising this blockade, that the gallant Euphranor, unsupported by his squadron, was overpowered with his ship and slain.[3] But at last Mithradates of Pergamum, a competent

---

[1] Cf. *Bell. Alex.* 9-11, where a very clear account is given of this engagement: the Roman author adds (15) that Euphranor was: *animi magnitudine ac virtute magis cum nostris hominibus quam cum Graecis comparandus.*

[2] Surely the legend that he saved his *Commentaries* at this moment by carrying them over his head while swimming for his life must have let loose the epigrammatists upon him, if he had indeed burnt the great Library. The saving of his one book from water by the man who destroyed myriads of others by fire would have afforded too tempting an exercise for these wits.

[3] *Bell. Alex.* 25.

general, was announced to be approaching by land, and the
Alexandrians, thinking that they would be stronger if they
had their king to command them, laid a plot to regain him.
They pretended that they wished for peace, but asked for
him to come out and discuss with them its conditions.
Caesar could not have been misled by these proposals, but
as he was not afraid of the king, who was young and
ignorant, and as he thought he should have a stronger
case against him and the people, and in favour of Cleopatra,
in prospect of their treachery, he sent him out, knowing
that, at all events, relief was at hand. The Egyptians at
once broke off all negotiations, and prepared to meet the
coming danger, for Mithradates had succeeded in storming
Pelusium, and had set out by the highroad to Memphis, to
the head of the Delta, where he could cross the river. He
succeeded in another action there, and crossed the river to
the west side.[1] Caesar who understood his movements,
whether by secret information, or with the instinct of a
general, made a feint by which he deceived his besiegers,
and landed a small force on the Libyan side of lake
Marea, from which he marched to join his approaching
succours. Caesar's progress, though laborious, must have
been very prompt, no doubt owing to the fine training of
his legionaries, for he outmarched the king, who had taken
the shorter and easier route by water to check Mithradates. It seems that all attempts to storm the fortress

---

[1] Josephus (*Antiqq.* xiv. §§ 1, 2) gives the whole credit of the campaign
to the Jew Antipater, who commanded (he says) the Jewish contingent
of Mithradates' forces, and not only won all the battles, but brought over
the Egyptian Jews to Caesar's side. Hirtius never mentions the Jew,
nor do I believe Josephus' story. Caesar's 'letter to the Sidonians'
which Josephus cites (xiv. 10, 1) gives the whole credit to Hyrcanus, and
speaks of his being sent by Caesar from Alexandria to meet Mithradates!
There is not a word here about Antipater.

in Alexandria had now ceased, the Egyptian army being concentrated under the king somewhere in the Delta to oppose the new invasion. Caesar came up just as the Egyptians were about to attack Mithradates, and effected the junction with this able officer.

While they hesitated he attacked them, and forced most of them into the river. Among the fugitives, the young king himself was drowned.[1] Caesar was now able to relieve his remaining troops still blockaded, by attacking Alexandria from the land-side. But the populace had abandoned all hope of success, and turned to prayers, carrying out the images of their gods to intercede for them. With his usual generosity, he forgave them without any measures of vengeance, and set the younger Ptolemy over them, as the nominal husband of Cleopatra, while he carried Arsinoe captive to Rome. He withdrew his cession of Cyprus,[2] as there was no longer any Ptolemaic prince to set over it, and for the sake of keeping the turbulent Alexandria in order, he left a strong garrison there under a son of his freed man Rufinus, who was not likely to trouble him with any aristocratic ambitions.[3]

§ 270. With his departure we again lose sight of Egypt,

---

[1] The narrative of this war is confused in our various sources, and they are so irreconcilable as to the exact order of the events, that I have only set forth the above as a probable arrangement of the facts. Certainty regarding them is not attainable, nor is it worth balancing the probabilities in this general history. It has been done by Bandelin *op. cit.*, Judeich *Caesar im Orient*, Stoffel *Hist. de Jules César*, and others.

[2] Mr. Poole (*Coins of the Ptolemies* p. lxxxiv.) thinks that Cyprian coins show some evidence of his nominees having already issued money as sovrans there. Others doubt the cession altogether, and think that if it did take place, Caesar was very glad to disown it.

[3] *Trium legionum, quas Alexandreae relinquebat, curam et imperium Rufini liberti sui filio, exsoleto suo, demandavit,* Suetonius *Divus Iulius* 76.

and cannot tell how Alexandria, or the upper country, accepted his settlement. In his great fourfold triumph (46 B.C.) when he paraded four foreign enemies of the Republic as if they had been his real foes, the princess Arsinoe, representing Egypt, excited great commiseration even among the Romans, as she was led along in chains.[1] We cannot but see the dark influence of Cleopatra here. Had she said one word against the public exhibition of her sister as a captive, Caesar would not have insisted; I am disposed to go further and say that had she not pressed him to do it, such a scene would not have taken place. But Cleopatra's hatred for her sister did not stop there.

A few months after Caesar's departure from Egypt she gave birth to a son, whom she alleged, without any immediate contradiction, to be the dictator's. The Alexandrians called him Caesarion, and she never swerved from asserting for him royal privileges. In formal inscriptions he is entitled Ptolemy, also Caesar, the god Philopator Philometor.[2] Her brother-husband was a child, and therefore did not count in the matter. We hear of no other lover, though it is impossible to imagine Cleopatra arriving at the age of twenty without providing herself with this luxury.[3] She was, how-

---

[1] Dio xliii. 19. Suetonius says he visited Upper Egypt with Cleopatra.

[2] Cf. the Theban stele at Turin, to be commented upon presently, and the Dendera texts in Baedeker's *Upper Egypt*.

[3] It is hard to explain the uncritical Suetonius in harmony with our other authorities: *quam denique accitam in urbem nonnisi maximis honoribus praemisque auctam remisit filiumque natum appellare nomine suo passus est. Quem quidem nonnulli Graecorum similem quoque Caesari et forma et incessu tradiderunt. M. Antonius adgnitum etiam ab eo senatui adfirmavit, quae scire C. Matium et C. Oppium reliquosque Caesaris amicos; quorum Gaius Oppius, quasi plane defensione et patrocinio res egeret, librum edidit, non esse Caesaris filium quem Cleopatra dicat* (*Divus Iulius* 52). He goes on to mention Helvius Cinna's proposal. The gossip about Cnaeus Pompey is probably groundless.

ever, afraid to let Caesar live far from her influence, and some time before his assassination, that is to say some time between 48 and 44 B.C., she came with the young king her brother to Rome, where she was received in Caesar's palace beyond the Tiber, causing by her residence there considerable scandal among the stricter Romans. Cicero confesses that he went to see her, but protests that his reasons for doing so were absolutely non-political. She apparently promised to get him some books from Alexandria, but she or her agent Ammonius failed in doing so.[1] Cicero found her haughty; he does not say she was beautiful and fascinating. We do not hear of any political activity on her part, though Cicero evidently suspects it; it is well nigh impossible that she can have preferred her very doubtful position at Rome to her brilliant life in the East. She was suspected of urging Caesar to move eastward the capital of his new empire, to desert Rome, and choose either Ilium, the imaginary cradle of his race, or Alexandria, as his residence.[2] She is likely to have encouraged at all events his expedition against the Parthians, which would bring him to Syria, whence she hoped to gain new territory for her son. The whole situation is eloquently, perhaps too eloquently, described by Merivale,[3]

---

[1] *Epp. ad Att.* xiv. 8, xv. 15. As I said before, Cicero makes no allusion to the destruction of the Alexandrian Library, when telling of these MSS. Plutarch mentions (*Antony* 58) that one of the charges made by Octavian against Antony was that he had given away to her as a gift the libraries in Pergamum amounting to 20 myriads of single books (βιβλίων ἁπλῶν). This, however, may have been to gratify the old jealousy felt against the rival library, not to supply what Alexandria had lost by fire. If the latter had been the case, we should probably have been told it.

[2] Cf. this gossip repeated by Nicolaus Damasc. *FHG* iii. 440, and Suetonius *Divus Iulius* 79.

[3] *Hist. of the Romans under the Empire* ii. pp. 430, 431.

for he weaves in many conjectures of his own, as if they were ascertained facts—

The colours of this imitation of a hateful original [the oriental despot] were heightened by the demeanour of Cleopatra, who followed her lover to Rome at his invitation. She came with the younger Ptolemaeus, who now shared her throne, and her ostensible object was to negotiate a treaty between her kingdom and the commonwealth. While the Egyptian nation was formally admitted to the friendship and alliance of Rome, its sovereign was lodged in Caesar's villa on the other side of the Tiber, and the statue of the most fascinating of women was erected in the temple of the Goddess of Love and Beauty. The connexion which subsisted between her and the dictator was unblushingly avowed. Public opinion demanded no concessions to its delicacy ; the feelings of the injured Calpurnia had been blunted by repeated outrage, and Cleopatra was encouraged to proclaim openly that her child Caesarion was the son of her Roman admirer. A tribune, named Helvius Cinna, ventured, it is said, to assert among his friends that he was prepared to propose a law, with the dictator's sanction, to enable him to marry more wives than one, for the sake of progeny, and to disregard in his choice the legitimate qualification of Roman descent. The Romans, however, were spared this last insult to their prejudices. The Queen of Egypt felt bitterly the scorn with which she was popularly regarded as the representative of an effeminate and licentious people. . It is not improbable that she employed her fatal influence to withdraw her lover from the Roman capital, and urged him to schemes of Oriental conquest to bring him more completely within her toils. In the meanwhile the haughtiness of her demeanour corresponded with the splendid anticipations in which she indulged. She held a court in the suburbs of the city, at which the adherents of the dictator's policy were not the only attendants. Even his opponents and concealed enemies were glad to bask in the sunshine of her smiles.

§ 271. When Caesar was assassinated, she was still at Rome, and had some wild hopes of having her son recognised by the Caesarians. But failing in this she escaped

secretly, and sailed to Egypt, not without causing satisfaction to cautious men like Cicero that she was gone.
The passage in which he seems to allude to a rumour that
she was about to have another child—another misfortune
to the state—does not bear that interpretation.[1] As he
says not a word concerning the young king Ptolemy, we
may assume that the youth was already dead, and that he
died at Rome. The common belief was that Cleopatra
poisoned him, as soon as his increasing years made him
troublesome to her. In her reign four years are assigned
to a joint rule with her elder brother, four more to that
with her younger, so that this latter must have died in the
same year as Caesar.

Cleopatra, watching from Egypt the great civil war
which ensued—summoned and commanded by the various
leaders to send aid in ships and money, threatened with
plunder and confiscation by those who were now exhaust-
ing Asia Minor and the islands with monstrous exactions
—had ample occupation for her talents in steering safely
among these constant dangers. Appian[2] says she pleaded
famine and pestilence in her country in declining the
demands of Cassius for subsidies. The latter was on
the point of invading Egypt, at the moment denuded of
defending forces, and *wasted with famine*, when he was
summoned to Philippi by Brutus. This statement has been
brought into connexion with the text of a stele at Turin,
which records the public spirit and self-sacrifice of a
certain Callimachus, a leading official at Thebes, apparently
in the tenth and second year of the joint reign of
Cleopatra Philopator and of Ptolemy Caesar, the god

---

[1] *Ad Att.* xiv. 20 *de regina velim* (sc. *scribas*, not *abortum*, though
nollem abortum is in the previous sentence).

[2] *Bell. Civ.* iv. 61, 63.

Philopator Philometor.[1] These virtues were shown when Thebes was in great difficulties, and the population in despair. It is perhaps negatively important to find that it is now a local official, not the king and queen, to whom the population look for help in days of need. Cleopatra seems to have excluded the Jews of Alexandria from the distributions of corn at this time, for which Josephus[2] reviles her, while admitting that Germanicus followed her precedent. The famine in question then probably dates 43-42 B.C.[3]

It was not till 41 B.C., after the decisive battle of Philippi, that the victorious Antony, turning to subdue the East to the Caesarian cause, held his *joyeuse entrée* into Ephesus,[4] and then proceeded to drain all Asia Minor of money for the satisfaction of his greedy legionaries, and his own still more greedy vices. Reaching Cilicia he sent an order to the queen of Egypt to come before him and explain her conduct during the late war, for she was reported to have sent aid to Cassius.

§ 272. The sequel may be told in Plutarch's famous narrative—

Dellius, who was sent on this message, had no sooner seen her face, and remarked her adroitness and subtlety in speech,

---

[1] The text was first printed with a brief commentary by A. Peyron (*Trans. of Turin Academy* vol. 34, 1829).

[2] *contra Apion.* c. ii. 5. Seneca *Quaest. Nat.* iv. 1.

[3] The text of the stele is given with an excellent commentary in *CIG* iii. 4957, but Franz makes no remark upon the peculiarly turgid style of the document, full of phrases foreign to sober prose, thus reminding us of the fact that Antony professed this style, of which I have given the extant specimen elsewhere (*Greek Life under Roman Sway* p. 162). Is it possible that he can already have set the fashion to the officials in Upper Egypt? If so, the document is probably to be dated as late as 37 B.C.

[4] Plutarch *Antony* 24.

than he felt convinced that Antony would not so much as think of giving any molestation to a woman like this; on the contrary, she would be the first in favour with him. So he set himself at once to pay his court to the Egyptian, and gave her his advice, 'to go,' in the Homeric style, to Cilicia, 'in her best attire,' and bade her fear nothing from Antony, the gentlest and kindest of soldiers. She had some faith in the words of Dellius, but more in her own attractions; which, having formerly recommended her to Caesar and the young Cnaeus Pompey, she did not doubt might yet prove more successful with Antony. Their acquaintance was with her when a girl, young, and ignorant of the world, but she was to meet Antony in the time of life when women's beauty is most splendid, and their intellects are in full maturity. She made great prepara-tion for her journey, of money, gifts, and ornaments of value, such as so wealthy a kingdom might afford, but she brought with her her surest hopes in her own magic arts and charms.

She received several letters, both from Antony and from his friends, to summon her, but she took no account of these orders; and at last, as if in mockery of them, she came sailing up the river Cydnus, in a barge with gilded stern and outspread sails of purple, while oars of silver beat time to the music of flutes and fifes and harps. She herself lay all along, under a canopy of cloth of gold, dressed as Venus in a picture, and beautiful young boys, like painted Cupids, stood on each side to fan her. Her maids were dressed like Sea Nymphs and Graces, some steering at the rudder, some working at the ropes.[1] The perfumes diffused themselves from the vessel to the shore, which was covered with multitudes, part following the galley up the river on either bank, part running out of the city to see the sight. The market-place was quite emptied, and Antony at last was left alone sitting upon the tribunal; while the word went through all the multitude that Venus was come to feast with Bacchus, for the common good of Asia.[2]   On

[1] There was no Egyptian feature in this show, which was purely Hellenistic.

[2] How easily such a belief started up in the minds of a crowd in the Asia Minor of that day, appears from *Acts* xiv. 11 *sq.*, where the crowd at Iconium, on seeing a cripple cured, at once exclaim that the gods are come down to them in the likeness of men, and call Barnabas

her arrival, Antony sent to invite her to supper. She thought it fitter he should come to her ; so, willing to show his good humour and courtesy, he complied, and went. He found the preparations to receive him magnificent beyond expression, but nothing so admirable as the great number of lights ; for on a sudden there was let down altogether so great a number of branches with lights in them so ingeniously disposed, some in squares, and some in circles, that the whole thing was a spectacle that has seldom been equalled for beauty.

The next day, Antony invited her to supper, and was very desirous to outdo her as well in magnificence as contrivance ; but he found he was altogether beaten in both, and was so well convinced of it, that he was himself the first to jest and mock at his poverty of wit, and his rustic awkwardness.[1] She, per- ceiving that his raillery was broad and gross, and savoured more of the soldier than the courtier, rejoined in the same taste, and fell into it at once, without any sort of reluctance or reserve. For her actual beauty, it is said, was not in itself so remarkable that none could be compared with her, or that no one could see her without being struck by it, but the contact of her presence, if you lived with her, was irresistible ; the attraction of her person, joining with the charm of her conversation, and the character that attended all she said or did, was something be- witching. It was a pleasure merely to hear the sound of her voice, with which, like an instrument of many strings, she could pass from one language to another ; so that there were few of the barbarian nations that she answered by an interpreter ; to most of them she spoke herself, as to the Ethiopians, Troglodytes, Hebrews, Arabians, Syrians, Medes, Parthians, and many others, whose language she had learnt ;[2] which was all the more surprising, because most of the kings her predecessors scarcely gave themselves the trouble to acquire the Egyptian tongue, and several of them quite abandoned the Macedonian.

Antony was so captivated by her, that, while Fulvia his wife maintained his quarrels in Rome against Caesar by actual force of arms, and the Parthian troops, commanded by Labienus

Jupiter, and Paul Mercurius, because he was the chief speaker, bringing sacrifices to offer to the Apostles.

[1] There is a description of these feasts in Athenaeus pp. 147-8.
[2] We have here the usual lies of courtiers.

(the king's generals having made him commander-in-chief), were assembled in Mesopotamia, and ready to enter Syria, he could yet suffer himself to be carried away by her to Alexandria, there to keep holiday, like a boy, in play and diversion, squandering and fooling away in enjoyments that most costly, as Antiphon says, of all valuables, time. They had a sort of company, to which they gave a particular name, calling it that of the Inimitable Livers.[1] The members entertained one another daily in turn, with an extravagance of expenditure beyond measure or belief. Philotas, a physician of Amphissa, who was at that time a student of medicine in Alexandria, used to tell my grandfather Lamprias, that, having some acquaintance with one of the royal cooks, he was invited by him, being a young man, to come and see the sumptuous preparations for dinner. So he was taken into the kitchen, where he admired the prodigious variety of all things; but particularly, seeing eight wild boars roasting whole, says he, 'Surely you have a great number of guests.' The cook laughed at his simplicity, and told him there were not above twelve to dine, but that every dish was to be served up just roasted to a turn, and if anything was but one minute ill-timed, it was spoiled. 'And,' said he, 'maybe Antony will dine just now, maybe not this hour, maybe he will call for wine, or begin to talk, and will put it off. So that,' he continued, 'it is not one, but many dinners must be had in readiness, as it is impossible to guess at his hour.' This was Philotas' story; who related besides, that he afterwards came to be one of the medical attendants of Antony's eldest son by Fulvia, and used to be invited pretty often, among other companions, to his table, when he was not dining with his father. One day another physician had talked loudly, and given great disturbance to the company, whose mouth Philotas stopped with this sophistical syllogism : ' In certain states of fever the patient should take cold water ; every one who has a fever is in a certain state of fever ; therefore in a fever cold water should always be taken.' The man was quite struck dumb, and

---

[1] We have independent evidence that this title really existed, for there is at Alexandria the pedestal of a statue of Antony, with the dedication to him as τον αμιμητον, τον ευεργετην, *Cat. du Musée d'Alexandrie* (1893).

Antony's son, very much pleased, laughed aloud, and said, 'Philotas, I make you a present of all you see there,' pointing to a sideboard covered with plate. Philotas thanked him much, but was very far from ever imagining that a boy of his age could dispose of things of that value. Soon after, however, the plate was all brought to him, and he was desired to set his mark upon it; and when he deprecated, and was afraid to accept, the present, 'What ails the wretch?' said he that brought it, 'do .you not know that he who gives you this is Antony's son, who is free to give it, if it were all gold? but if you will be advised by me, I would counsel you to accept of the value in money from us; for there may be amongst the lot some antique or famous piece of workmanship, which Antony would be sorry to part with.' These anecdotes, my grandfather told us, Philotas used frequently to relate.

To return to Cleopatra; Plato admits four sorts of flattery, but she had a thousand. Were Antony serious or disposed to mirth, she had at any moment some new delight or charm to meet his wishes; at every turn she was upon him, and let him escape her neither by day nor by night. She played at dice with him, drank with him, hunted with him; and when he exercised in arms, she was there to see. At night she would go rambling with him to joke with people at their doors and windows, dressed like a servant woman, for Antony also went in servant's disguise, and from these expeditions he always came home very scurvily answered, and sometimes even beaten severely, though most people guessed who it was. However, the Alexandrians in general liked it all well enough, and joined good humouredly and kindly in his frolic and play, saying they were much obliged to Antony for acting his tragic parts at Rome, and keeping his comedy for them. It would be trifling without end to be particular in relating his follies, but his fishing must not be forgotten. He went out one day to angle with Cleopatra, and, being so unfortunate as to catch nothing in the presence of his mistress, he gave secret orders to the fishermen to dive under. water, and put fishes that had been already taken upon his hooks; and these he drew in so fast that the Egyptian perceived it. But, feigning great admiration, she told everybody how dexterous Antony was, and invited them next day to come and see him again. So, when a number of them had come on board the fishing boats, as soon as he had let down his hook, one of her servants was beforehand with his divers, and fixed upon his hook a salted fish from Pontus. Antony, feeling his line taut, drew up the prey, and when, as may be imagined, great laughter ensued : ' Leave,' said Cleopatra, ' the fishing-rod, autocrat, to us poor sovereigns of Pharos and Canopus ; your game is cities, kingdoms, and continents.' [1]

I do not crave the reader's indulgence for delaying over these trivial details. I would there were more of them in the history of the Ptolemies to give some hold for our imagination in reconstructing an image of the times. But Plutarch does not mention the most tragic and the most characteristic proof of Cleopatra's complete conquest of Antony. Among his other crimes of obedience, he sent by her orders and put to death the princess Arsinoe, who, knowing well her danger, had taken refuge as a suppliant in the temple of Artemis Leucophryne at Miletus.[2]

§ 273. It is not our duty to follow the various complications of war and diplomacy, accompanied by the marriage with the serious and gentle Octavia, whereby the brilliant but dissolute Antony was weaned, as it were, from his follies, and persuaded to live a life of public activity. Whether the wily Octavian did not foresee the result, whether he did not even sacrifice his sister to accumulate odium against his dangerous rival, is not for us to determine. But when it was arranged (in 36 B.C.) that Antony should lead an expedition against the Parthians, any man of ordinary sense must have known that he would come within the reach of the eastern Siren, and was sure to be again attracted by her fatal voice. It is hard to account

---

[1] *Antony* cc. 25-29.

[2] Cf. Appian *Bell. Civ.* v. 9, who adds some important details ; Josephus *c. Ap.* ii. 5 (in the Latin version) ; and Dio xlviii. 24, who says τοὺς ἀδελφούς, as if including the younger Ptolemy, her brother.

for her strange patience during these four years. She had borne twins to Antony, probably after the meeting in Cilicia. Though she still maintained the claims of her eldest son Caesarion to be the divine Julius' only direct heir, we do not hear of her sending requests to Antony to support him, or that any agents were working in her interests at Rome. She was too subtle a woman to solicit his return to Alexandria. There are mistaken insinuations that she thought the chances of Sextus Pompey, with his naval supremacy, better than those of Antony, but these stories refer to his brother Cnaeus, who visited Egypt before Pharsalia.[1]

§ 274. It is probably to this pause in her life, as we know it, that we may refer her activity in repairing and enlarging the national temples. The splendid edifice at Dendera, at present among the most perfect of Egyptian temples, bears no older names than those of Cleopatra and her son Caesarion,[2] and their portraits represent the latter as a growing lad, his mother as an essentially Egyptian figure, conventionally drawn according to the rules which had determined the figures of gods and kings for 1500 years. Under these circumstances it is idle to speak of this well-known relief-picture as a portrait of the queen. It is no more so than the granite statues in the Vatican (above, p. 116) are portraits of Philadelphus and Arsinoe. The artist had probably never seen the queen, and if he had, it would not have produced the slightest alteration in his drawing.[3]

---

[1] Plutarch, above, and Shakespeare *Antony and Cleopatra* iii. 13, and Gutschmid (Sharpe ii. 52).

[2] Traces of Cleopatra and her brothers are to be found at Soohag.

[3] Ebers has assumed (in the preface to his *Cleopatra*) that the colossal pair, hand in hand, found at Alexandria in 1892, of which the female figure is fairly preserved, represent Antony and Cleopatra.

We can tell far better from the extant coins[1] what her type was, though these too are very prone to have given an idealised likeness. Plutarch expressly says that it was not in peerless beauty that her fascination lay, but in the combination of more than average beauty with many other personal attractions. The Egyptian portrait is likely to confirm in the spectator's mind the impression derived from Shakespeare's play,[2] that Cleopatra was a swarthy Egyptian, in strong contrast to the fair Roman ladies, and suggesting a wide difference of race. She was no more an Egyptian than she was an Indian, but a pure Macedonian, of a race akin to, and perhaps fairer, than the Greeks.

§ 275. No sooner had Antony reached Syria than the fell influence of the Egyptian queen revived. In the words of Plutarch—

But the mischief that thus long had lain still, the passion for Cleopatra, which better thoughts had seemed to have lulled and charmed into oblivion, upon his approach to Syria, gathered strength again, and broke out into a flame. And, in fine, like Plato's restive and rebellious horse of the human soul, flinging off all good and wholesome counsel, and breaking fairly loose, he sends Fonteius Capito to bring Cleopatra into Syria. To whom at her arrival he made no small or trifling present, Phoenicia, Coele-Syria, Cyprus, great part of Cilicia, that side of Judaea which produces balm, that part of Arabia where the Nabathacans extend to the outer sea[3]—profuse gifts

---

[1] Cf. that given at the end of this chapter, which represents an intellectual head, but not a beautiful face.

[2] Cf. the opening scene of *Antony and Cleopatra*, ' His goodly eyes —now turn the office and devotion of their view upon a tawny front ' ; and again, ' to cool a gipsy's lust ' ; and again, IV. xii. 28 ' Like a right gipsy.' Possibly the word *gipsy* may have expressed its derivation to the poet, and may only mean *Egyptian;* but the gipsy type must have also been before his mind.

[3] In fact, the old Ptolemaic Empire as it had been under Ptolemy Euergetes I.

which much displeased the Romans. For although he had invested several private persons with great governments and kingdoms, and bereaved many kings of theirs, as Antigonus of Judaea, whose head he caused to be struck off (the first example of that punishment being inflicted on a king), yet nothing stung the Romans like the shame of these honours paid to Cleopatra. Their dissatisfaction was augmented also by his acknowledging as his own the twin children he had by her, giving them the names of Alexander and Cleopatra, and adding, as their surnames, the titles of Sun and Moon.

After much dallying the triumvir really started for the wild East, whither it is not our business to follow him. Cleopatra he sent home to Egypt, to await his victorious return, and it was on this occasion that she came in state to Jerusalem to visit Herod the Great [1]—probably the most brilliant scene of the kind which had taken place since the Queen of Sheba came to learn the wisdom of Solomon. But it was a very different wisdom that Herod professed, and in which he was verily a high authority, nor was the subtle daughter of the Ptolemies a docile pupil, but a practised expert in the same arts of cruelty and cunning, wherewith both pursued their several course of ambition, and sought to wheedle from their Roman masters cities and provinces. The re-union of Antony and Cleopatra must have greatly alarmed Herod, whose plans were directly thwarted by the freaks of Antony, and he must have been preparing at the time to make his case with Octavian, and seek from his favour protection against the new caprices of the then lord of the East.

The scene at Herod's palace must have been inimitable. The display of counter-fascinations between these two tigers; their voluptuous natures mutually attracted; their hatred giving to each that deep interest in the other which so often turns

[1] Josephus *Antt.* xv. 4, 2.

to mutual passion while it incites to conquest ; the grace and
finish of their manners, concealing a ruthless ferocity ; the
splendour of their appointments—what more dramatic picture
can we imagine in history !

We hear that she actually attempted to seduce Herod, but
failed, owing to his deep devotion to his wife Mariamme.
The prosaic Josephus adds that Herod consulted his council
whether he should not put her to death for this attempt
upon his virtue.   He was dissuaded by them on the ground
that Antony would listen to no arguments, not even from
the most persuasive of the world's princes, and would take
awful vengeance when he heard of her death.   So she was
escorted with great gifts and politenesses back to Egypt.

Such, then, was the character of this notorious queen.
But her violation of temples and even of ancient tombs for
the sake of treasure must have been a far more public and
odious exhibition of that want of respect for the sentiment
of others which is the essence of bad manners.[1]

§ 276. As is well known, the first campaign of Antony
against Armenians and Parthians was a signal failure, and
it was only with great difficulty that he escaped the fate of
Crassus.   But Cleopatra was ready to meet him in Syria
with provisions and clothes for his distressed and ragged
bataillons, and he returned with her to spend the winter
(36-5 B.C.) at Alexandria.   She thus snatched him again
from his noble wife Octavia, who had come from Rome
to Athens with succours even greater than Cleopatra had
brought.   This at least is the word of the historians who
write in the interest of the Romans, and regard the queen
of Egypt with horror and with fear.

The new campaign of Antony (34 B.C.) was apparently

[1] *The Greek World under Roman Sway* pp. 166-7.   More recently
E. Renan gave a very brilliant picture of Herod and his policy, on the
same lines, in the January number of the *Revue des deux Mondes* for
1894.   It is doubtful whether this was the first meeting (39 B.C.) of
these sovrans.   For according to Josephus *B. J.* i. 14, 18, Herod had
visited Egypt, probably before this date.

more prosperous, but it was only carried far enough to warrant his holding a Roman triumph at Alexandria[1]— perhaps the only novelty in pomp which the triumvir could exhibit to the Alexandrian populace, while it gave the most poignant offence at Rome. It was apparently now that he made that formal distribution of provinces which Octavian used as his chief *casus belli.*

Nor was the division he made among his sons at Alexandria less unpopular; it seemed a theatrical piece of insolence and contempt of his country. For, assembling the people in the exercise ground, and causing two golden thrones to be placed on a platform of silver, the one for him and the other for Cleopatra, and at their feet lower thrones for their children, he proclaimed Cleopatra queen of Egypt, Cyprus, Libya, and Coele-Syria, and with her conjointly Caesarion, the reputed son of the former Caesar. His own sons by Cleopatra were to have the style of 'king of kings'; to Alexander he gave Armenia and Media, with Parthia, so soon as it should be overcome; to Ptolemy, Phoenicia, Syria, and Cilicia. Alexander was brought out before the people in Median costume, the tiara and upright peak, and Ptolemy, in boots and mantle and Macedonian cap done about with the diadem; for this was the habit of the successors of Alexander, as the other was of the Medes and Armenians. And, as soon as they had saluted their parents, the one was received by a guard of Macedonians, the other by one of Armenians. Cleopatra was then, as at other times when she appeared in public, dressed in the habit of the goddess Isis, and gave audience to the people under the name of the New Isis. . . .

This over, he gave Priene to his players for a habitation, and set sail for Athens, where fresh sports and play-acting employed him. Cleopatra, jealous of the honours Octavia had received at Athens (for Octavia was much beloved by the Athenians), courted the favour of the people with all sorts of attentions. The Athenians, in requital, having decreed her

---

[1] The Armenian Artabazus was led in chains after his conqueror, Appian *Hist. Parth., sub fin.*

public honours, deputed several of the citizens to wait upon her at her house; amongst whom went Antony as one, he being an Athenian citizen, and he it was that made the speech. . . .

The speed and extent of Antony's preparations alarmed Caesar, who feared he might be forced to fight the decisive battle that summer. For he wanted many necessaries, and the people grudged very much to pay the taxes; freemen being called upon to pay a fourth part of their incomes, and freed slaves an eighth of their property, so that there were loud outcries against him, and disturbances throughout all Italy. And this is looked upon as one of the greatest of Antony's oversights, that he did not then press the war. For he allowed time at once for Caesar to make his preparations, and for the commotions to pass over. For while people were having their money called for, they were mutinous and violent; but, having paid it, they held their peace. Titius and Plancus, men of consular dignity and friends to Antony, having been ill-used by Cleopatra, whom they had most resisted in her design of being present in the war, came over to Caesar, and gave information of the contents of Antony's will, with which they were acquainted. It was deposited in the hands of the vestal virgins, who refused to deliver it up, and sent Caesar word, if he pleased, he should come and seize it himself, which he did. And, reading it over to himself, he noted those places that were most for his purpose, and, having summoned the senate, read them publicly. Many were scandalised at the proceeding, thinking it out of reason and equity to call a man to account for what was not to be until after his death. Caesar specially pressed what Antony said in his will about his burial; for he had ordered that even if he died in the city of Rome, his body, after being carried in state through the forum, should be sent to Cleopatra at Alexandria. Calvisius, a dependant of Caesar's, urged other charges in connexion with Cleopatra against Antony; that he had given her the library of Pergamus, containing two hundred thousand distinct volumes; that at a great banquet, in the presence of many guests, he had risen up and rubbed her feet, to fulfil some wager or promise; that he had suffered the Ephesians to salute her as their queen; that he had frequently at the public audience of kings and princes received amorous messages written in tablets made of onyx and crystal, and read them openly on the tribunal ; that when Furnius, a man of great authority and eloquence among the Romans, was pleading, Cleopatra happening to pass by in her litter, Antony started up and left them in the middle of their cause, to follow at her side and attend her home.[1]

§ 277. We are not further concerned with the Roman side of the great quarrel. When war was declared, Antony sought to gain the support of the East in the conflict. He made alliance with a Median king who betrothed his daughter to Cleopatra's infant son Alexander ; but he made the fatal mistake of allowing Cleopatra to accompany him to Samos, where he gathered his army, and even to Actium, where she led the way in flying from the fight, and so persuading the infatuated Antony to leave his army and join in her disgraceful escape.

Historians have regarded this act of Cleopatra as the mere cowardice of a woman who feared to look upon an armed conflict and join in the din of battle. But she was surely made of sterner stuff. She had probably computed with the utmost care the chances of the rivals, and had made up her mind that, in spite of Antony's gallantry, his cause was lost.[2] If she fought out the battle with her strong contingent of ships, she would probably fall into Octavian's hands as a prisoner, and would have no choice between suicide or death in the Roman prison, after being exhibited to the mob in Octavian's triumph. There was no chance whatever that she would have been spared, as was her sister Arsinoe after

---

[1] Plutarch *Ant.* 54-8. Cf. Lumbroso *Egitto* p. 135, on Calvisius' falsehoods.

[2] Dion says (li. 15) that Antony was of the same opinion, and went into the battle intending to fly ; but this does not agree with his character or with the facts.

Julius Caesar's triumph, nor would such clemency be less hateful than death. But there was still a chance, if Antony were killed or taken prisoner, that she might negotiate with the victor as queen of Egypt, with her fleet, army, and treasures intact, and who could tell what effect her charms, though now full ripe, might have upon the conqueror? Two great Romans had yielded to her, why not the third, who seemed a smaller man?

This view implies that she was already false to Antony, and it may well be asked how such a charge is compatible with the affecting scenes which followed at Alexandria, where her policy seemed defeated by her passion, and she felt her old love too strong even for her heartless ambition? I will say in answer that there is no more frequent anomaly in the psychology of female love, than a strong passion coexisting with selfish ambition, so that each takes the lead in turn, nay, even the consciousness of treachery may so intensify the passion as to make a woman embrace with keener transports the lover whom she has betrayed, than one whom she has no thought of surrendering.[1] There are moreover in these tragedies unexpected accidents, which so affect even the hardest nature, that calculations are cast aside, and the old loyalty resumes a temporary sway. Nor must we fail to

---

[1] This mixture of contrasted feelings has been noticed long ago by Des Cartes : *Par exemple, lorsqu'un mari pleure sa femme morte, laquelle (ainsi qu'il arrive quelquefois) il serait fâché de voir ressuscitée, il se peut faire que son cœur est serré par la tristesse que l'appareil des funerailles et l'absence d'une personne à la conversation de laquelle il était accoutumé excitent en lui, et il se peut que quelques restes d'amour ou de pitié qui se présentent à son imagination tirent de véritables larmes de ses yeux, nonobstant qu'il sente cependant une joie secrète dans le plus intérieur de son âme, l'émotion de laquelle a tant de pouvoir, que la tristesse et les larmes qui l'accompagnent ne peuvent rien diminuer de sa force* (*Passions de l'âme*, ii. art. cxlvii.)

insist again upon the traditions wherein this last Cleopatra
was born and bred.   She came from a stock whose women
played with love and with life as if they were mere
counters.   To hesitate whether such a scion of such a
house would have delayed to discard Antony and to assume
another passion, is to show small appreciation of the effects
of heredity and of example.   Dion tells us[1] that she
arrived in Alexandria before the news of her defeat, pretended a victory, and took the occasion of committing
many murders, in order to get rid of secret opponents, and
also to gather wealth by confiscation of their goods.   For
both she, and Antony, who came along the coast of Libya,
seem still to have thought of defending the inaccessible
Egypt, and making terms for themselves and their children
with the conqueror.   But Antony's efforts completely failed;
no one would rally to his standard.   And meanwhile the false
queen had begun to send presents to Caesar, and encour-
age him to treat with her.   But when he bluntly proposed
to her to murder Antony as the price of her reconciliation
with himself, and when he even declared by proxy that he
was in love with her, he clearly made a rash move in this
game of diplomacy, though Dion[2] says he persuaded her of
his love, and that accordingly she betrayed to him the
fortress of Pelusium, the key of the country.   Dion also
differs from Plutarch in repeatedly ascribing to Octavian
great anxiety to secure the treasures which Cleopatra had
with her, and which she was likely to destroy by fire, if
driven to despair.

§ 278. The historian may well leave to the biographer,
nay to the poet, the affecting details of the closing scenes
of Cleopatra's life.   In the fourth and fifth acts of *Antony
and Cleopatra*, Shakespeare has reproduced every detail of

[1] li. 5.   [2] li. 8.

Plutarch's narrative, which was drawn from that of her physician Olympos.[1] Her fascinations were not dead, for they swayed Dolabella to play false to his master so far as to warn her of his intentions, and leave her time for her dignified and royal end. But if these Hellenistic queens knew how to die, they knew not how to live. Even the penultimate scene of the tragedy, when she presents an inventory of her treasures to Octavian, and is charged by her steward with dishonesty, shows her in uncivilised violence striking the man in the face, and bursting into indecent fury, such as an Athenian, still less a Roman, matron would have been ashamed to exhibit. Nor is there any reason to doubt the genuineness of this scene, though we must not be weary of cautioning ourselves against the hostile witnesses who have reported to us her life. They praise nothing in her but her bewitching presence, and her majestic death.

After her repast, Cleopatra sent to Caesar a letter which she had written and sealed ; and, putting every body out of the monument but her two women, she shut the doors. Caesar, opening her letter, and finding pathetic prayers and entreaties that she might be buried in the same tomb with Antony, soon guessed what was doing. At first he was going himself in all haste, but, changing his mind, he sent others to see. The thing had been quickly done. The messengers came at full speed, and found the guards apprehensive of nothing ; but on opening the doors, they saw her stone-dead, lying upon a bed of gold, set out in all her royal ornaments. Iras, one of her women, lay dying at her feet, and Charmion, just ready to fall, scarce able to hold up her head, was adjusting her mistress's diadem. And when one that came in said angrily, 'Was this well done of your lady, Charmion ?' 'Perfectly well,' she answered, 'and as became the daughter of so many kings' ; and as she said this, she fell down dead by the bedside.

[1] *Antony* 82.

§ 279. Even the hostile accounts cannot conceal from us that both in physique and in intellect she was a very remarkable figure, exceptional in her own, exceptional had she been born in any other, age. She is a speaking instance of the falsehood of a prevailing belief, that the intermarriage of near relations invariably produces a decadence in the human race. The whole dynasty of the Ptolemies contradicts this current theory, and exhibits in the last of the series the most signal exception. Cleopatra VI. was descended from many generations of breeding-in, of which four exhibit marriages of full brother and sister. And yet she was deficient in no quality physical, or intellectual, which goes to make up a well-bred and well-developed human being. Her morals were indeed those of her ancestors, and as bad as could be, but I am not aware that it is degeneration in this direction which is assumed by the theory in question, except as a consequence of physical decay. Physically, however, Cleopatra was perfect. She was not only beautiful but prolific, and retained her vigour, and apparently her beauty, to the time of her death, when she was nearly forty years old.

§ 280. Though the dynasty closes with Cleopatra, we must not omit to notice the fortunes of her children. If there be one redeeming point about her character, it is her constant love and care for Caesarion, her eldest and Caesar's son, whom she associated with her in the sovranty, whose figure she engraved on the national monuments, whose life and interests she strove to safeguard in every extremity. Nor do we hear that she ever diminished his claims in the interests of Antony's children, who might well have shown some jealousy of the young prince. Caesarion is one of those figures about whom we should gladly learn more, but about whom history preserves an obstinate silence.

It is a case like that of the son of Alexander the Great and Roxane, whose life is hidden from us, though his titles to fame are not only his superb origin, but the gigantic heritage of which he was defrauded, and the captivity and early death to which his bitterest foe consigned him. Yet who had better claims to be known of all men than the young Alexander? So it is with Caesarion. He had reached an age when several of his dynasty had not only sat upon the throne, but led armies, begotten children, and engaged in councils of state.[1] Yet not one word of his appearance, of his habits, of his betrothal in marriage to any princess, is recorded. We are only told by Dion that upon their final return to Alexandria, Antony and Cleopatra had his eldest son Antyllus (Antonius), and her eldest Caesarion, declared *ephebi*, that the populace might regard them as men, fit to rule if any casualty removed their parents. This, he adds, was the cause of both their deaths at Octavian's hands.

§ 281. When the day of Actium had made Octavian master of the Mediterranean, Cleopatra's first thought was of the Red Sea and the far Ethiopian lands, whither many expeditions had gone from Egypt, and which seemed to promise a safe refuge from the turmoils of the Hellenistic and Roman worlds.

When Antony came into Africa, he sent on Cleopatra from Paraetonium into Egypt, and staid himself in the most entire solitude that he could desire, roaming and wandering about with only two friends, one a Greek, Aristocrates, a rhetorician, and the other a Roman, Lucilius, of whom we have elsewhere spoken, how, at Philippi, to give Brutus time to escape, he suffered himself to be taken by the pursuers, pretending he was Brutus. Antony gave him his life, and on this account he remained true and faithful to him to the last.

---

[1] But see the third note on p. 491.

But when even the officer who commanded for him in Africa, to whose care he had committed all his forces there, took them over to Caesar, he resolved to kill himself, but was hindered by his friends; and coming to Alexandria, he found Cleopatra busied in a most bold and wonderful enterprise. Over the small space of land which divides the Red Sea from the sea near Egypt, which may be considered also the boundary between Asia and Africa, and in the narrowest place is not much above three hundred furlongs across, over this neck of land Cleopatra had formed a project of dragging her fleet, and setting it afloat in the Arabian Gulf, thus to secure herself a home with her soldiers and her treasure on the other side, where she might live in peace, far away from war and slavery. But the first galleys which were carried over being burnt by the Arabians of Petra, and Antony not knowing but that the army before Actium still held together, she desisted from her enterprise, and gave orders for the fortifying of all the approaches to Egypt. But Antony, leaving the city and the conversation of his friends, built him a dwelling-place in the water, near Pharos, upon a little mole which he cast up in the sea, and there, secluding himself from the company of mankind, said he desired nothing but to live the life of Timon; as indeed, his case was the same, and the ingratitude and injuries which he suffered from those he had esteemed his friends, made him hate and mistrust all mankind.

It seems from this narrative that the canal of Philadelphus was no longer passable for ships, and this again suggests that the later Ptolemies had found the desert roads to the Nile (from Berenike and Myos Hormos to Koptos) more practical than the dangerous navigation of the Red Sea.[1] Presently she sent away her son Caesarion, now a lad of 17 years, to the far Berenike, to hide him from his enemies under the care of his tutor. But this faithless knave, that he might curry favour with the conqueror, brought the lad

---

[1] Above, § 84. Dion speaks of the fleet which the Arabs burned being built on the Red Sea coast, not transported from the Mediterranean.

back, when Octavian cruelly put him to death.[1] The conqueror acknowledged then the asserted parentage of the divine Julius, and could not brook in the world a nearer heir to the great Dictator.

As we hear that he only put to death one son of Antony, Antyllus (who had been declared a hereditary prince), the rest remain to be accounted for. But history tells us nothing of their fate save that the young princess, called Cleopatra after her mother, was married to Juba, the literary king of Mauretania, a friend and companion in arms of Octavian, who came with him to Egypt, and was probably struck with her beauty and impressed with the great traditions of her race. Dion adds that Octavian allowed Juba and his wife to carry off her two brothers, Alexander and Ptolemy, with them to their African home.

§ 282. In his settlement of Egypt, Augustus acknowledged fully the practical wisdom of the Ptolemies in their treatment of the country. It has been said that they considered it as little more than a huge private estate, to be administered for the profit of the owner. If so, Augustus, when he had conquered Cleopatra, took over her property as belonging to him personally. He gave the Senate no control of it whatever; he would not even allow a single senator to visit the country, without a personal passport from himself. All the treasure which he found heaped up there by Cleopatra, all the yearly income in corn and money, he added to his private fortune. But we do not hear that he found abuses to rectify, or antiquated arrangements to annul. Though in all the crowd of business papyri in our museums,

---

[1] Plutarch (*Antony* 81) charges the tutor of Antyllus, Theodoros, with the murder of this boy, whom he betrayed to the soldiers (what soldiers?). He adds that it was the epigram of Areios, οὐκ ἀγαθὸν πολυκαισαρίη, which cost Caesarion his life.

hardly one, so far as I know, comes to us from this generation—a strange accident—yet we are justified in saying that
all the internal administration remained as it had been
under the Ptolemies, nay even the building of temples to
the local gods whom the Romans did not know, went on
as systematically under the Caesars as it had done under
the Ptolemies. The names of all the emperors down to
Decius are found contorted into hieroglyphics at Esneh and
at Dendera. The Alexandrians are left without a free constitution. The imperial control of science and letters is not
changed. It was from Alexandria that Caesar had borrowed
the great reform of the Calendar, still called after his name ;[1]
it was from Alexandria that he imported the surveyors, who
were to make a scientific inventory of the great Estate
called the Roman Empire. It was from Alexandria that
the whole financial administration was borrowed, and applied
to all the imperial domains throughout the Empire.[2] The
free distribution of corn, so notorious at Rome in the
Gracchan times, was probably an Alexandrian benevolence
of the Ptolemies copied by Roman demagogues. Nay
more, there are evidences that not a few Hellenistic features
of etiquette found their way to Rome from the court of
Alexandria. For the etiquette of the Ptolemies was a reflex
of the old splendour of the Macedonian Conqueror, and
there is no doubt that even still Alexander was regarded
as the ideal of everything that was imperial. Augustus
was far more ready to copy Alexander than to copy
Caesar.

But these things are beyond the limits assigned to this
history. The bare mention of them, however, is not out of
place as an apologia for the sovrans whom modern historians

[1] Cf. above, appendix to Chapter VI., for the details in the Canopus
decree of 238 B.C. [2] Mommsen *RG* v. 560.

have called a set of idle and vicious despots.   Strabo found
the country not recovering from the exhaustion of Ptolemaic
oppressors under the beneficent sway of Augustus, but
enjoying peace, and flourishing with plenty under the new
government which had changed nothing beyond substituting
the Emperor's viceroy for the old royalty.

§ 283. If then the rule of the Ptolemies was a centralised
despotism, where the interests of the Crown were everything, and those of the people nothing, it must at least be
admitted that there never was a more intelligent despotism,
or one which understood more clearly that the interests of
the one cannot be secured without consulting those of the
other.   If the taxes levied by the Ptolemies seem enormous,
I have produced evidence [1] to show that those exacted from
Palestine by the Seleukids were apparently as exorbitant;
there remains also this curious negative evidence to ex-
culpate the Ptolemies, that in the scores of papyri treating
of the local administration, among the many complaints
and petitions addressed to the Crown, we have not found
a single protest that the burden of taxation was intolerable,
or that the State exacted its debts with cruelty and injustice.
It may be urged that the native Egyptians were, like the
Syrians, *patientissimum genus hominum*; but how does this
agree with the obstinate insurrections against such of the
Ptolemies as strained their power, and alienated the sentiments of their subjects?   For the natives had by no
means lost that spirit of resistance to oppression, which
leads to dangerous revolutions.   Of their readiness to lay
formal complaints before the king we have ample evidence.
We hear indeed of petty exactions, individual acts of violence
on the part of subordinate officials, but of any extended
oppression, or of the misery consequent upon it, we have

[1] Above, § 117.

no charge, nor can we even infer it as indirectly suggested by our evidence.

As it is the nature of gossip to degenerate into scandal, not to rise into appreciation, so it seems to be the bent of the later Greek historians to chronicle the vices rather than the virtues of men. 'The fierce light that beats upon the throne' was never fiercer than in those days of sentimental republicanism; of idle regrets for imaginary liberties. If we had only Tacitus to tell us of the early Caesars, would we suspect many of them of having been wise and humane administrators? Thus it may be that the recorded vices of the Ptolemies have so obscured their better qualities as to produce a picture permanently darkened, and which we can hardly hope to clear of its ugly shadows. But the achievements of that dynasty cannot be set aside. They were the ablest, the most successful, and therefore the most enduring of all the Successors of Alexander.

COIN OF CLEOPATRA VI.

ADDITIONAL NOTES AND ILLUSTRATIONS

Page 21. The problem as to the formulae used by Philadelphus in his dating of documents is fully discussed in my
Introduction to *The Revenue Papyrus of Ptolemy Philadelphus*,
published by the Clarendon Press, 1895.

The two dates (8th and 11th years) of Ptolemy son of
Ptolemy found at Lissa (in Lycia) which Mr. Hicks refers to
the third Ptolemy, I refer to the second.

Page 30. I should have added to the first note, that the indifferent use of Σ and C occurs in the well-known inscription
from Philae of Euergetes II. (cf. § 229), and this suggests to
me that possibly the soldiers of this king, who went so far into
Nubia, may be the very men who carved their names at Wadi-
Halfa. If so it is fresh evidence of his far-reaching power.

Page 37. The reader who desires to study the many speculations on allusions in Callimachus' hymns to contemporaneous
events, should read Bruno Ehrlich *de Call. hymnis quaest.
chronologicae* Breslau 1894.

Page 49. Under the events of 309 B.C. Diodorus says (xx.
27) 'Ptolemy king of Egypt learning that his local strategi
(τοὺς ἰδίους στρατηγούς), or the particular strategi set over each
city, had lost cities in Cilicia, set out with a force, and took by
blockade Phaselis, then passing on to Lycia stormed Xanthus,
which was garrisoned by Antigonus. Then attacking Kaunos
he took the town, and the two citadels with their garrisons,
the Heracleum by storm, the Persicum by the surrender of its
garrison. Then sailing to Kos he sent for Ptolemy the nephew
of Antigonus, who had been entrusted by the latter with a
command. This Ptolemy abandoned his uncle, and came
over to king Ptolemy, sailing from Chalcis to Kos. At first
the king treated him well, but seeing him set up, and seducing

the officers by talk and bribes to make a party of his own, he determined to forestall him, and made him drink hemlock; his forces he beguiled with fair promises (δημαγωγήσας) and persuaded them to be embodied among his own troops.' It appears from an inscription at Kos (Paton No. 52) that Kaunos was henceforth governed for Egypt by a local βασιλεύς. We also know that Philocles, king of Sidon, acted as στρατηγός for Ptolemy in this campaign.

Ibid. The murder of Cleopatra may not have taken place till 308 B.C. Gutschmid notes that her sister Thessalonika (after whom the well-known city, now Salonika, was called) was still alive and the wife of Casander. She did not die till 296 B.C.

Page 79. The resolutions of the artists of Ptolemais have been printed by E. Miller in *BCH* ix. 137 *sqq.*

Page 87. It appears from Mr. Poole's researches, that the coinage of Ptolemy Soter shows three marked stages; one according to the Attic standard, then a lighter one according to the Rhodian, followed by a still lighter drachme, to correspond with the Phoenician. This downward scale is not in quality of silver, but in weight. It has been held by some that these successive stages in lightening the coins point to an appreciation of silver during this reign. Political and commercial reasons afford a far better explanation. After starting with the Attic standard, as that of the highest traditions, Ptolemy probably found the Rhodian commerce and the Rhodian bankers so much more important that it was both an inconvenience and a loss to maintain any but the Rhodian standard. Later in his reign, we find Syrian policy becoming the uppermost in his mind; perhaps also he desired closer relations with the Eastern powers and their trade, and so was induced to pay the Phoenicians a very solid compliment. But these are as yet only conjectures.

Page 106. Regarding the partial abdication of Ptolemy Soter, an inscription printed by Dittenberger *Syll.* i. 249, containing an honorary decree of this very date at Athens (prob. 287 B.C.) has πρεσβευσας δε προς τον βασιλεα τον πρεσβυτερον Πτολεμαιον, which seems to me to imply that he was still alive, and still regarded as king together with his son.

Page 115. Bruno Ehrlich (*de Callim. hymnis* etc. p. 7) in discussing the date of Callimachus' *hymn to Zeus*, and the meaning of the various veiled flatteries therein contained, holds that while Keraunos was reconciled with his brother as soon as he had seized the crown of Macedon (Justin xvii. 2, § 9), the others remained in Egypt, and did not begin their conspiracies till after the king's second marriage, which he thinks caused all manner of plots on the part of the first queen Arsinoe. He thinks the hymn, which commemorates the accession to power of Zeus, who was not the eldest brother, was written about 283 B.C., before Philadelphus' reconciliation with Keraunos, before the revolt of his brothers, and before even the first marriage of Philadelphus, which he (most improbably) puts in 281 B.C., and after the death of King Lysimachus. Any one who reads his careful essay will see how confused the whole matter is made by the speculations of the learned. To base arguments upon the veracity of a court poet is of course absurd ; to determine *a priori* his amount of tact is nearly as absurd, for he may have found out beforehand how much the king would tolerate.

Page 122. Far from desiring to support Pyrrhus against Rome, it was apparently in 274 B.C. that Ptolemy sent an embassy to congratulate the Romans upon their success, and to make alliance with them. The embassy, received with great distinction by the Romans, was followed by a counter-embassy to Alexandria, and it is stated by Pliny (*HN* xxxiii. 3, 13) that it was from this visit that the Romans learned (in 269 B.C.) to coin silver, called consular denarii. This interchange of civilities, which secured the neutrality of Philadelphus in the ensuing first Punic War, when the Carthaginians sought a loan from him, is mentioned by Livy *Epit.* xiv ; Val. Max. iv. 3 ; Dio Cass. Frag. 147 and *Sicilica* fr. 1.

Page 127. Regarding the great temple of Isis at Philae, which was begun, though apparently not finished, by Philadelphus, it is not certain that it was founded late in his reign ; there is even an argument against a late date to be drawn from the Aswân stele commented on in § 235. It appears from this stele that Ptolemy II. must have ordained the association of the Ptolemies with the local god Chnum or Chnubo, who was identified with Amon, and had a temple there. The fact that the series appears to start from the gods Adelphi, omitting Alexander and the gods Soteres, points to the probability that at the time of the foundation, Soter had not been formally deified. In this case the temple would have had its foundation before ∠ 27 of Philadelphus.

The worship of Isis, the Egyptian deity specially favoured by this king, is shown not only by his cartouche (on which he appears as *beloved of Isis*) but by this temple, and one of far greater splendour which he built to her in the Delta, not far from Sebennytus, known as the temple of Hebt, and by the Romans as the Iseum. The ruins and rubbish cover 400 paces in circumference (cf. Baedeker's *Lower Egypt* p. 441).

These Egyptian foundations—we can also attribute to him a consecration of himself and his descendants as θεοὶ σύνναοι with Amon at Thebes—show that the king was not absolutely devoted to a Hellenistic policy in Egypt. Indeed apart from his general character, and his displays at Alexandria, we can only point to his restoration of the Hellenion at Naukratis as indicating special favours to the old Greek population in Egypt.

Page 150. The friendly relations of Ptolemy II. with Athens are not only attested by the statues of him and his wife which Pausanias saw at Athens, but by many gifts of various kinds, for which the Athenian gratitude was shown, no doubt, by honorary decrees. Unfortunately all the material evidences of these things are lost, nor do I know of a single Ptolemaic inscription found at Athens. There were tribes for some time at Athens called Πτολεμαίς and Βερενικίς, the former in honour of the 2nd Ptolemy (according to Pausanias), but whether the other was established in honour of the 1st or 3rd queen we do not know.

Page 152. The inscriptions of the artists of Dionysus (above p. 79) speak of a worship of the gods Adelphi at Ptolemais, and during their reign. If Ptolemy Soter was not deified till ∠ 27 of the reign, then Ptolemy II. went to Upper Egypt earlier, for even at Philae the priests of Chnum are priests of the gods Adelphi etc., but not of the gods Soteres.

Page 171. I think that 247 B.C. is the preferable date for the battle of Andros, and that it was probably in consequence of it that Philadelphus was able to grant cities like Telmessus to a Syrian grandee, who had helped his cause. This person, Ptolemy son of Lysimachus, controlled the town in the 7th year of Euergetes ; cf. *BCH* xiv. 162.   Ptolemy son of Ptolemy in that inscription is surely the second Ptolemy, nor am I aware that any other Ptolemy was so entitled without further specification.

Page 181.   The term ἐπιμελητής, at least in Rhodian Greek, meant clearly a Special Commissioner or Resident, sent to a foreign city under Rhodian control, to watch its loyalty, and to act as umpire in local disputes.   It was a vaguer term than most of those quoted in the text, and implied general authority from the commissioning power (cf. Holleaux in *BCH* xvii. 56). Whether this was so in Egypt seems doubtful.

Page 188.   The arguments I have brought forward on the succession of Ptolemy III. to the sovranty of Cyrene in my Introduction to *The Revenue Papyrus* are against the alteration of the date of Magas' death, and make it more certain that the crisis in Cyrene was not 250, but 258-7 B.C.

Page 196.   The delay of Euergetes' marriage, after he had obtained the royalty of Cyrene, and indeed the lateness of his marriage, have been the main difficulty in accepting the chronology which I have preferred.   But this very difficulty has suggested to me an important fact hitherto overlooked.   *It was not the habit of Ptolemaic crown princes to get married before they succeeded to their throne.*   This is so in the case of Philadelphus, of Euergetes I., of Philopator, of Euergetes II., negatively of Caesarion, and probably of the other princes who had attained puberty before their fathers died.   There must have been some law or tradition of the old Pharaonic royalty on account of which the wife of a prince royal could not be elevated to the dignity of reigning queen.   For no mere accident can account for this strange absence of *married* crown princes. Thus Berenike II. was probably not made queen of Egypt till Philadelphus, her father-in-law, was dead, and the veracity of the *Coma Berenices* as to her recent marriage in 246 B.C. may be admitted.

Page 253.   Upon the whole character of this army we can still read with profit Droysen *de Lagidarum regno*, etc. in his *Kleine Schriften* ii. 377 *sq*.   He maintains (against Letronne) the right sense of κάτοικοι, which cannot mean natives, as Revillout has recently translated it.

Page 271, *note* 1.   The inscription in question is however

dated the 7th year of Euergetes I., and applies to Telmessus;
cf. *BCH* xiv. 162. There is also a text from Eriza, which
was on the inner frontier of Lycia and Caria, which may
date from this reign, and shows that the sway of Egypt
extended up to the mountain passes at least. Cf. *BCH* xv.
556 οι εν τηι περι Εριζαν υπαρχιαι | φυλακιται και οι κατ-
οικουντες | εν Μοξουπολει και Κριθινιηι | Μηνωδορον Ζηθου
Αδραμυττηνον | τον επι των προσοδων δια την | προς α[υτους
ευ]νοιαν και . . . V. Berard, the editor, absurdly supposes
that this officer was a τελώνης.

Page 296. Droysen *de Lag. regno* § 30 endeavours to get
rid of the difficulties regarding Lepidus' tutorship by referring it
to a later senator of the name, and making his duties apply
not to Epiphanes, but to Philometor, in 180 B.C. This escape
does not appear to me satisfactory (cf. Mommsen *RG* i. 699).
I think Livy xlii. 6 *Alexandriam iidem [legati] ad Ptolemaeum
renovandae amicitiae causa proficisci iussi* [173 B.C.] would be
absurd, if the king had been under Roman tutelage. In
Polybius xxviii. 1, Lepidus appears as the *adviser* at Rome,
while Q. Marcius settles the dispute.

Page 300. Something may here be added concerning the
campaign of Antiochus with his fleet to the coast of Asia
Minor in 197 B.C. Having secured Coele-Syria, he next proceeded to take the coast cities, sending a land-army to Sardis
to await him. But as he was besieging Coracesium, after
subduing a number of strongholds and cities on his way, he
was met by a bold ultimatum from the Rhodians, that they
would resist him if he came westwards of the Chelidonian isles.
This they did in the interest of Rome, to prevent any junction
with Philip. But when the battle of Cynoscephalae had prevented this danger, they contented themselves with saving
from Antiochus the Ptolemaic cities. Livy says their help
and advice were the cause of liberty to Kaunos, Myndos,
Halicarnassos, and Samos, though they are described as *in
dicione Ptolemaei.*

Page 306. It was apparently at this time that the Rhodians,
being allowed to acquire a *Peraea* by Rome, bought from
Ptolemy's generals the town of Kaunos for 200 talents. This
town they had saved from Antiochus III. in 197 B.C., and
were the cause of its liberty. Now, about 189 B.C., they

bought it for themselves. This is shown by Holleaux *BCH* xvii. 56, who aptly quotes Appian *Mith.* 23 Καύνιοι ὑποτελεῖς Ῥοδίοις ἐπὶ τοῦ Ἀντιόχου πολέμου γενόμενοι.

Page 335. The sequel of the quotation ' to meet Antiochus . . .' should perhaps have been quoted, if it were only for the sake of Naukratis.

' While Antiochus was occupying Egypt, he was visited by the Greek envoys sent to conclude terms of peace. He received them courteously, devoted the first day to giving them a splendid entertainment, and on the next granted them an interview, and bade them deliver their instructions. The first to speak were the Achaeans, the next the Athenian Demaratus, and after him Eudemus of Miletus. And as the occasion and subject of their speeches were the same, the substance of them was also nearly identical. They all laid the blame of what had occurred on Eulaeus, and referring to Ptolemy's youth and his relationship to himself, they entreated the king to lay aside his anger. Thereupon Antiochus, after acknowledging the general truth of their remarks, and even supporting them by additional arguments of his own, entered upon a defence of the justice of his original demands. He attempted to establish the claim of the king of Syria on Coele-Syria, " insisting upon the fact that Antigonus, the founder of the Syrian kingdom, exercised authority in that country ; and referring to the formal cession of it to Seleucus, after the death of Antigonus, by the sovereigns of Macedonia. Next he dwelt on the last conquest of it by his father Antiochus ; and finally he denied that any such agreement was made between the late king Ptolemy and his father as the Alexandrian ministers asserted, to the effect that Ptolemy was to take Coele-Syria as a dowry when he married Cleopatra, the mother of the present king." Having by these arguments not only persuaded himself, but the envoys also, of the justice of his claim, he sailed down the river to Naucratis. There he treated the inhabitants with humanity, and gave each of the Greeks living there a gold piece, and then advanced towards Alexandria. He told the envoys that he would give them an answer on the return of Aristeides and Thesis, whom he had sent on a mission to Ptolemy ; and he wished, he said, that the Greek envoys should all be cognisant and witnesses of their report.'

I think this passage proves that the Greek population of Naukratis was small, and in the midst of a native population. For however ostentatious Antiochus IV. may have been, he would hardly throw away any large part of his war-chest in Egypt at that moment.

Page 337. It is to be noted that these two kings did not give their dates separately, as, for example, Cleopatra III. and Alexander I. did in subsequent times, but that they and their sister were together called the gods Philometores, and appear to have begun their joint dating afresh from the time of the compromise. It was not till Euergetes was cast out that Philometor resumed his dating from his own accession.

Ibid. It is not without great reluctance that I differ from my friend Professor Wilcken's reconstruction of this complicated war. I take the course of events to be probably as follows, premising that none of our authorities is aware (so far as I know) of more than two invasions of Egypt by Antiochus Epiphanes. I regard the first invasion (172-0) to have had two stages or acts ; first comes the battle at Pelusium, and defeat of Philometor. It seems to me most probable that it was in his first despair at this defeat that the youth gave up all hopes of reigning, and set off to live a life of seclusion in Samothrace. Thus Antiochus for the moment found Egypt without a king, and advanced to Memphis. Meanwhile two new events altered all his plans. He seems to have got possession of Philometor on sea by means of his now superior fleet, and the young king was probably brought to him at Memphis or Pelusium. At the same time the Alexandrians, learning of their king's flight, at once set up Euergetes II. in his place. Thus Antiochus found himself on the one hand baulked of his prize, so far as he seemed to have conquered Egypt, and on the other he had in his hands the strongest card he could play against the new boy-king. He now proclaimed that his object was to bring back Philometor to his rightful throne. This was the excuse he publicly gave (1) for continuing his occupation of Egypt, (2) for advancing upon Alexandria. His pretext *reducendi regis* does not imply that he went home and came back again. Euergetes tried, with his usual vigour, a diversion with his fleet at Pelusium, and had he succeeded Antiochus might have found his retreat cut off. But by a naval victory Antiochus kept his communications open, and proceeded to besiege Alexandria. Whether all the Greek embassies which came to treat with him came now or upon his renewed invasion I cannot tell. Probably they offered mediation on both occasions. But though Euergetes was besieged in Alexandria, the Syrian army was probably too small for a regular investment, and very possibly the Jews in Egypt may have induced the Jews in Palestine to threaten Antiochus' retreat. At all events he was obliged to retire, leaving Philometor at Memphis as nominal king, and garrisoning strongly the frontier fort of Pelusium. On his way home he paid his first hostile visitation to Jerusalem. All this ended in 169 B.C. at latest. The remainder of the story, the reconciliation of the brothers, the renewed invasion, and the interference of the Romans are not matters of dispute.

Page 372. In corroboration of my favourable estimate of the character of Philometor, I will here quote a text found at Delos, and published in *BCH* xiii. 231. It is a dedication to show the gratitude of certain Egyptians.

[επει] Πτολεμαιος βασ. οσιος και ευσεβης και παντων
ανθρωπων ημερωτατος εποησατο την τε φιλιαν και την ειρηνην
κατα παντα χρησαμενος τοις πραγμασι μεγαλοψυχως προαι-
[ρουμε]νος εν οις μαλιστα χαριζεσθαι Ρωμαιοις, οπως ουν και
οι συμμαχησαντες [εν] Κυπρωι βασιλει Πτολεμαιωι και μετε-
σ[χη]-οτες των ενδοξων κτλ.

It is hardly possible to refer this inscription to any other time and circumstances than the last struggle for Cyprus between Philometor and Euergetes II., when Philometor used his victory so moderately and generously. This text seems to contrast his mildness by implication with the cruelty and harshness of his brother. It also corroborates what some historians have said regarding his fear of further Roman interference.

Ibid. There is also another vaguer and more indirect testimony to the king's urbanity to Greek people in an inscription recently found at Delphi and published in *BCH* xviii. 251, by M. Louis Couve. In it a certain Seleukos son of Bithys is granted privileges etc. for his hospitalities to the Delphian embassy which went to this Ptolemy. The same Seleukos was afterwards governor of Cyprus, under the succeeding Ptolemy (*CIG* 2622), but near the beginning of his reign, when the two Cleopatras are named with him.

Pages 391 *and* 393 *note* 1. I have refrained from drawing any very decided conclusions regarding the fortunes of Cleopatra II. from the evidence before us, which is almost altogether derived from the dating of demotic papyri, with two or three Greek documents. Letronne, Lepsius and Revillout have all assumed that when one Cleopatra appears, after the year 140 at all events, it must mean the younger queen, the king's niece, but that whenever two appear, as they often do, specified as his sister and his wife, we have a moment when his divorced sister was again recognised. Thus they have attempted to frame a history of this oscillation between one queen and two, which I think quite unwarranted. Here is the sort of evidence given by Revillout (*RE* iii. 6, note) : Cleopatra II. had been, he says, associated with her first husband Philometor in ∠16-21 of his reign. But already in the 29th (really the 4th) of Euergetes we already find two Cleopatras following his name. This then seems to prove his second marriage as having taken place within four years of his ultimate accession upon his brother's death. But the very next year (∠30) we find only one Cleopatra in a protocol. ∠34 again gives us two, ∠35 only one, ∠37 again two, ∠40-45 only one. From ∠46 on to the end of his reign, both queens appear. During the gap ∠40-46 he was expelled from Egypt, and yet during this period Theban contracts mention him with one Cleopatra, in this case surely the reigning queen Cleopatra II. There are even certain documents dated in the reign of Cleopatra only, year 2, which Revillout now justly attributes to the reign of Cleopatra II., when her husband was exiled (*RE* vi. 154 ; vii. 40). One of these in Greek says της ταραχης παυσαμενης, at Thebes, so that her accession was probably accompanied with disturbances even in the upper country.

But I feel certain from the perpetual changing from one to two queens, that we have before us mere inaccuracies of the scribes, who copied sometimes from an earlier document with one queen, sometimes from one with two. These inaccuracies may fairly be inferred from the frequent mistakes in the titles of kings and queens that we can still detect. Thus Philometor and his wife are addressed both as θεοι ευχαριστοι (Paris

Pap. 29, 12), and apparently as θεοι μεγαλοι ευεργεται on an inscription of Methana. In two hieroglyphic inscriptions at Ombos, Cleopatra III. and Berenike III. are called θεα Φιλαδελφος and θεα Φιλοπατωρ, and the latter in a Leyden papyrus η θεα Φιλαδελφος. Soter II. is called Philadelphus (Letronne i. 64). We seem to find that any of the titles of the preceding sovrans might be applied to any king or queen, by way of politeness.

The variations in the lists concerning Eupator are well known; we have moreover cases (*BCH* ix. 141 *sq.*) where the lists of Ptolemaic θεοὶ σύνναοι are shortened; we have a priest of Soter and Epiphanes who appears, not only on contracts of the years 6, 11, 23 of Philometor, but in a Greek text. Another Greek text (ibid. p. 143) gives us the deified kings in wrong order, placing Philometor, then reigning, after Soter, and the priestess with like disorder in the queens she serves.

These facts lead me to mistrust these strings of titles, unless there be independent evidence to corroborate their variations.

Page 447. It should be said here in connexion with § 262, that it was probably during Pompey's preparation for the war. that he sent his son Cnaeus to visit Egypt and bring up subsidies of ships and money. At this time Pompey's name was so great in the East that his ultimate success against Caesar must have seemed certain. Then it was (49 B.C.) that Cleopatra sought to fascinate the elder son of the future lord of the Roman empire. This story was so probable that it was easy to invent, and we have no better evidence for it than the allusions of Plutarch. Cn. Pompey was killed at the battle of Munda in 45 B.C.

INDEX

THE END

Printed by R. & R. CLARK, LIMITED, *Edinburgh*

BY THE SAME AUTHOR.

A HISTORY OF CLASSICAL GREEK LITERA-
TURE. By the Rev. J. P. MAHAFFY, M.A., D.D.,
Fellow and Professor of Ancient History in Trinity College,
Dublin, and Hon. Fellow of Queen's College, Oxford. In
two Vols. Vol. I. The Poetical Writers. In Two Parts.
Part I. Epic and Lyric. Part II. Dramatic. Third
Edition, revised and enlarged. Crown 8vo. 4s. 6d. each
Part. Vol. II. The Prose Writers. Part I. Herodotus
to Plato. Part II. Isocrates to Aristotle. Crown 8vo.
4s. 6d. each Part.

CLASSICAL ANTIQUITIES. I. Old Greek Life. Pott
8vo. 1s.

GREEK LIFE AND THOUGHT FROM THE AGE
OF ALEXANDER TO THE ROMAN CONQUEST.
Crown 8vo. 12s. 6d.

THE GREEK WORLD UNDER ROMAN SWAY,
FROM POLYBIUS TO PLUTARCH. Crown 8vo.
10s. 6d.

RAMBLES AND STUDIES IN GREECE. With
Illustrations. New Edition. With a Map. Crown 8vo.
10s. 6d.

SOCIAL LIFE IN GREECE FROM HOMER TO
MENANDER. Third Edition. Crown 8vo. 9s.

PROBLEMS IN GREEK HISTORY. Crown 8vo.
7s. 6d.

THE DECAY OF MODERN PREACHING: an Essay.
Crown 8vo. 3s. 6d.

THE PRINCIPLES OF THE ART OF CONVERSA-
TION. Second Edition. Crown 8vo. 4s. 6d.

———————

SKETCHES FROM A TOUR THROUGH HOL-
LAND AND GERMANY. By J. P. MAHAFFY and
J. E. ROGERS. With Illustrations by J. E. ROGERS.
Extra Crown 8vo. 10s. 6d.

MACMILLAN AND CO., LONDON.

BOOKS ABOUT GREEK LIFE AND LITERATURE.

THE HISTORY OF GREECE FROM ITS COMMENCE-
MENT TO THE CLOSE OF THE INDEPENDENCE OF
THE GREEK NATION. By ADOLPH HOLM. Translated
from the German. In four Vols. 8vo. Vol. I. up to the end of
the Sixth Century, B.C. 6s. net. Vol. II. The Fifth Century,
B.C. 6s. net. Vol. III. [*Shortly.*

SELECT PASSAGES FROM ANCIENT WRITERS,
illustrative of the History of Greek Sculpture. By H. STUART
JONES, Fellow of Trinity College, Oxford. Extra Crown 8vo.
7s. net.

THE GROWTH AND INFLUENCE OF CLASSICAL
GREEK POETRY. Lectures delivered in 1891 on the Percy
Turnbull Memorial Foundation in the Johns Hopkins University.
By R. C. JEBB, Litt.D. Crown 8vo. 7s. 6d. net.

THE ATTIC ORATORS, FROM ANTIPHON TO
ISAEUS. By R. C. JEBB. Litt.D., Regius Professor of Greek,
and Fellow of Trinity College, Cambridge, and M.P. for the
University. Second Edition. 2 Vols. 8vo. 25s.

SELECTIONS FROM THE ATTIC ORATORS. Antiphon,
Andokides, Lysias, Isokrates, Isaeus. Being a companion volume
to the "Attic Orators from Antiphon to Isaeus." Edited with
Notes. By R. C. JEBB, Litt.D., M.P. Second Edition. Fcap.
8vo. 5s. [*Classical Series.*

GREEK LITERATURE. By R. C. JEBB, Litt.D., M.P.
Pott 8vo. 1s. [*Literature Primers.*

MODERN GREECE; two lectures delivered before the
Philosophical Institution of Edinburgh. With papers on "The
Progress of Greece" and "Byron in Greece." By R. C. JEBB,
Litt.D., M.P. Crown 8vo. 5s.

PLATO AND PLATONISM. A Series of Lectures by
WALTER PATER, Fellow of Brasenose College, Oxford; Author of
"Imaginary Portraits," "Marius the Epicurean," etc. Extra
Crown 8vo. 8s. 6d.

ASPECTS OF THE GREEK GENIUS. By S. H.
BUTCHER, M.A., Professor of Greek, University of Edinburgh.
Second Edition, revised. Crown 8vo. 7s. net.

STUDIES OF THE GODS IN GREECE AT CERTAIN
SANCTUARIES RECENTLY EXCAVATED. Being eight
Lectures given in 1890 at the Lowell Institute. By LOUIS DYER,
B.A., Oxon., late Assistant Professor in Harvard University.
Extra Crown 8vo. 8s. 6d. net.

MYTHOLOGY AND MONUMENTS OF ANCIENT
ATHENS. Being a Translation of a Portion of the "Attica" of
Pausanias. By MARGARET DE G. VERRALL. With Introductory
Essay and Archaeological Commentary by JANE E. HARRISON,
Author of "Myths of the Odyssey," "Introductory Studies in Greek
Art." With Illustrations and Plans. Crown 8vo. 16s.

MACMILLAN AND CO., LONDON.

5/6/09